For Connie & Sam Perkins,

with appreciation
& I'm so happy
that *Rose Diptych for Lannis*
is with you!

My Best!

[illegible]

Reflections of Nature:
Paintings by
Joseph Raffael

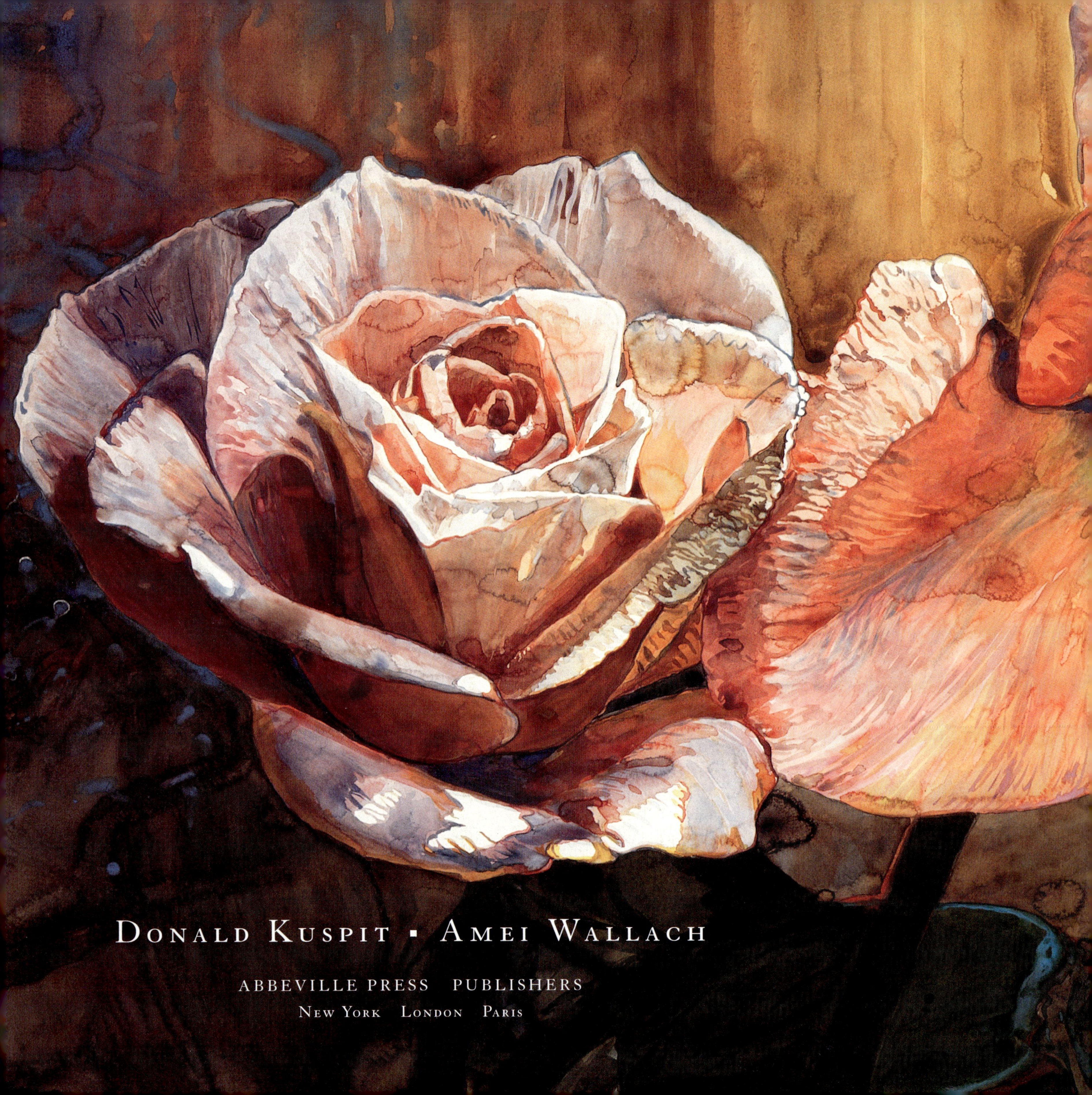

DONALD KUSPIT • AMEI WALLACH

ABBEVILLE PRESS PUBLISHERS
NEW YORK LONDON PARIS

Reflections of Nature: Paintings by Joseph Raffael

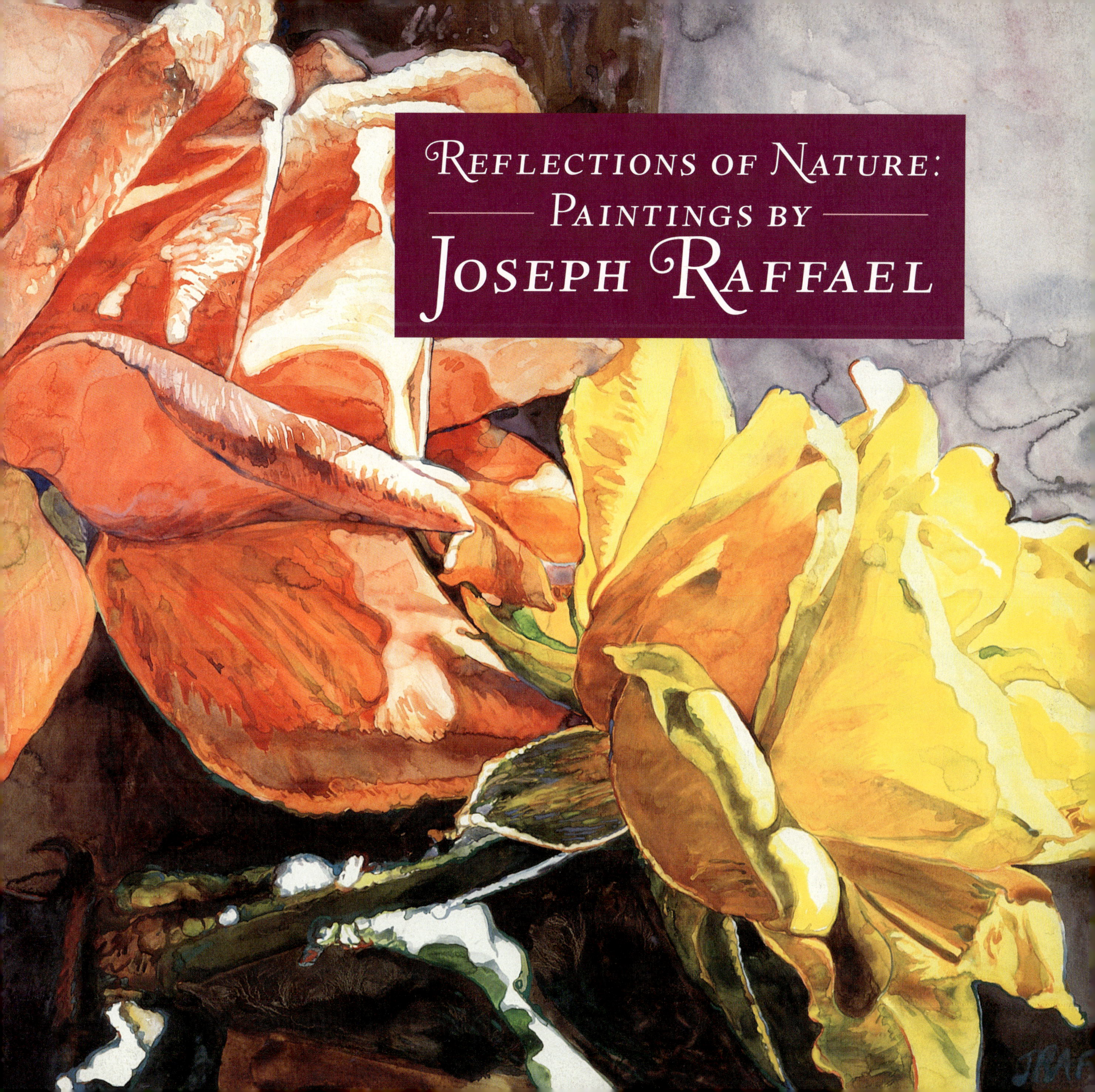

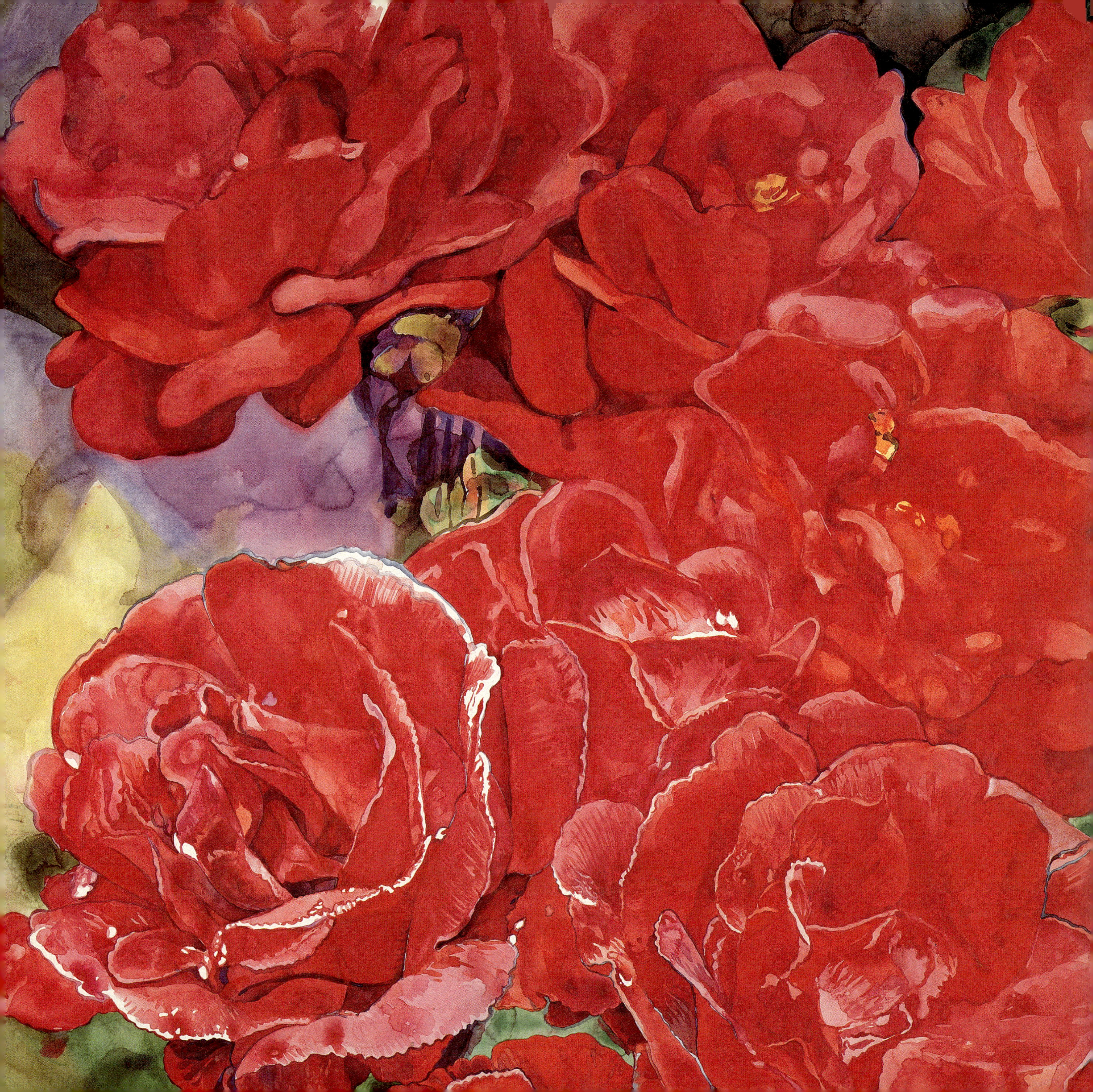

Contents

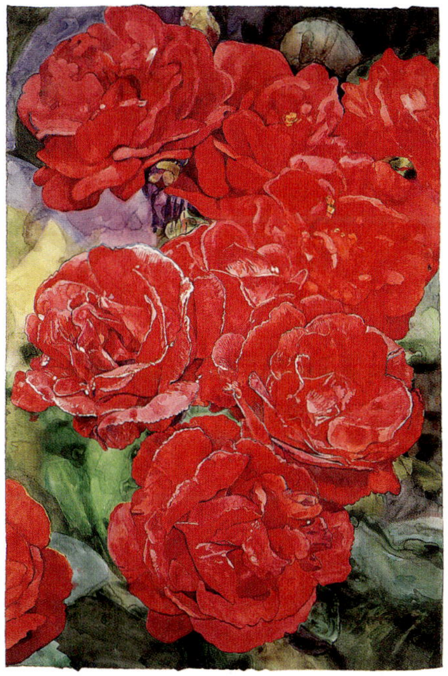

Joseph Raffael: The Nature of Beauty
Amei Wallach
7

The Water and Shore Paintings
"The rivers shine and hold their mirrors up"
21

The Flower and Leaf Paintings
"Mazily dewed and mauved in bloom"
39

The Animal Paintings
"Things to be cherished like the thought of heaven"
59

The Lily and Fish Paintings
"In its watery radiance"
75

The Sacred Symbol Paintings
"Sacrament and celebration"
95

The Lannis Paintings
"The woman in sunshine"
107

Diary of a Painting
Joseph Raffael
115

Raffael's Metaphysics of Nature
Donald Kuspit
123

An Autobiographical Chronology
Joseph Raffael
171

Selected Bibliography
183

Index
188

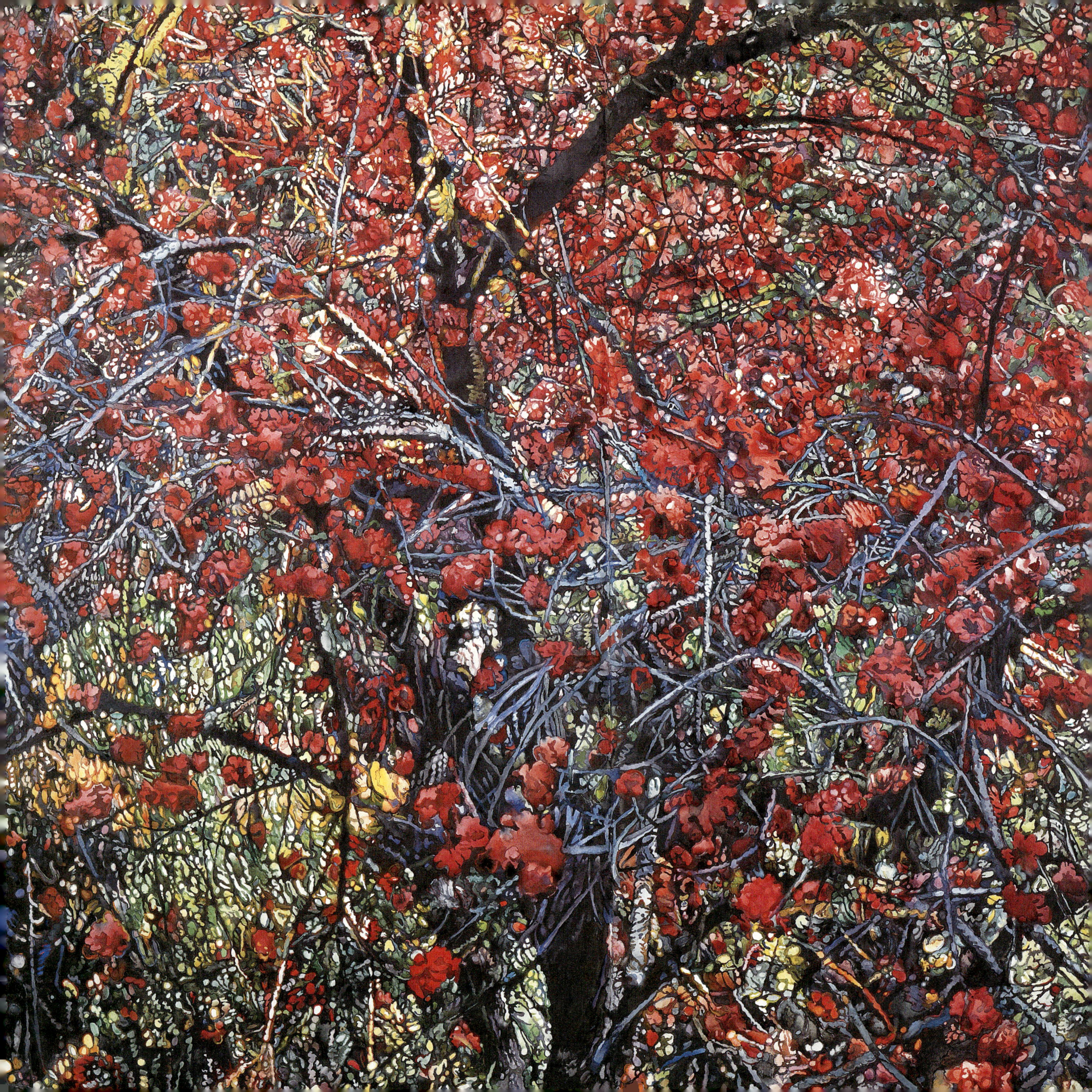

Joseph Raffael: The Nature of Beauty

Amei Wallach

The place to begin is where Joseph Raffael begins, with an experience framed, as in a photograph.

Joseph and Lannis Raffael are having lunch at an insubstantial metal table in their garden on the Côte d'Azur. As in a Raffael painting, the west-slanting sun is backlighting a white iris to improbable incandescence. Joseph Raffael is wearing a straw hat with a broad brim that projects latticework shadows onto his face, covering his eyes like a mask. Behind him the sun throws into high relief other scenes from Raffael paintings: leafed branches entangled in a Wedgwood sky, Lannis's garden abloom in jumbled excess, the glitter of unruly water. There is more to this moment than a photograph could capture. There is the vegetarian food, ecumenically spiced with California chiles and the herbs of Provence; raised French voices on the other side of the hedge; airplanes and seagulls overhead; dogs and cats underfoot.

"Beauty!" Raffael shouts at one of the dogs, who has erupted in woeful barking. Beauty ceases. Raffael nods. The latticed shadow descends to his lips in the manner of Ingrid Bergman's veil in *Casablanca,* a scene altogether familiar to an aficionado who sees upward of three hundred movies a year, always in theaters.

On his rambles through Dutch thickets, California deserts, and his own garden, Raffael takes scores of photographs, close-up and oddly composed: a patch of forest undergrowth, branching cherry blossoms, carp in a dappled lily pond. These are notes on a moment in time, detailed and particular—because in the next moment light and sense will alter. A few of these stills of stopped action find their way into the studio, to be tacked on the wall. At some point Raffael chooses one and projects the slide from which it comes onto paper or canvas to outline his painting.

1. Detail of *12 March,* 1997
See plate 2

A single sense engaged specifically enough summons an experience in its faceted entirety. It is the unique whole experience that interests Raffael. "When I paint nature, I begin with an image, but then what I'm really showing the viewer who wants to see it is the nature of one human being—my nature," he says. "I'm trying to get the feeling of what this flower means to me."[1] He means literally this iris, this carp, at this moment, rooted in the documentation of a photograph, repossessed by the process of painting.

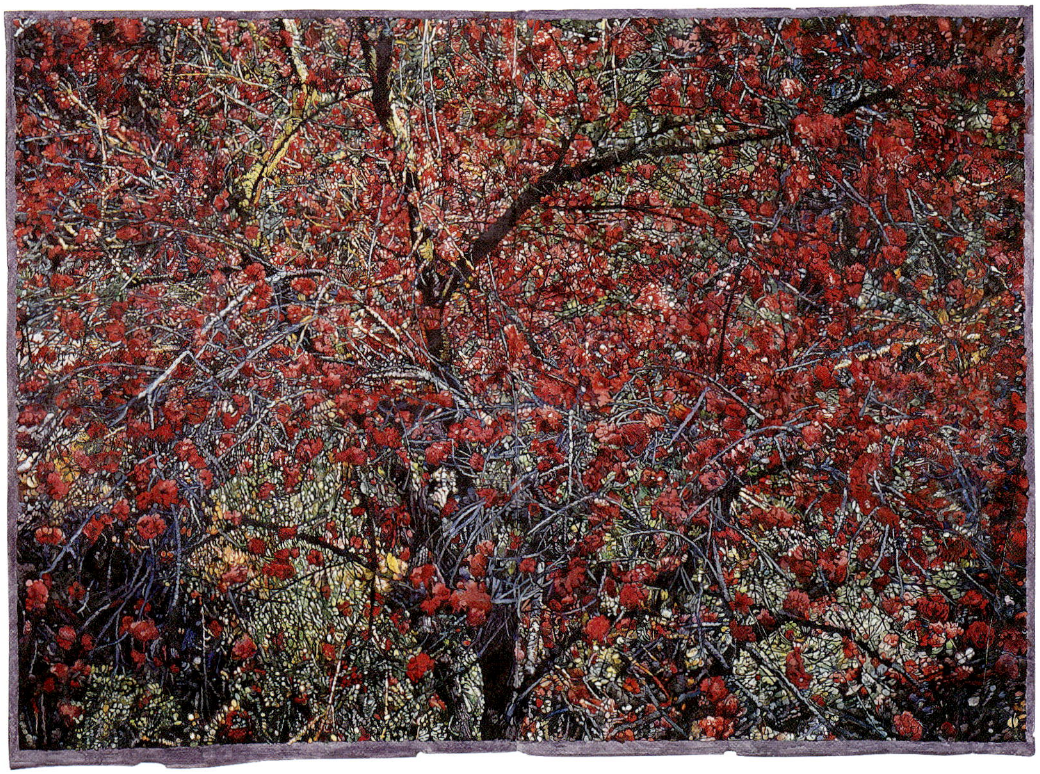

2. *12 March,* 1997. Watercolor on paper, 65½ x 89 in. (166.4 x 226.1 cm). Private collection; Courtesy of Nancy Hoffman Gallery, New York

"I always call it documentation, they happen to be slides. It's like a truth; the slide is a fiction of the truth. Then I continue the fiction, when I get into starting to work. What I always notice is that there are these incredible shapes. I probably have done a hundred fish and there's no two at all alike. Whereas the mind, on its own, no matter who the person is, no matter how talented, versatile, and able—can't replicate a fish. You could do a fish, but it would be a stylization of a fish. It would be a cliché, it would be limited. I feel very humble in front of nature and expressing it is a sacramental activity."

Raffael projects the slide he has chosen onto a sheet of paper or a length of canvas, tacked onto the wall. Standing in the color-stained light of the projector, he traces each minute outline of each leaf, vein, mottled patch. He calls this his "map." He lays the map on the table, and then, taking tiny brushes, outlines and fills each complex penciled shape with infinitesimal gradations of color. "Even if I have to make an expanse of one color, it's always with a small brush, because to go from A to X I feel there has to be psychic energy. I like all the differentiations from one point to another."

As an artist, Raffael is at once outside tradition and firmly within it. His technique can be traced to the moment when Edgar Degas took note of the horse-racing photographs by Eadweard Muybridge. Raffael's view of art and the world is as

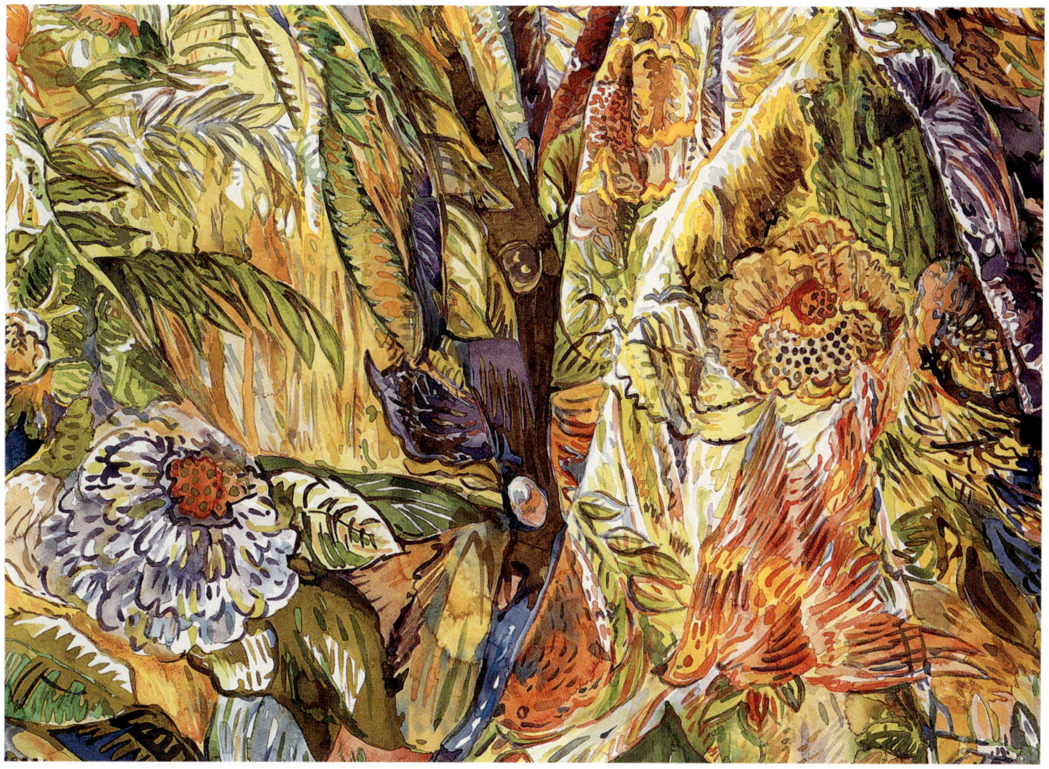

3. Detail of *Lannis in Sieste XIV*
See plate 110

American as New England transcendentalism. He is an altogether twentieth-century incarnation of a pragmatic romanticism out of Ralph Waldo Emerson and Henry David Thoreau. Nature "is the organ through which the universal spirit speaks to the individual, and strives to lead back the individual to it,"[2] Emerson wrote.

By the middle of the nineteenth century, American painters deflected from the portrait and the history painting by Emerson's angle of vision searched for immanence in the rivers of the East and the mountains of the West. Robert Hughes has called Raffael "a very American figure recognizable from his 19th-century prototypes along the Hudson River and the Yosemite Valley, the painter as Italian altar boy in the cathedral of nature."[3]

Nature in Raffael's twentieth-century cathedral is transfused with the theories of Carl Jung; the teachings of Krishnamurti, Gurdjieff, and Tibetan Buddhism; the poetry of Rainer Maria Rilke and Wallace Stevens. Plus a touch of can-do California mysticism. "To be religious you don't have to be a part of a religion," Raffael says. He dropped the *e* from Raffaele, the name he was born with, after a numerologist recommended the change. Raffael looks for spiritual connections in the deaths that have punctuated his life: he almost died when he was seven, his mother died when he was fourteen, he nearly died again when he was thirty, and his father died the next year; his son Matthew died in 1980, Lannis nearly died in 1993.

"I was always an artist, and then there were these things that deepened one and deepened the artist at the same time. The thing about painting is that it's an activity, and it's about life and death."

The tradition of painting nature as sacrament and individual testament stretches far beyond the nineteenth century. Edward Hopper seems astonishingly close to Raffael in his statement of 1933, the year Raffael was born: "My aim in painting has always been the most exact transcription possible of my most intimate impressions of nature. If this end is unattainable, so it can be said, is perfection in any other ideal of painting or in any other of man's activities."[4]

In the following decades, the language of feeling became an embarrassment in aesthetic discourse; when emotion recently reemerged, it was as angst and the search for identity. Only now is beauty beginning to be reconstituted as a fitting goal for art at the end of the twentieth century, at a time when passion is the stuff of television talk shows. But Raffael has long been making beautiful paintings with passionate convic-

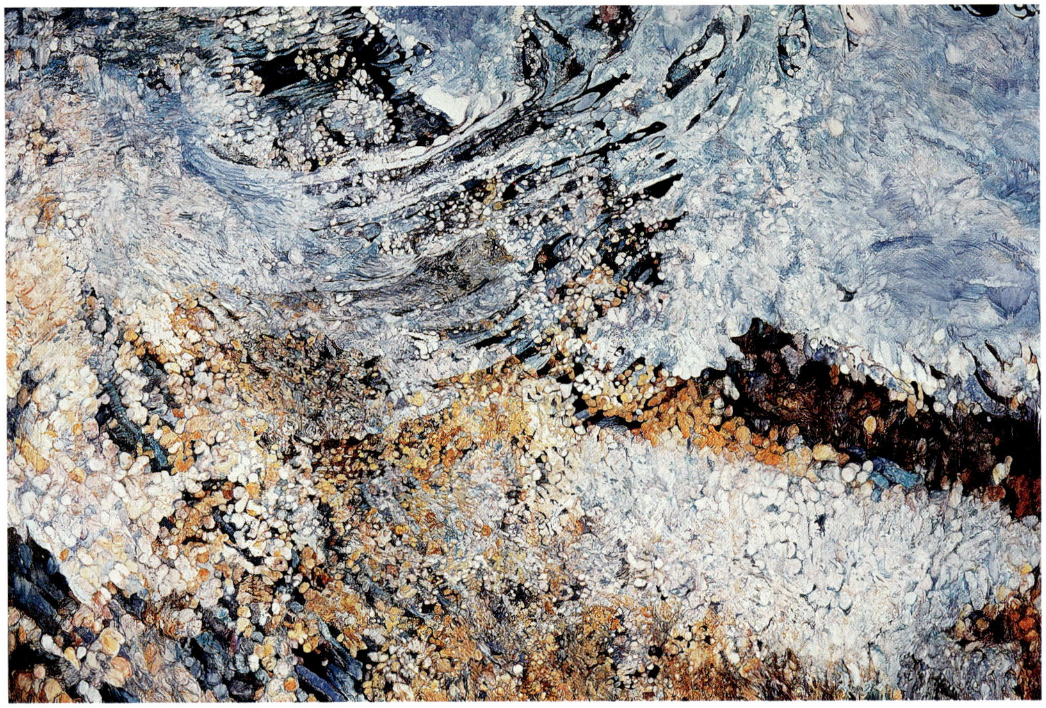

4. *Water Painting III,* 1973
Oil on canvas, 78 x 114 in. (198.1 x 289.5 cm)
Jane and John Fitz Gibbon, Pilot Hill, California

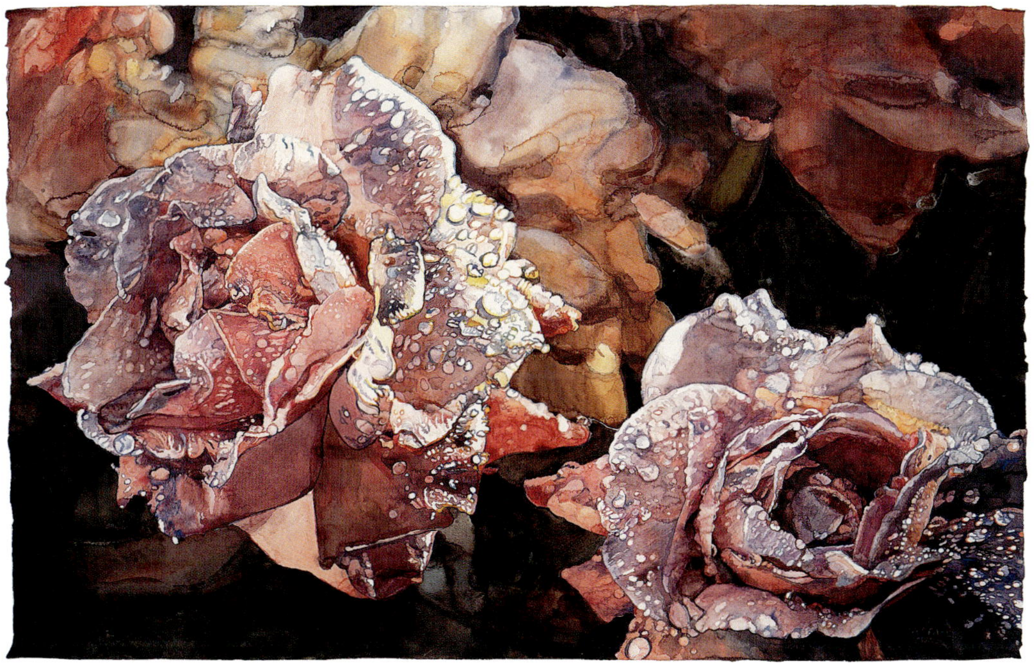

5. *The Garden after the Rain,* 1990
Watercolor on paper, 44 x 68 in.
(111.7 x 172.7 cm)
Philbrook Museum of Art,
Tulsa, Oklahoma

tion. His unembarrassed subject is nature—its specificity, variety, and powers of transfiguration. The content of his paintings is flux. Exactness of observation is essential to painting flux without bathos. The rocks in his rivers will submerge and reemerge, the foam will subside, the riffs and rills will be flattened and edged under by overbearing waves. His flowers are at the stage of ultimate voluptuousness; his birds transiently alight. To be in a Raffael painting is to be in the moment. And Raffael fully intends his viewers to be in his paintings.

He accomplishes this with a cinematographer's sense of color, scale, and incident and with a filmmaker's ease with emotion. The photograph may be his tool, but film, that most twentieth-century of arts, animates his aesthetic. His color is Technicolor—higher, more outrageously various, more fuschia, aquamarine, chartreuse, mandarin, and marigold than even nature is accustomed to. His space is Cecil B. DeMille space, and we are the Egyptian army crashing headlong into the Red Sea. His viscous surfaces slip and slide. They elude our ability to stop the action, to focus the sea of incident, color, shape, and the tumultuous transparencies that immerse us in that rare occurrence in the late twentieth century: a unique, firsthand experience.

It is as difficult to grasp Raffael's most ambitious paintings from a reproduction as it is to comprehend *Casablanca* from a film still. You'd miss S. Z. Sakall checking for his wallet after Peter Lorre bumps into him, or a rapt Paul Henreid conducting *La Marseillaise.* Too much is going on to be reduced to a glance or a single image. You have to be there, in real time. "Perhaps the truth depends on a walk around the lake."[5]

By the time Raffael began studying at New York's Cooper Union School of Art in the early 1950s, Wallace Stevens, Jung, and Buddhism as taught by Daisetz T. Suzuki at Columbia University were the intellectual air that avant-garde painters breathed. "I am nature," Jackson Pollock had declared, meaning that he was of nature, not merely an outside observer. In fact, Pollock's view of nature had a great deal in common with the nineteenth-century landscape painters' quest to find God in Old Faithful. The Museum of Modern Art's Bicentennial exhibition, *The Natural Paradise: Painting in America, 1800–1950,* persuasively made the point that to seek the sublime in nature had been a central purpose of American painting, up to and including Abstract Expressionism. In that exhibition, the orange light suffusing Mark Rothko's *Number 22, 1949* bore a decided kinship to Albert Bierstadt's *Sunset in the Yosemite Valley* (1868). The elongated horizontal rhythms of Pollock's *Summertime (Number 9A, 1948)* suggested the space and flow of Frederic Edwin Church's *Niagara Falls* (1857).

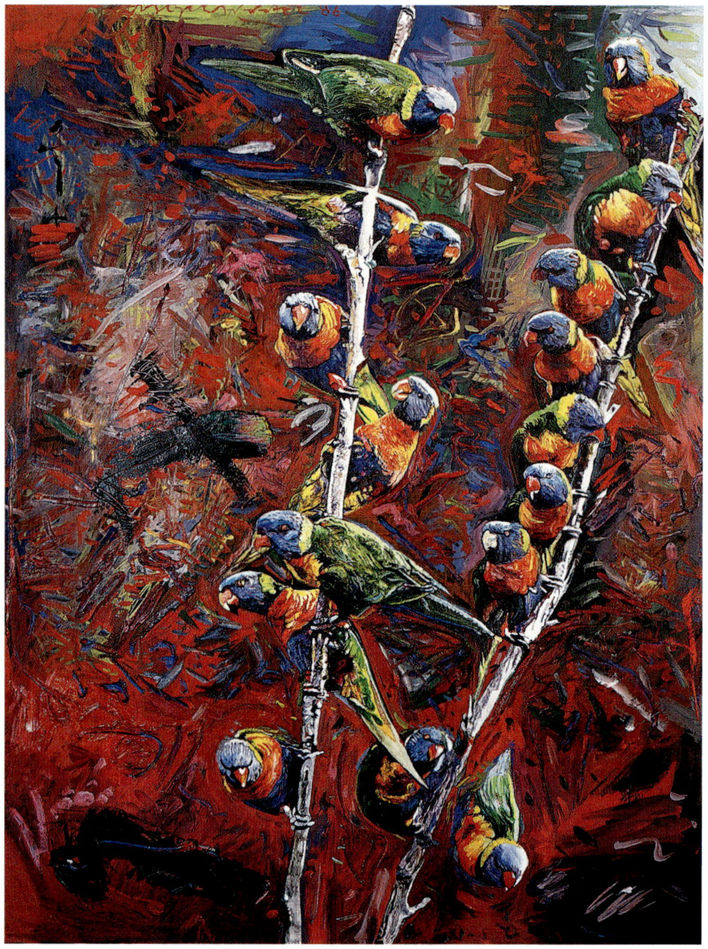

6. *Restoring,* 1986
Oil on canvas, 44 x 32 in. (111.7 x 81.2 cm)
Private collection

"My concern is with the rhythms of nature . . . the way the ocean moves. . . . The ocean is what the expanse of the west was for me. . . . I work from the inside out, like nature,"[6] Pollock was quoted as saying in the catalog. But in the 1950s a generation of younger painters mistook a manner of painting for its moral ambition. The Abstract Expressionism of Pollock, Willem de Kooning, Philip Guston, and the other painters Raffael admired, and whose example freed him to experience the act of painting as possibility, was hardening into an academy.

It was at this point that Raffael left town. It has been a lifelong habit of his to leave just as he is melding into the artistic mainstream. Not long after his art catches the attention of other artists, critics, or museums, it seems, he changes zip code and changes the subject. "I've always had to separate myself from the crowd. I guess there's this pattern of leaving something when it has reached a kind of maturity. Maybe it's the life and death theme. We were talking about how a flower goes through a cycle—maybe it's trying to protect the plant, the artist as plant."

In 1954, with a great deal of help from Bernard Chaet, his instructor at the Yale University–Norfolk School of Music and Art in Connecticut, Raffael entered graduate school at Yale and came under the influence of Josef Albers. Albers himself may be most noted for his investigations into color through the painted medium of stacked minimal squares, but his teaching, honed in the *gesamtkunst* world of the Bauhaus, was more catholic. "We want a student who sees art as neither a beauty shop nor imitation of nature . . . but as a spiritual documentation of life,"[7] he wrote. He taught that "color is the most relative medium in art,"[8] and that under no circumstances should an artist get on any aesthetic bandwagon. Robert Rauschenberg, who had studied with Albers at Black Mountain College and (like Raffael) "found his criticism so excruciating and so devastating that I never asked for it," also learned that "what he taught had to do with the entire visual world."[9]

Raffael returned to New York from Yale in 1956, in time for the exhibitions with which Jasper Johns and Rauschenberg challenged the all-pervasive influence of abstraction by introducing images into their paintings (although he didn't see their work until the early 1960s). On a Fulbright Fellowship in Italy, Raffael continued painting abstractions, as he had at Yale, but now with a suggestion of flowers. "I realized that what I always appreciated in life was the color and form and life in nature, but what I was doing was extracting the art elements from the nature experience. I was a young being who painted, rather than a being who was describing some very intimate realities."

Back in New York, Raffael once again had a near-death experience, this time from hepatitis. When he returned to painting in 1963, he began to arrange fragmented images, disturbing emblems of dreams and daily life, on white canvas, in a manner that was suggestive of contemporaneous images by artists such as Rauschenberg but far more austere in execution and psychologically charged in tone. The minute Raffael attracted some notice with these paintings—in exhibitions at the Stable Gallery in 1965 and 1966—he left town again, to teach at the University of California at Davis. It was after his first encounter with California, after meeting the artists William Allan and William T. Wiley and discovering that art and life existed outside the New York art world, that Raffael, back in Manhattan at the age of thirty-four, began what would become a lifelong enterprise: to probe the nature of beauty through the act of painting. And that is where this book begins.

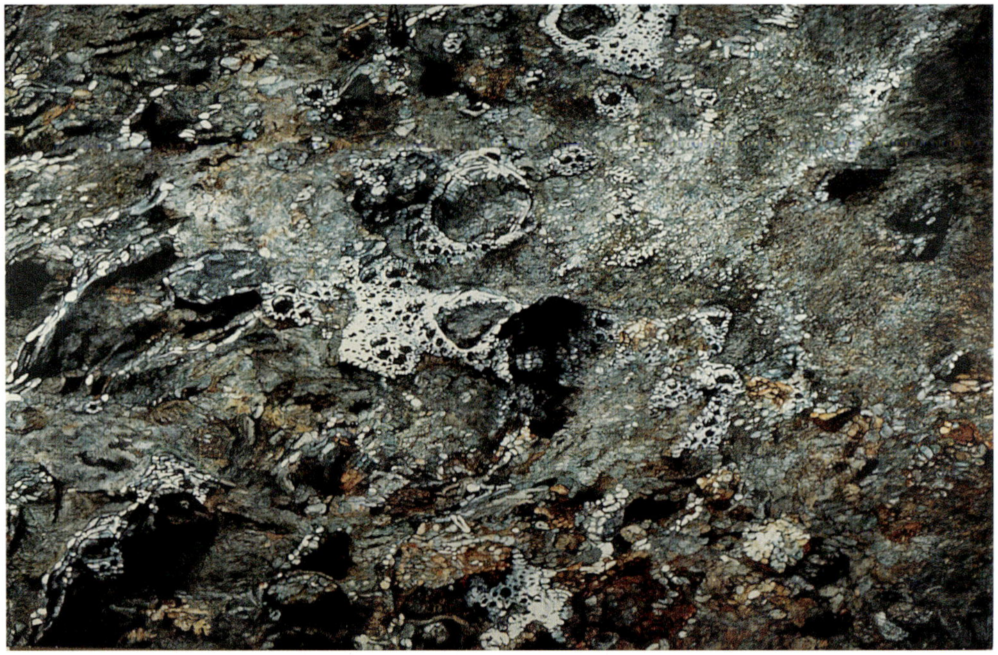

7. *Highland Magic,* 1975
Oil on canvas, 8 x 12 ft. (2.43 x 3.65 m)
Private collection; Courtesy of Nancy Hoffman Gallery, New York

By 1971, when Raffael painted *Lizard* (plate 56) and *Lion* (plate 57)—those archetypal images at opposite ends of the animal world—Chuck Close was making his deadpan frontal portraits of his friends "Kent" and "John." Though both artists worked from photographs, the differences were considerable. Close's approach was objective, his interest was in perception, his portraits were based on the grid, and he took care to make his color as bloodless and impersonal as color in mechanical reproduction. Raffael's interest was in the emotional impact of these implacable animal heads on himself and his viewers. The paintings were built from discrete shapes he mapped by tracing a projected slide, and on closer inspection they reveal miniature passages of abstract painting. His color was lush.

For the first and last time in his life, Raffael was identifiable as part of a movement—a New Realism that was briefly broad enough to encompass not only Close's complexity but also the high-gloss urban records of Richard Estes. The next year Raffael jettisoned the frontal image, which honored the denizens of nature in cinematic closeup, and entered the landscape.

As a child spending summers in Cutchogue, Peconic, and Mattituck, Long Island, Raffael would sit and gaze at Long Island Sound, enveloped in sky, water, and shoreline. "The water was flat, it had color on it, it was always changing. Sometimes you could see those big, strange, seaweedy round rocks that were on the floor of the water." Jackson Pollock's "I am nature" seemed to infuse the paintings that Raffael began to make of water observed from the viewpoint of gazer or diver in midair, a vantage that made scene and artist/viewer inseparable. Childhood memory congealed in such extraordinary paintings as *Highland Magic* (plate 7), in which rocks and water become at once pockmarked and smoothly transparent abstraction, conveying both the specific

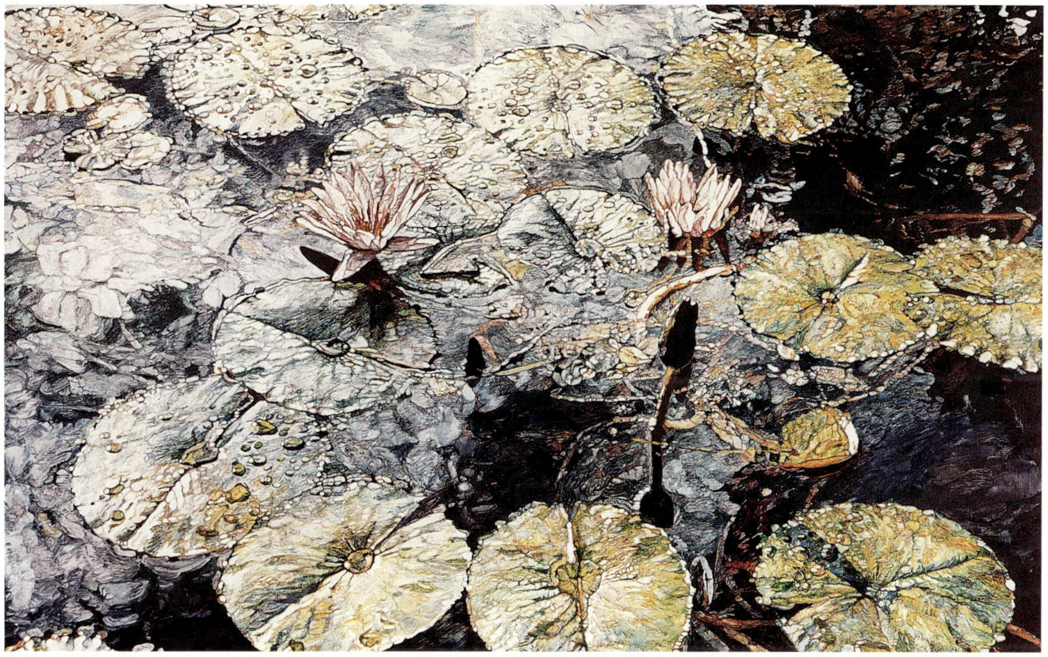

8. *Lily Painting: Hilo II,* 1975
Oil on canvas, 84 x 132 in. (213.3 x 335.2 cm)
Oakland Museum of California; Gift of the Collectors Gallery, Oakland Museum Association, and the National Endowment for the Arts

sensation of mist and a metaphor for the shoals and speed of life. That year, 1975, with photographs of a lily pond taken in Hawaii, Raffael reintroduced identifiable images, as in *Lily Painting: Hilo II* (plate 8). The lily is an emblem of interrelatedness, so inextricable from its surroundings that figure and ground are simply separate configurations of his discrete lozenges of abstraction and color. Then, as now, Raffael's paintings took nature as their form and abstraction as their means. They can be read either as whole or as fragmented into thousands of prismatic effects, which, like Thoreau, float with "the impetus derived from the earth and the system, a subjective heavily laden thought, in the midst of an unknown and infinite sea."[10]

In 1978 and 1979 *Joseph Raffael: The California Years, 1969–1978,* organized by Thomas H. Garver for the San Francisco Museum of Modern Art, traveled through the West and Midwest. Shortly after that, Raffael's world fell apart. He separated from his wife of thirteen years, Judy Davis. And their son Matthew was killed in an automobile accident. Raffael locked himself into his studio, curtained the doors and windows, and made a series of excruciatingly expressive and symbolic paintings of himself naked and alone, or naked, dying, and being reborn. When these paintings were exhibited at the Nancy Hoffman Gallery in New York, in 1984, they looked right at home in the midst

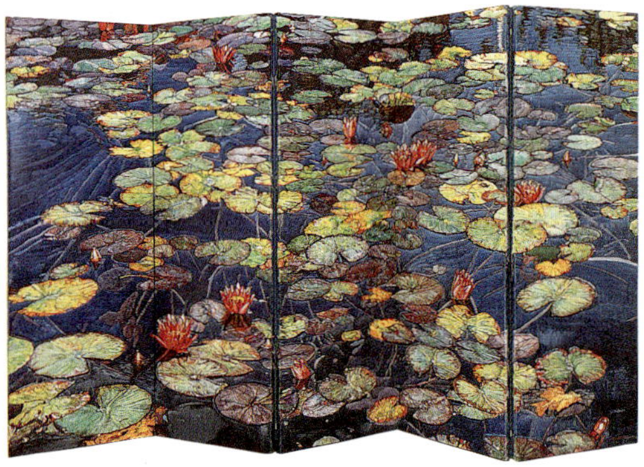

9, 10. *Renewal,* 1995
Acrylic on canvas, 5 panels: 77 x 129 in.
(195.5 x 327.6 cm)
Private collection

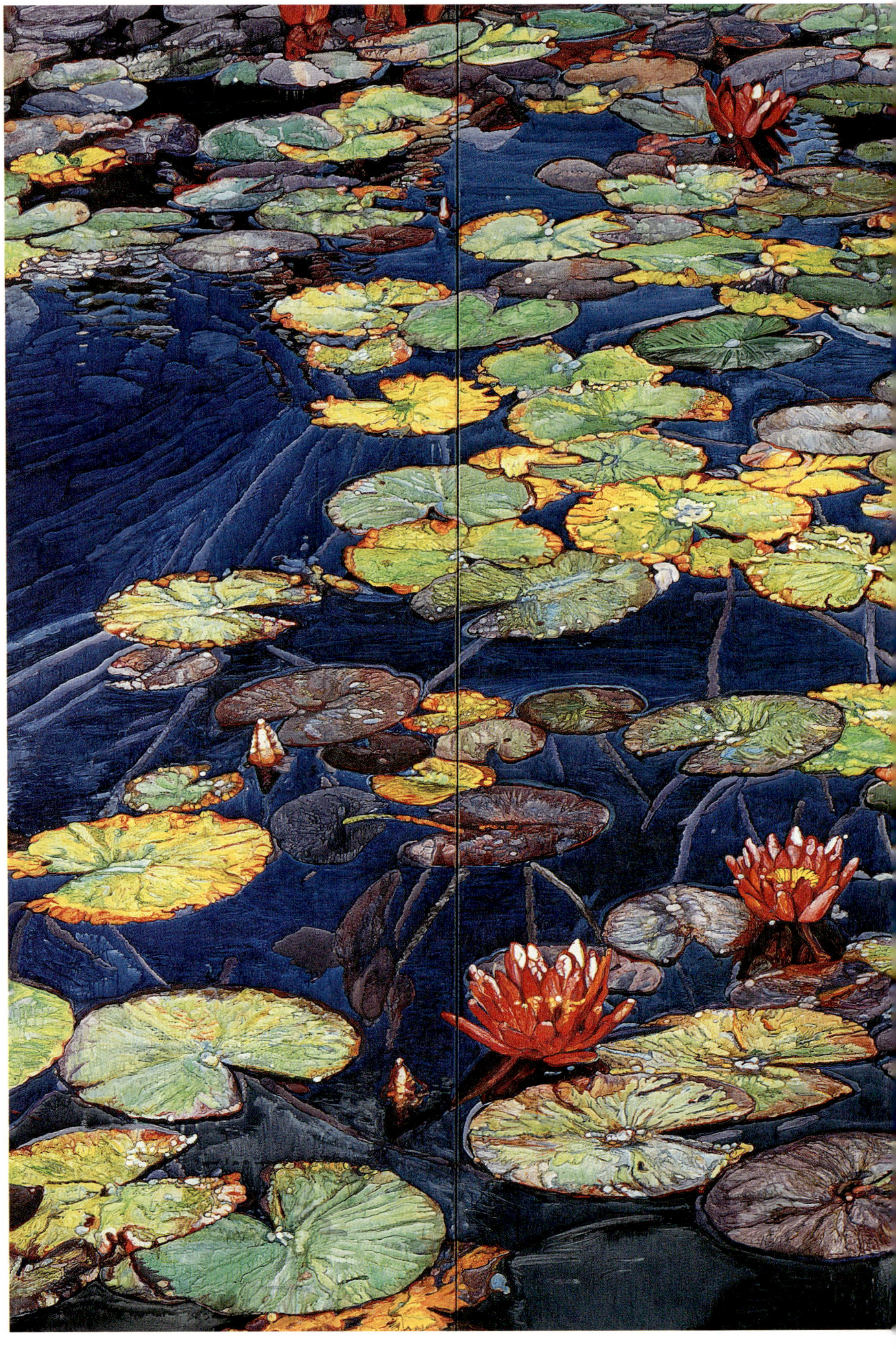

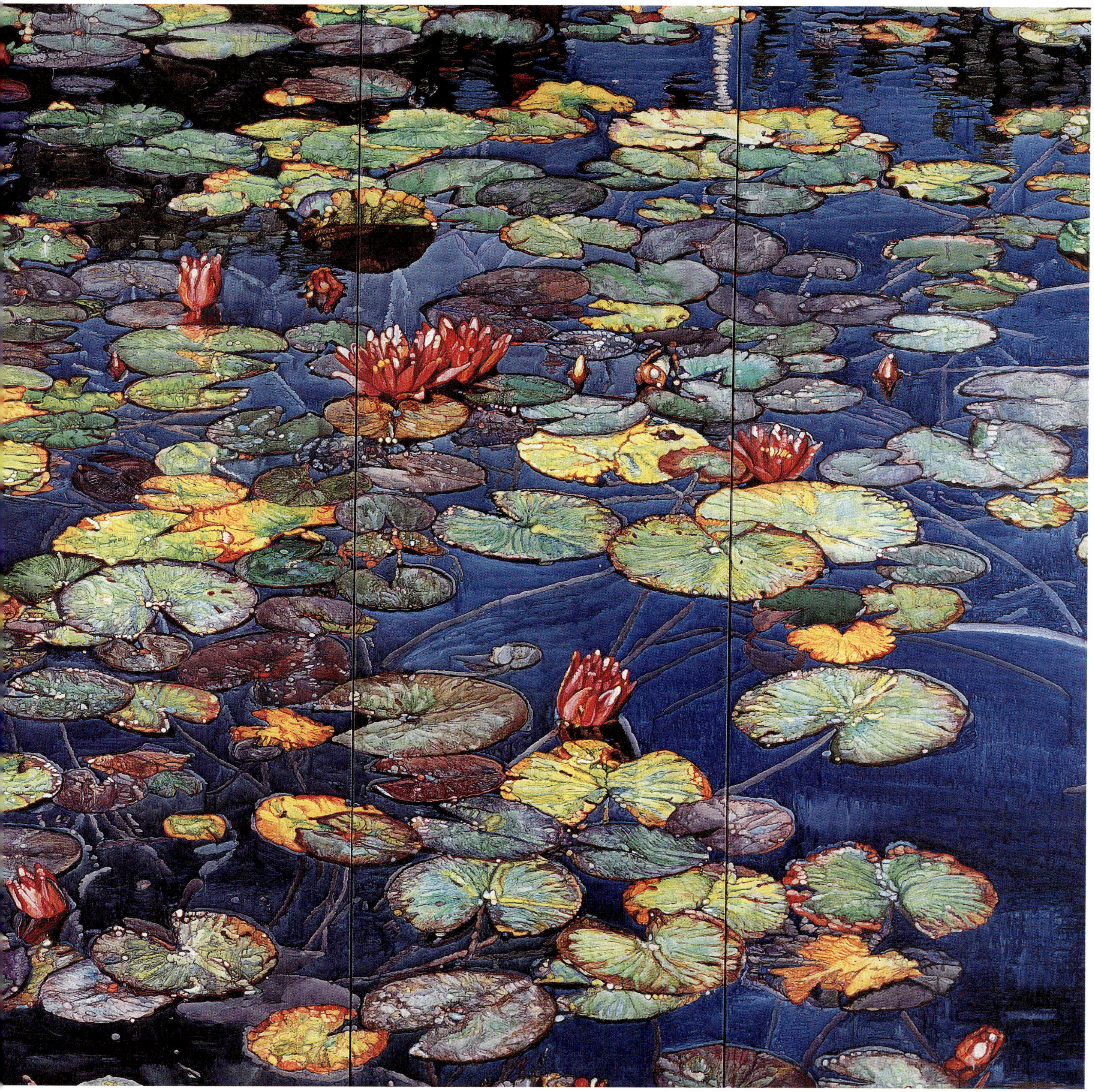

of the frenzied Expressionist picture-making exemplified by Julian Schnabel and Francesco Clemente. Raffael hardly noticed. Like Wallace Stevens, he focused on his new manner of wrestling with the ways art-making could transform the observed and experienced world.

. . . the poem makes meanings of the
rock,
Of such mixed motion and such imagery
That its barrenness becomes a thousand things
And so exists no more.[11]

In 1986 Raffael married Lannis Wood, a spiritual teacher, who had three children, as he did. "It's like being married to your Zen teacher," he says with comical pride. Together they determined that what was needed for his art was to strip himself of all outward concerns with community and ambition. They moved to France, where painting became the core around which their days are constructed, even to the extent that they sleep on a mattress in his studio.

During their years together Raffael has experimented—with subject, with medium, and with meaning. His responses to Lannis's near death in 1993 have been as disparate as the five-part acrylic screen *Renewal* (plates 9 and 10) and the watercolor triptych *May 4th* (plate 120). The lily pads in *Renewal* traverse its glistening surface in extravagantly colored jubilation. *May 4th* simultaneously explodes and implodes from the central coot's nest, which paradoxically anchors and is subsumed by its volatile, contradictory universe.

At a moment when many artists are struggling with the basic question—can painting have relevance in our multimedia times?—Raffael continues to demonstrate that the brush is as equal to the task of conjuring the sublime at the end of the twentieth century as it was when Thoreau homesteaded Walden or the Chinese master Fan Kuan traveled the mountains and streams of the Northern Sung dynasty.

Notes

1. Joseph Raffael, conversation with Amei Wallach, Cap d'Antibes, France, April 1997. Unless otherwise indicated, all Raffael quotes are from this source.
2. *The Selected Writings of Ralph Waldo Emerson,* ed. Brooks Atkinson (New York: Modern Library, 1950), p. 34; in Barbara Novak, *Nature and Culture* (New York: Oxford University Press, 1986), p. 7.
3. Robert Hughes, "A Note on Joseph Raffael," in *Joseph Raffael: The California Years, 1969–1978* (San Francisco: San Francisco Museum of Modern Art, 1978), p. 28.
4. Hopper, "Notes on Painting," in *Edward Hopper* (New York: Museum of Modern Art, 1933), p. 17; in Kynaston McShine, ed., *The Natural Paradise: Painting in America, 1800–1950* (New York: Museum of Modern Art, 1976), p. 109.
5. Wallace Stevens, "Notes toward a Supreme Fiction," in *Wallace Stevens: The Collected Poems* (New York: Vintage Books, 1990), p. 386. My chapter titles are also taken from *Wallace Stevens: The Collected Poems.* "The rivers shine," from "The Dove in the Belly," p. 366; "Mazily dewed," from "The Comedian as the Letter C," p. 41; "Things to be cherished," from "Sunday Morning," p. 67; "In its watery radiance," from "Sea Surface Full of Clouds," p. 99; "Sacrament and celebration," from "Comedian as the Letter C," p. 39; and "The Woman in Sunshine," title of poem, p. 445.
6. Pollock, c. 1955–56, in B. H. Friedman, *Jackson Pollock: Energy Made Visible* (New York: McGraw Hill, 1972), p. 228; in McShine, ed., *Natural Paradise,* p. 109.
7. Josef Albers, "Concerning Art Instruction," *Black Mountain College Bulletin,* no. 2 (June 1934): 393; in Mary Emma Harris, "Josef Albers: Art Education at Black Mountain College," in *Josef Albers: A Retrospective* (New York: Solomon R. Guggenheim Museum, 1988), p. 51.
8. Color notes by Irene Cullis, in Harris, "Josef Albers," pp. 53, 55.
9. Rauschenberg, in Calvin Tomkins, *The Bride and the Bachelors: Five Masters of the Avant-Garde* (New York: Viking Press, 1968), p. 199; in Harris, "Josef Albers," p. 55.
10. Thoreau, entry for August 13, 1838, in *The Journal of Henry D. Thoreau,* ed. Bradford Torrey and Francis H. Allen (New York: Dover, 1962), vol. 1, p. 34; in McShine, ed., *Natural Paradise,* p. 79.
11. Stevens, "The Rock," in *Wallace Stevens: The Collected Poems,* p. 527.

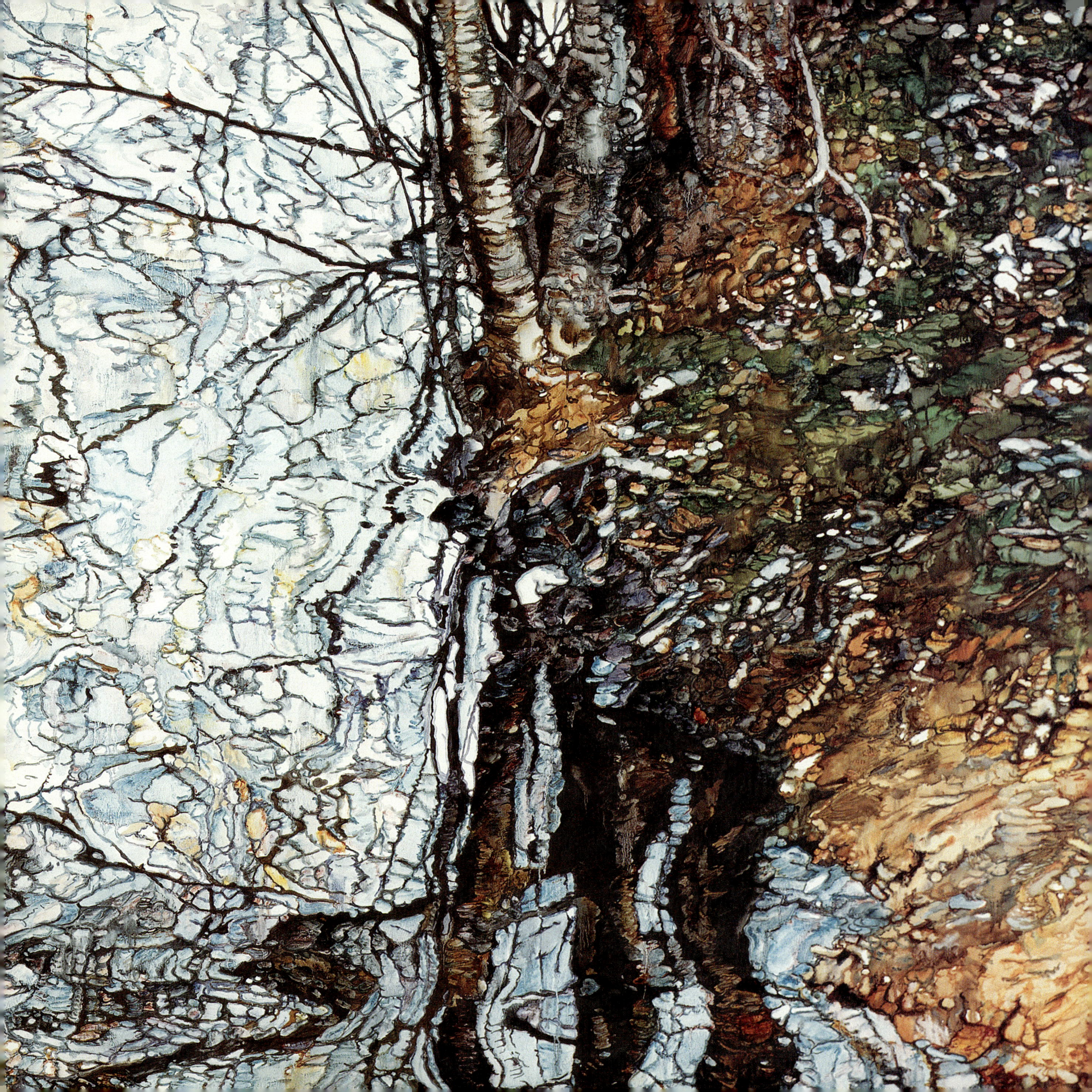

The Water and Shore Paintings

"The rivers shine and hold their mirrors up"

When Joseph Raffael paints water, he paints light and movement. The light is transparent, it glitters, it moves as the water moves. There is a great deal of slippage in this light. It loses itself in the depth and reflects off the surface. The surface appears gelatinous, seems to slide, submerge, to surf the light. When he paints the shore, he paints substantiality, he separates grasses and defines roots.

In *Blue Pond, Winter Shore* (plate 28), Raffael painted both. The way he recalls it,

> It was December in California. The grasses were still green, there were fallen leaves, some trunks; the brown at the bottom is an eaten-away bank from this river. The earth part on the right is some kind of reality, although very complex. The whole left part of the painting is blue, the blue water with reflections of trees in it, and branches. So what's happening in the scene is that everything's still on the right, but the water is moving in myriad ways. I love that water. I would say this is a real good self-portrait of my mind. It's like zingzingzingzing rrrrrrr! It's static a lot of the time, like the water, so many little things going on.

The line between image and abstraction is porous in Raffael's water paintings, even when, as in *Galactic Waters III* (plate 12), a duck treads these waters. Consider the duck as the eyeball in Thoreau's notion of a lake as "earth's eye, looking into which the beholder measures the depth of his own nature." Because the water stretches in all directions, this duck seems alone in an infinite universe. In fact, though, it floats on a lake, an altogether finite and prosaic universe—unless one is Thoreau/Raffael, in which case, "Nothing so fair, so pure, and at the same time so large, as a lake, perchance lies on the surface of the earth."[1]

11. Detail of *Blue Pond, Winter Shore*, 1977
See plate 28

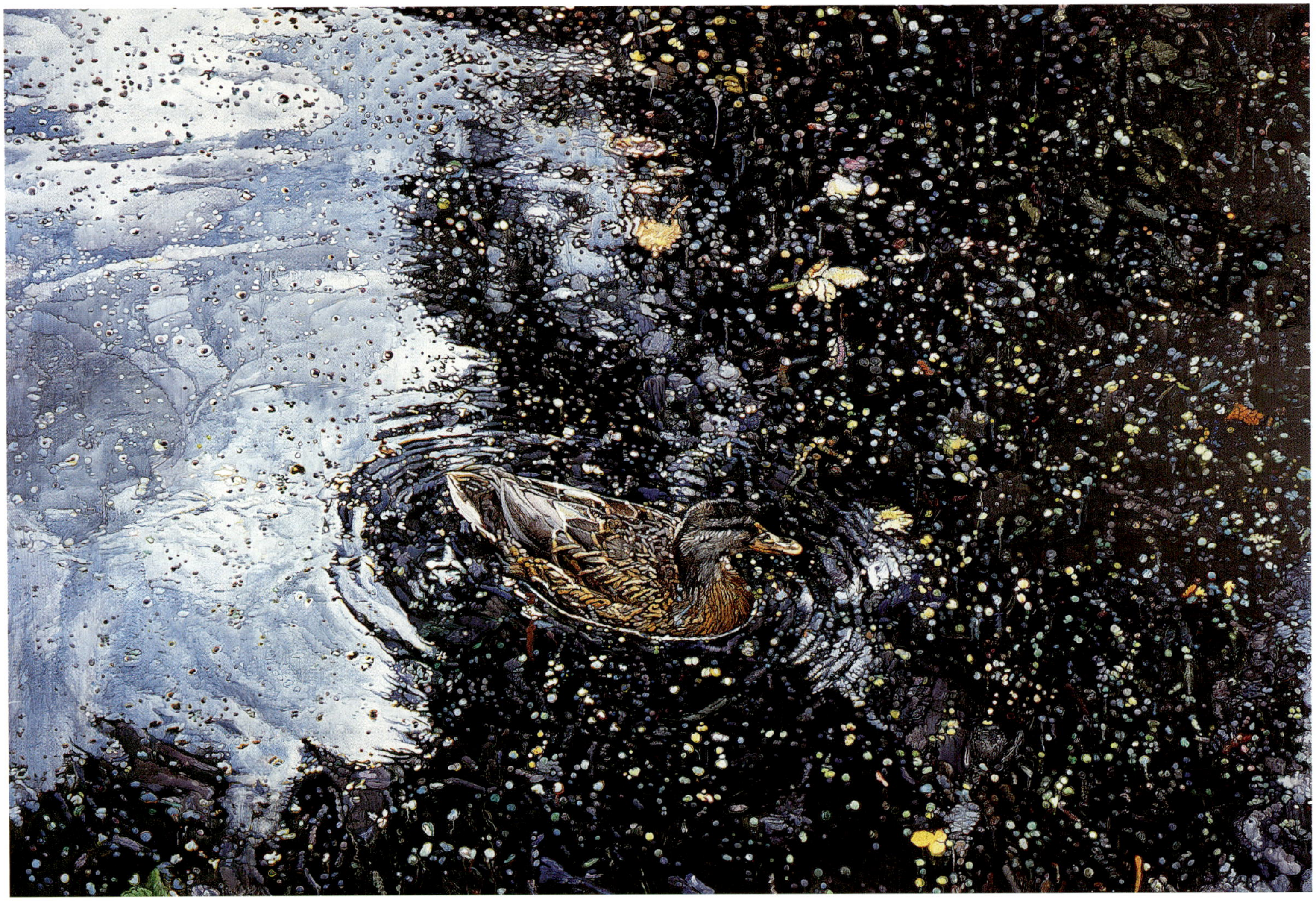

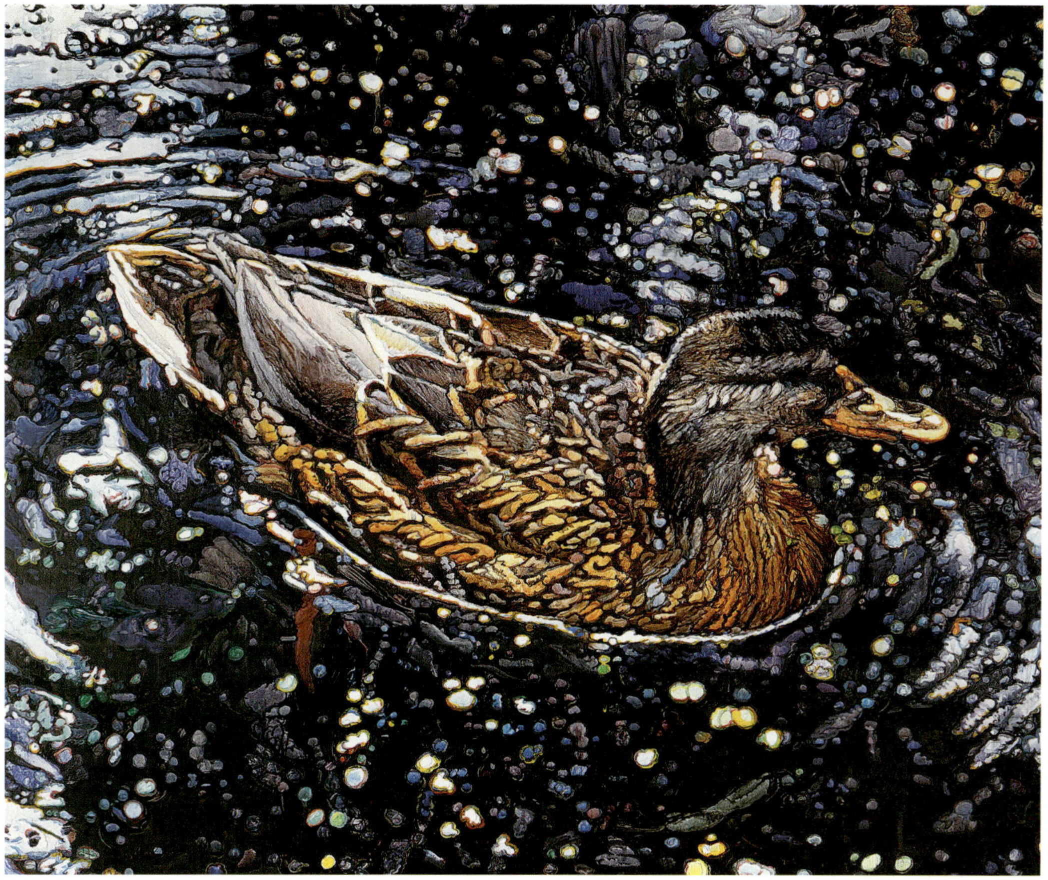

OPPOSITE
12. *Galactic Waters III,* 1995
Acrylic on linen, 57 x 82½ in.
(144.7 x 209.5 cm)
Courtesy of Nancy Hoffman Gallery,
New York

ABOVE
13. Detail of *Galactic Waters III*

Pointillist prisms of light trouble the surface of the water and animate layers upon layers beneath. There is a play between surface and depth that is at once formal and metaphysical. The duck is advancing from luminous blue currents into these darkening depths, in a rippled path of its own making. "The mystery," says Raffael, "is being a human being, finding oneself in this universe, and trying to make head or tail of it."

For nearly a decade, in the 1980s, Raffael did not make water paintings. While he was grappling with the realities of the life he was remaking, he painted what was around him: Lannis, their children, sacred symbols, flowers, and animals. Then, in 1989, he began to ponder evening light on the North Sea within a series of paintings he called Soyez mystérieuses. This, he explains, is the feminine form of the command, "Be mysterious!" At the time, Raffael was particularly interested in Vincent van Gogh and

Paul Gauguin, and Gauguin had written "Soyez mystérieuses" on some of his paintings. Raffael was at a moment when it was a mystery to him what the next painting would be. He had been wanting to make his way back to painting water, and it was this feminine form that particularly intrigued him. "I'm very interested in the feminine, the experience of the feminine within myself and the experience of the feminine outside myself."

The water paintings of the 1970s had been muscular. But in *Soyez mystérieuses VIII* of 1989 (plate 14), a horizontal path of blue separates a vertical band of rosy creases constructed of innumerable points of color and light. Raffael made his way back to water paintings by exchanging the hurly-burly for the hush.

NOTE

1. Henry David Thoreau, *Walden* (1854; reprint, New York: Mentor, 1942), pp. 128–29; in Kynaston McShine, ed., *The Natural Paradise: Painting in America, 1800–1950* (New York: Museum of Modern Art, 1976), p. 102.

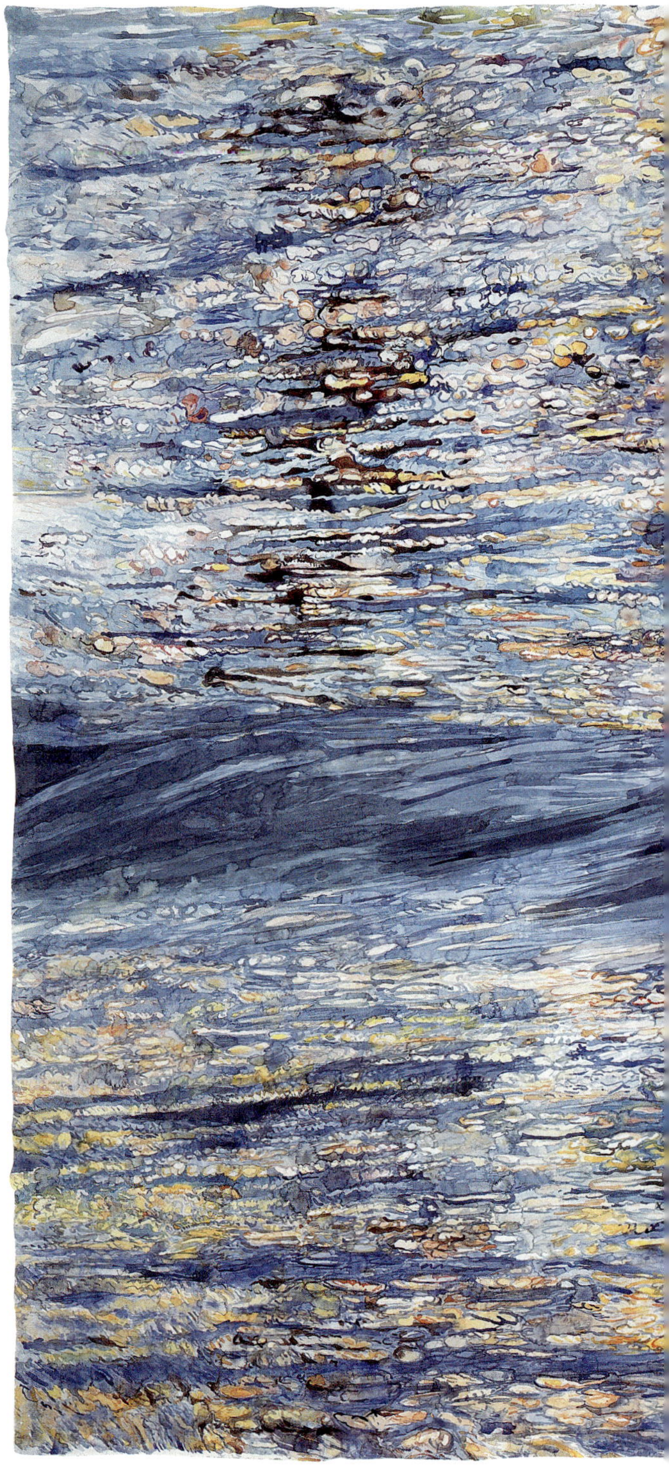

14. *Soyez mystérieuses VIII,* 1989
Watercolor on paper, triptych: 75¾ x 114 in.
(192.3 x 289.5 cm)
Orlando Museum of Art, Orlando, Florida;
Acquisition Trust Purchase, 1989

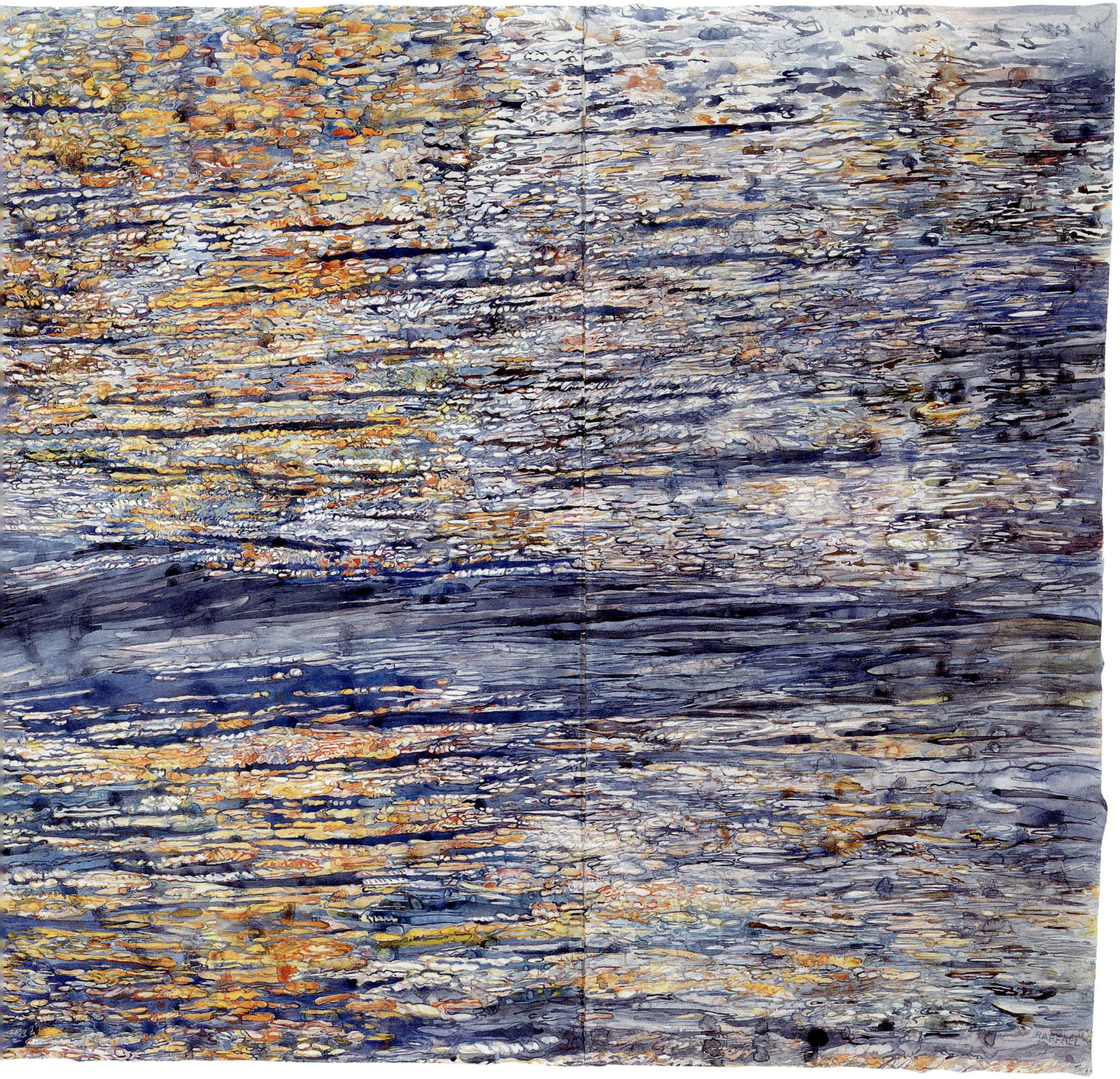

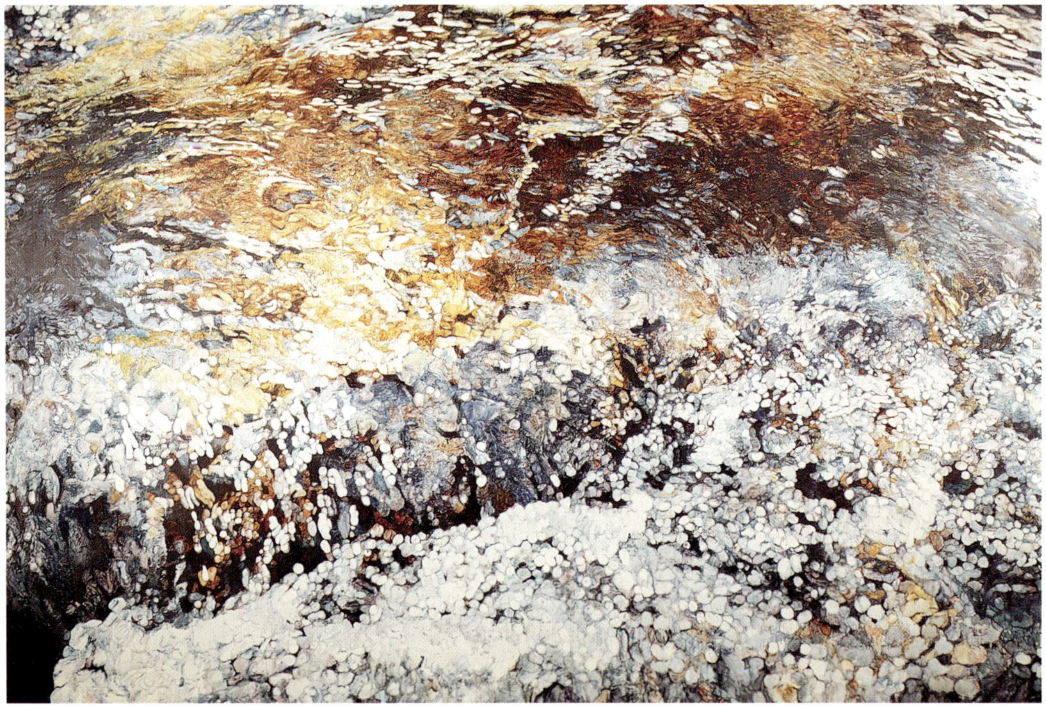

15. *Water Painting II,* 1973
Oil on canvas, 78 x 114 in. (198.1 x 289.5 cm)
BankAmerica Corporation Art Collection, San Francisco

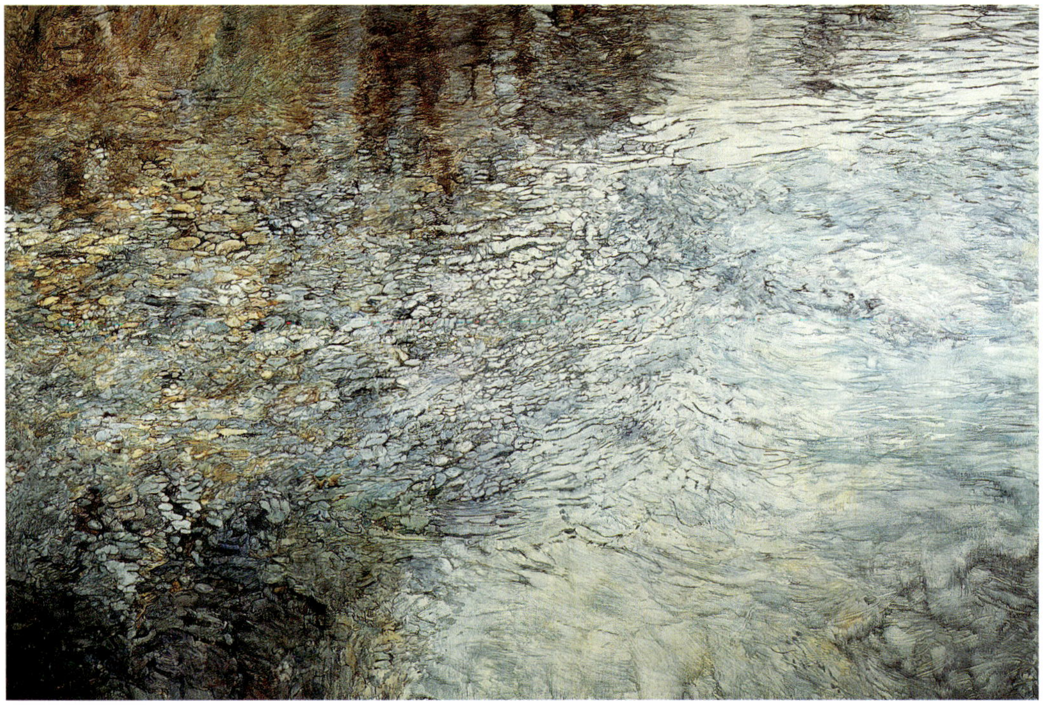

16. *Water Painting V,* 1973
Oil on canvas, 78 x 114½ in. (198.1 x 290.2 cm)
Whitney Museum of American Art, New York; Purchase

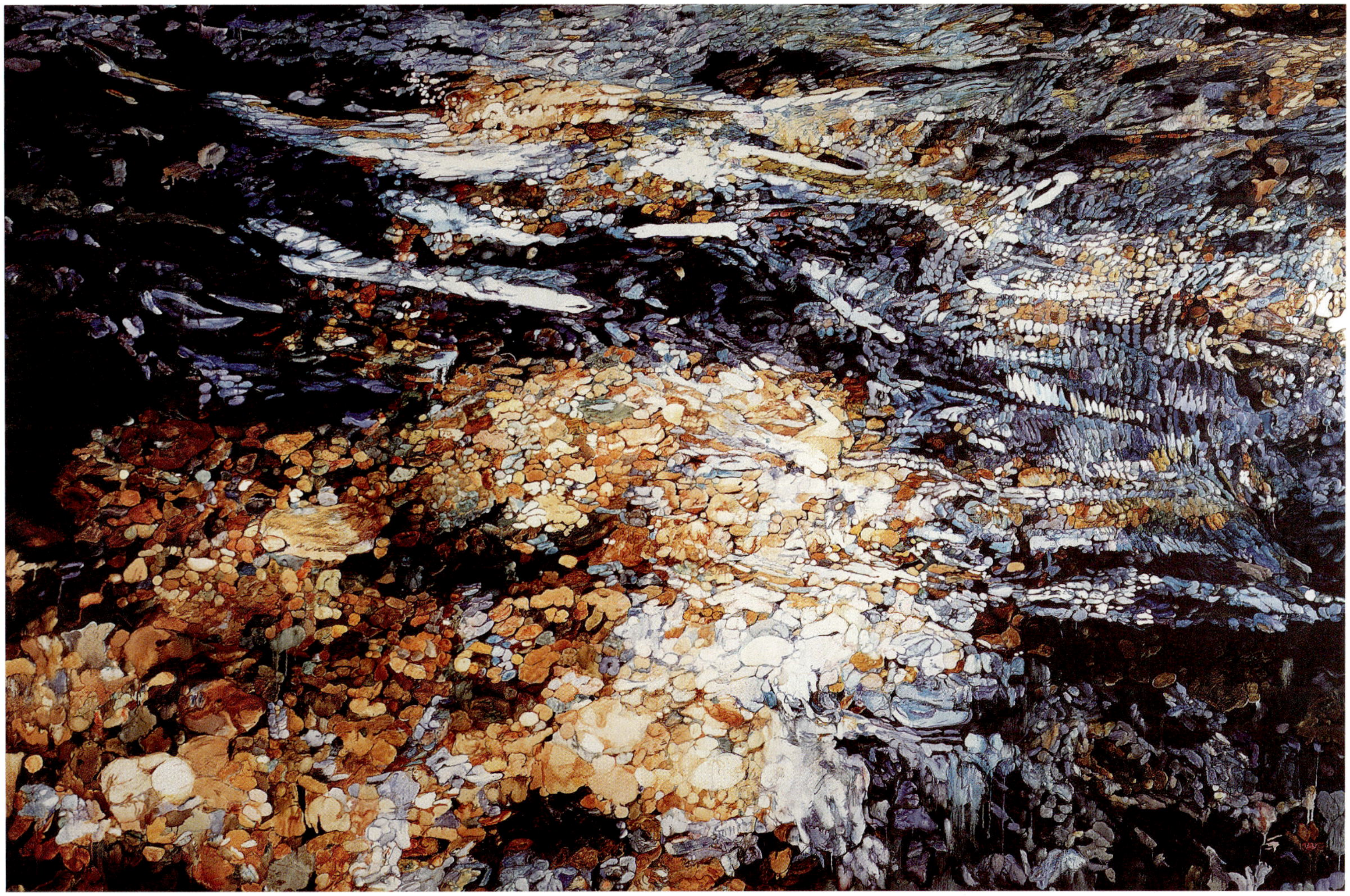

17. *Water Painting VI,* 1973
Oil on canvas, 78 x 114 in.
(198.1 x 289.5 cm)
Private collection, New York

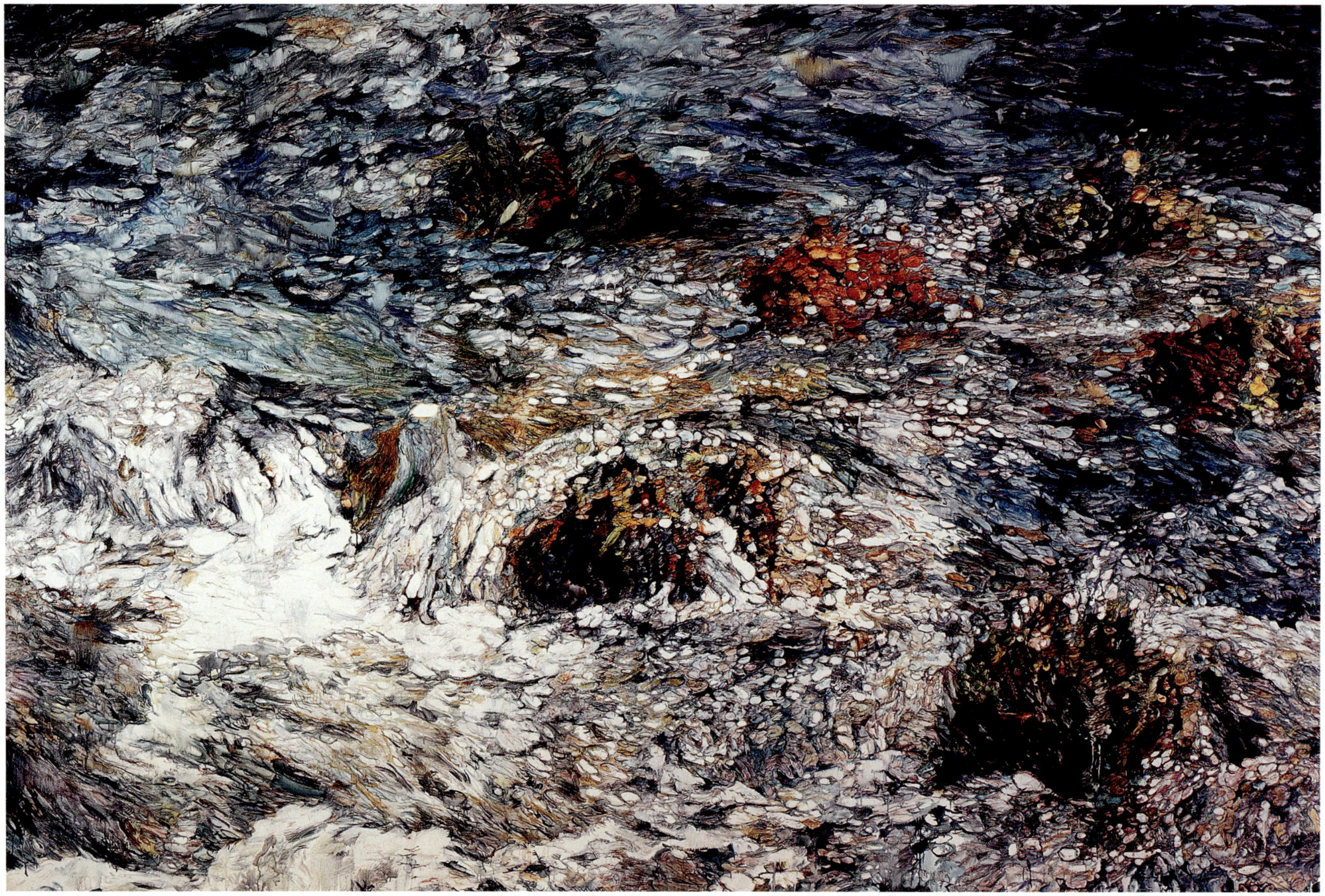

18. *Paper Mill Creek,* 1974
Oil on canvas, 78 x 114 in.
(198.1 x 289.5 cm)
Butler Institute of American Art,
Youngstown, Ohio

RIGHT
19. *Scottish Falls,* 1974
Oil on canvas, 78 x 114 in.
(198.1 x 289.5 cm)
Mr. and Mrs. Marshall Bennett, Chicago

BELOW
20. *Black Craig Bubbles,* 1974
Oil on canvas, 66 x 108 in.
(167.6 x 274.2 cm)
Private collection

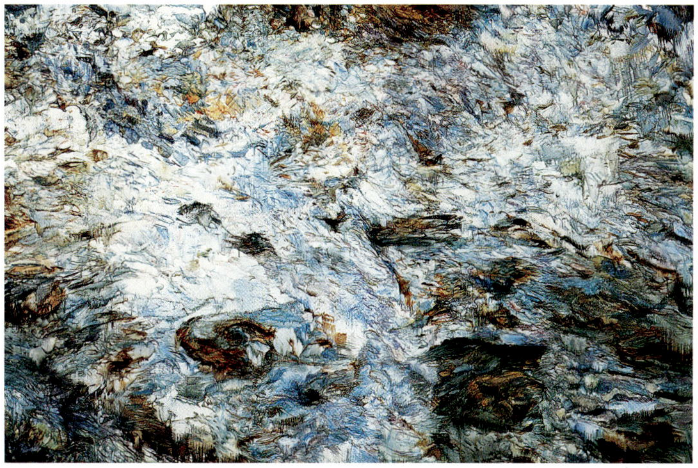

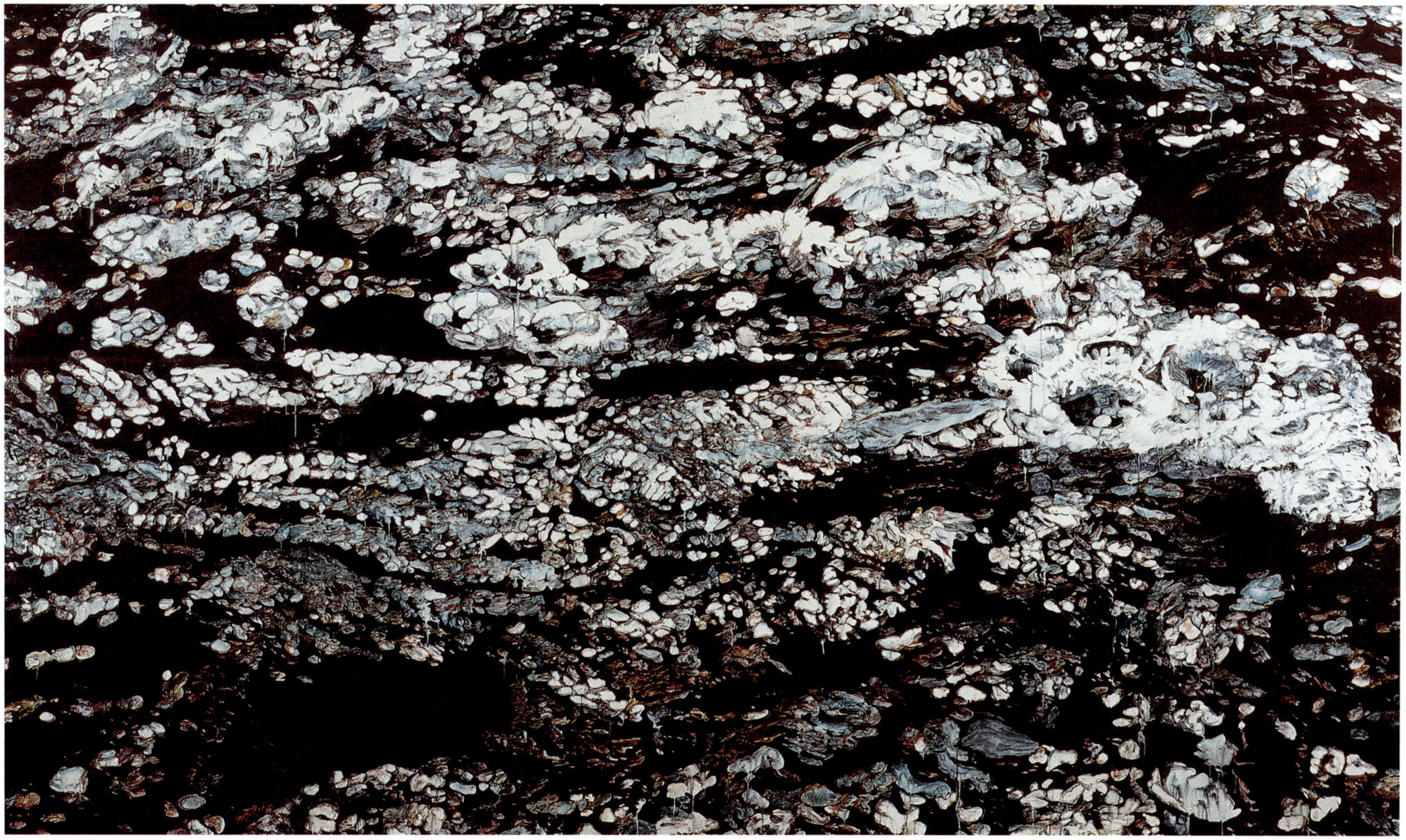

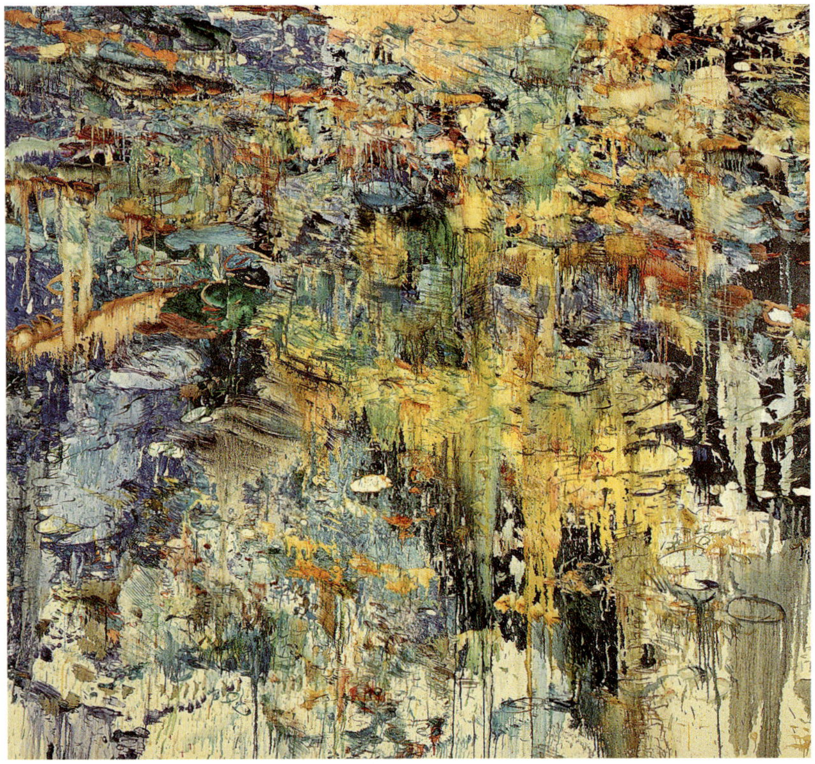

LEFT

21. *Fourth of July,* 1974
Oil on canvas, 78 x 84 in. (198.1 x 213.4 cm)
Joseph and Lannis Raffael, Cap d'Antibes, France

BELOW

22. *Island Magic,* 1975
Oil on canvas, 84 x 132 in. (213.3 x 335.2 cm)
Private collection

OPPOSITE

23. *Kona,* 1975
Oil on canvas, 90 x 66 in.
(228.5 x 167.6 cm)
Private collection, California

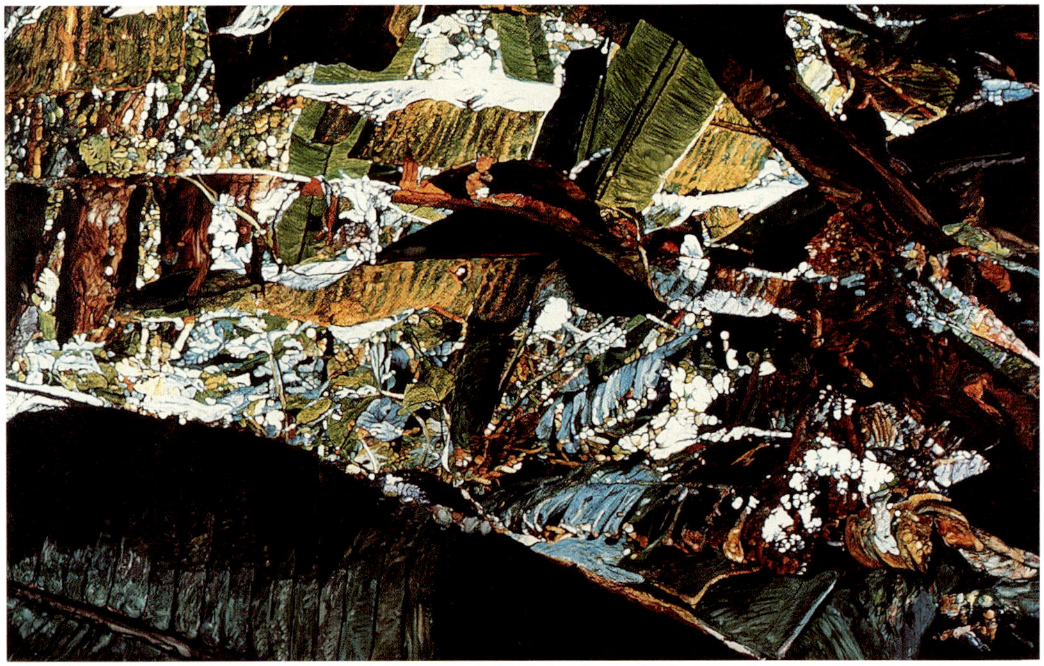

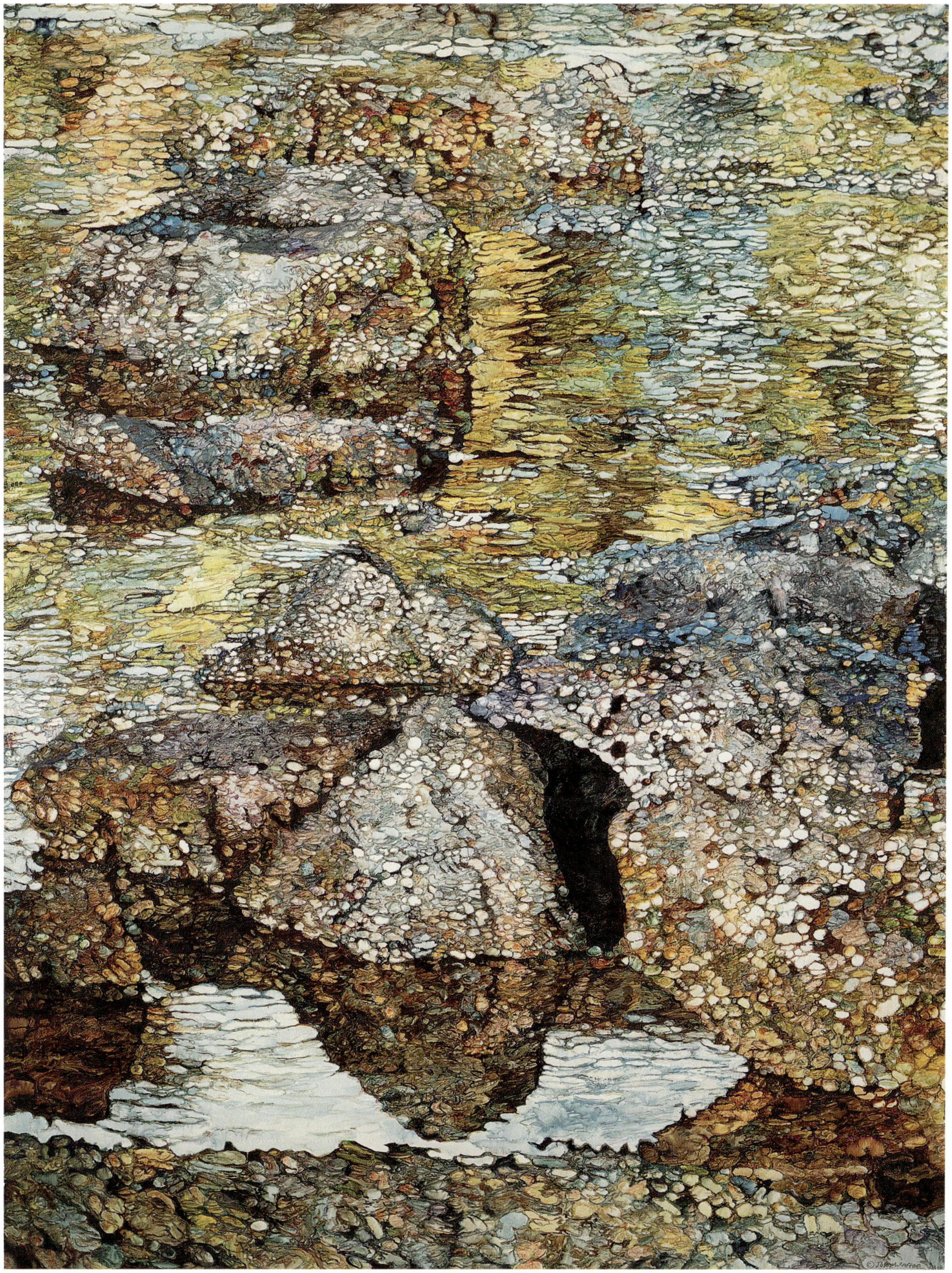

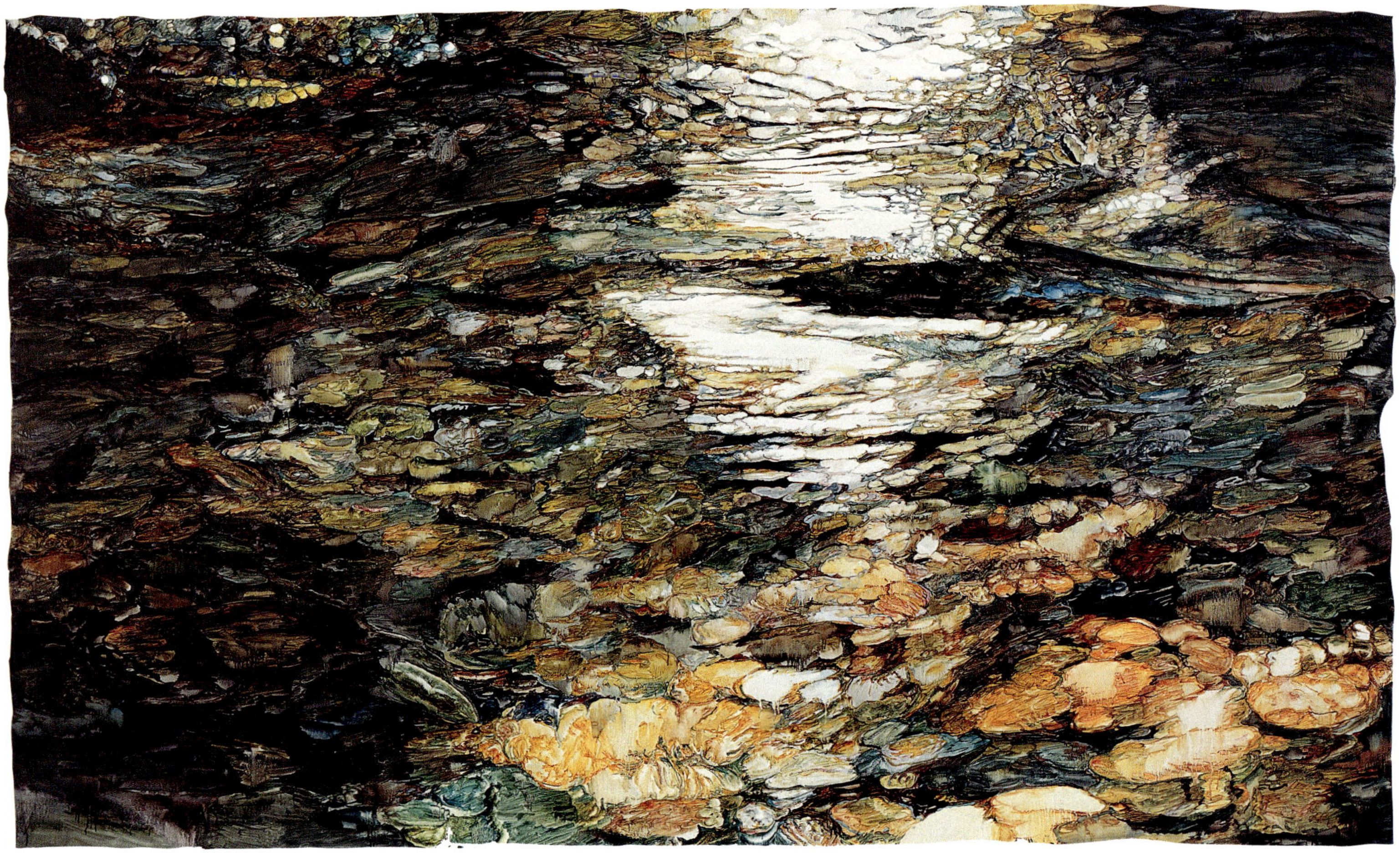

ABOVE

24. *Muir Creek IV,* 1976
Oil on canvas, 72 x 108 in. (182.8 x 274.2 cm)
Private collection

OPPOSITE

25. *Muir,* 1979
Oil on canvas, 78 x 93 in. (198.1 x 236.2 cm)
Public collection, Chicago

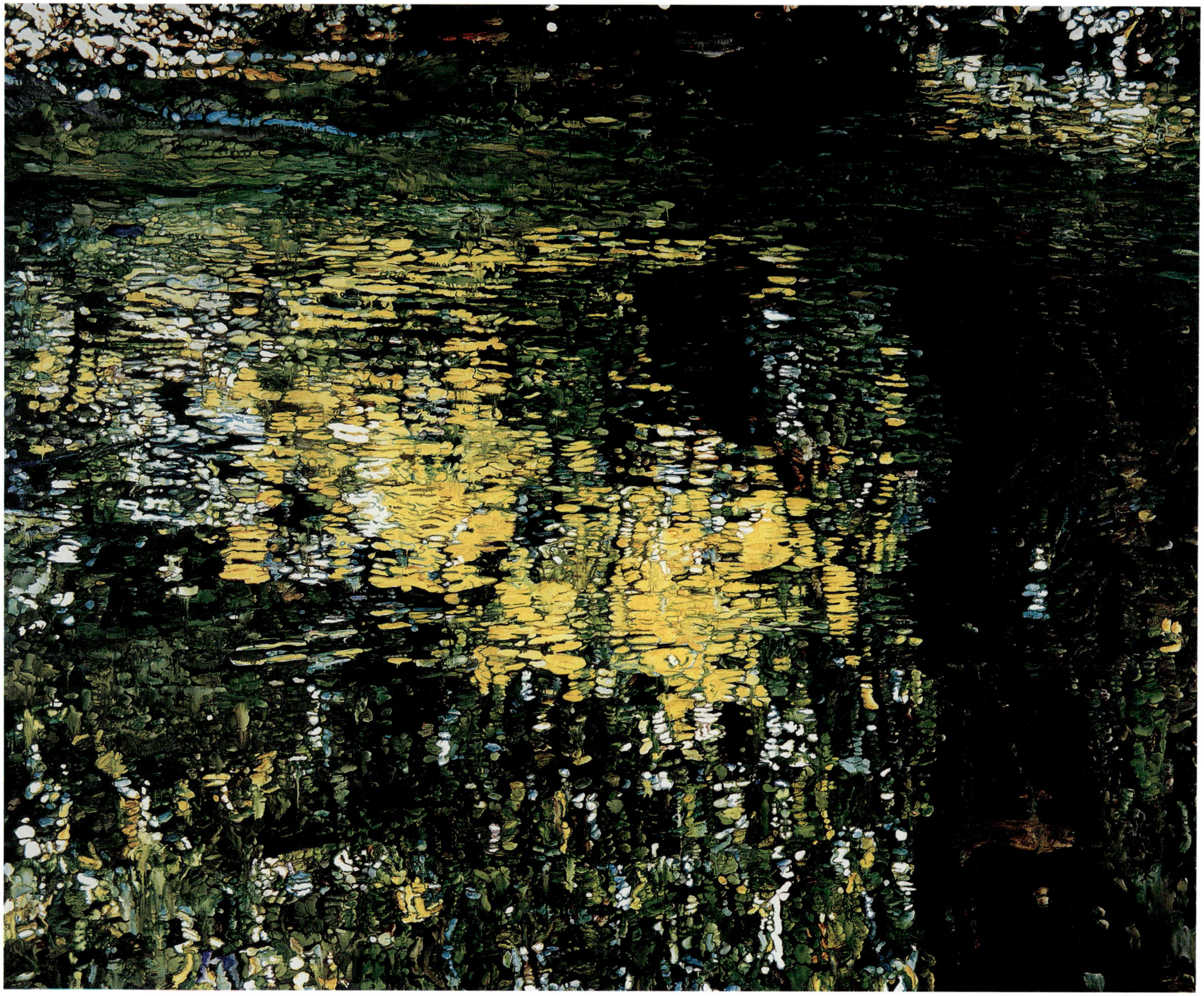

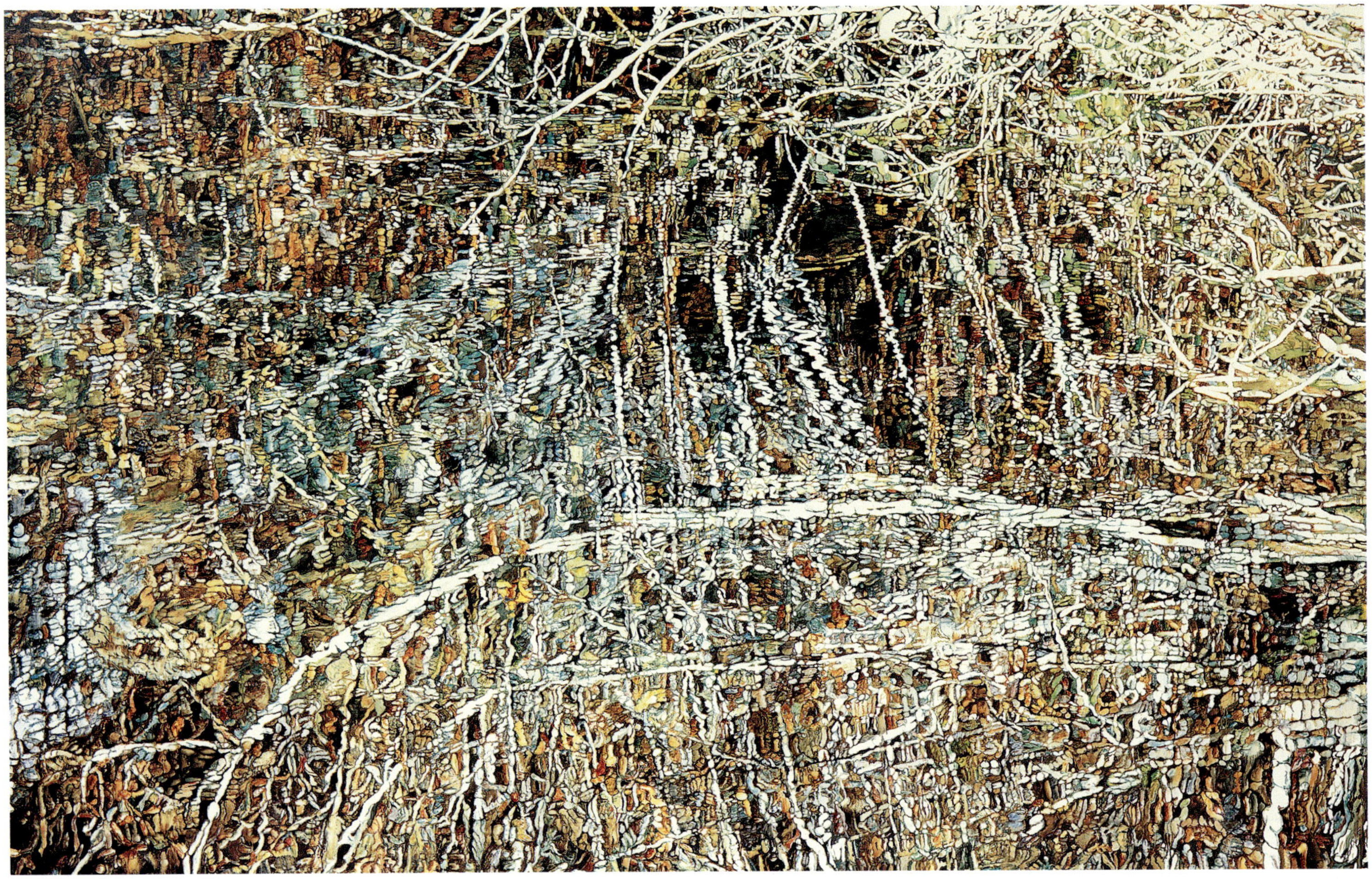

26. *Ch'i,* 1977
Oil on canvas, 8 ft. 2 3/16 in. x 12 ft. 3 in.
(2.5 x 3.73 m)
Brauer Museum of Art, Valparaiso, Indiana; Valparaiso University Sloan Fund Purchase

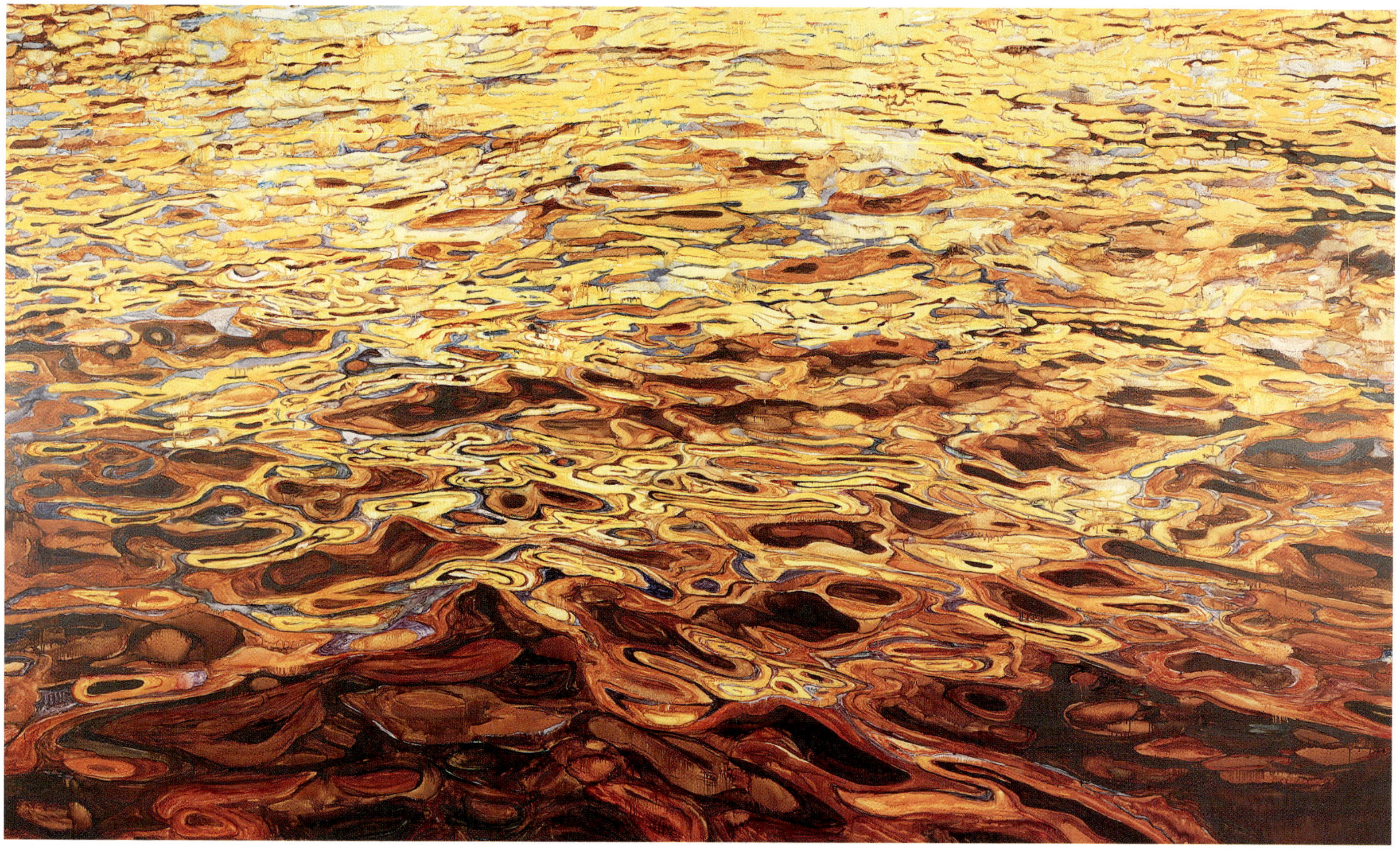

27. *Sunset on South China Sea II,* 1978
Oil on canvas, 78¼ x 126¼ in.
(182.8 x 304.7 cm)
Denver Art Museum; Anonymous gift

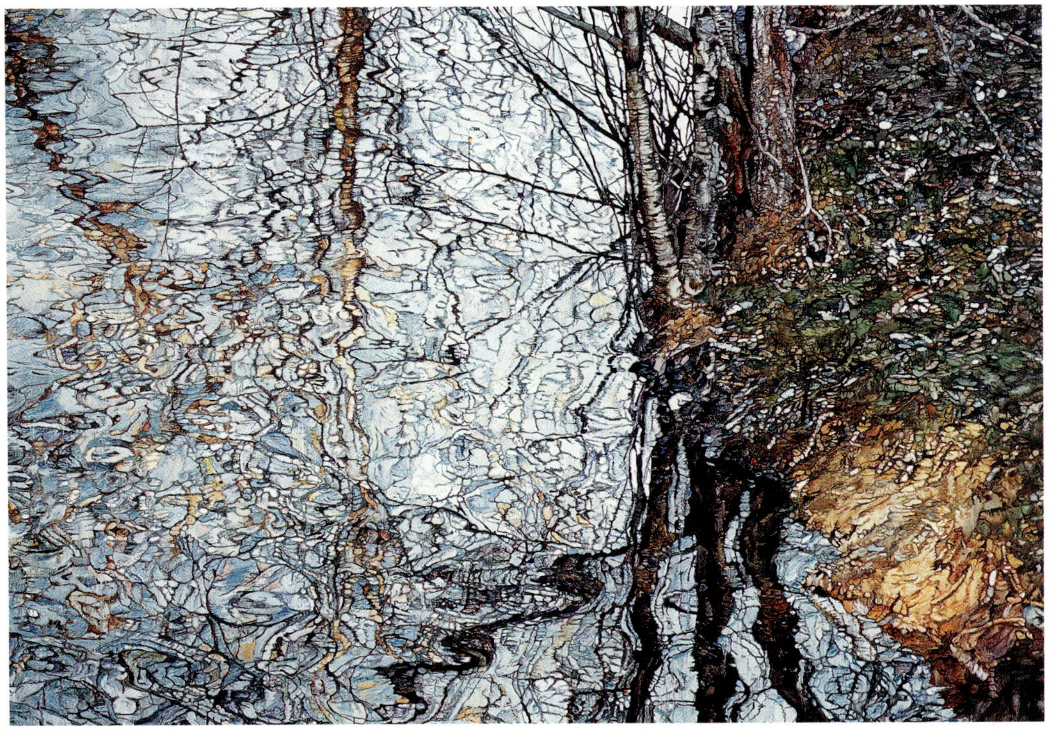

28. *Blue Pond, Winter Shore,* 1977
Oil on canvas, 78 x 114 in. (198.1 x 289.5 cm)
J. B. Speed Art Museum, Louisville, Kentucky

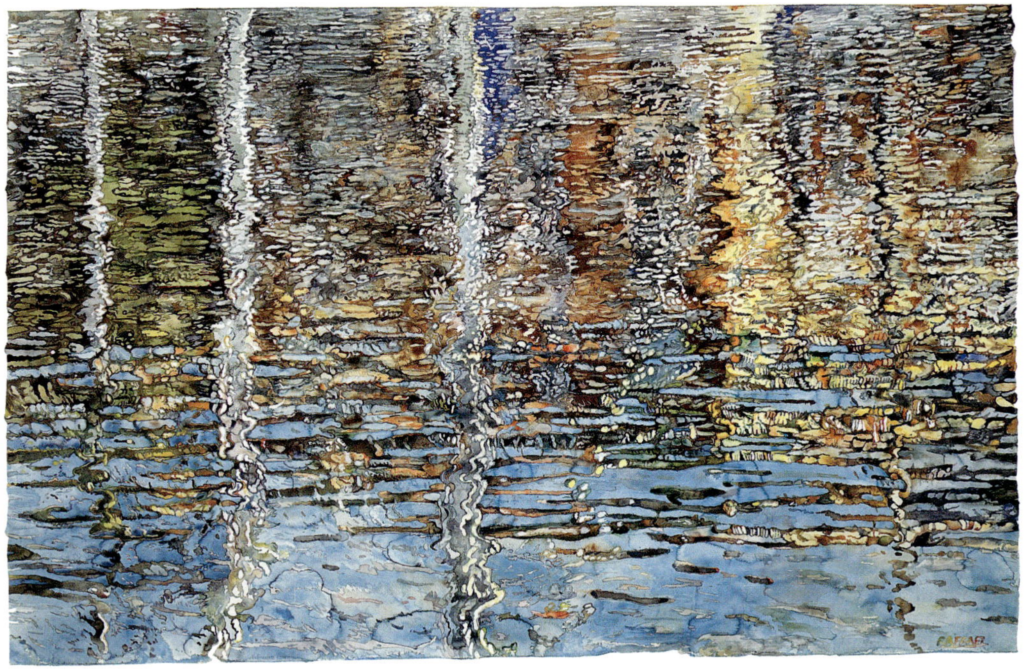

29. *Water and Reflections,* 1992
Watercolor on paper, 52¼ x 81 in. (132.7 x 205.7 cm)
Private collection, Hobe Sound, Florida

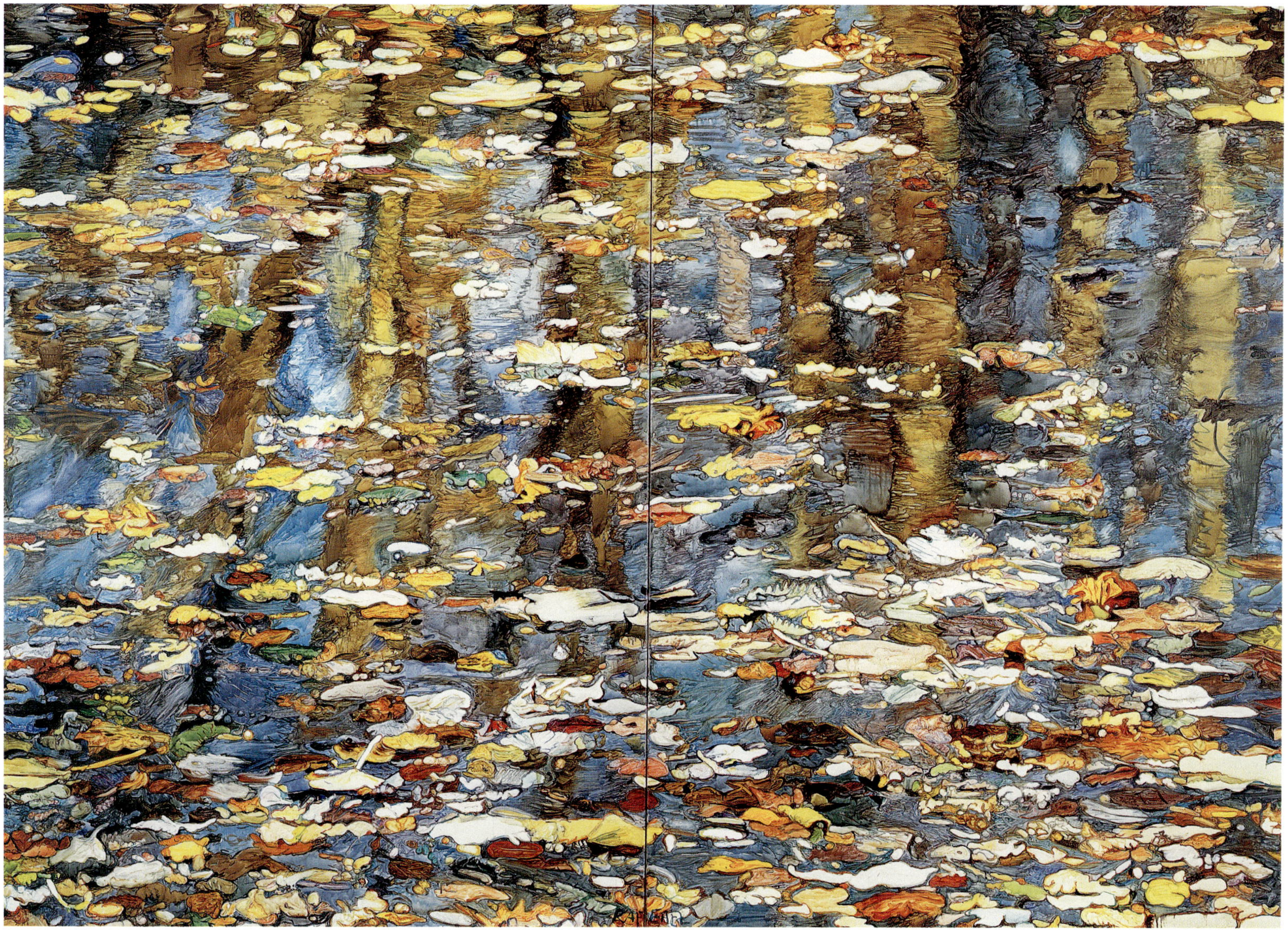

30. *Reflection,* 1988
Oil on canvas, 76¾ x 102½ in.
(194.9 x 260.3 cm)
Private collection

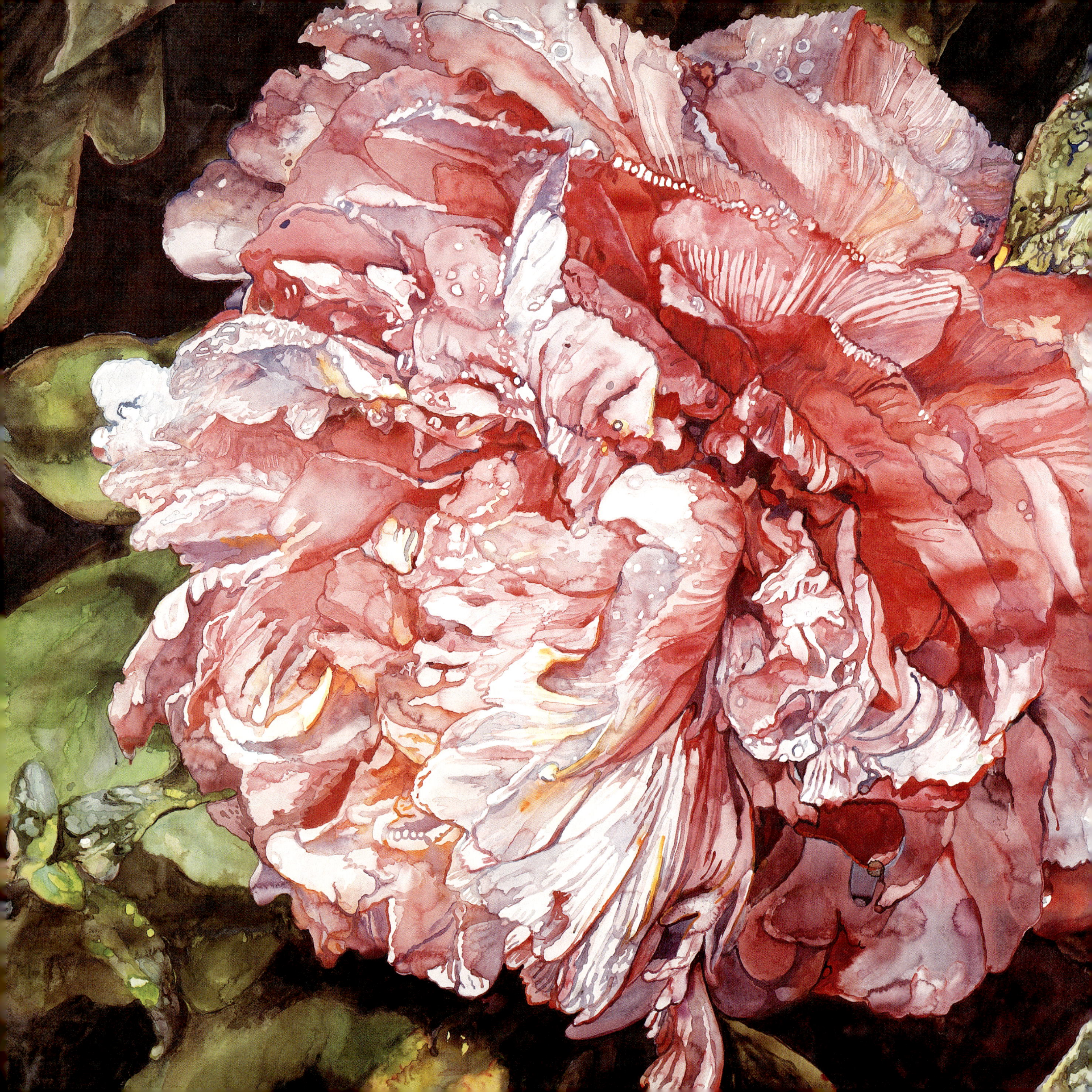

The Flower and Leaf Paintings

"Mazily dewed and mauved in bloom"

31. Detail of *After the Rain: A Peony and Its Leaves,* 1993
See plate 51

Raffael's predilection for translucence and the effects it can achieve in paint is nowhere more evident than in his flower paintings. He fixes his flowers at the moment when they are infused by the sun, like alabaster. Or he contemplates them in the morning dew or after a rain, so that it is the drops of water that become transparent, that shimmer and reflect and permit him to record each infinitesimal change in color and weight and lucidity.

For a great many years now Raffael has been accustomed to switching between oil and watercolor for both his major paintings and his smaller works, no matter what the subject or size. In France he added acrylic to his repertoire. He considers watercolor as capable of monumentality as either oil or acrylic. A watercolor is not to him, as it is to most painters and curators, a work on paper. It is a painting. Watercolor is also the medium best suited to his flower paintings, though even here he uses it interchangeably with oil.

"Basically what I started wanting to do was to make my oil paintings look like these watercolors I was mixing on the plates. So I started painting in oils very, very thinly. That got my painting to look different from anybody else's, because not only was it very transparent, but it had all those colors and a lot of runniness and complexity, which I liked. Not only was I painting complex images, they were being painted in a complex medium, with little brushes."

The painter William Allan showed him how to use the smooth side of the Arches paper, where the color would stay more on the surface. It was also Allan who had given him the photographs of water that instigated Raffael's water paintings. Two of Raffael's most stirring flower and leaf paintings are watercolors. In *Matthew's Branch*

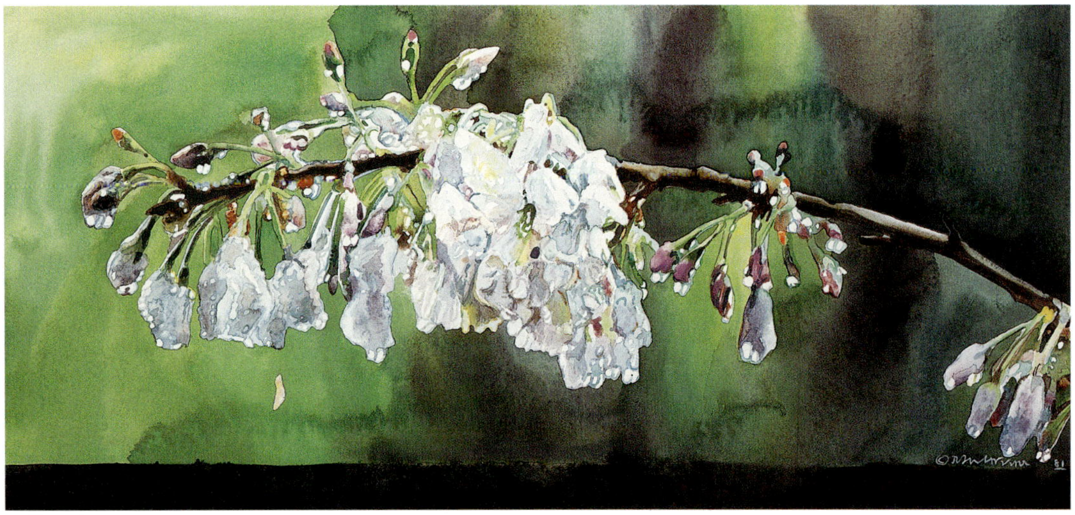

(plate 32) he permitted the colors to overlap and to soak into the paper with unpredictable effect, puddling and staining the paper with muted greens, grayed-down blues, and ruptured browns. Even this dolorous background, however, achieves an incandescent glow that backlights the diaphanous pinks and whites of a weeping branch of cherry blossoms. Across the bottom is a rough black stripe.

"A friend had given us a tree to honor Matthew. This was a year to the day after he died, and the tree blossomed for the first time. The dark stripe across the bottom, that's just one of the things an artist does, there's no explanation. But it's perfect now seeing it twenty years later. It's sort of like a weeping stripe, a mourning stripe."

Renewal is less apparently the subject in *Metamorphose* (plate 33), though the title gives the sense away. It is named after *Metamorphoses,* a piece by Béla Bartók. This is a monumental painting, grandly conceived, baroque in its opulence and lavishness of space. Its focus is a vine in the full flush of autumn decay. The painting is vertical, like a Chinese landscape. The leaves spill as in a waterfall; they are perforated, veined, ablaze with what Emily Dickinson called "the ecstasy of death." Except that the complex contemplation of these leaves is like the reading of a Chinese scroll. One travels along the scroll in a journey, which, in the case of Raffael's autumnal painting, will end next spring in a landscape familiar, but altered.

Take note: this is hardly Thoreau's untrammeled nature. Raffael's flowers are almost never in the wild; unlike his untamed water, they are planted and tended, already altered by the hand of the artist (and that of the artist's wife in the garden).

ABOVE
32. *Matthew's Branch,* 1981
Watercolor on paper, 14 x 30 in.
(35.5 x 76.1 cm)
Joseph and Lannis Raffael,
Cap d'Antibes, France

OPPOSITE
33. *Metamorphose,* 1996
Watercolor on paper, 66 x 44½ in.
(167.6 x 113 cm)
Courtesy of Nancy Hoffman Gallery,
New York

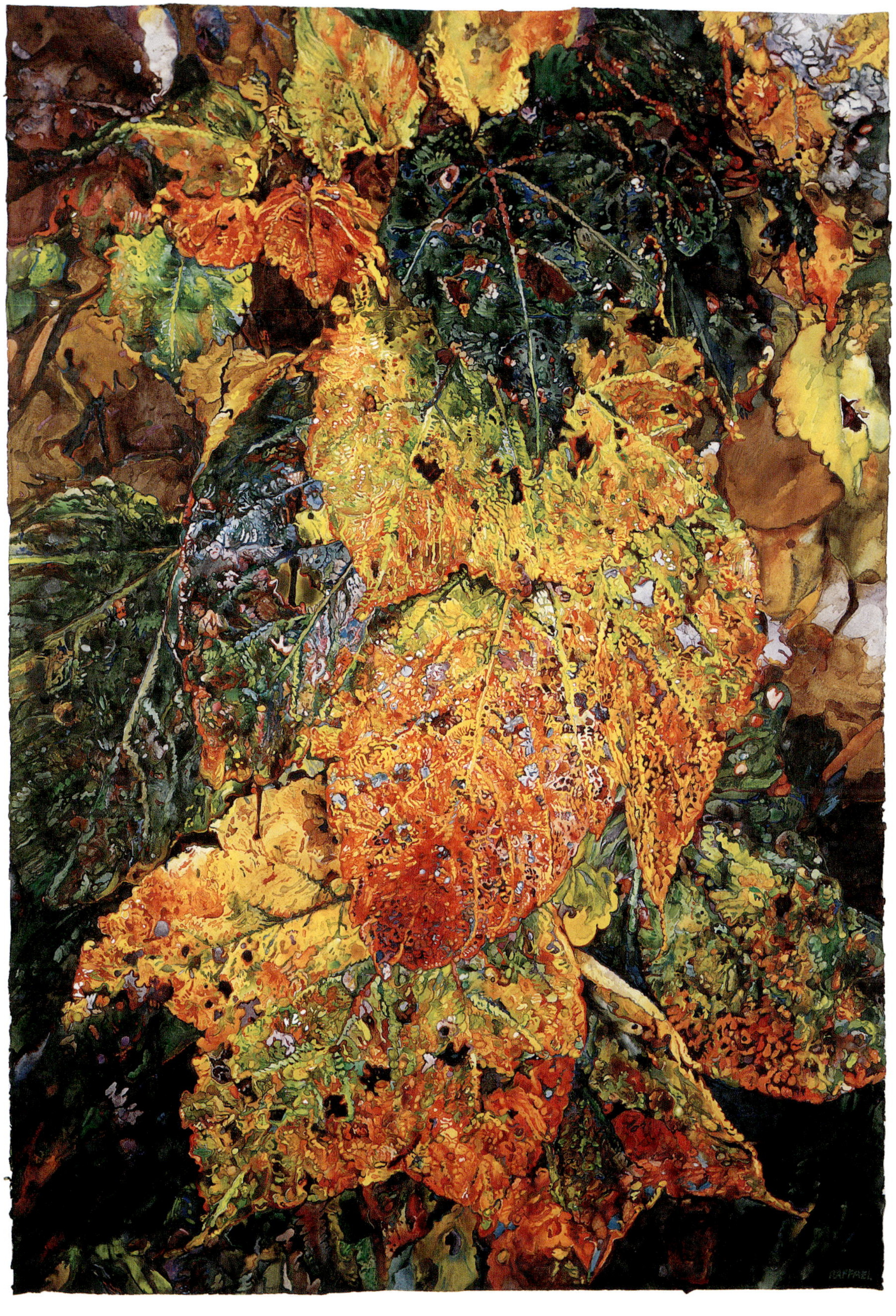
RAFFAEL

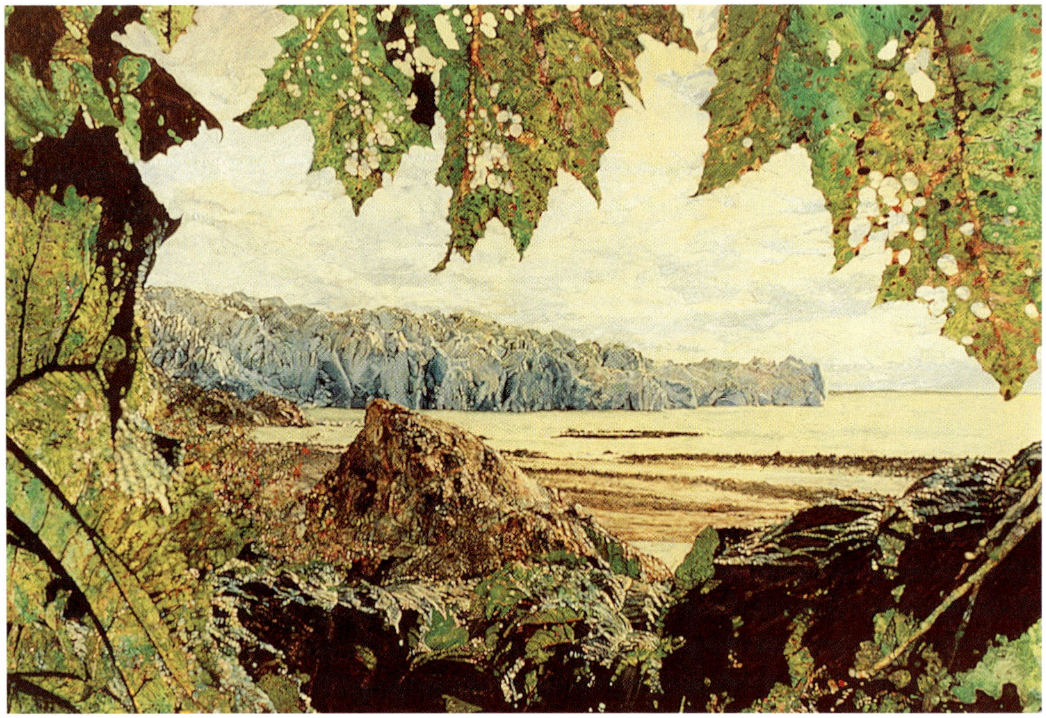

LEFT

34. *Landscape,* 1972
Oil on canvas, 92 x 132 in.
(233.6 x 335.2 cm)
The Robert B. Mayer
Family Collection, Chicago

BELOW

35. *Black Spring,* 1976
Oil on canvas, 6 x 18 ft. (1.82 x 5.48 m)
Private collection

OPPOSITE

36. *Along the Secret Path,* 1980
Watercolor on paper, 52 x 42½ in.
(132 x 107.9 cm)
Mr. and Mrs. John D. Nichols

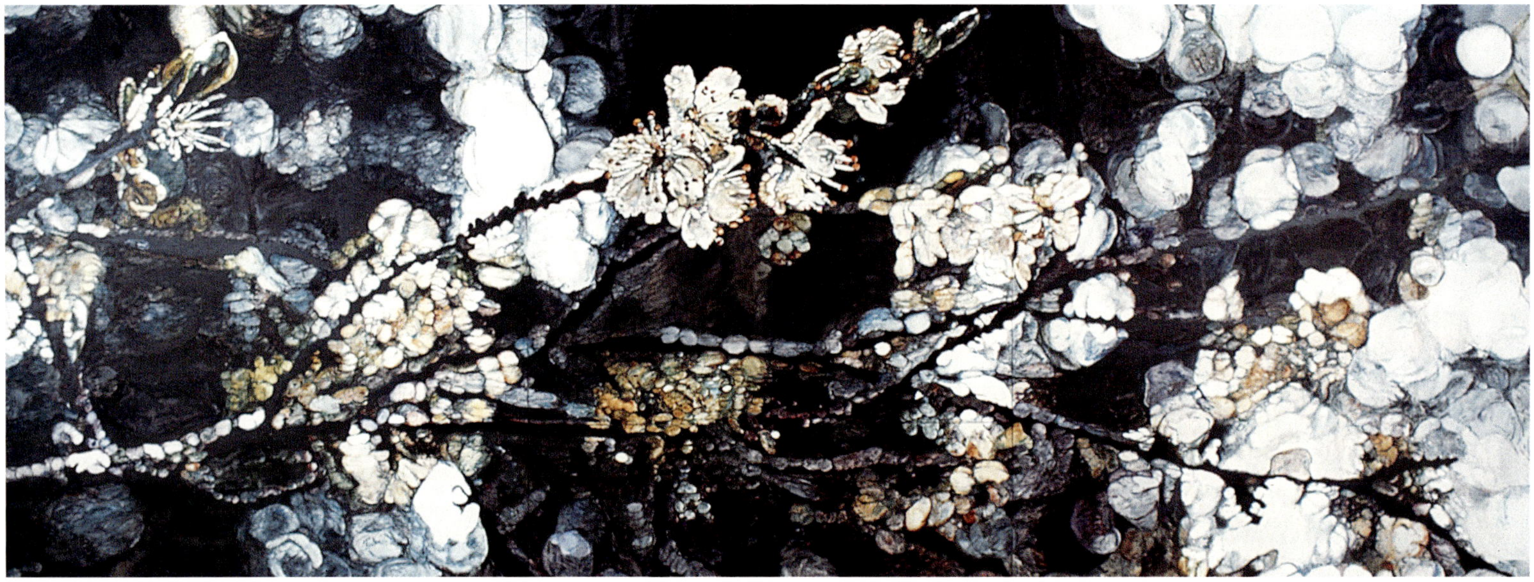

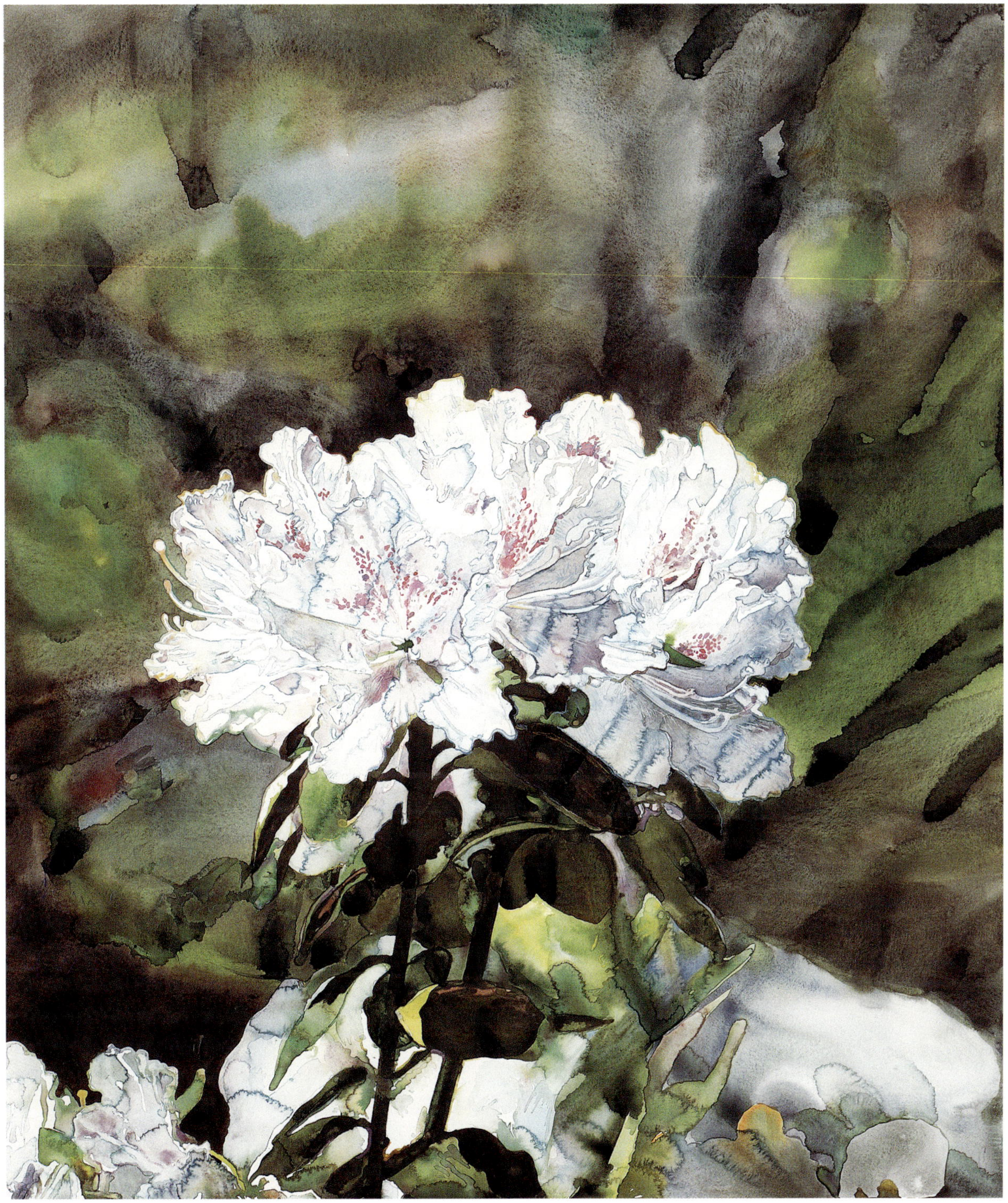

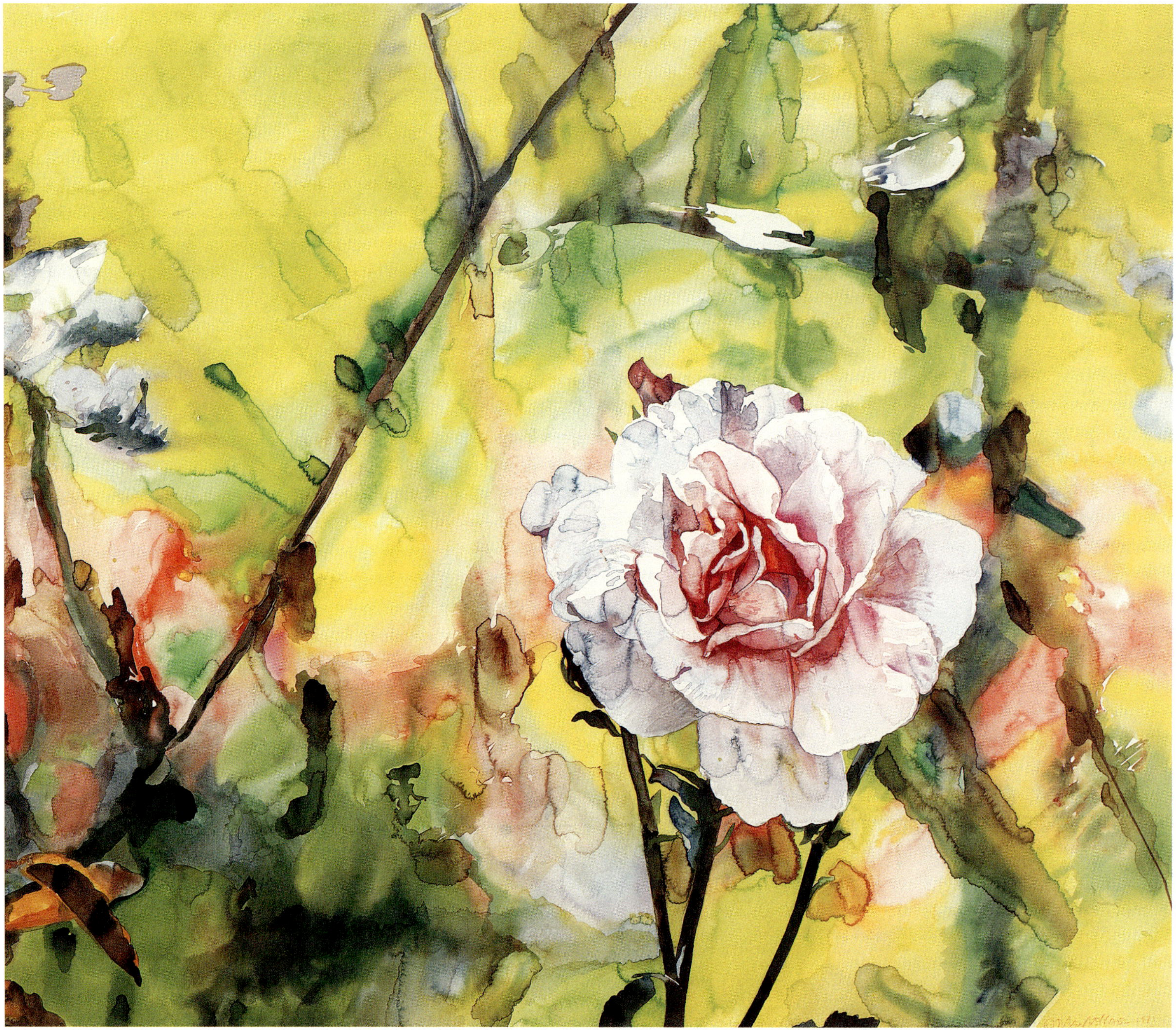

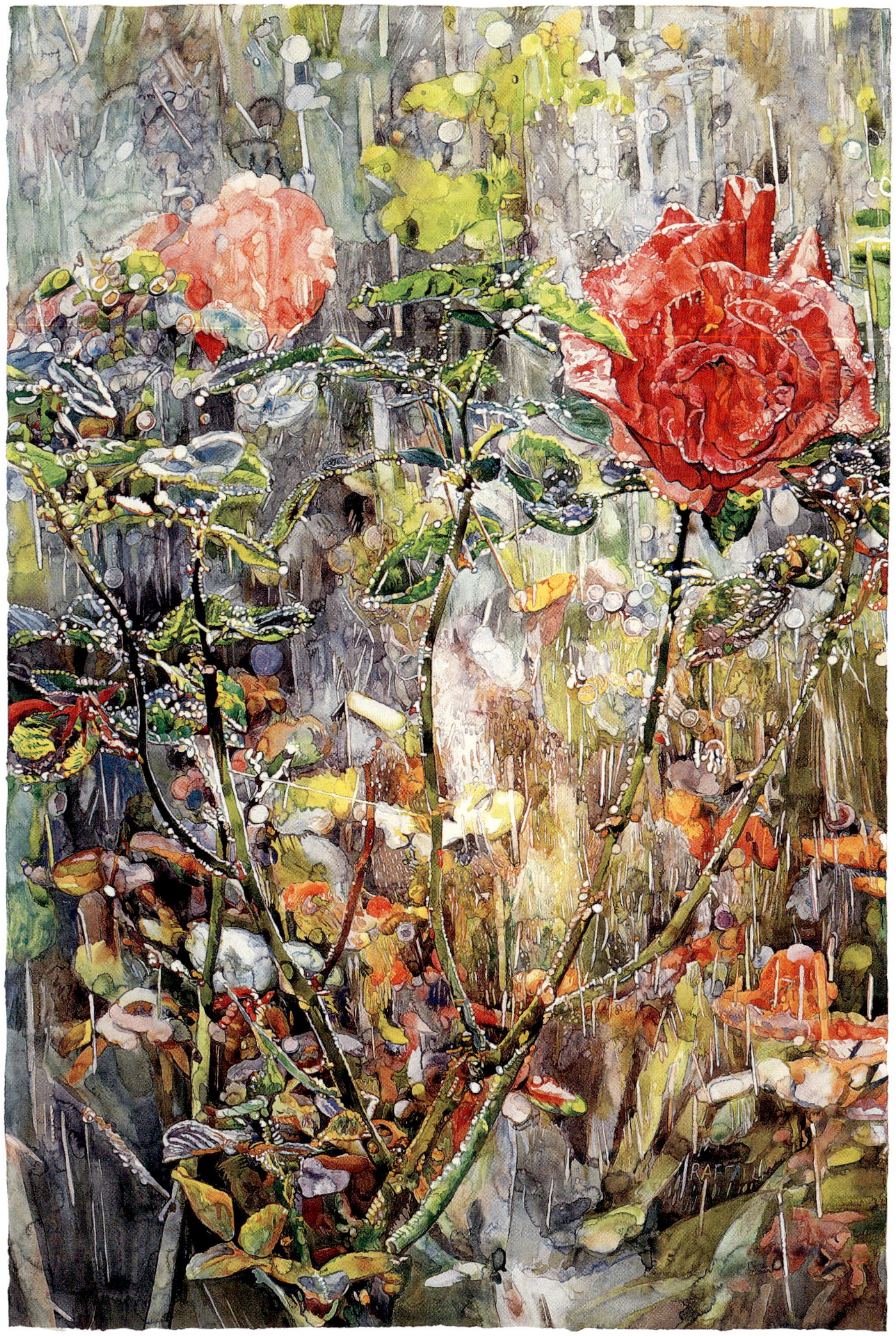

OPPOSITE

37. *Rose Outside Matisse Museum Garden, Nice, July 1981,* 1981
Watercolor on paper, 43¾ x 49½ in.
(111.1 x 125.7 cm)
Private collection

RIGHT

38. *Soyez mystérieuses X,* 1989
Watercolor on paper, 68 x 45 in.
(172.7 x 114.2 cm)
Private collection; Courtesy of
Nancy Hoffman Gallery, New York

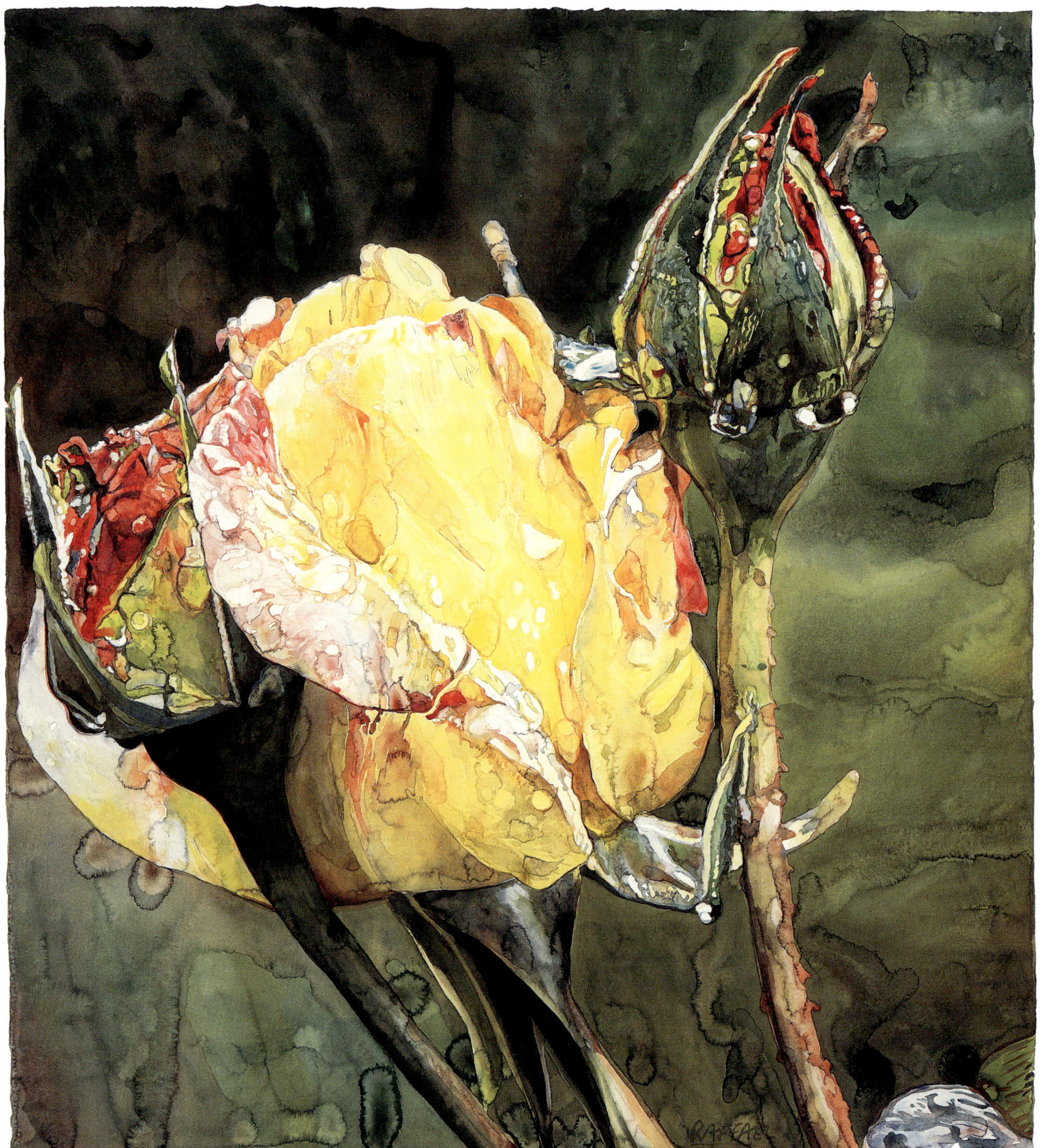

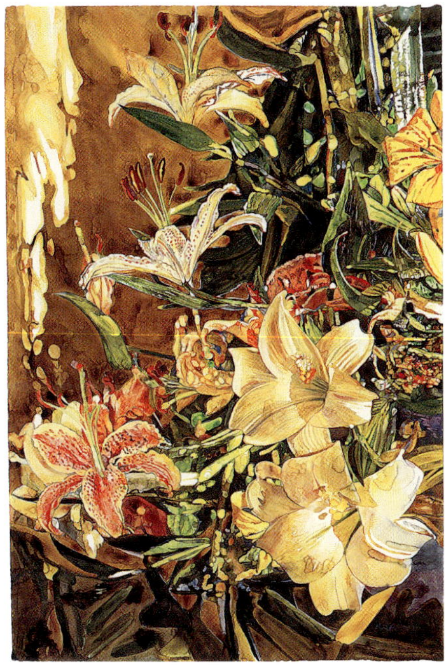

OPPOSITE

39. *Rose Awakening,* 1990
Watercolor on paper, 51¼ x 45½ in.
(130.1 x 115.5 cm)
Private collection

ABOVE

40. *Winter Gift,* 1990
Watercolor on paper, 69 x 44½ in.
(175.2 x 113 cm)
Corporate collection, Illinois

RIGHT

41. *Autumn Bouquet,* 1989
Watercolor on paper, 67 x 45 in.
(170.1 x 114.2 cm)
Bobbi and Walter Zifkin

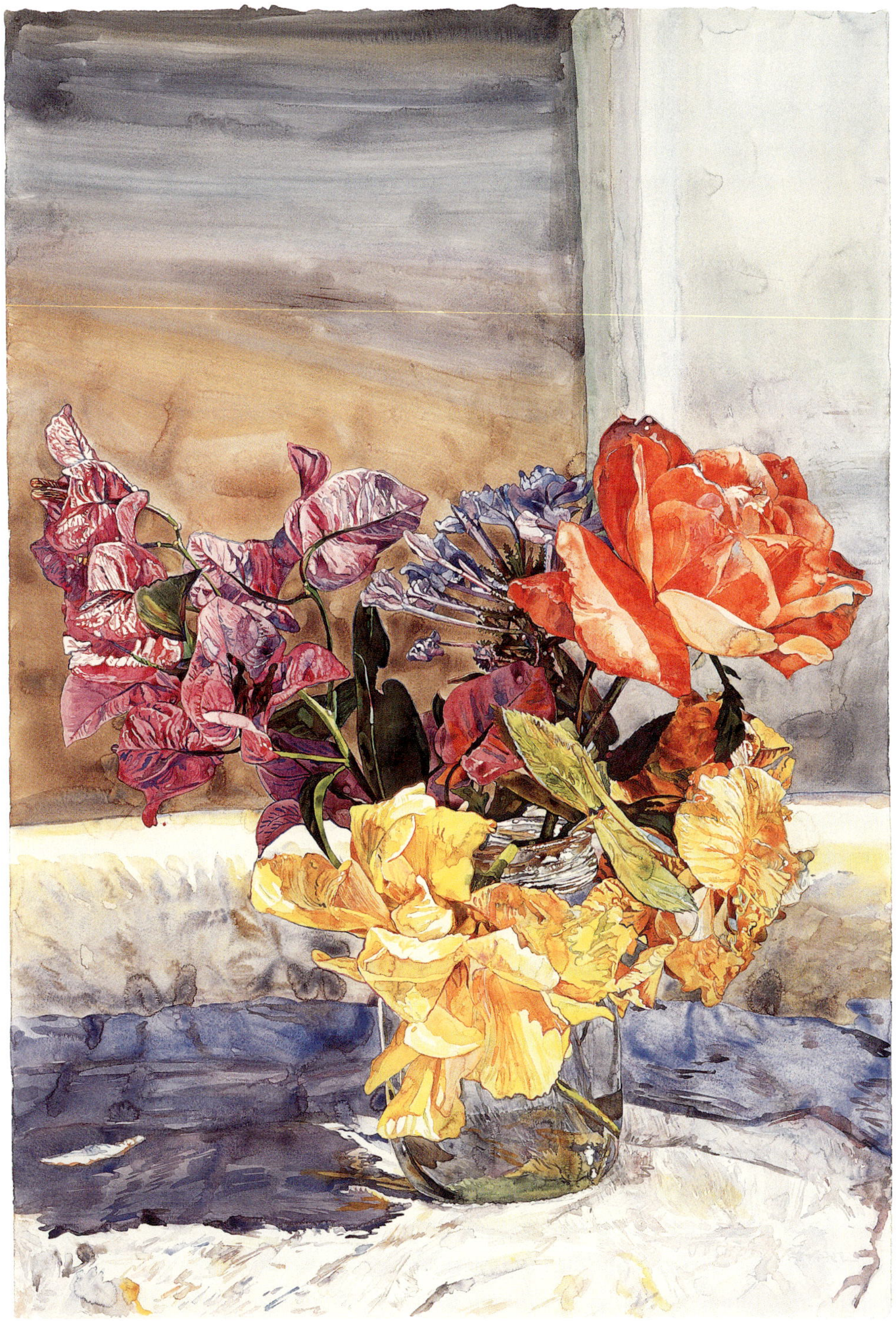

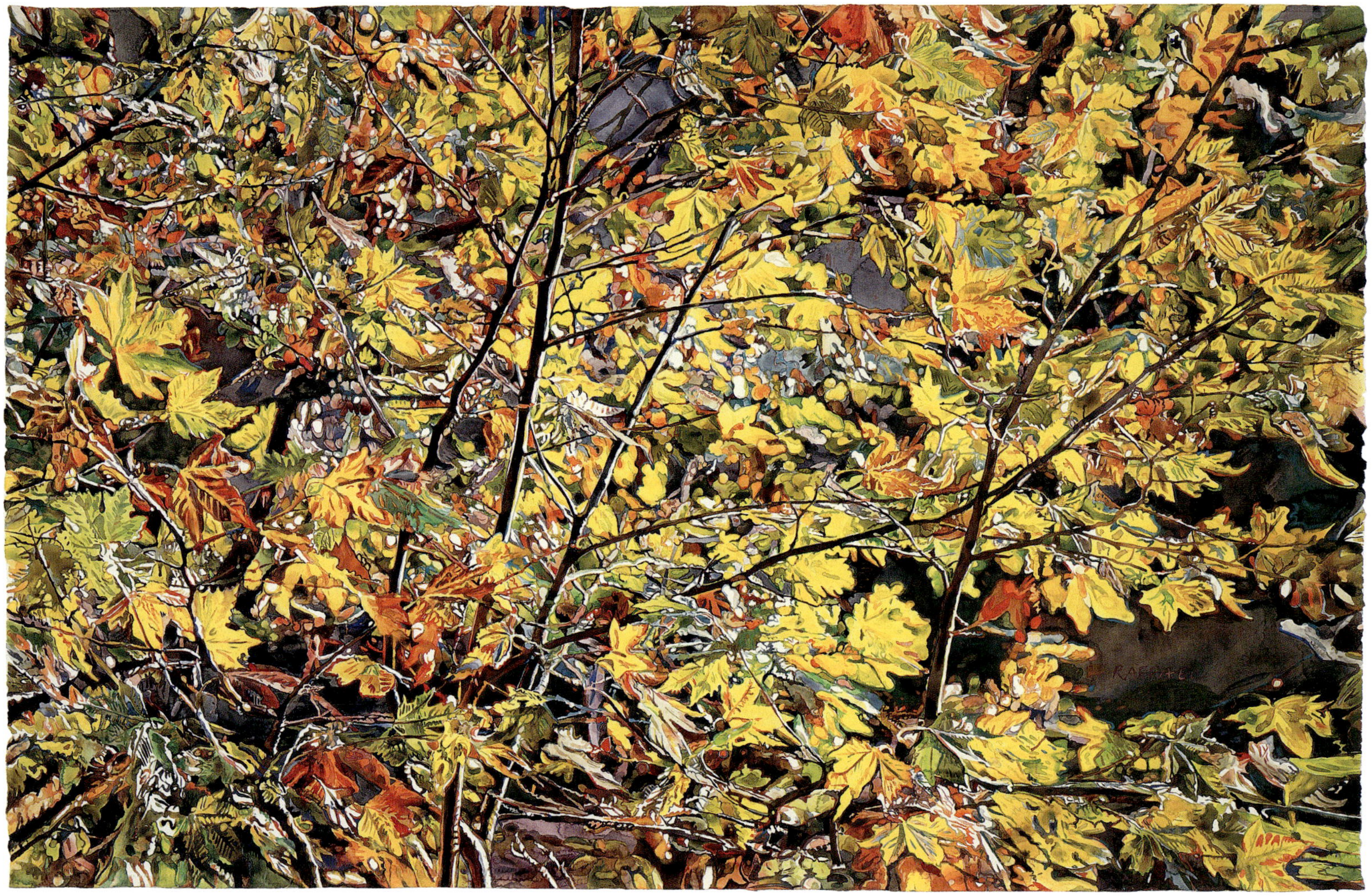

42. *Provençal Autumn: Vaucluse,* 1990
Watercolor on paper, 44½ x 67½ in.
(113 x 171.4 cm)
The Capital Group Companies, Inc.,
Los Angeles

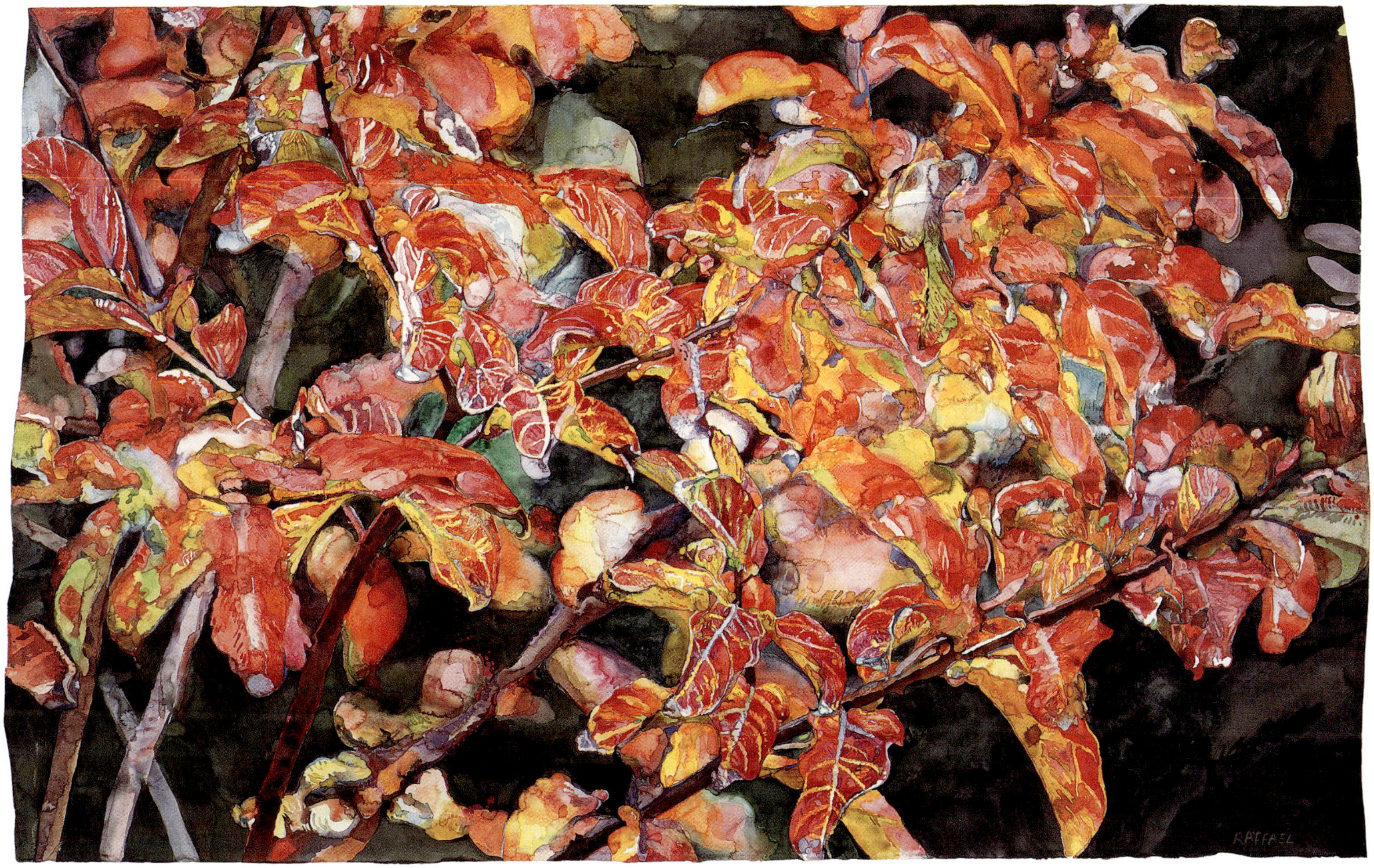

43. *Site Charmant, Autumn,* 1990
Watercolor on paper, 44½ x 70 in.
(113 x 177.7 cm)
Doctors Satish and Phiroza Modi

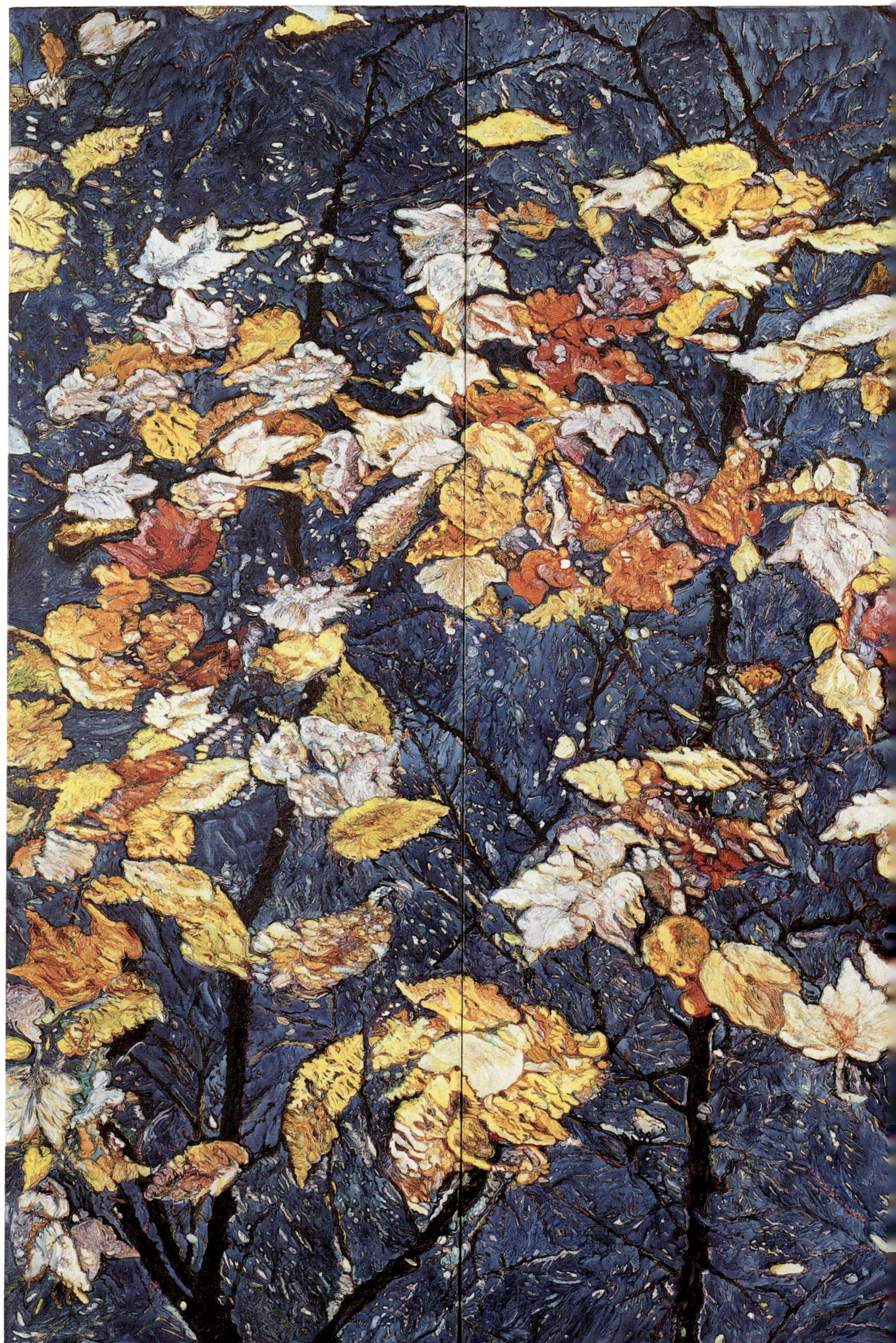

44. *Le 2 Novembre II,* 1991
Oil on linen, 5 panels: 77 x 128 in. (195.5 x 325 cm)
Courtesy of Nancy Hoffman Gallery, New York

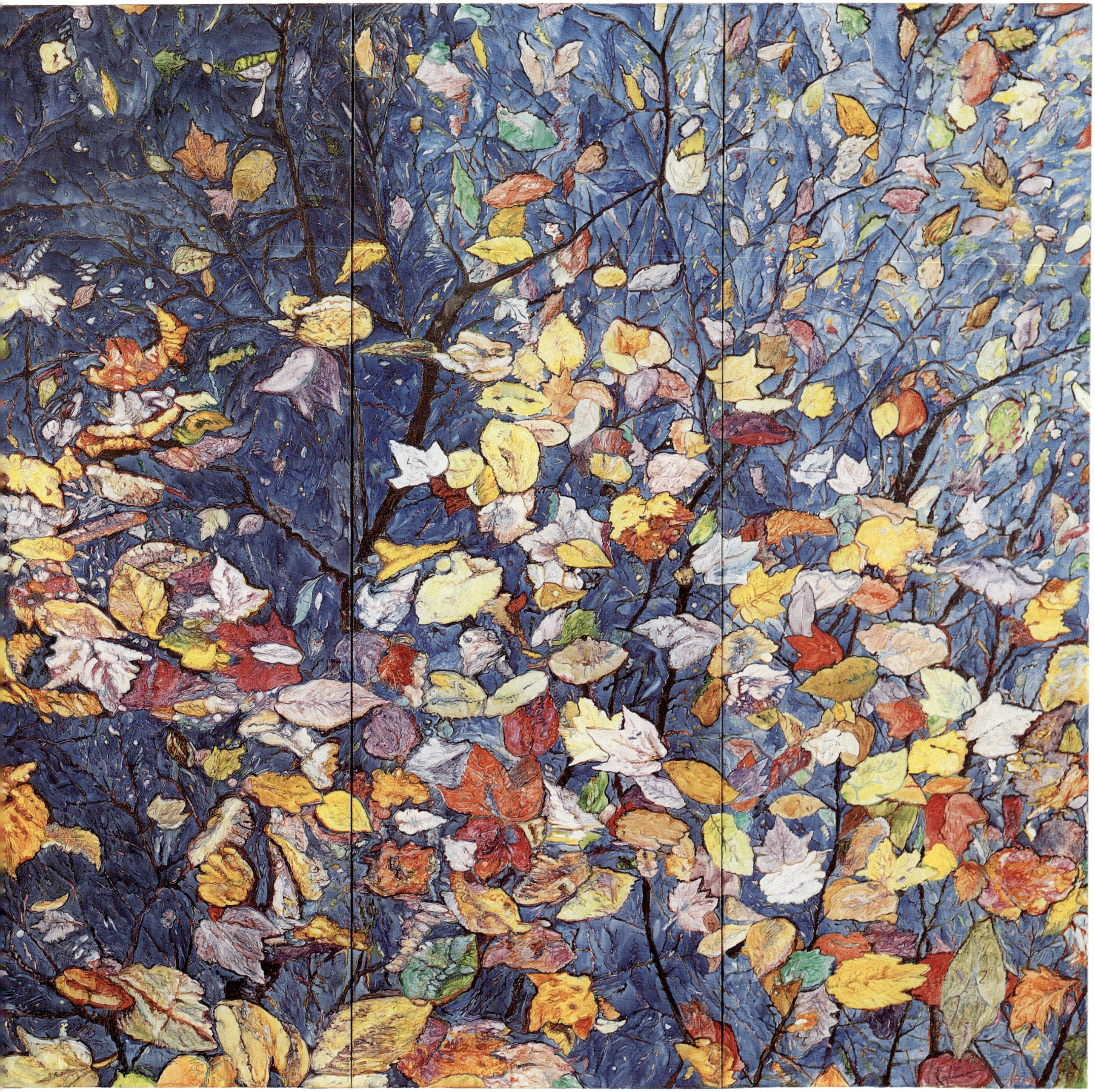

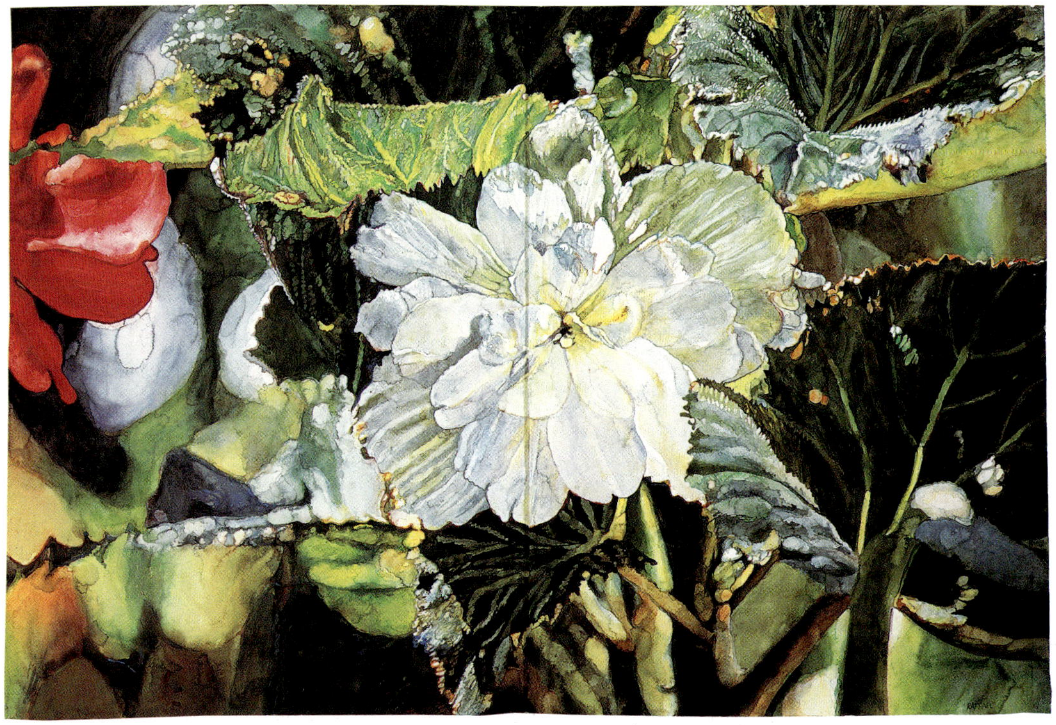

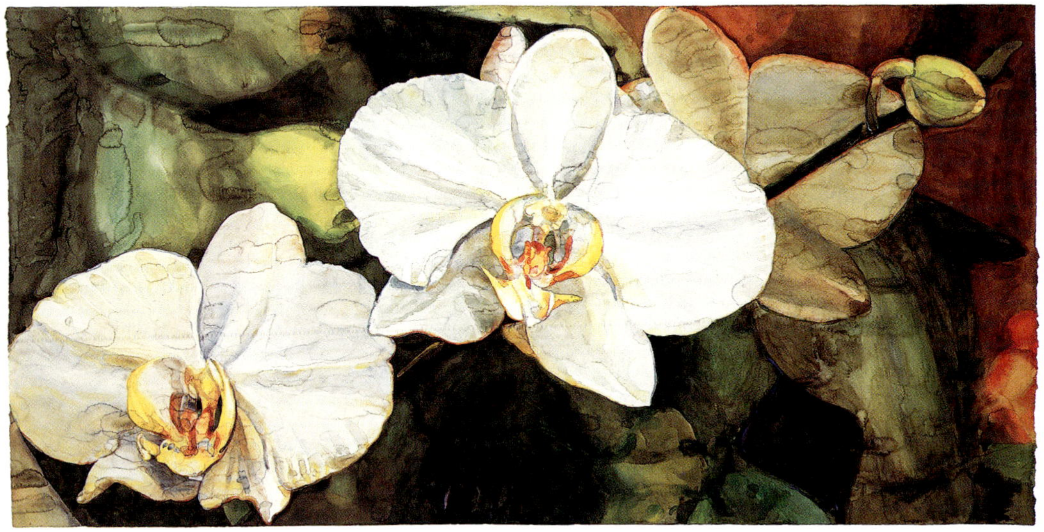

LEFT

45. *Begonia Diptych,* 1992
Watercolor on paper, diptych: 55 x 79¼ in.
(139.6 x 201.2 cm)
Private collection; Courtesy of Keny Galleries, Columbus, Ohio

BELOW

46. *Orchid Bridge,* 1991
Watercolor on paper, 45 x 87½ in.
(114.2 x 222.2 cm)
Private collection, New York

OPPOSITE

47. *Rose for Lannis Diptych,* 1993
Watercolor on paper, diptych: 59½ x 61 in.
(151.1 x 154.9 cm)
Sam and Connie Perkins,
Longboat Key, Florida

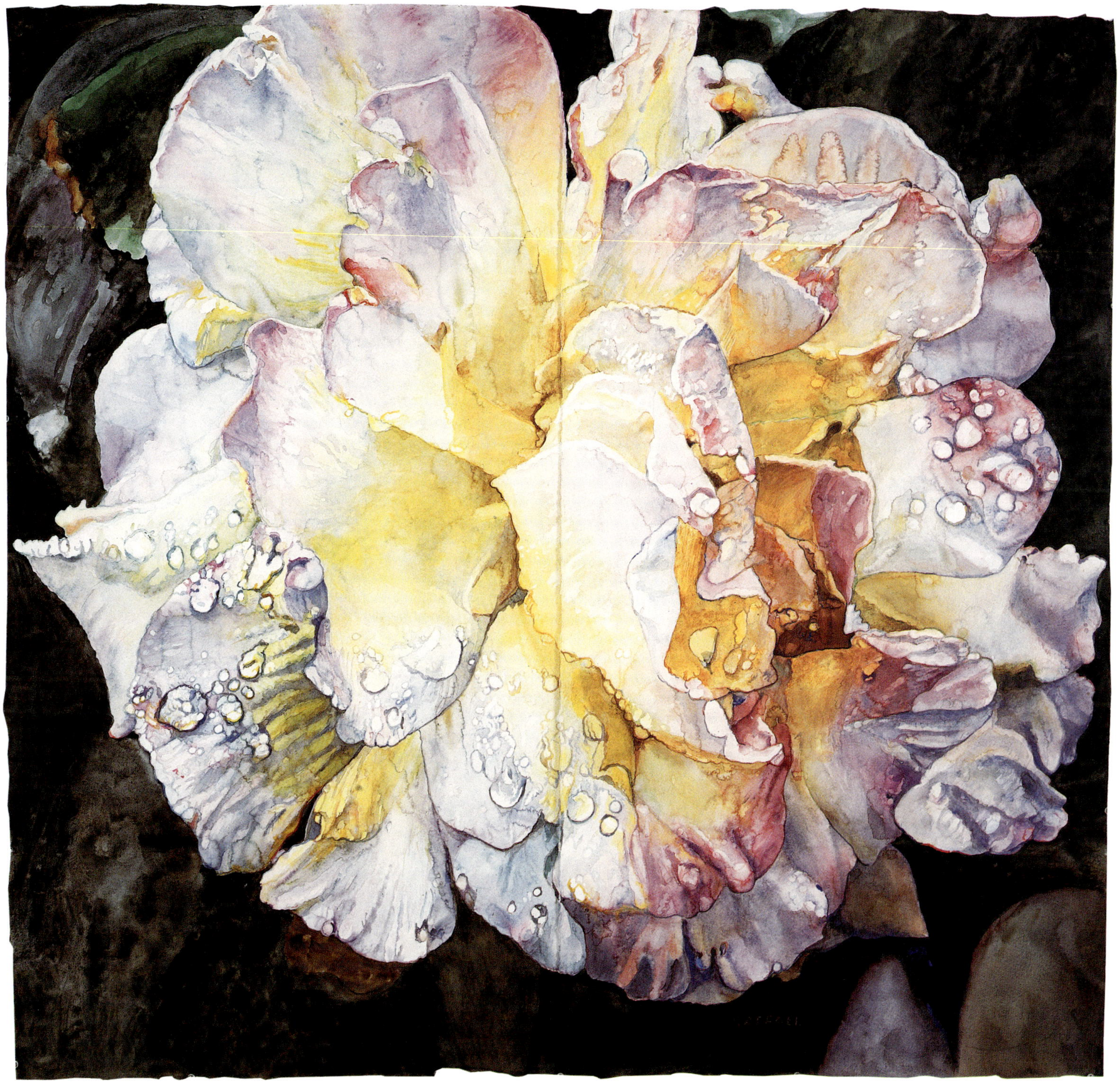

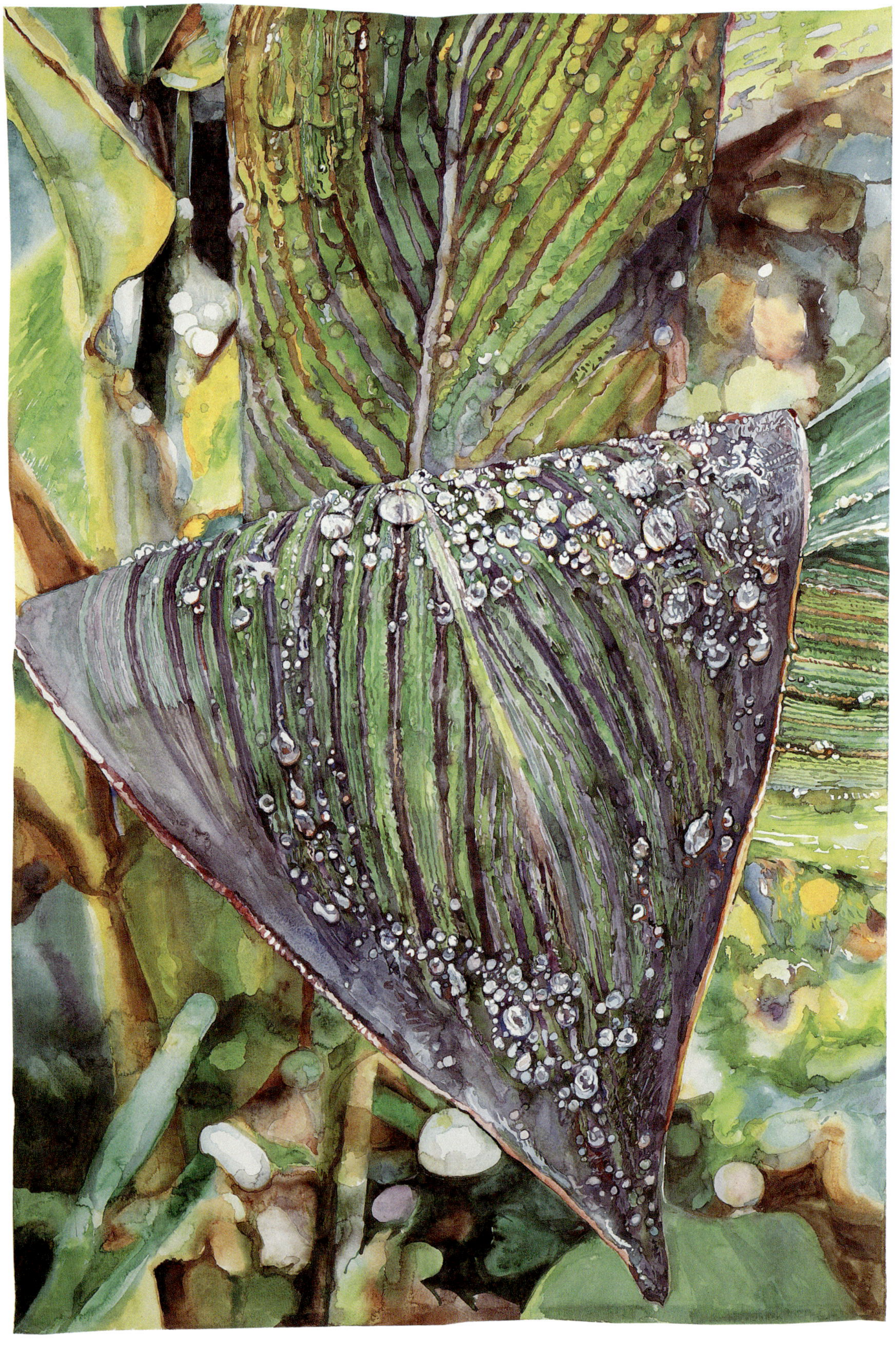

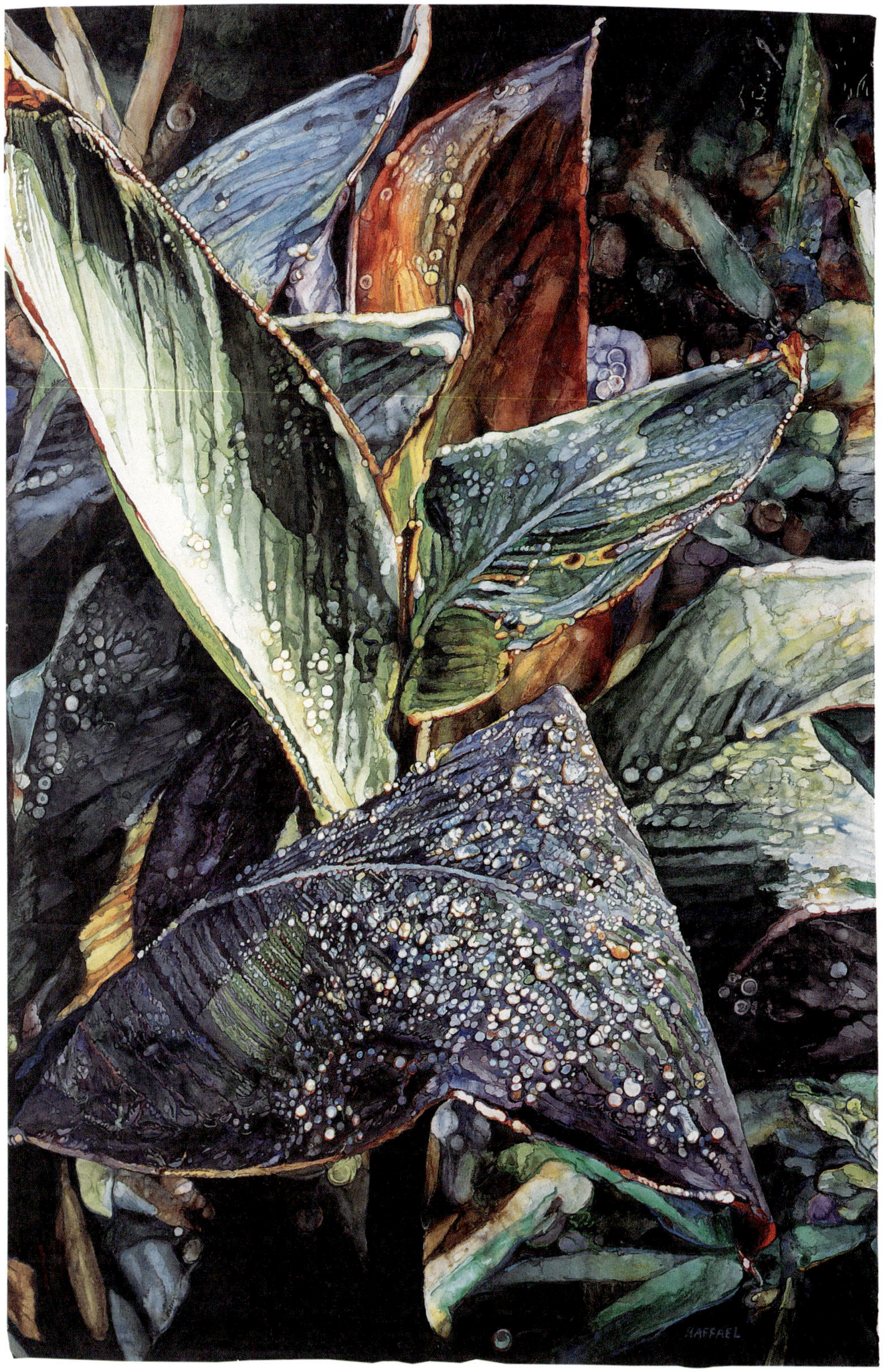

OPPOSITE

48. *Canna Leaf after the Rain,* 1992
Watercolor on paper, 58 x 38½ in.
(147.3 x 97.7 cm)
Commerce Bancshares, Inc.,
Kansas City, Missouri

RIGHT

49. *Vernal Equinox after the Blooming,* 1995
Watercolor on paper, 70 x 45 in.
(177.7 x 114.2 cm)
Courtesy of Nancy Hoffman Gallery,
New York

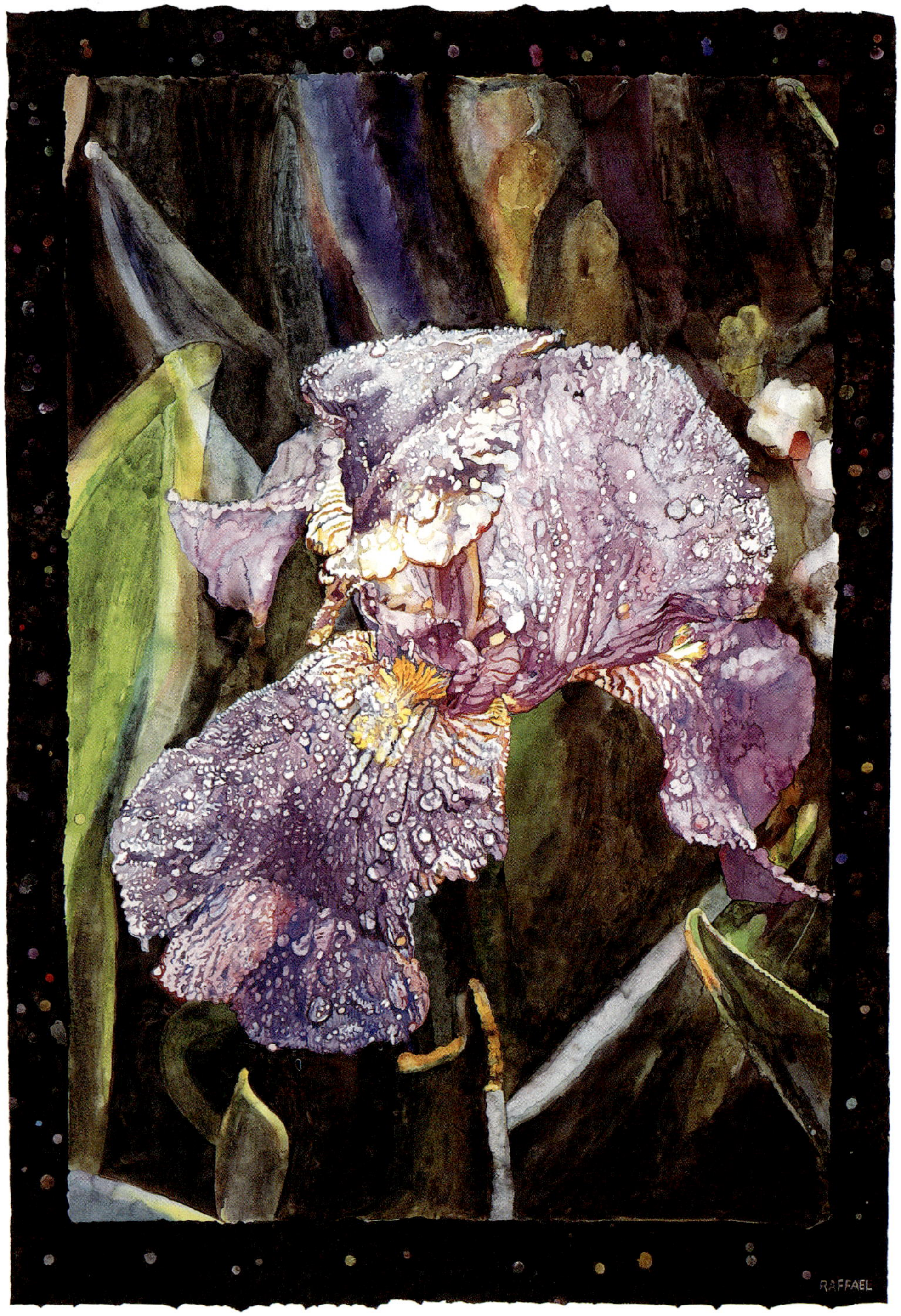

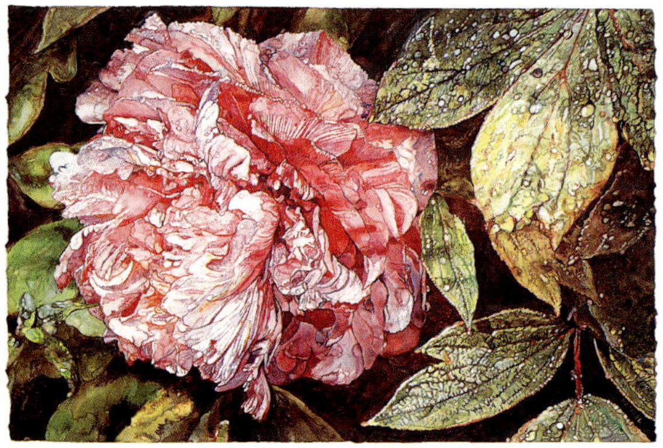

LEFT

50. *After the Rain: An Iris with Border,* 1993
Watercolor on paper, 66 x 44½ in.
(167.6 x 113 cm)
The Seavest Collection

ABOVE

51. *After the Rain: A Peony and Its Leaves,* 1993
Watercolor on paper, 44½ x 65 in. (113 x 165 cm)
Betta Clair

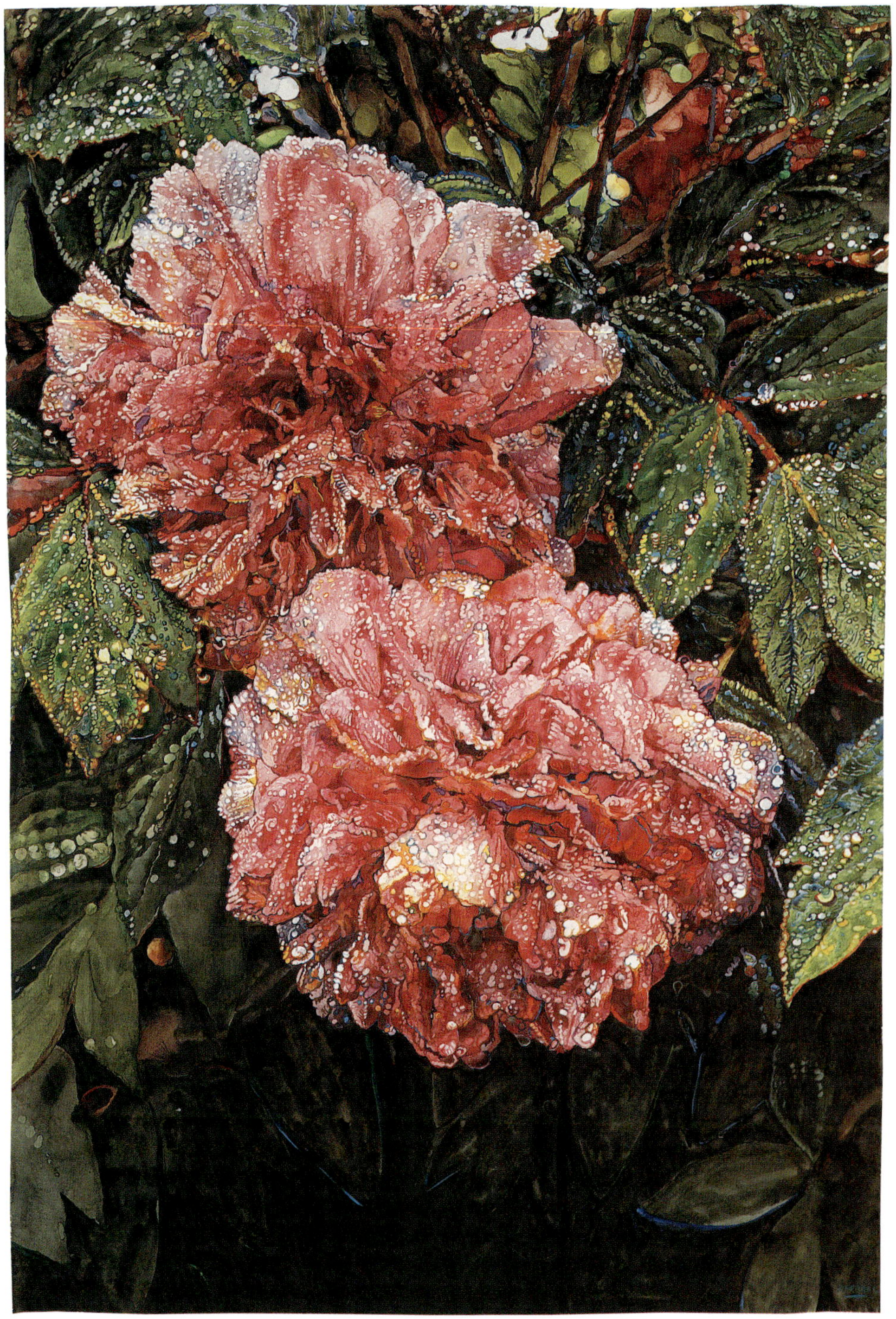

52. *Quietude,* 1996
Watercolor on paper, 67 x 44½ in.
(170.1 x 113 cm)
Private collection, New York

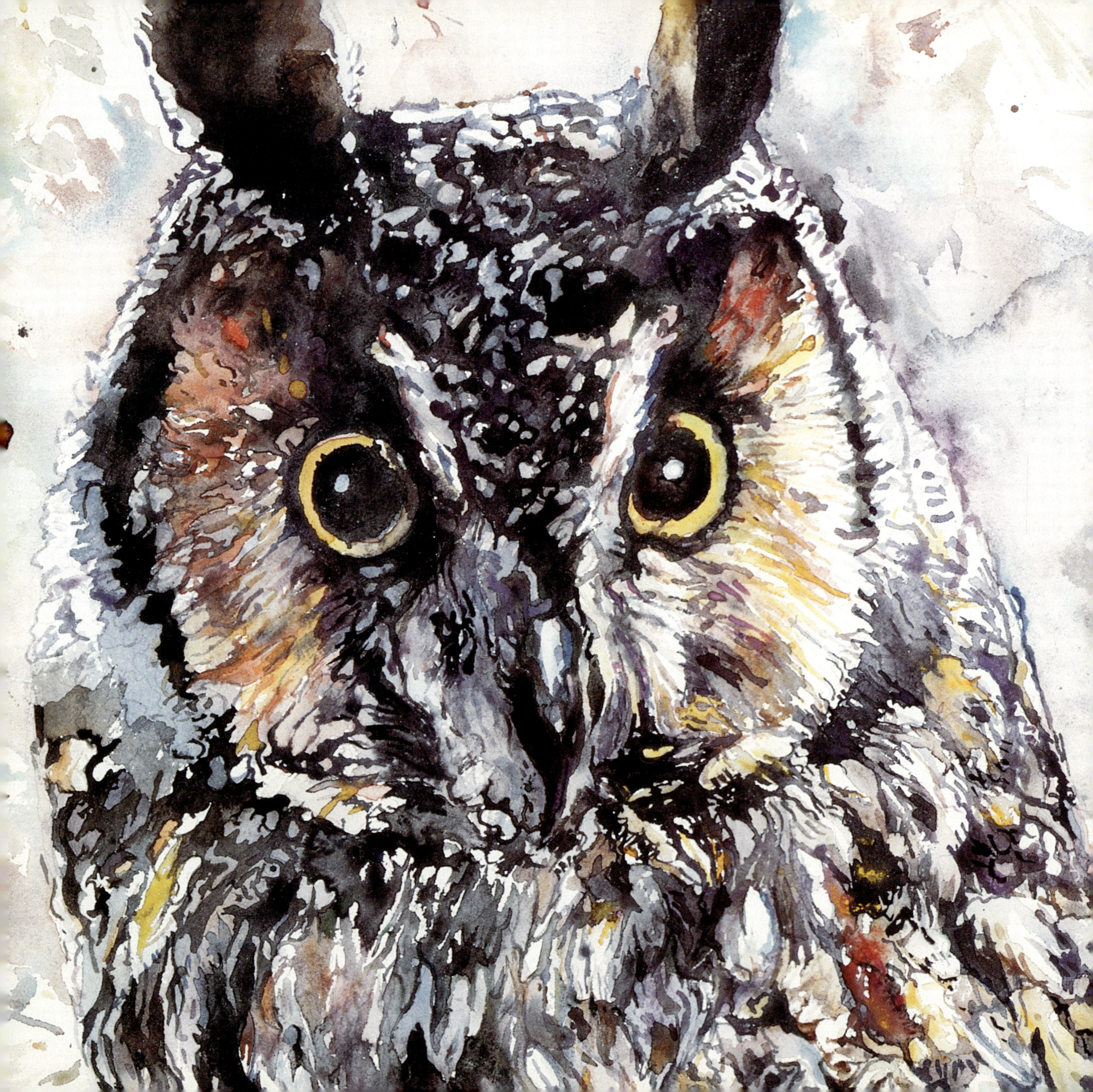

The Animal Paintings

"Things to be cherished like the thought of heaven"

53. Detail of *Spirit (Owl)*, 1985
See plate 67

Of all the subjects Raffael paints, his animals (until the recent paintings of his cats Tigre and Fumé) have been the farthest from the real world, the most heraldic and theatrical. This is particularly true of the paintings from his New Realism period, the *Lizard* and *Lion* of 1971 (plates 56 and 57). Seen straight on and up close in Technicolor verisimilitude, the lizard is otherworldly, at once cosmic and comical. The lion, highlighted and haloed like an icon, could easily pose for the MGM logo. These are not the animals of nature but animals as brought to you through the medium of celluloid, larger than life, flamboyant as a melodrama, redolent of danger and mystery. They are a Steven Spielberg version of an animal, isolated, enhanced, and enshrined.

To Raffael this approach is a means of "honoring" them, to use a word he relishes. But he honors these animals as representatives of nature rather than as nature itself. Like the statues of the Buddha that have also been a recurring theme for him, the animals serve as messengers from another world. Once his attention turned to landscape and nature became his subject, the animals shed their star status and became part of the scenery. When they began to make their presence felt once more in such paintings of 1976 as *A Frog in Its Pond* (plate 137) and *Mallard* (plate 68), they surfaced as only slightly more solid elements of the water, only somewhat more fixed than the incessant currents. Now they seemed like characters in a Greek tragedy, at once at the mercy of the elements and the chief players in the drama. They seldom face front or hog the spotlight. They are distinguished from the field of water and color in which they float neither by line nor color but only by minute changes in the discrete abstract passages that define them.

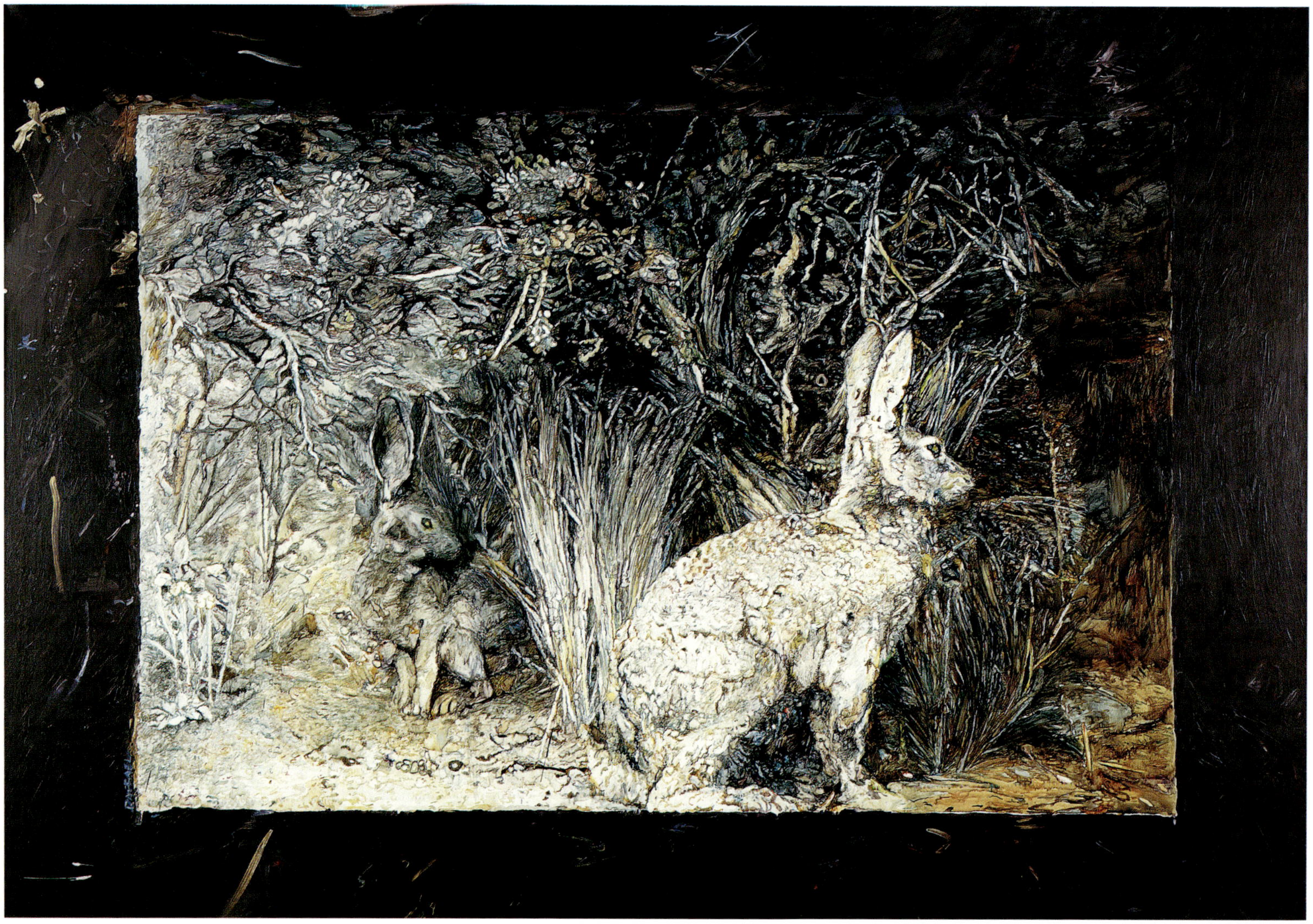

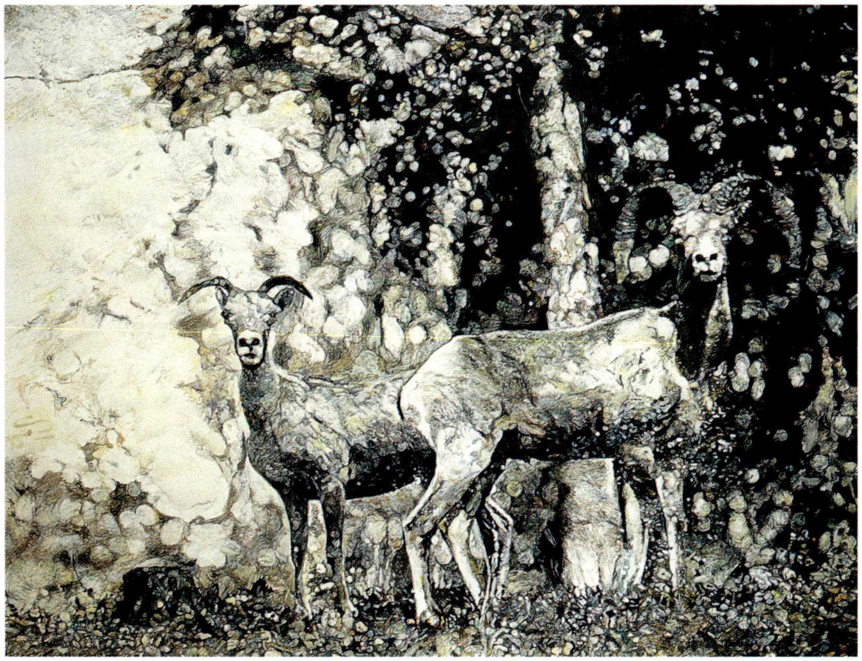

OPPOSITE
54. *Out of the Thicket,* 1985
Oil on canvas, 69 x 98 in.
(175.2 x 248.9 cm)
Private collection; Courtesy of
Nancy Hoffman Gallery, New York

ABOVE
55. *The Clearing,* 1985
Oil on canvas, 65 x 84 in.
(165 x 213.3 cm)
Private collection

In 1985, as Raffael was beginning to emerge from a life that had come to an end and was forming a new one, animals became his agents of expression once again. The emotion of Greek tragedy was replaced by the symbolism of a medieval passion play, in which the animals played assigned roles of despair, hope, and transformation. In *Re-Entry (Moth)* (plate 152) the moth, floating in intergalactic space, is seen from above, its wings spread to reveal mottled markings the color of dried wounds. In *Spirit Bird* (plate 148), the medium—which is watercolor—asserts itself in infinitesimally modulated passages, so subtle and so transparent that the bird does, indeed, suggest a spirit in formation. As with so many of Raffael's most successful paintings, both space and movement can be read on diverse levels. The bird seems at once to dissolve into and emanate from its translucent habitat. "This is definitely a self-portrait," says Raffael. "It's what I feel like when I'm out at night getting wood or putting garbage out, and I feel the air around me, and I feel the quiet and I feel nature."

What are perhaps his most stagy renditions of animals are also his most stunning. In the twin double portraits *Out of the Thicket* (plate 54) and *The Clearing* (plate 55), Raffael went to unaccustomed lengths to emphasize the artificiality of the image. In both cases, he began with black-and-white photographs, which he made into color slides. "All this color came from the process, and it added auras and vibrations. So that's what I painted."

There is a connection in these paintings both to the history of art-making and to time past. The muted aquas, greens, and browns with which Raffael replicates black-and-white tones suggest old etchings; the shallow space of the action recalls Nicolas Poussin. In *Out of the Thicket,* the adamant profile of the larger rabbit pays homage to Albrecht Dürer. This crystallized moment in which two rabbits peer into a daunting future clarifies what has occurred before. It is a reaffirmation of the central role of painting in the artist's life with his new partner.

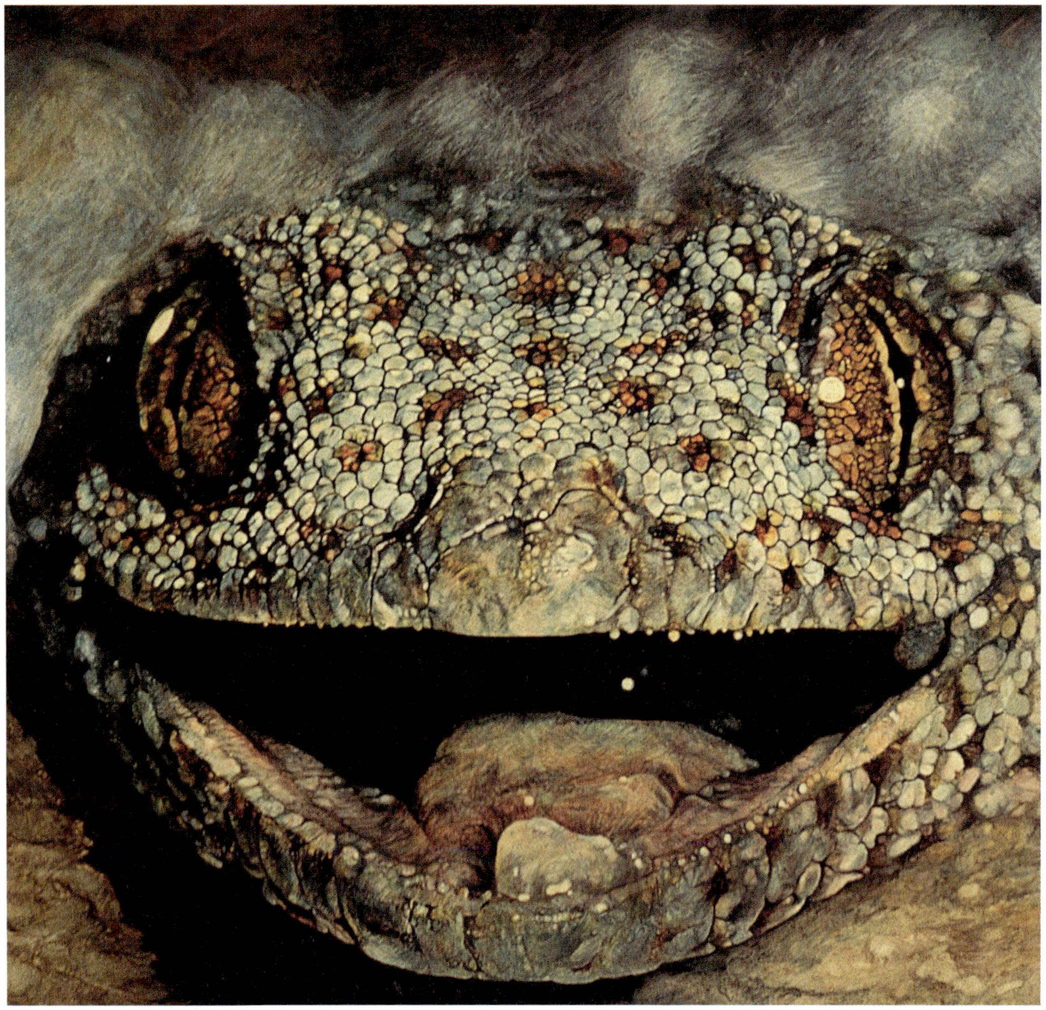

LEFT
56. *Lizard,* 1971
Oil on canvas, 84 x 84 in. (213.3 x 213.3 cm)
Private collection

OPPOSITE
57. *Lion,* 1971
Oil on canvas, 84 x 84 in. (213.3 x 213.3 cm)
Robert E. Abrams, New York

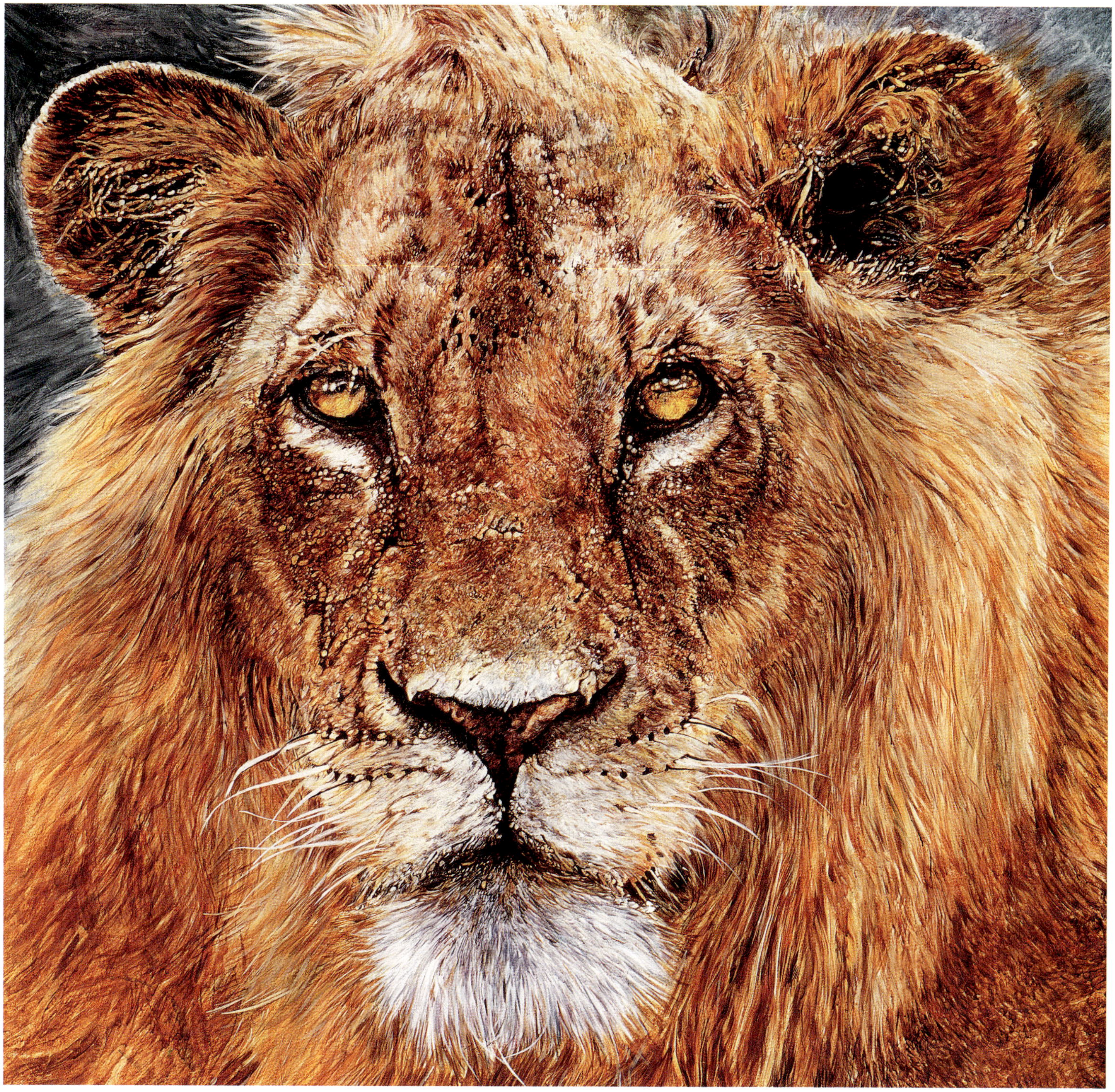

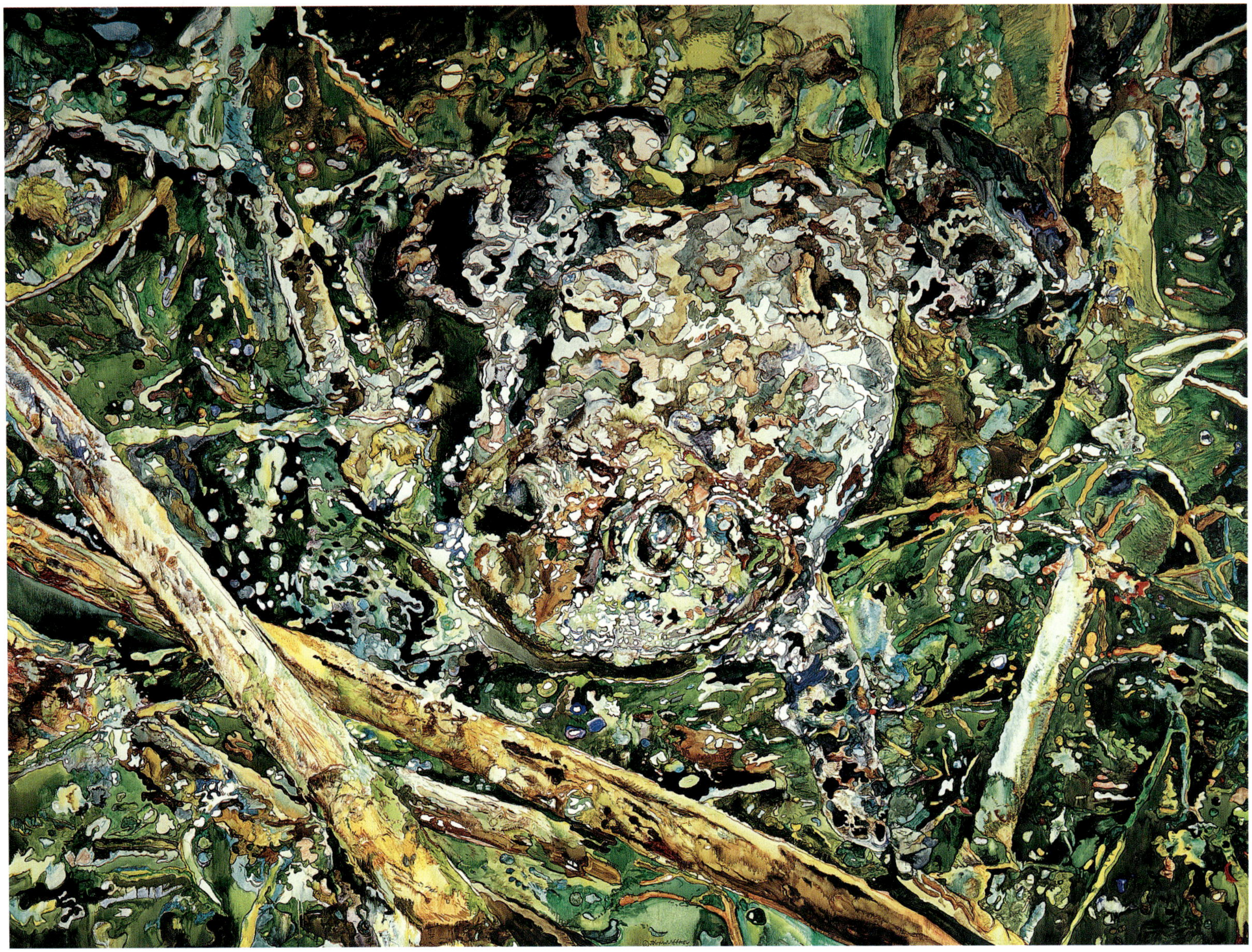

58. *Season of the Frog,* 1979
Oil on canvas, 90 x 120 in. (228.5 x 304.7 cm)
Private collection; Courtesy of
Nancy Hoffman Gallery, New York

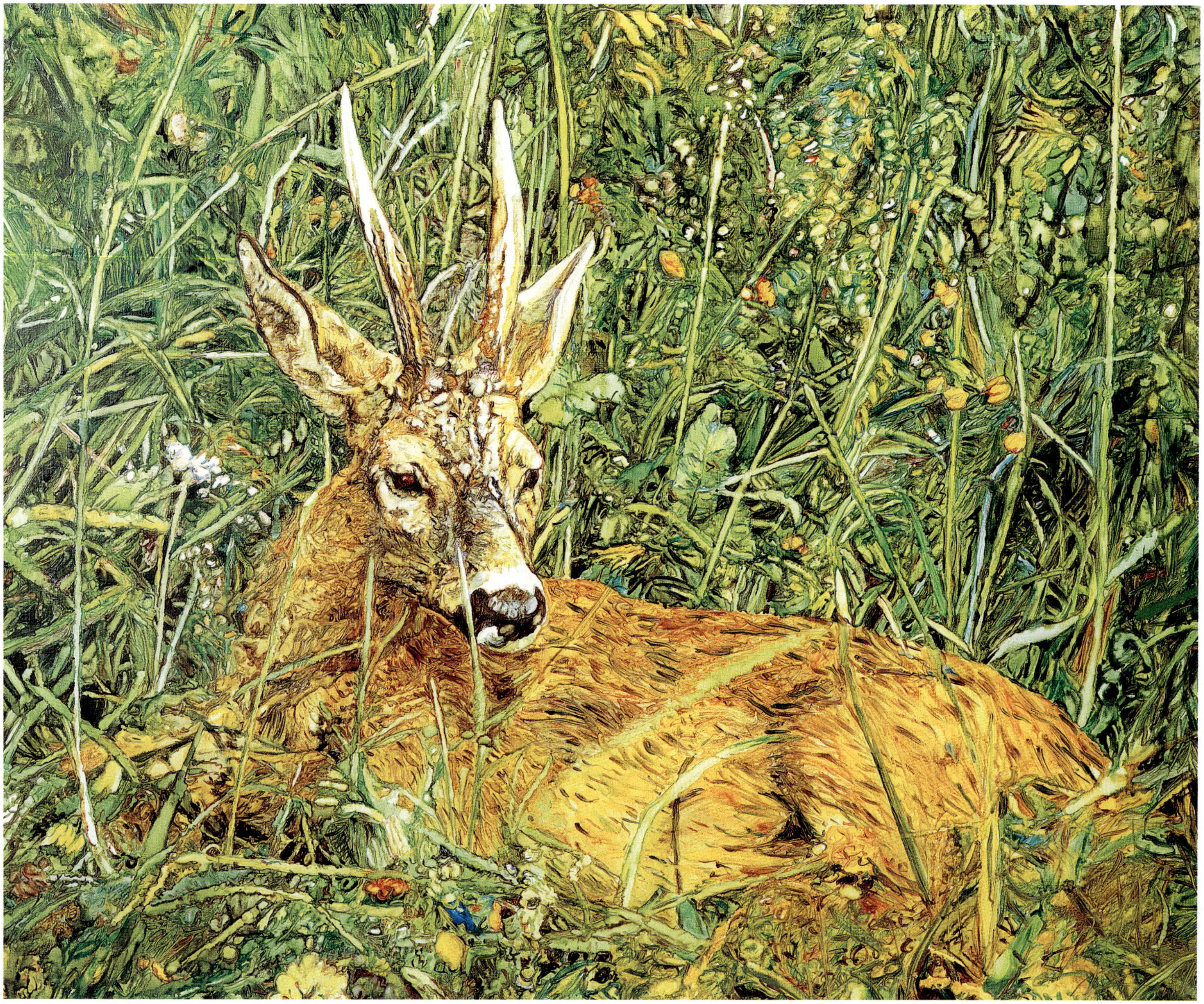

59. *Antelope in High Grass,* 1986
Oil on linen, 21¼ x 25½ in. (53.9 x 64.7 cm)
Joseph and Lannis Raffael,
Cap d'Antibes, France

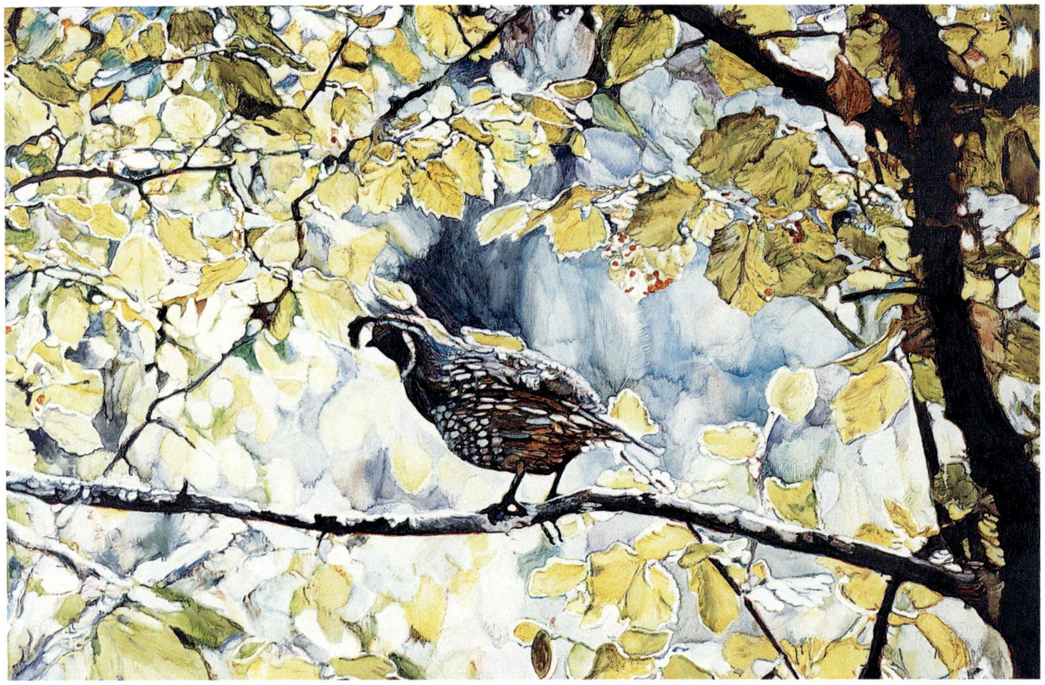

60. *Quail,* 1979
Oil on canvas, 48 x 72 in. (121.9 x 182.8 cm)
Mrs. William C. Janss, Sun Valley, Idaho

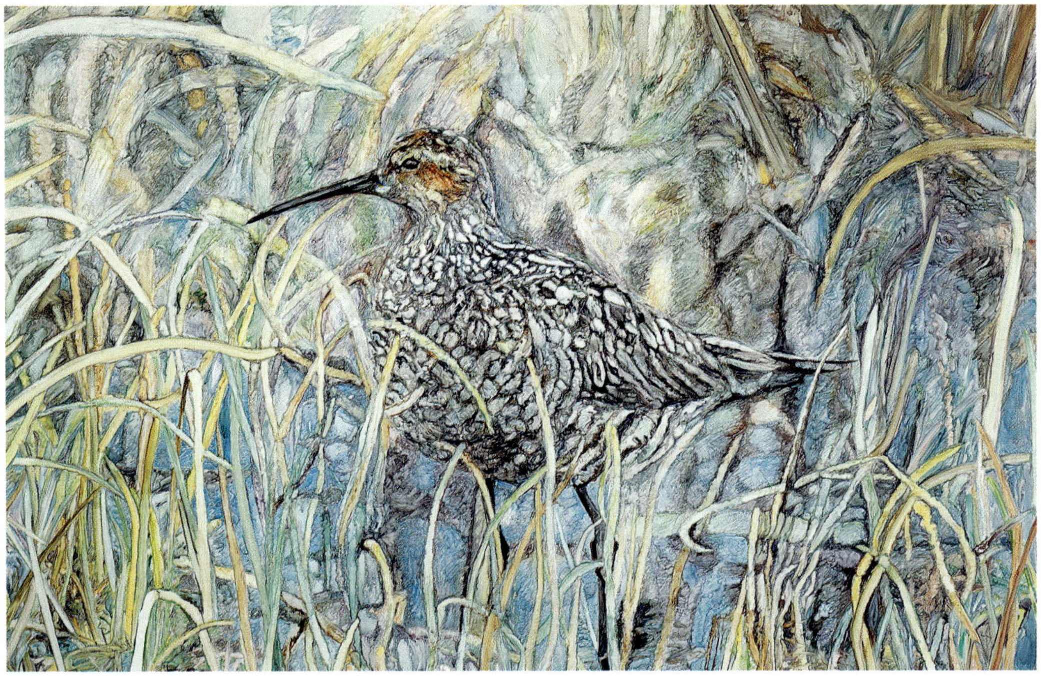

61. *Bird in the Marsh,* 1991
Oil on linen, 51¼ x 76¾ in. (130.1 x 194.9 cm)
Joseph and Lannis Raffael,
Cap d'Antibes, France

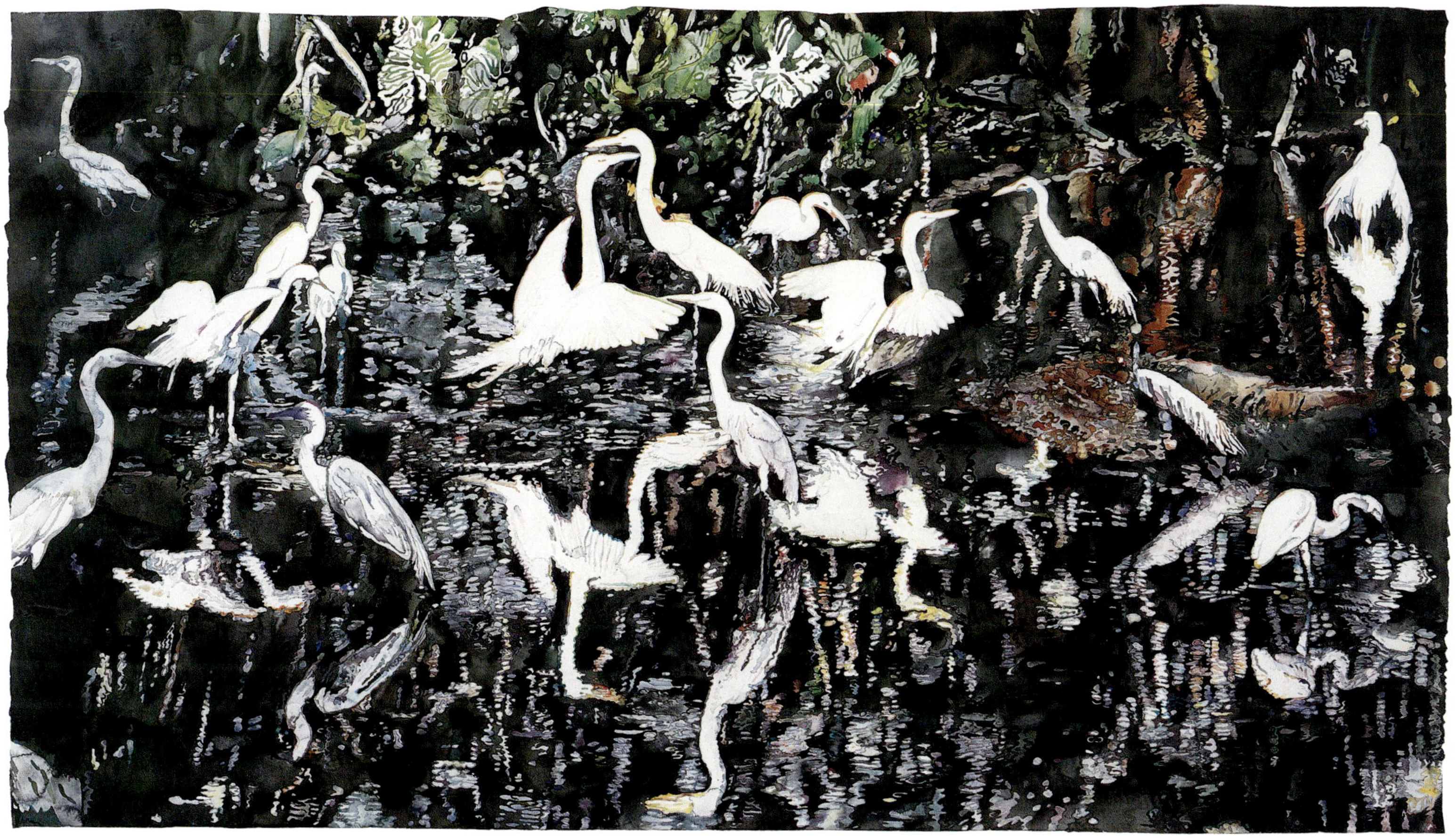

62. *Cranes,* 1987
Watercolor on paper, 40½ x 70 in.
(102.8 x 177.7 cm)
Sidney and George Perutz

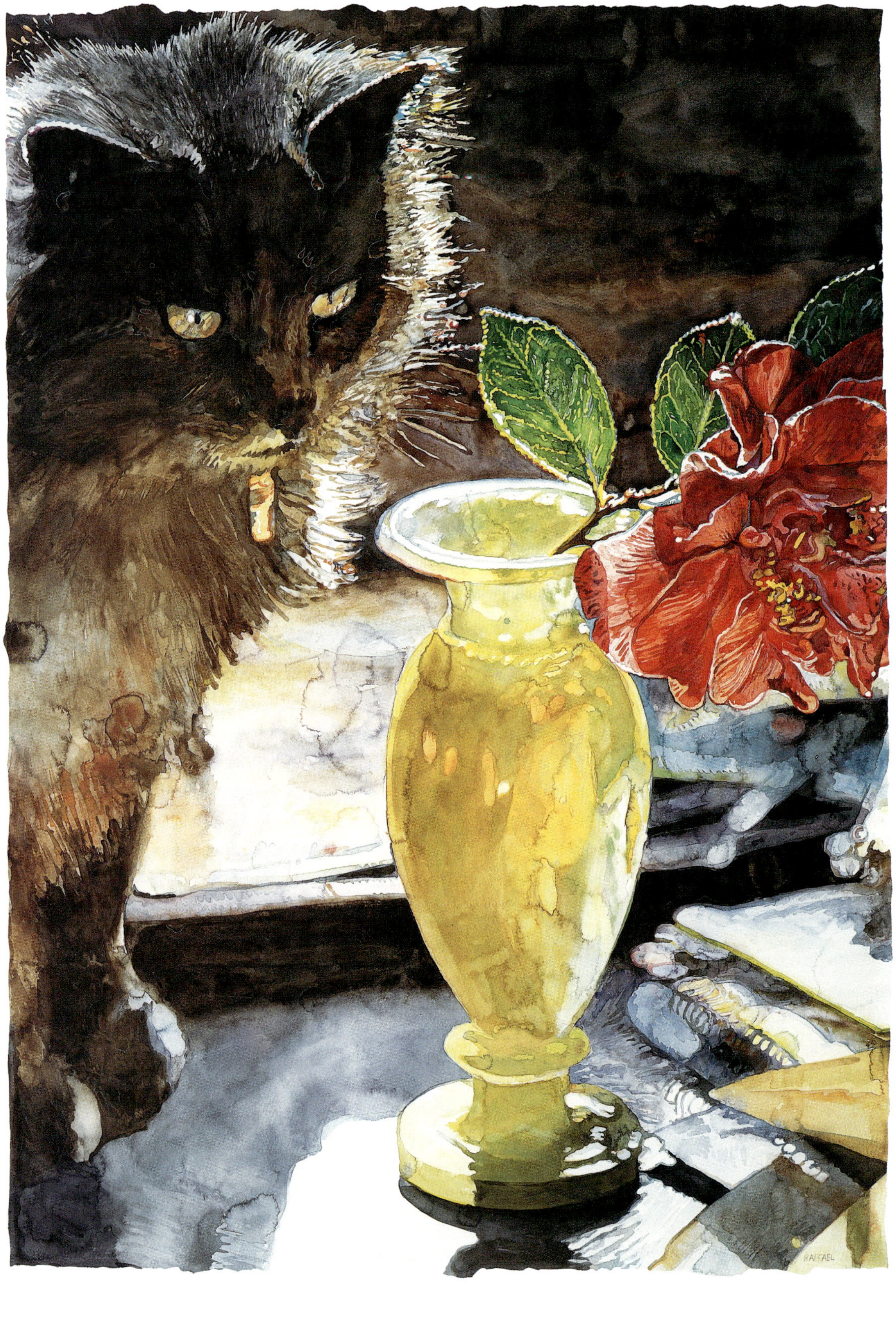
RAFFAEL

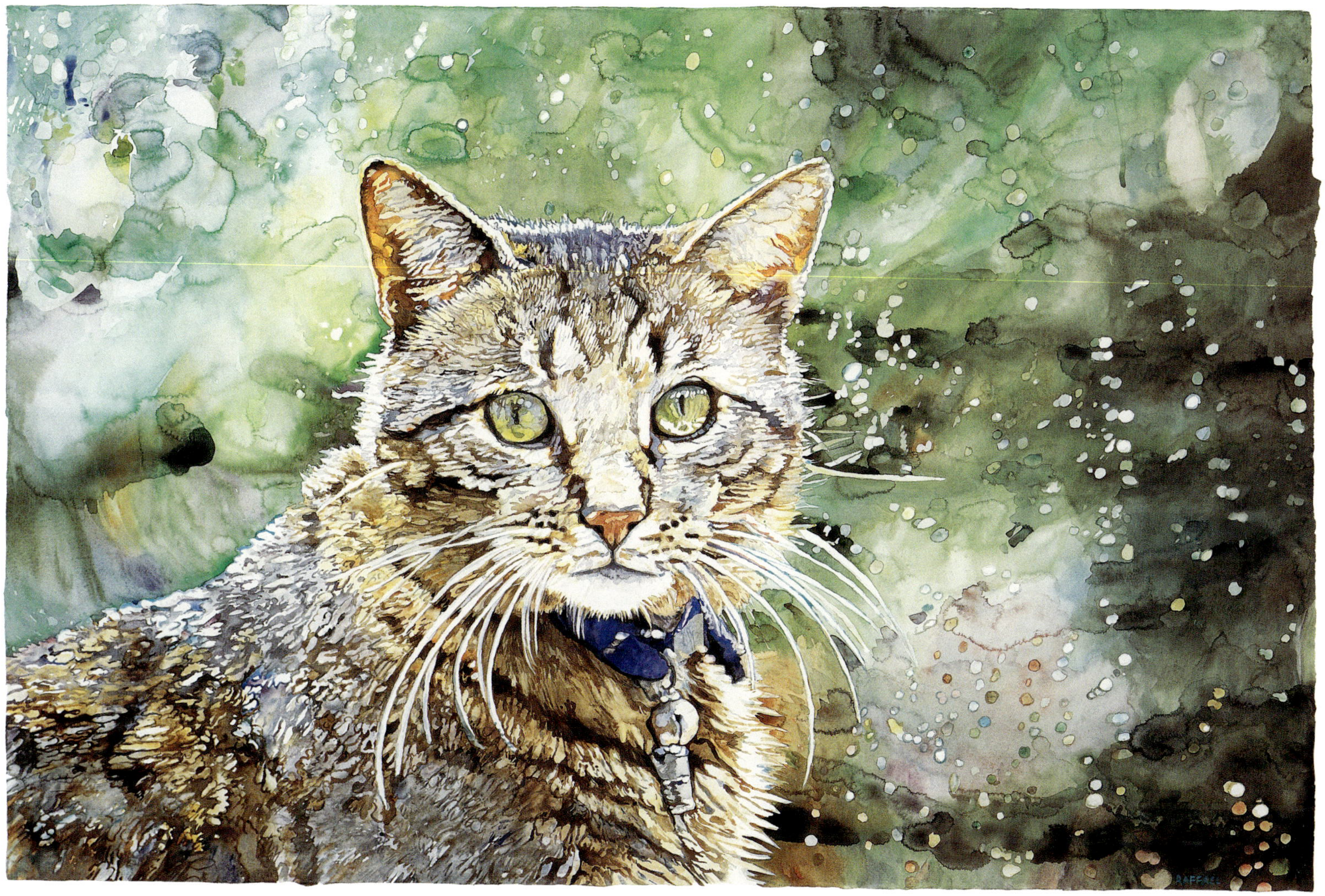

OPPOSITE

63. *Fumé with Vase and Camellia,* 1991
Watercolor on paper, $49\frac{3}{4}$ x $34\frac{1}{8}$ in.
(126.3 x 86.6 cm)
Oprah Winfrey, Chicago

ABOVE

64. *Tigre's Dream,* 1992
Watercolor on paper, $43\frac{1}{2}$ x $64\frac{1}{4}$ in.
(110.4 x 163.1 cm)
Mr. and Mrs. Richard Aron

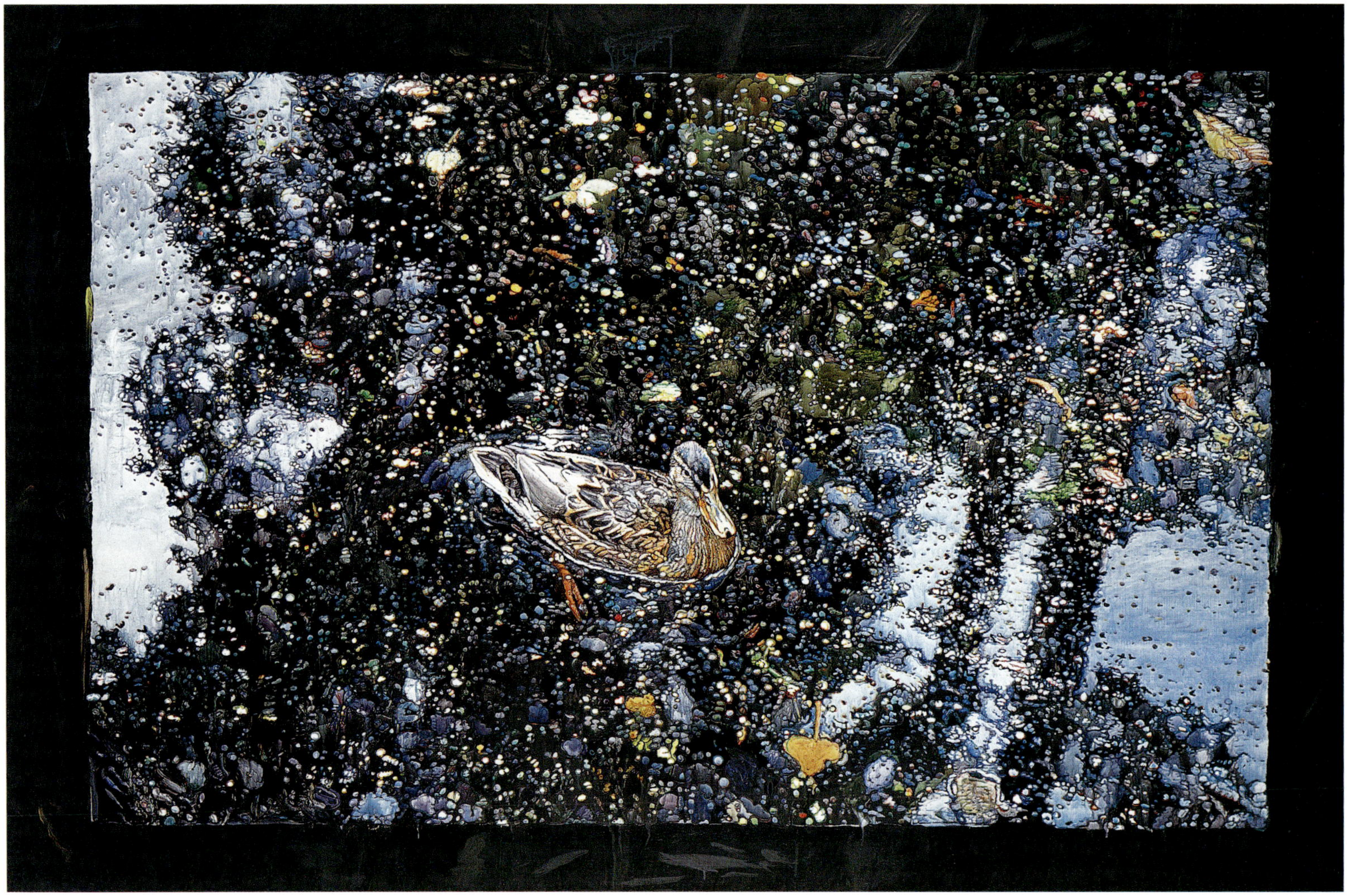

65. *Galactic Waters II,* 1995
Acrylic on canvas, 51 x 77 in. (129.5 x 195.5 cm)
Courtesy of Nancy Hoffman Gallery,
New York

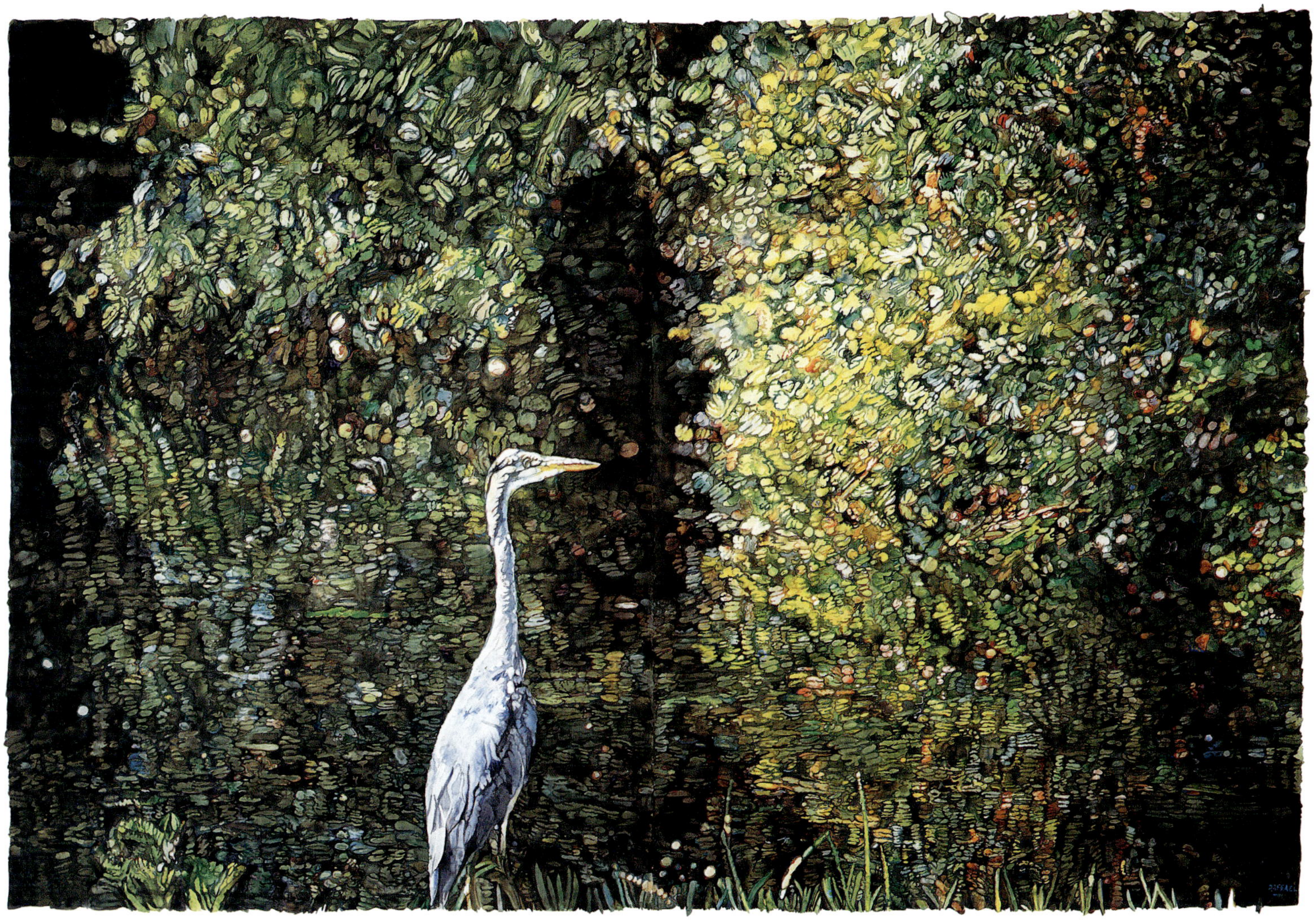

66. Heron's Vision, 1996
Watercolor on paper, diptych: 60½ x 86½ in.
(153.6 x 219.6 cm)
Private collection, Providence, Rhode Island

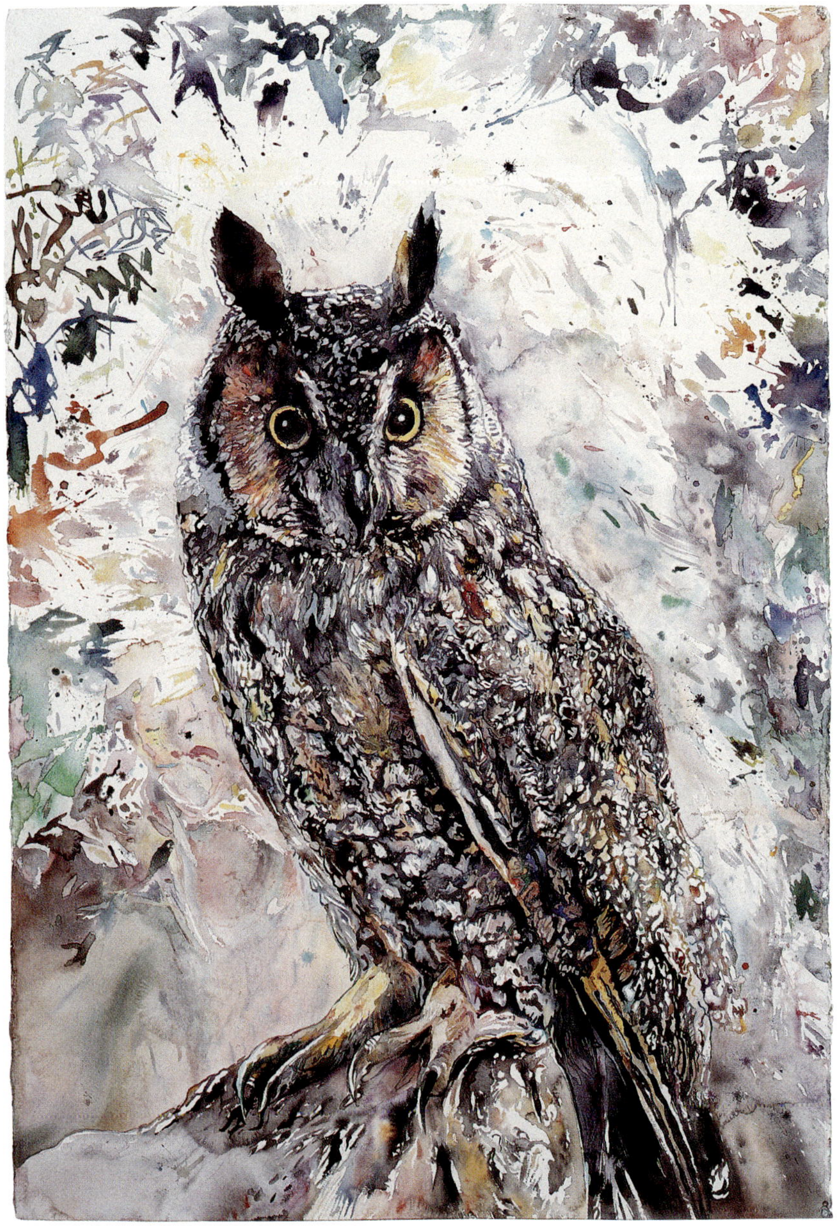

LEFT

67. *Spirit (Owl)*, 1985
Watercolor on paper, 60 x 40 in.
(152.4 x 101.6 cm)
Robert E. Abrams, New York

BELOW

68. *Mallard,* 1976
Oil on canvas, 66 x 108 in. (167.6 x 274.3 cm)
Private collection

OPPOSITE

69. *Twilight,* 1996
Watercolor on paper, diptych: 68½ x 87 in.
(173.9 x 220.9 cm)
Courtesy of Nancy Hoffman Gallery,
New York

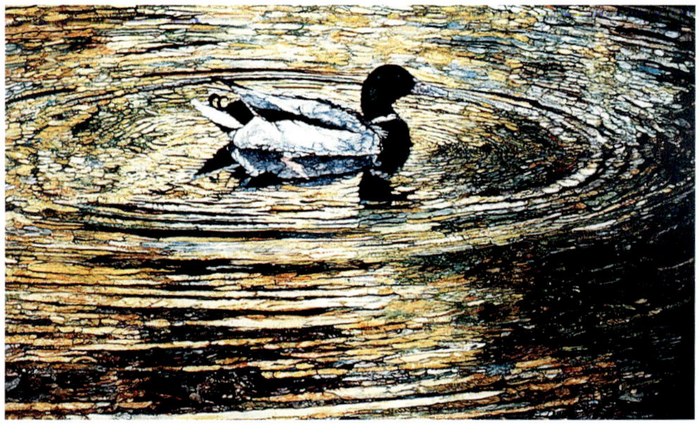

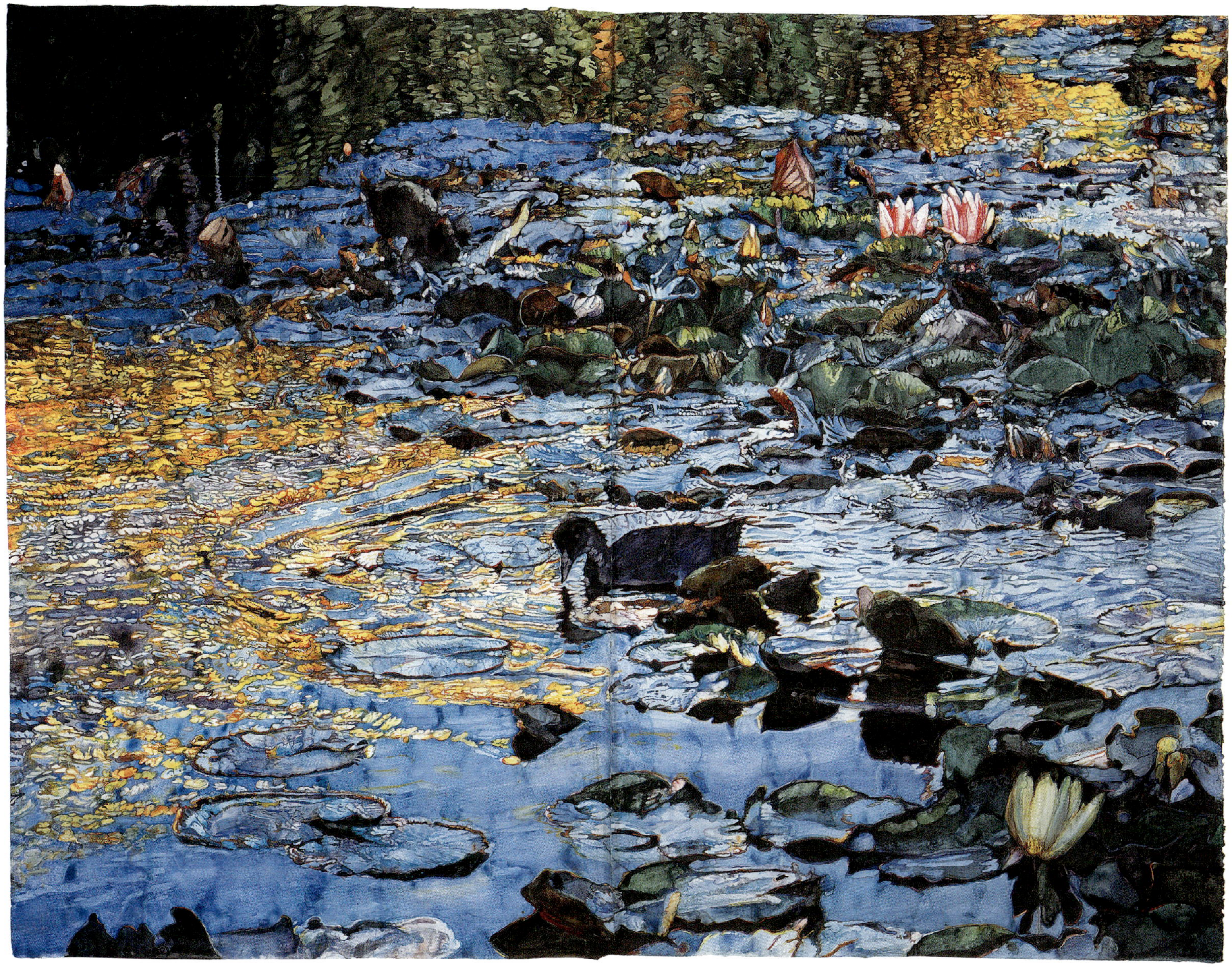

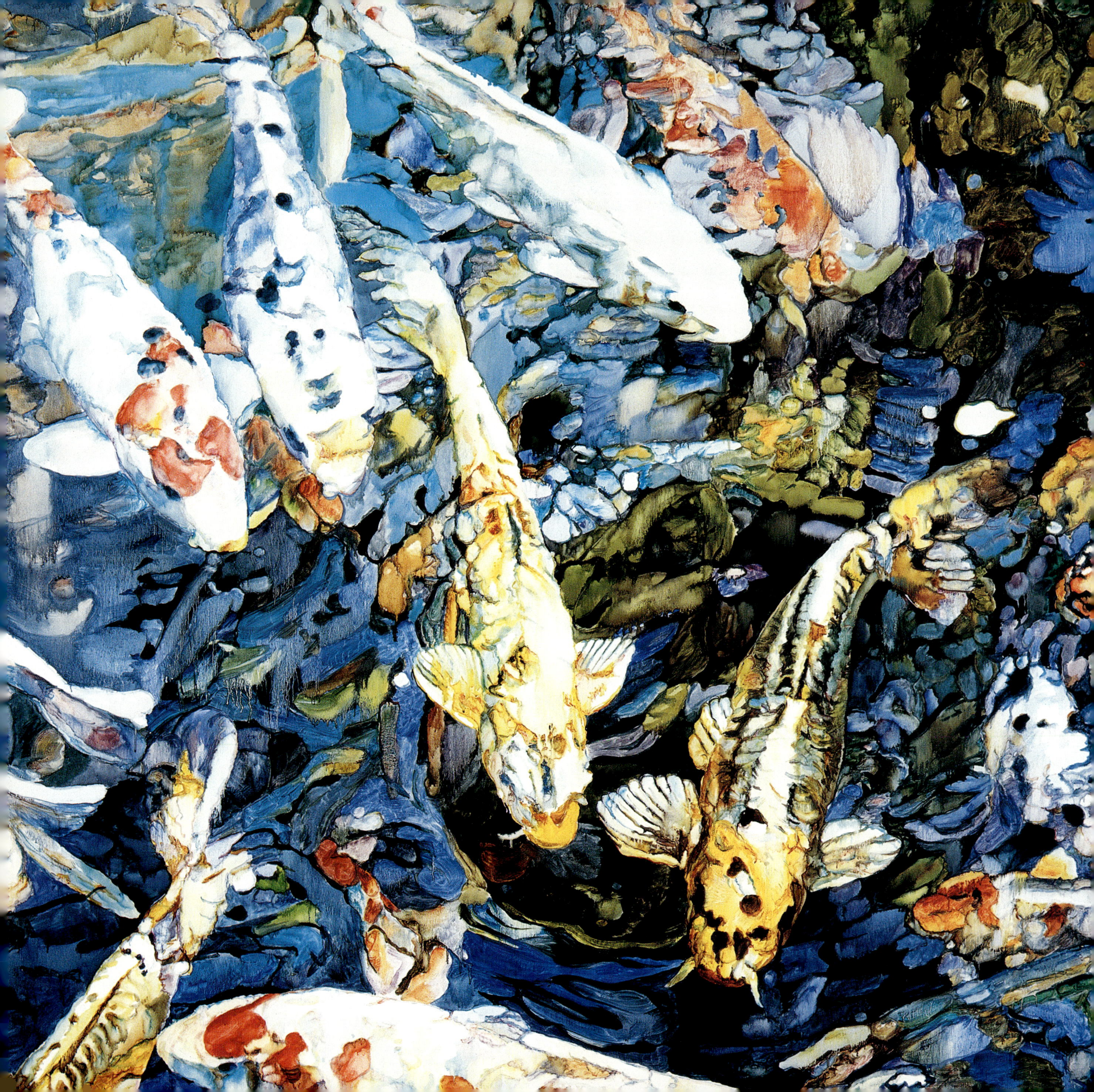

The Lily and Fish Paintings

"In its watery radiance"

70. Detail of *Fish Spirit,* 1978
See plate 86

Raffael's lily and fish paintings are complementary aspects of the same phenomenon. Both lilies and fish are born, reside, and die in water; they both alter and are altered by the uncountable ways light penetrates water or reflects off it. Fish move through water, which illuminates them with color, burnishing them to a phosphorescent sheen. Lily pads ride water and accumulate it; they soak up light and darken it. Lily flowers reflect back light and render water droplets luminous. Fish function for Raffael like stained-glass windows, altering and refracting light. Lilies, like the gold in a Cimabue halo, are a means of achieving radiance. The spiritual implications are not accidental. Lilies and fish signify mystery above and mystery below.

As with so many of his other recurring themes, Raffael began painting lilies and fish in the late 1970s. At about the same time, Post-Minimalist painters in New York were experimenting with inserting figures into what had been uninflected abstract grounds. Raffael had been schooled by Josef Albers in the gestalt theory that there is no background or foreground, only interconnections. So it was a logical step for him to begin introducing fish and lilies into his water paintings. But only in the last four years have these images become so numerous and so loaded. A great many of the paintings that Raffael made after Lannis was rushed to the hospital in August 1993 and almost died there have been of lilies and of fish. They have been exaltations of her recovery, odes to endurance, celebrations of life.

One of the first of this series was *Lily Pond, Lannis, Light and Shadow Diptych* (plate 71). It is difficult to disentangle the lily pads from their shadows on the glassine water—life and death have become interchangeable. At the center of the painting is a pink lily, bleached in light. The only other blooming lilies are to its left and to its right, as on a cross. "This to me is a very serious painting," says Raffael. "It's like Uccello's horses and riders. It's a very serious, structured painting. People could see it only as lilies, but this is also like the Sacred Heart of the Cross," the Catholic church he attended during his boyhood summers on Long Island's North Fork.

Summer Fish II (plate 88) is, in a sense, a companion piece to *Metamorphose* (plate 33). It, too, is vertical; its stacked, crisscrossing fish are in autumnal colors; its theme is darkness and luminescence and the quickness with which the one can transmogrify into the other.

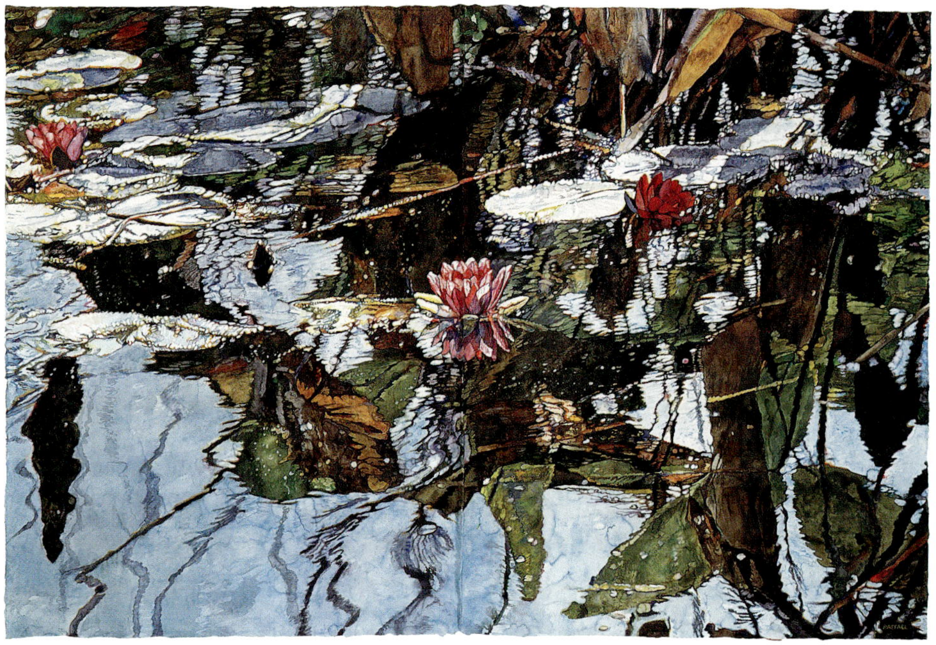

ABOVE

71. *Lily Pond, Lannis, Light and Shadow Diptych,* 1993
Watercolor on paper, diptych: 61¼ x 88½ in. (155.5 x 224.7 cm)
Dale Scott Yamane, Yardley, Pennsylvania

OPPOSITE

72. *Hommage au Printemps II,* 1997
Watercolor on paper, 62½ x 44½ in. (158.7 x 113 cm)
Courtesy of Nancy Hoffman Gallery, New York

In the spring of 1997 Raffael taped two just-finished paintings of fish on his wall (plate 72). Both were framed in thick contrasting borders, flecked in confetti colors—a device he had used to great effect in *Out of the Thicket* (plate 54). In this case, however, the colors took a hint from the combinations of hues that Lannis had painted their house, with yellow window frames on Matisse-blue walls and arches of burgundy to offset green rooms. The photographs from which the paintings came had been taken within minutes of one another. In one the fish is half-doused in shadow. In the other it has emerged into clear water.

The paintings were still on the wall when Raffael embarked on a new painting. This time the photograph from which he had begun was not his own. He had asked Lannis to scout for scenes on a recent solo trip to Bali, and he chose a vertical photograph of a pond filled with lotus leaves—growing, rotting, reflected, splashing raindrops in spiraling complexity. He traced each tiny permutation onto paper, laid the paper on the table, and then began to fill in with watercolor. As was his habit, he worked close up, unfurling and rescrolling the paper as he went along so that he never saw the picture whole as he worked. In the photograph the colors were greens, yellows, and murky browns. The colors he began to apply with a thin brush, wet so that the edges ran together, were pink, baby blue, chartreuse, orange, tangerine, and aqua (plate 92).

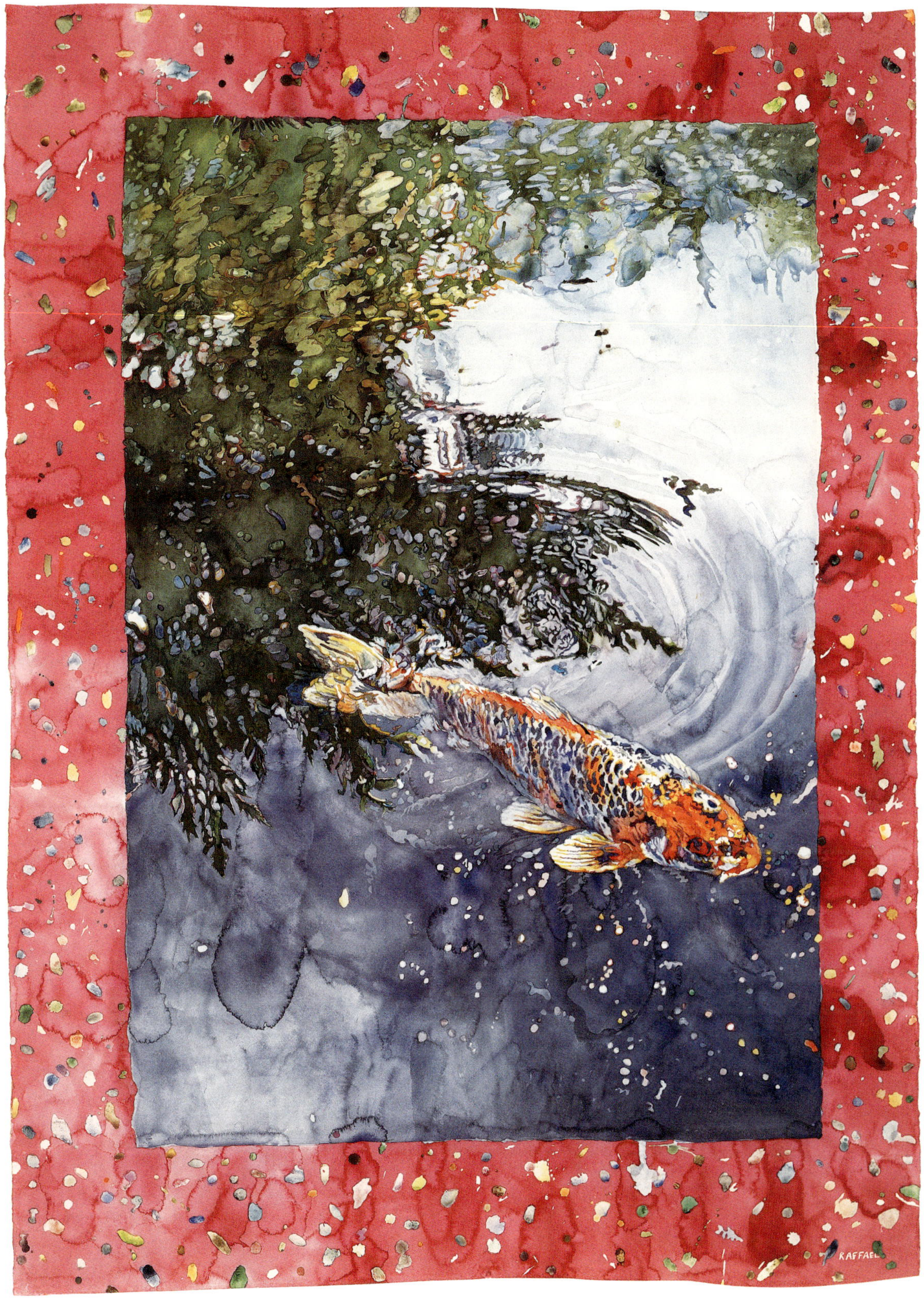
RAFFAEL

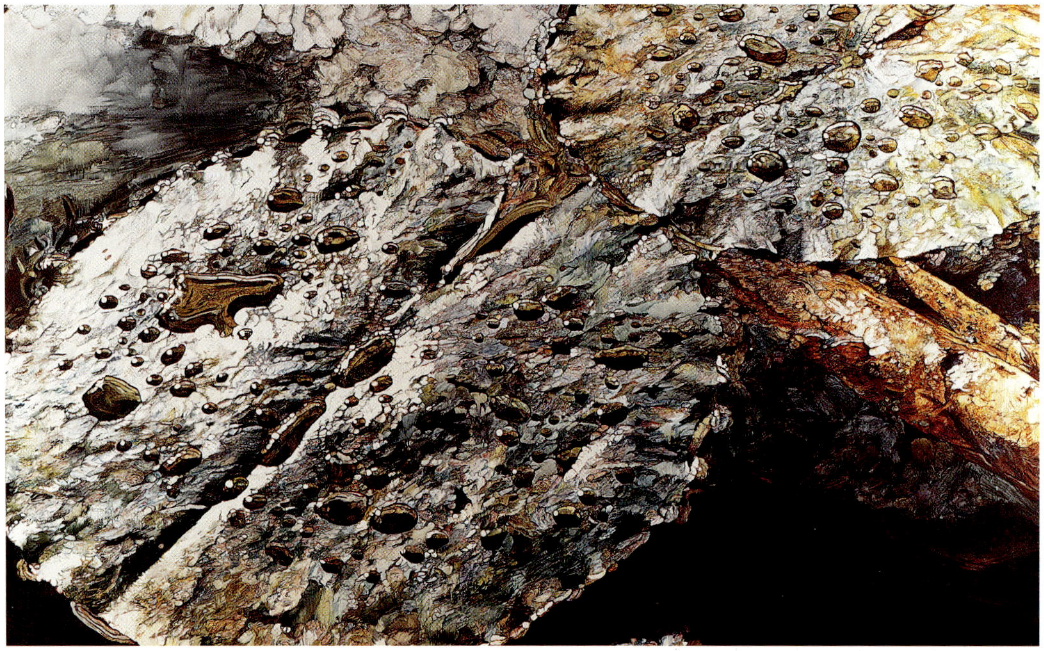

73. *Lily Pads and Leaf,* 1975
Oil on canvas, 84 x 132 in. (213.3 x 335.2 cm)
Harris Bank Collection, Chicago

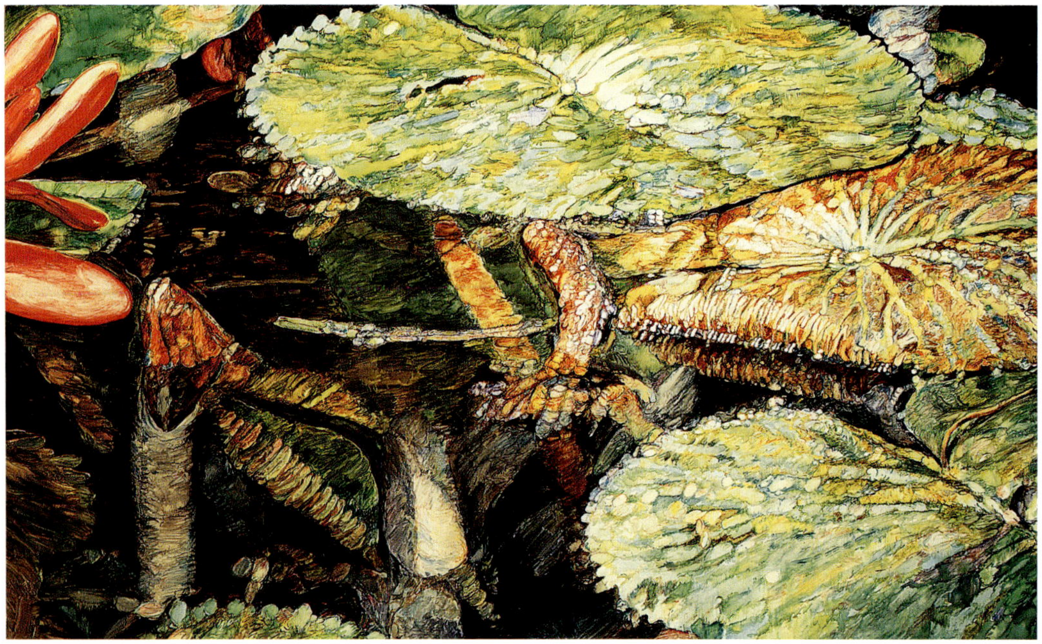

74. *Lily Pond II,* 1976
Oil on canvas, 90 x 114 in. (228.5 x 289.5 cm)
Private collection, Hobe Sound, Florida

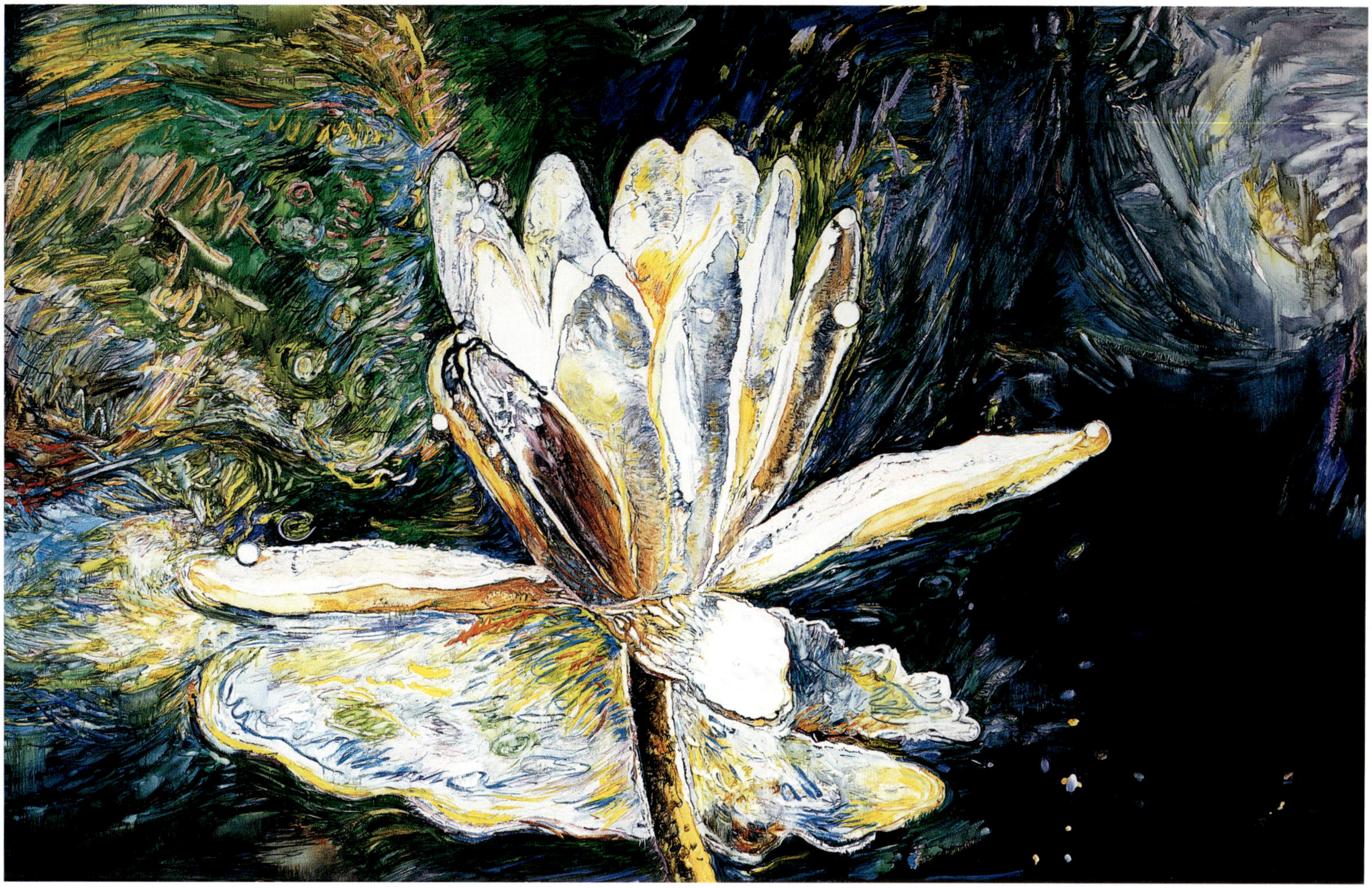

75. *New Lily,* 1979–80
Oil on canvas, 84 x 127¼ in.
(213.3 x 323.1 cm)
Mr. and Mrs. John D. Nichols

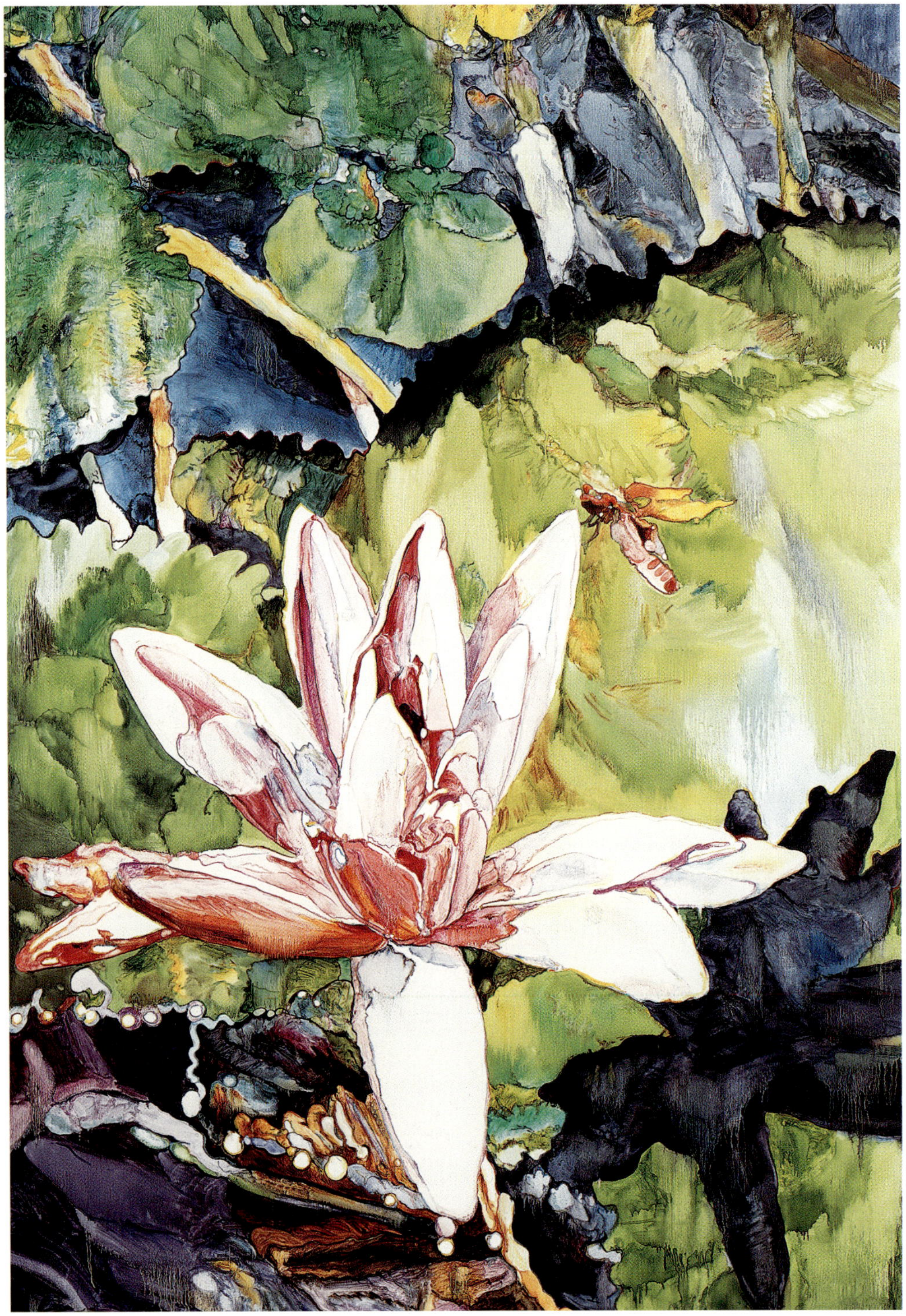

LEFT

76. *Lily with Dragonfly,* 1980
Oil on canvas, 72 x 48 in. (182.8 x 121.9 cm)
Private collection

OPPOSITE

77. *Listening Lily,* 1976
Watercolor on paper, 30 x 40 in.
(76.2 x 101.6 cm)
Private collection

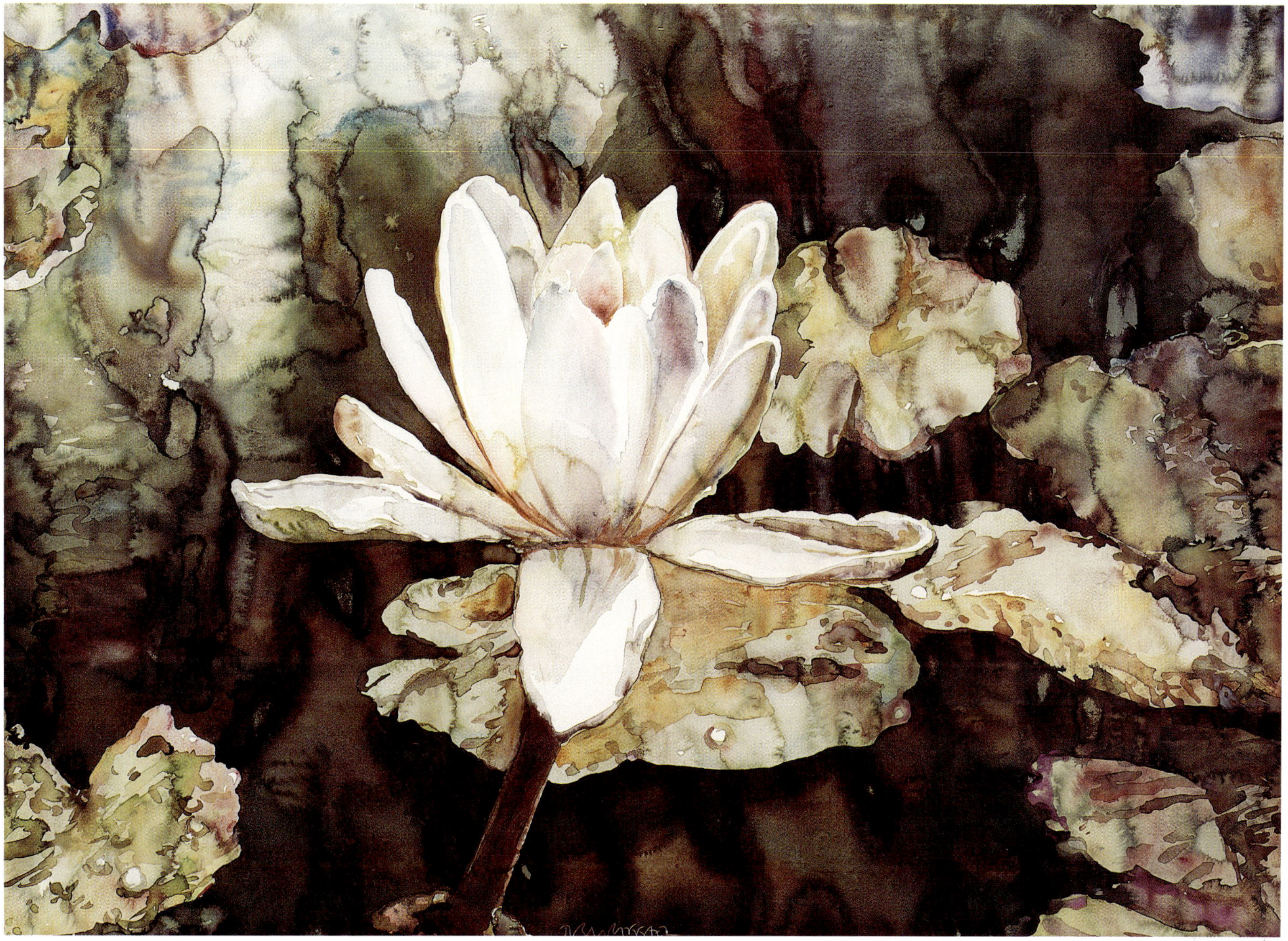

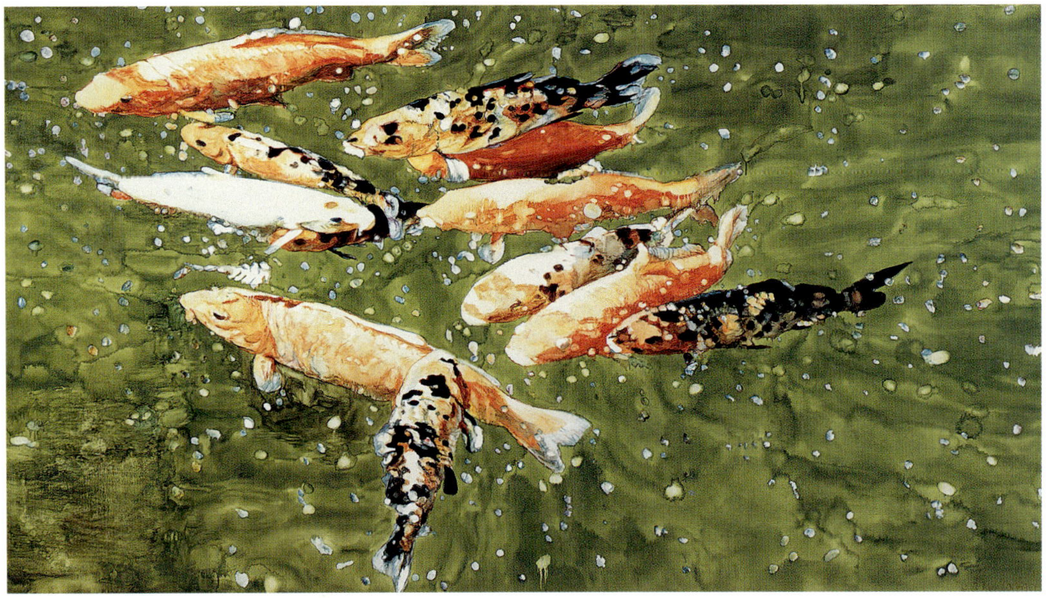

78. *Eleven Fish,* 1978
Oil on canvas, 48 x 84 in. (121.9 x 213.3 cm)
The Cleveland Museum of Art;
Gift of Rod Jacobson

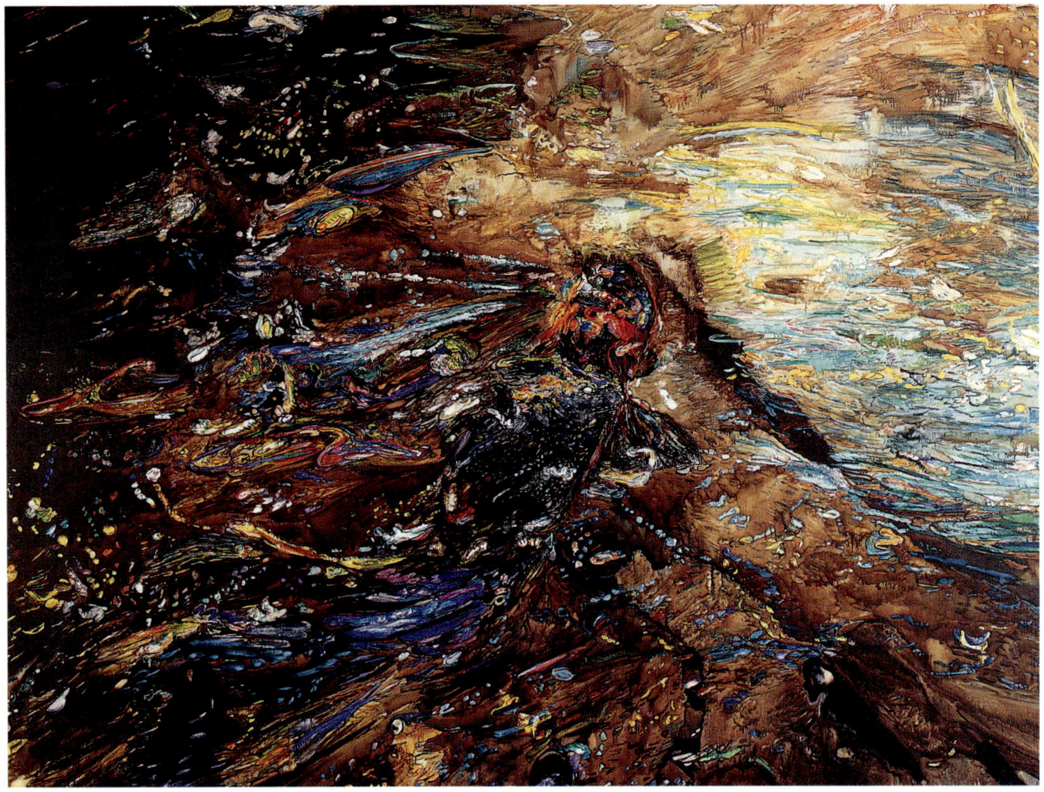

79. *Fish Dream,* 1979
Oil on canvas, 72 x 96 in. (182.8 x 243.8 cm)
Joseph and Lannis Raffael,
Cap d'Antibes, France

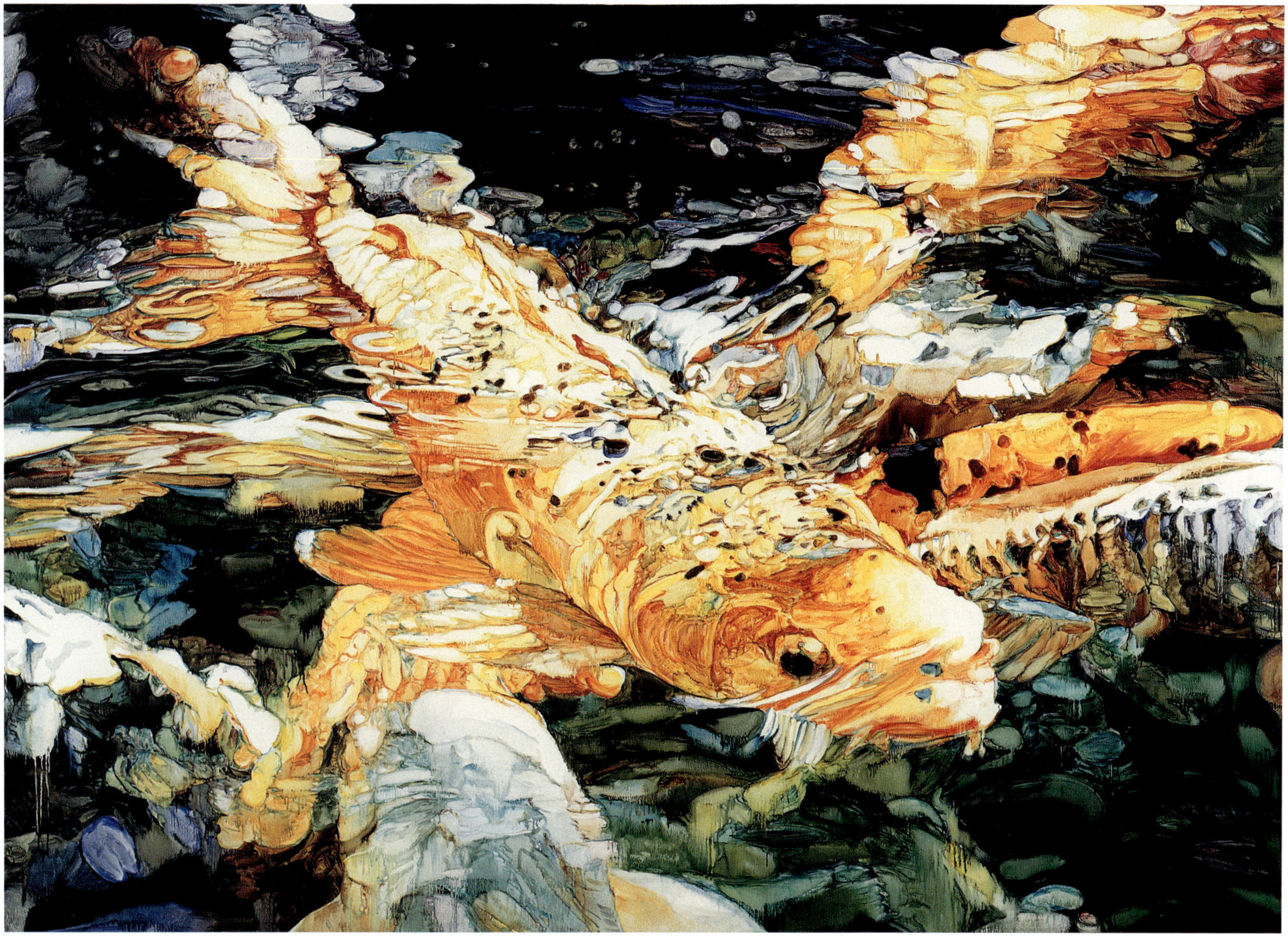

80. *Orange Fish,* 1979
Oil on canvas, 66 x 90 in. (167.6 x 228.5 cm)
Sidney and George Perutz

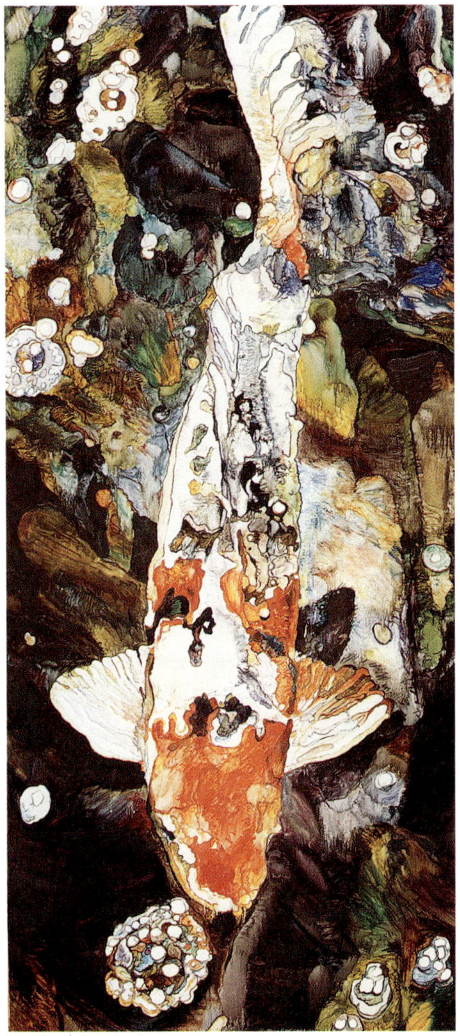

LEFT
81. *Celebration,* 1980
Oil on canvas, 96 x 40¾ in. (103.4 x 243.8 cm)
Mr. and Mrs. Walter J. Haas, San Francisco

BELOW
82. *Spirit Pond,* 1980
Watercolor with pastel on paper,
44¾ x 52¼ in. (113.6 x 132.7 cm)
Dr. Rosenberg, Orinda, California

OPPOSITE
83. *Luminous Pond,* 1980
Watercolor on paper, 54 x 44½ in.
(137.1 x 113 cm)
The Mann Collection,
Highland Park, Illinois

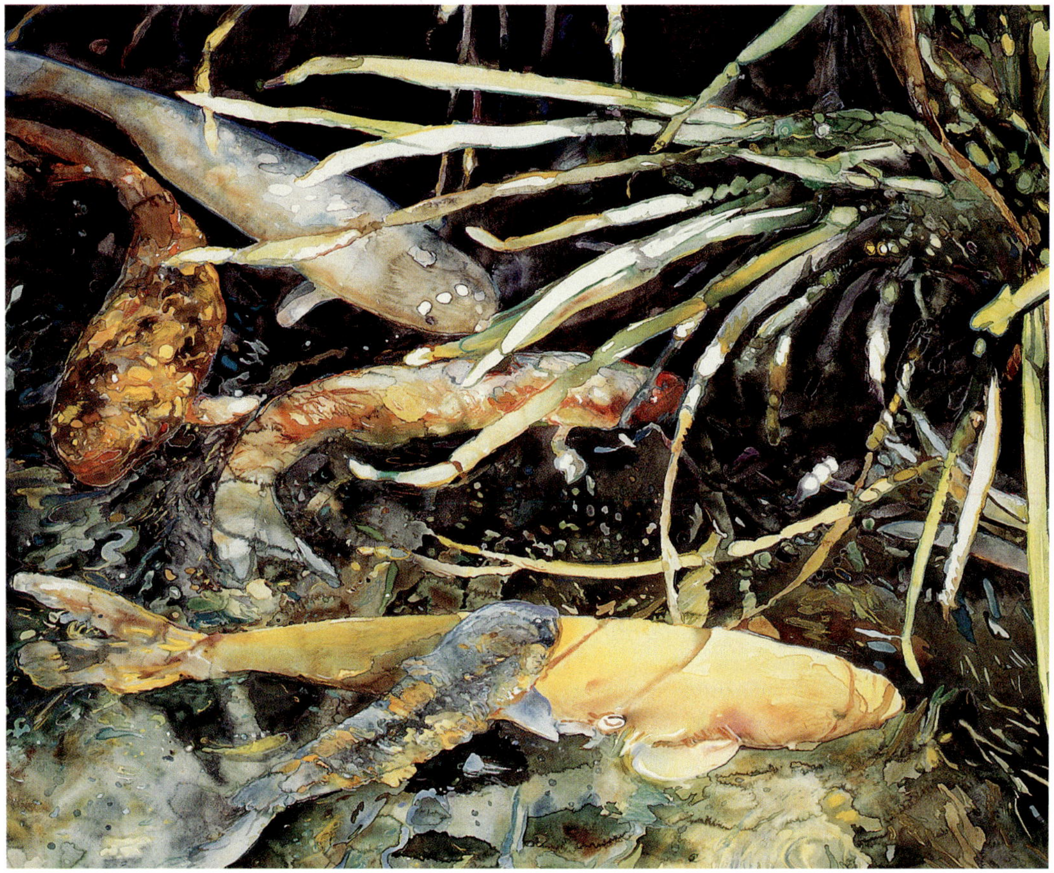

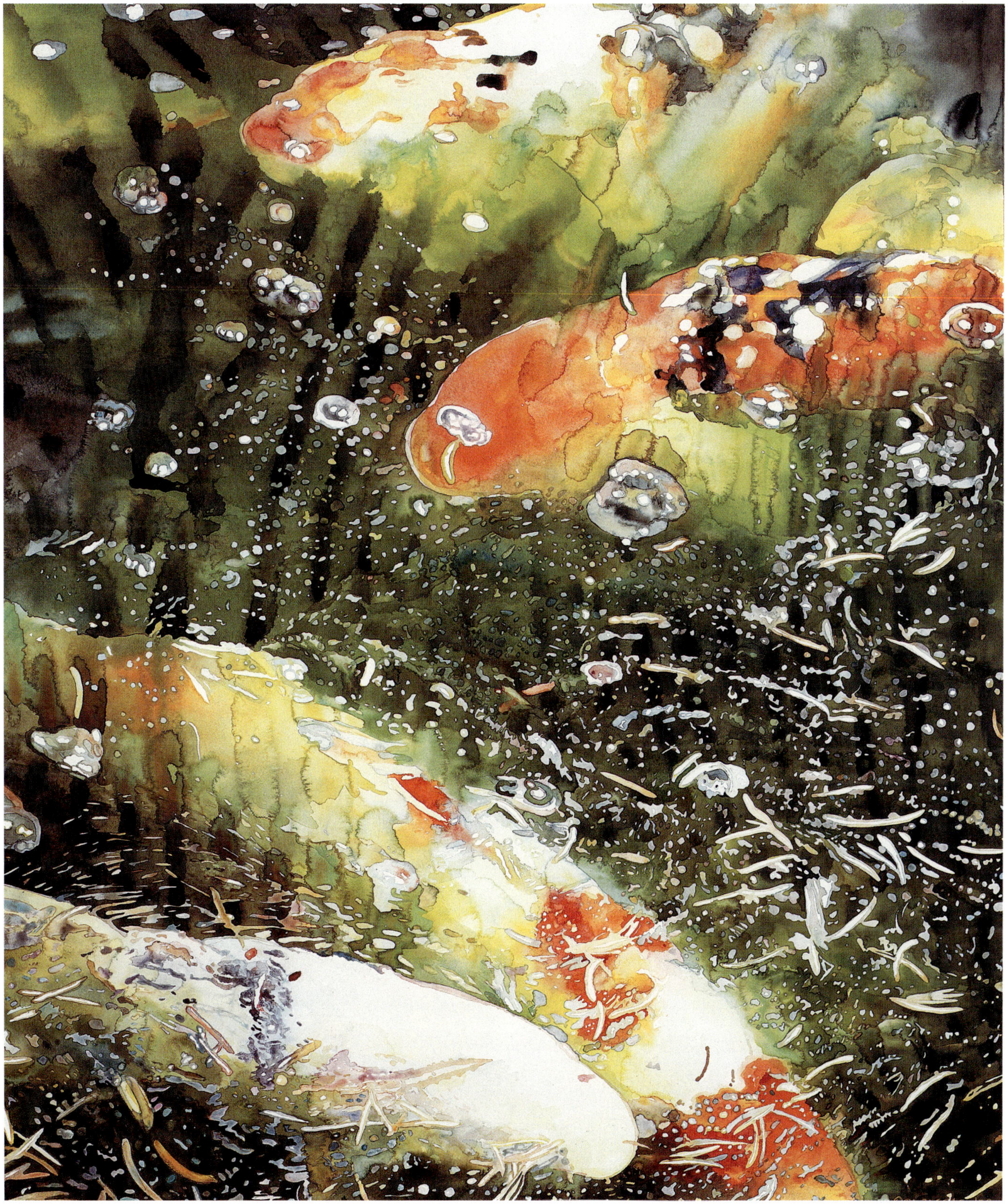

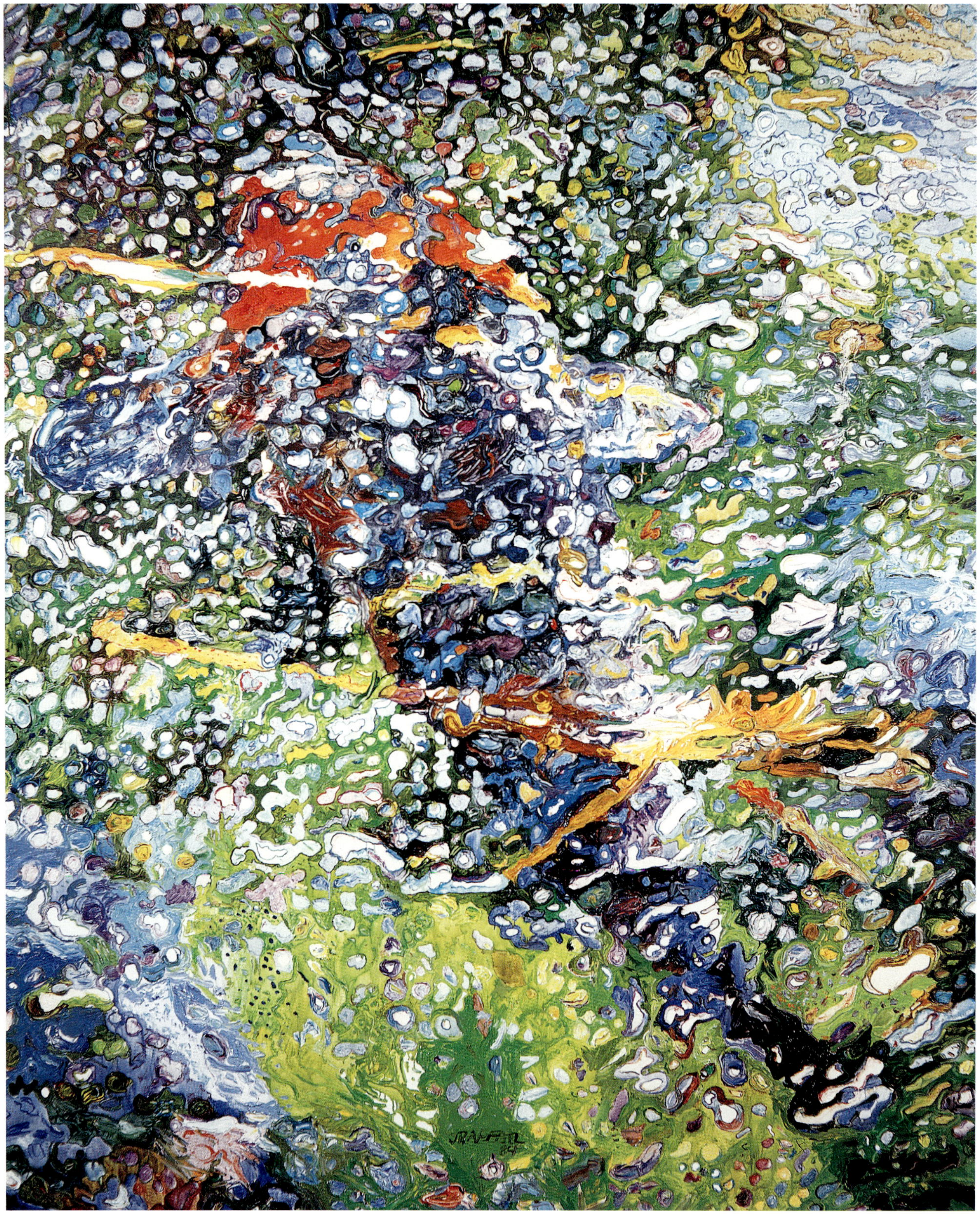

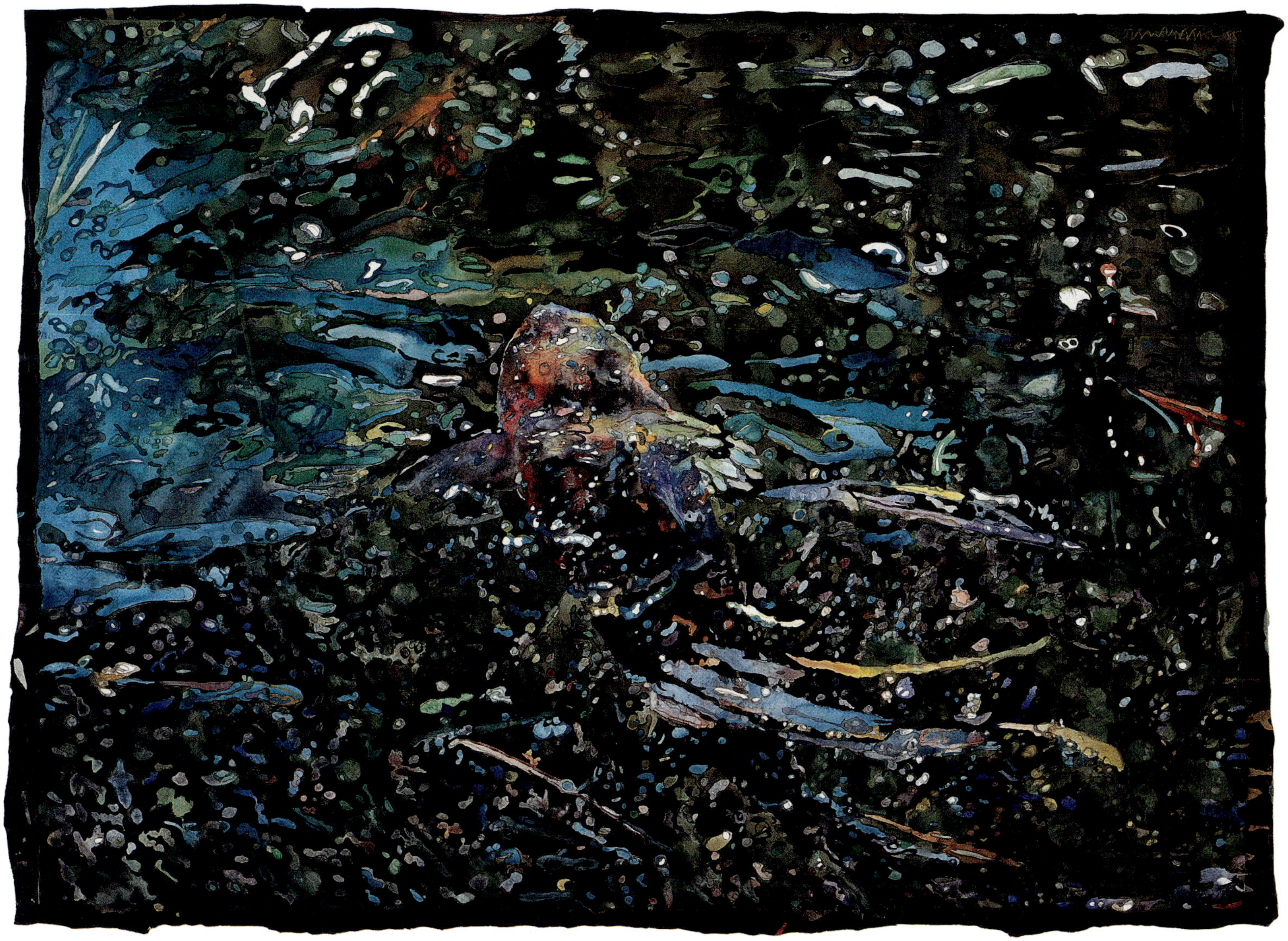

OPPOSITE

84. *Wind on Water Spring,* 1984
Oil on canvas, 84 x 66 in. (213.3 x 167.6 cm)
Portland Art Museum, Portland, Oregon;
Gift of Mr. and Mrs. William A. Small, Jr.

ABOVE

85. *Water with Fish,* 1985
Watercolor on paper, 29 x 38¾ in. (73.6 x 98.4 cm)
Pennsylvania Academy of the Fine Arts,
Philadelphia; John S. Phillips Fund

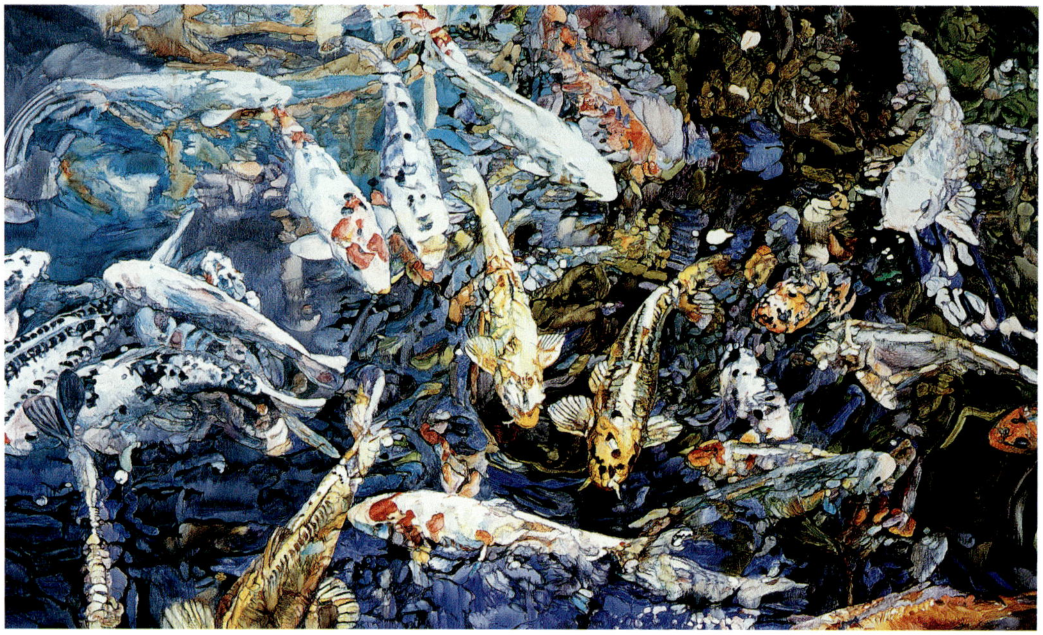

LEFT

86. *Fish Spirit,* 1978
Oil on canvas, 72 x 120 in.
(182.8 x 304.7 cm)
Barbara Fendrick,
Chevy Chase, Maryland

BELOW

87. *Solstice,* 1993
Watercolor on paper, 44½ x 66½ in.
(113 x 168.6 cm)
Courtesy of Nancy Hoffman Gallery,
New York

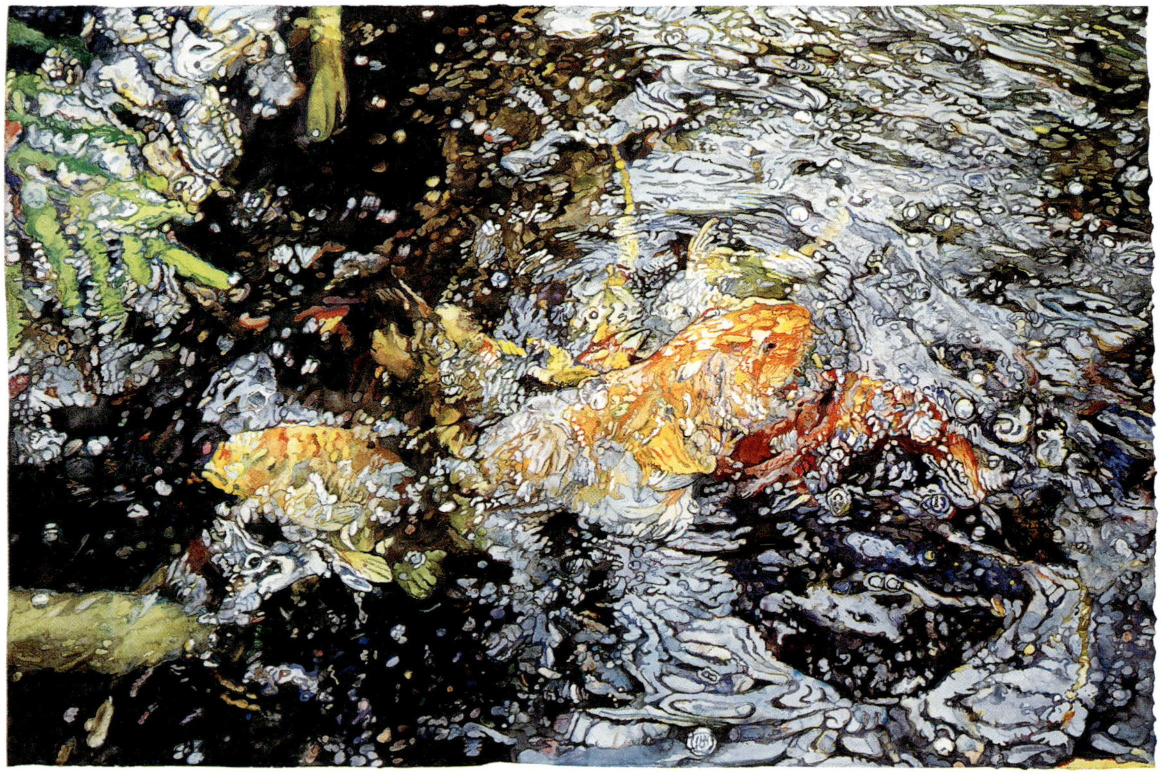

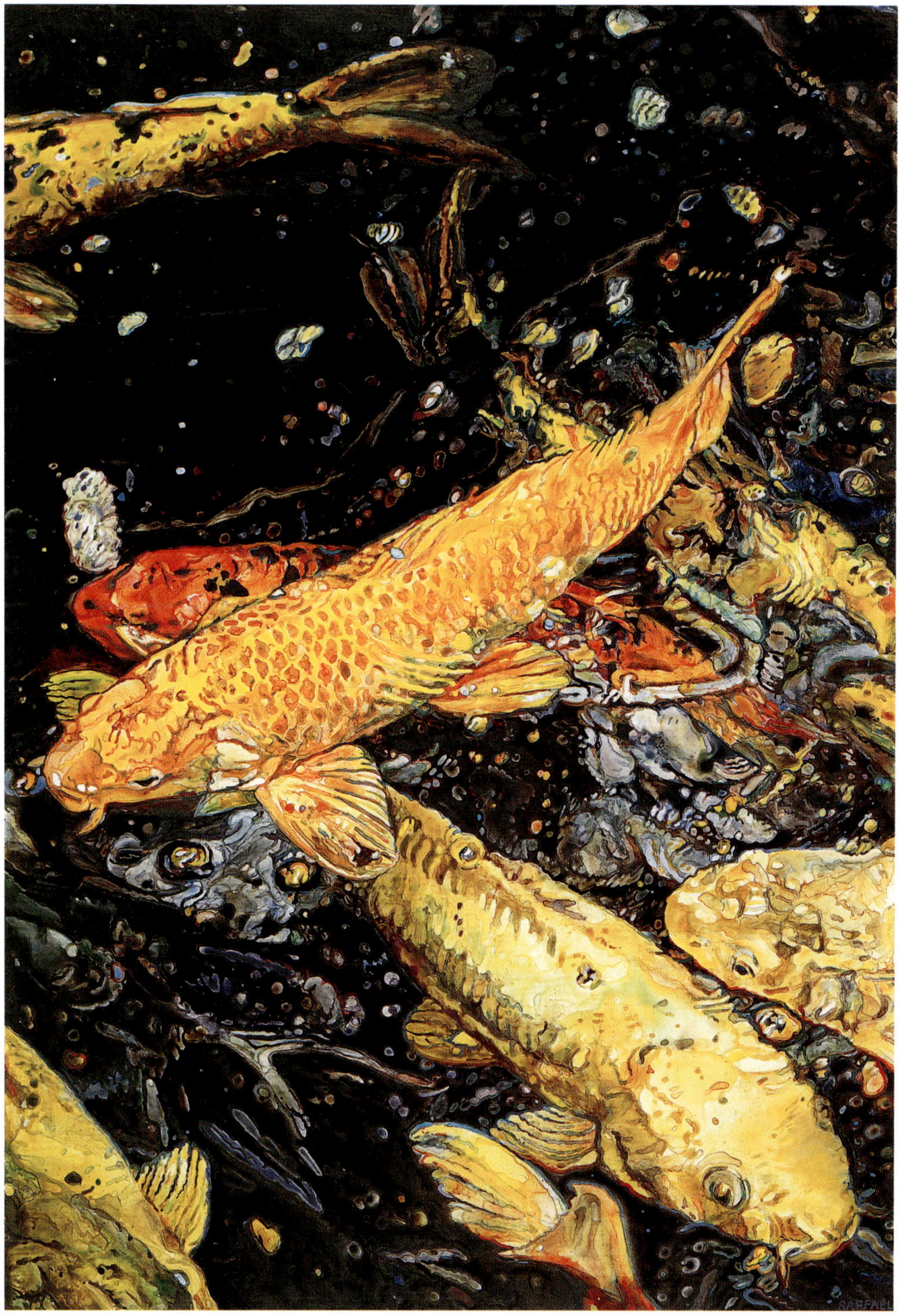

88. *Summer Fish II,* 1995
Acrylic on canvas, 32 x 21¼ in.
(81.2 x 53.9 cm)
Private collection

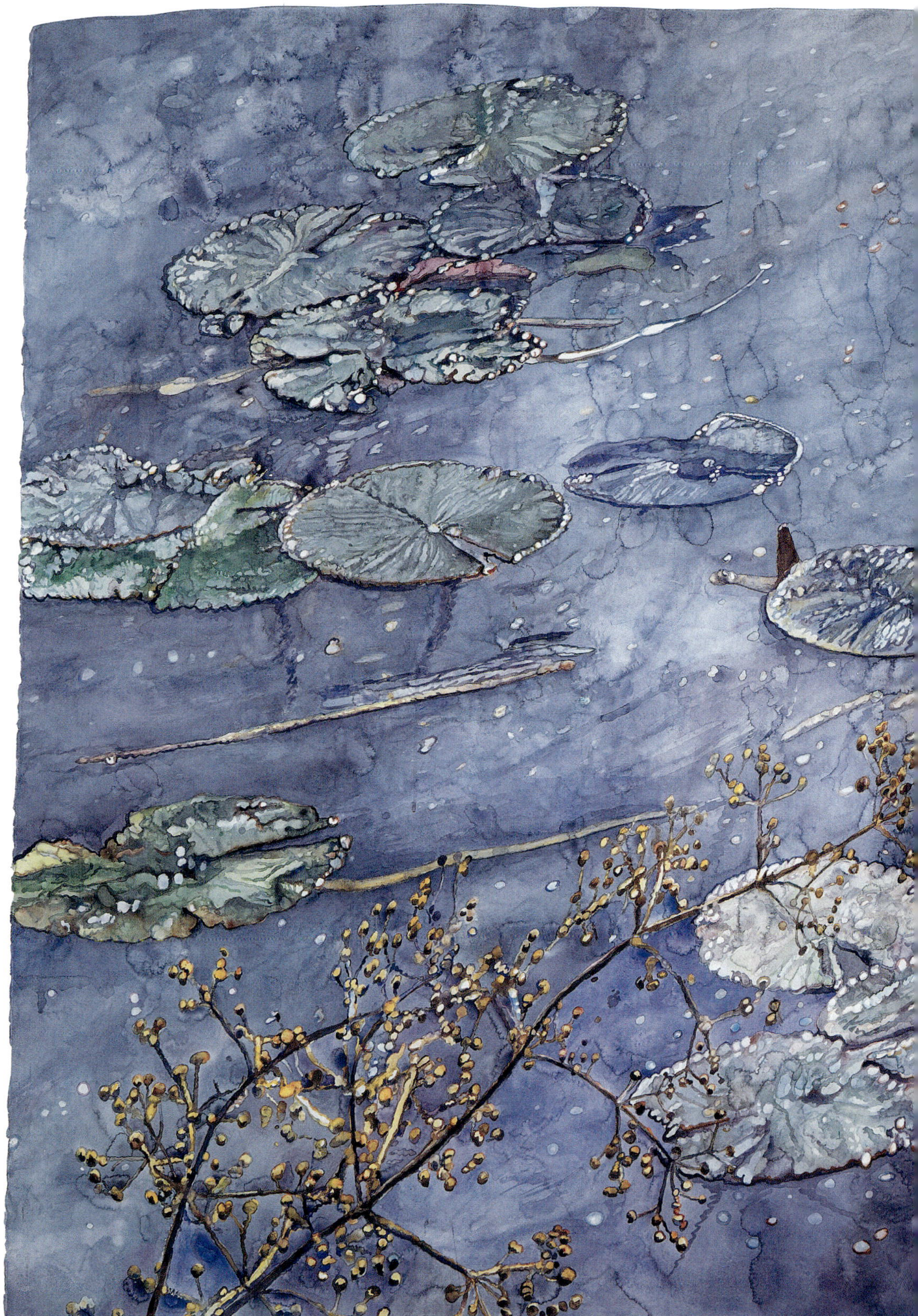

89. *Lily Pond, Lannis, Restoration,* 1993
Watercolor on paper, diptych: 64½ x 88¾ in.
(163.8 x 225.4 cm)
Private collection, Hobe Sound, Florida

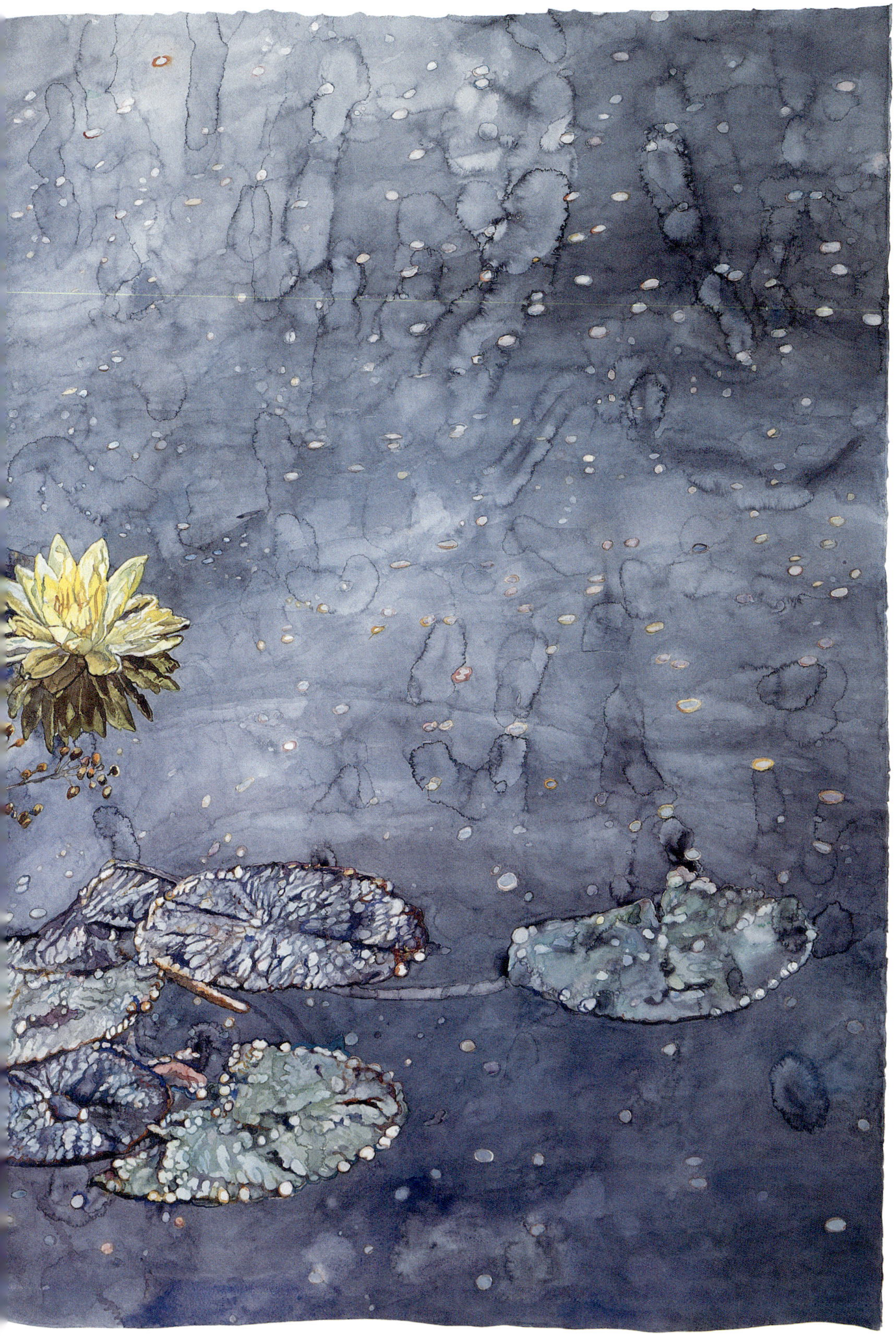

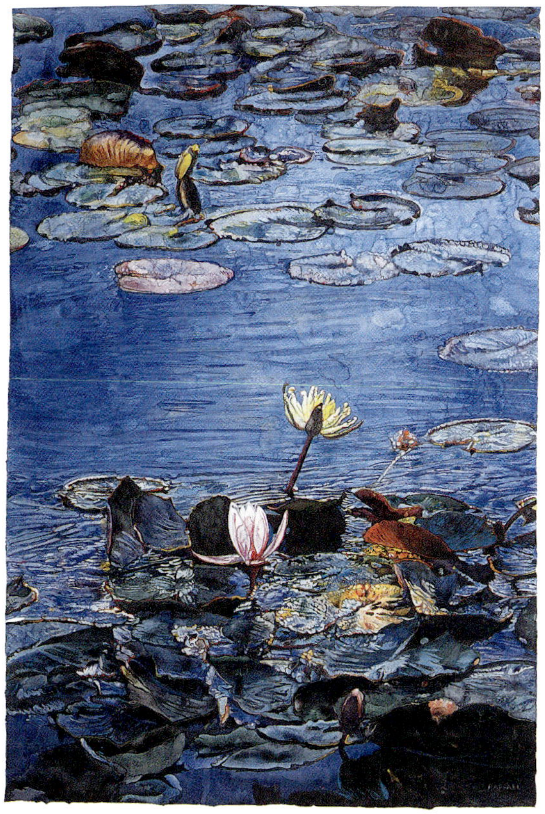

90. *Lilies Dreaming,* 1997
Watercolor on paper, 68 x 44½ in.
(172.7 x 113 cm)
Private collection

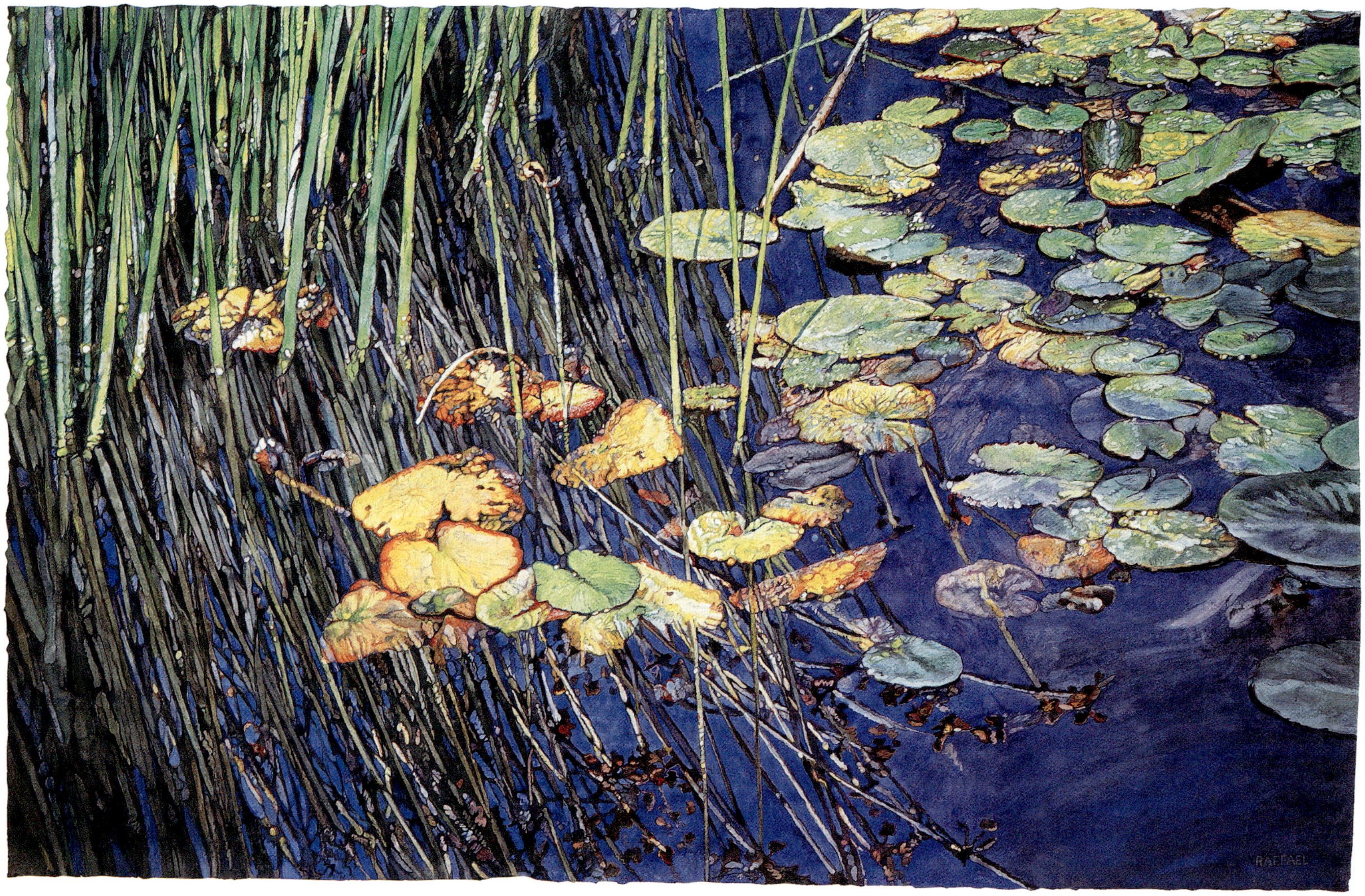

ABOVE

91. *The Colour of Transition,* 1994
Watercolor on paper, 44½ x 68 in.
(113 x 172.7 cm)
The Capital Group Companies, Inc.,
Los Angeles

OPPOSITE

92. *La Magie de Bali,* 1997
Watercolor on paper, 58¼ x 44¾ in.
(147.9 x 113.6 cm)
Private collection, Chicago

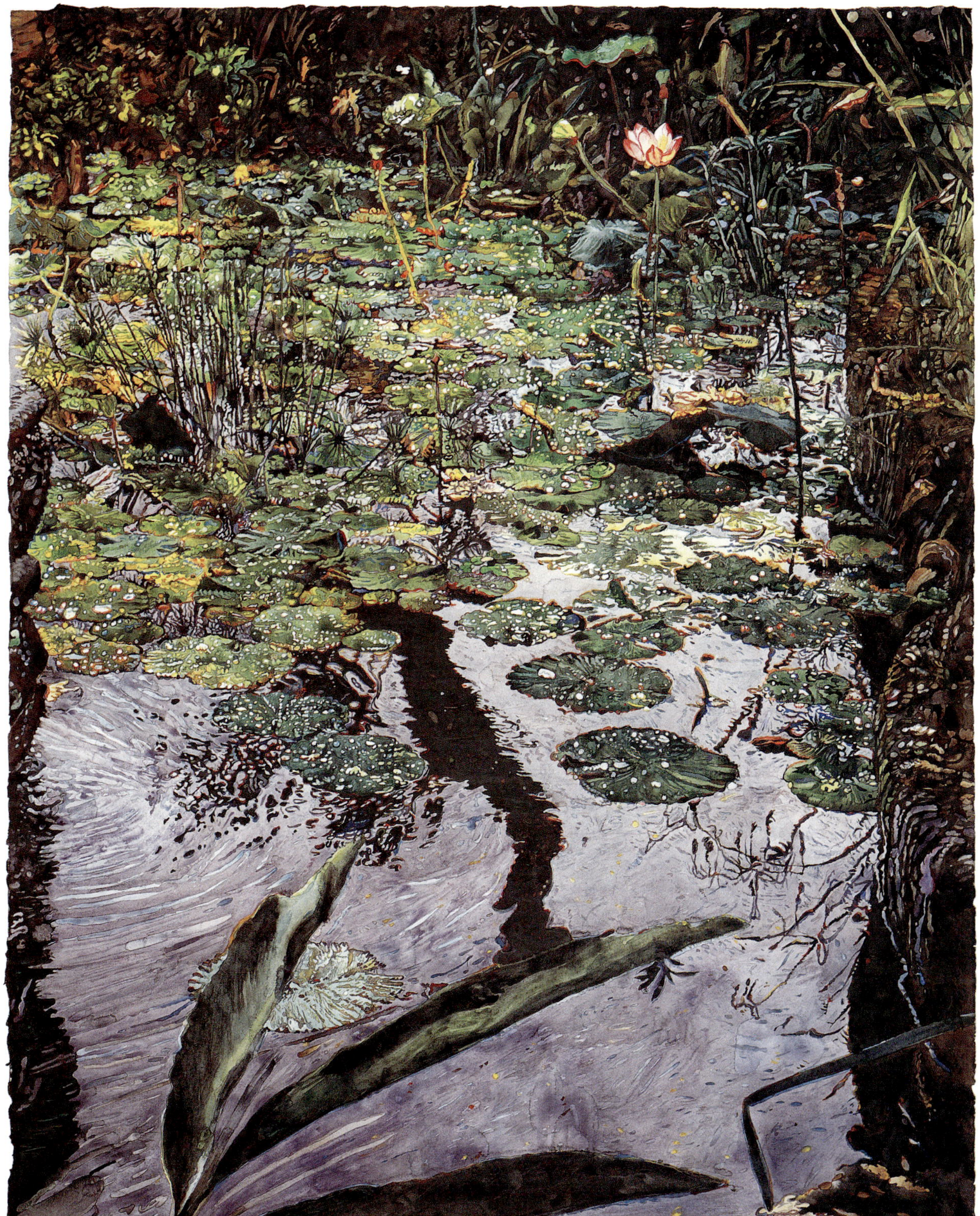

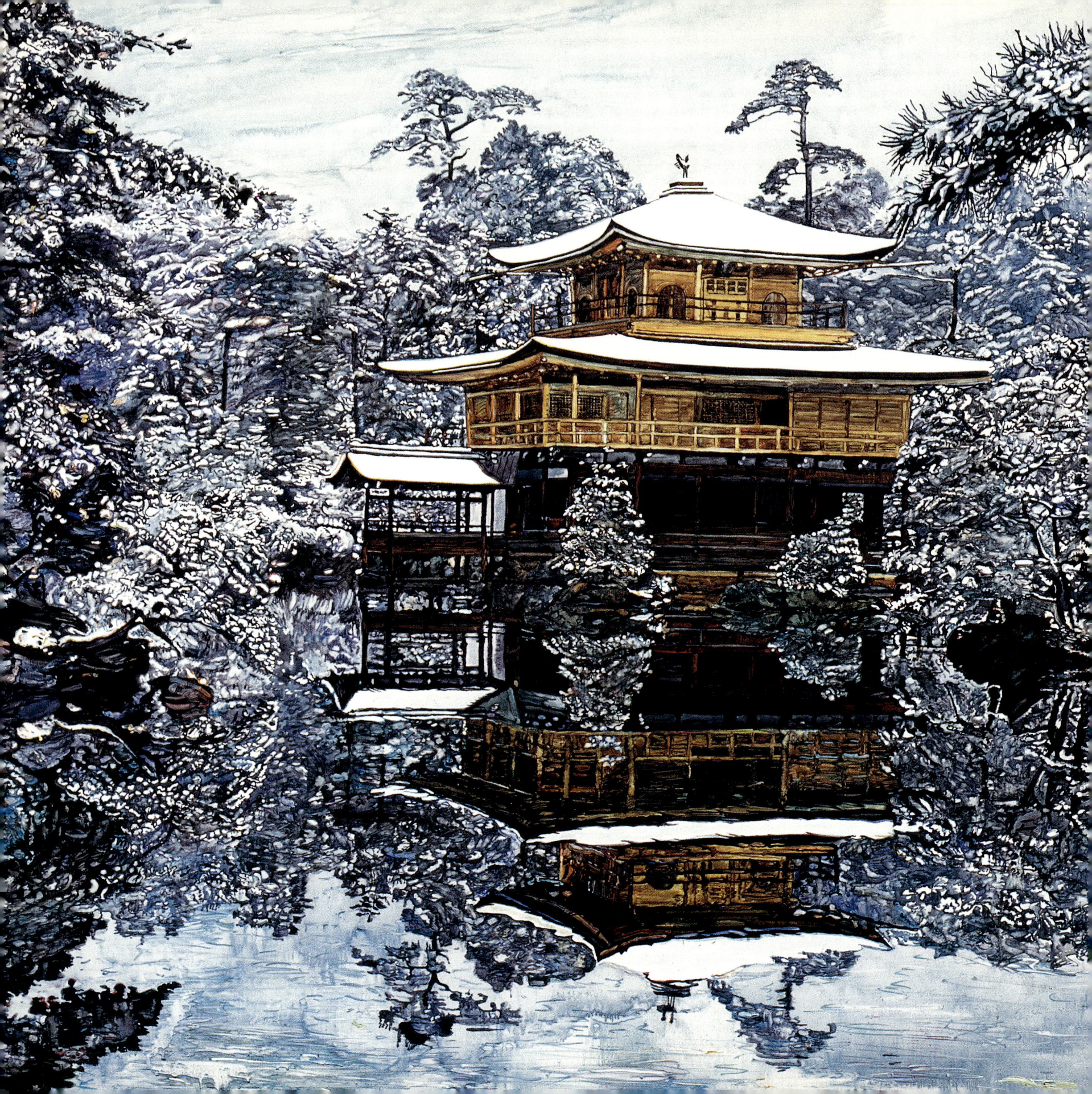

The Sacred Symbol Paintings

"Sacrament and celebration"

Raffael does not consider himself a practicing Buddhist—more a seeker after salient truths. But a recurrent theme in his paintings has been Buddhist temples and statues of the Buddha as well as of the rather more approachable Hindu deity Ganesh. He chooses Japanese themes, he has said, because, "When I look at Japan, the aesthetic aspect of Japan, it seems to me there has been a creative union in which person and nature have been able to interweave together, and become one in balance and harmony. There is a synthesis of beauty, strength, and form. An equilibrium."[1]

Equilibrium was a hard-won prize after years of turmoil when Raffael painted *Marriage* (plate 103), in 1986, to honor his marriage to Lannis. It is a painting that accents tranquillity with gaiety, but as in a reverie. He had never seen the Golden Temple, which is pictured in this work on a snowy day when fir trees are reflected in the pond whose edge is our vantage point. A breeze is ruffling lilac ripples. On the other side the temple gleams—at once precious object, spiritual goal, and fantastic dream. This dream, like all of Raffael's dreams, is a vision of painting. It is played out in the broad border—a rhapsody of spring-colored brush strokes, overlays, and drips. Neither the decisively rendered temple in its snowy landscape nor the extravagantly giddy border could comfortably stand on its own. The poetry—the art—lies in the marriage between them.

In the life Joseph and Lannis Raffael live together now, they are surrounded by statues of Buddha—outdoors in the garden, large and small indoors. "It's like art for us, and yet they also have something we respond to." The statue of a smiling Blue Buddha on their sideboard holds a photograph of their first grandchild in his arms and is encircled by candles, which Lannis lights every day. In 1990 Ganesh found his way into a

93. Detail of *Marriage,* 1986
See plate 103

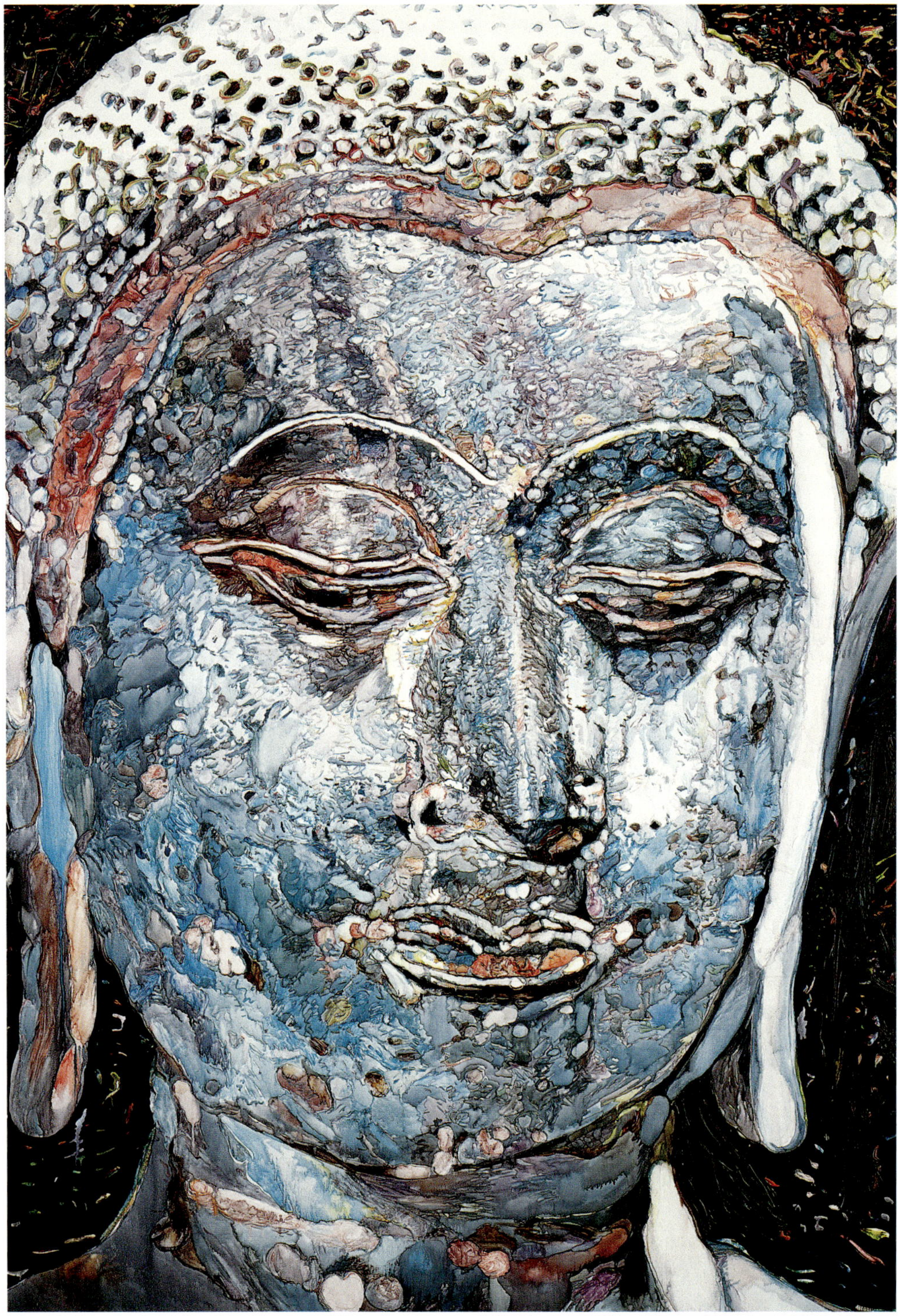

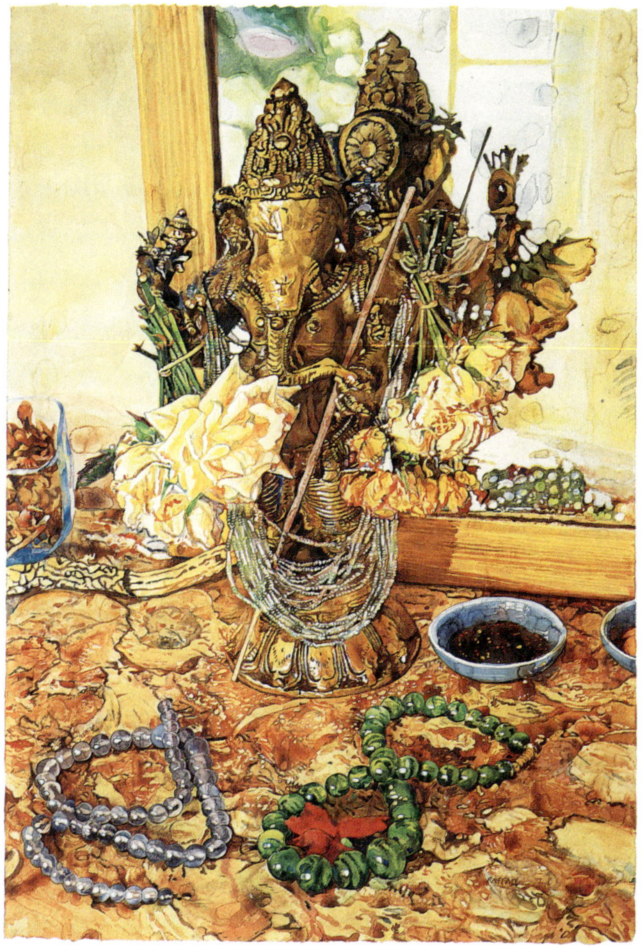

painting (plate 95), flourishing in opulent golds and rich oranges, light gleaming off his metallic skin and reflected in the mirror behind him. Surrounding him are flowers and offerings of beads that give Raffael an excuse to paint transparency and flash. This Ganesh is as sumptuous as any peony in a garden and an equally commonplace yet miraculous fact of life.

When Raffael painted a portrait of the Buddha in 1985 (plate 94), he returned to the frontality of his earlier animal portraits but without the theatrical derring-do. His Buddha signifies calm, as a Buddha should; the painting is as much in praise of the beauty of the statue as of the god who inspired it. The painting serves as an allegory of the sacredness of art. Like a mallard in a pond, the Buddha is bound by its universe, but one that is infinite, stretching blackly behind him. And unlike the mallard, he has been twice transformed by art—once in bronze, once in oil so thinly laid on that it soaks into puddles of blue and light motes of pink.

In Raffael's pantheon, nature itself is the sacred symbol and sacred place, "the teacher or mirror or instructor." The man-made shrines and statues, like Raffael's paintings, are translators of experience, "evidences of the basic nature of the universe," of "the ecstasy of being in nature and seeing something that touches us so. . . . To me the painting is to describe ecstasy."

OPPOSITE
94. *Buddha,* 1985
Oil on canvas, 72 x 48 in.
(182.8 x 121.9 cm)
Joseph and Lannis Raffael,
Cap d'Antibes, France

ABOVE
95. *Ganesh,* 1990
Watercolor on paper, 67½ x 44½ in.
(171.4 x 113 cm)
Lannis Raffael,
Cap d'Antibes, France

NOTE

1. Raffael, in Nancy Hoffman, "Interview with Joseph Raffael," in *Joseph Raffael: A Dream Remembered* (New York: Nancy Hoffman Gallery, 1986), p. 13.

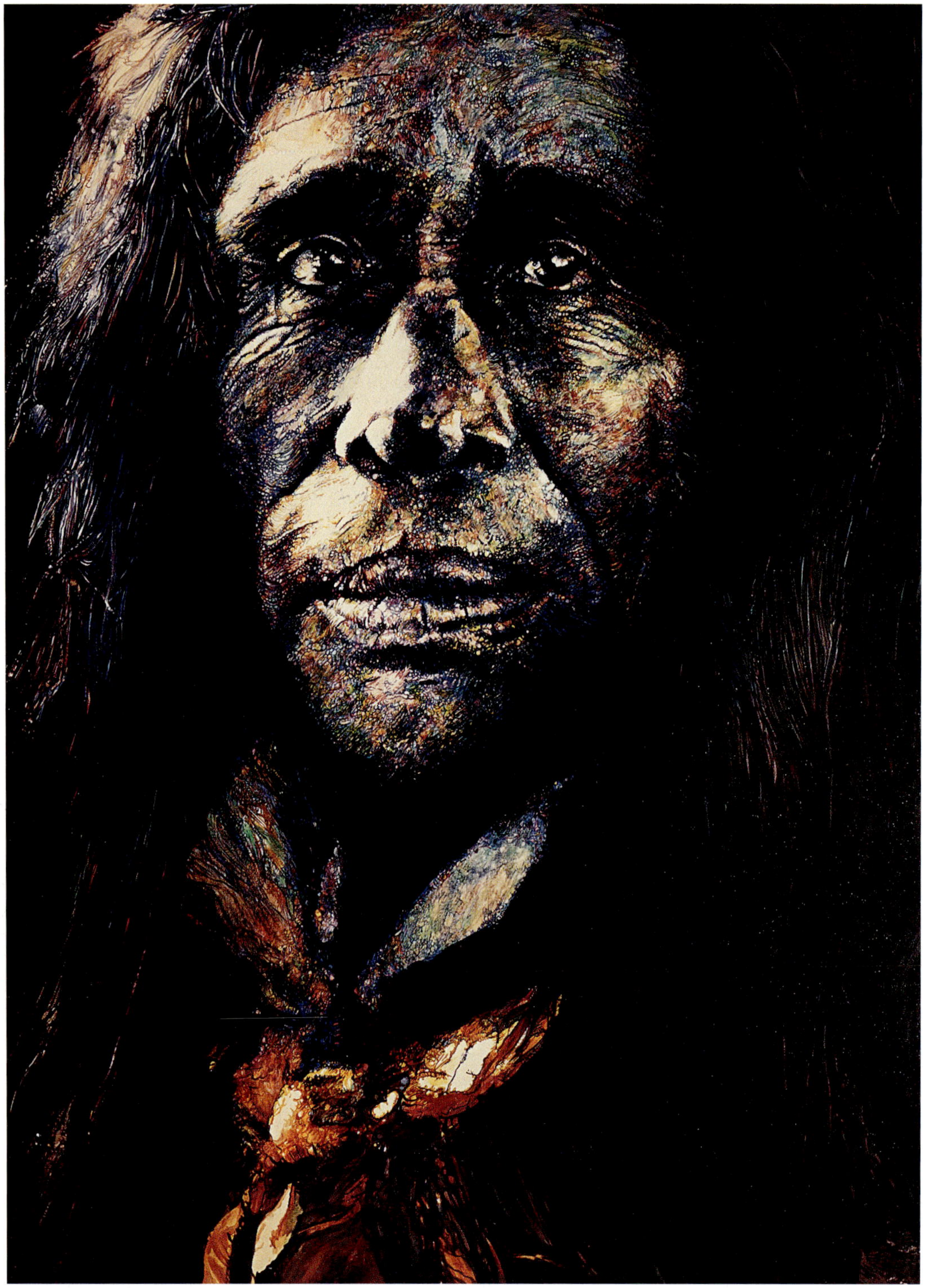

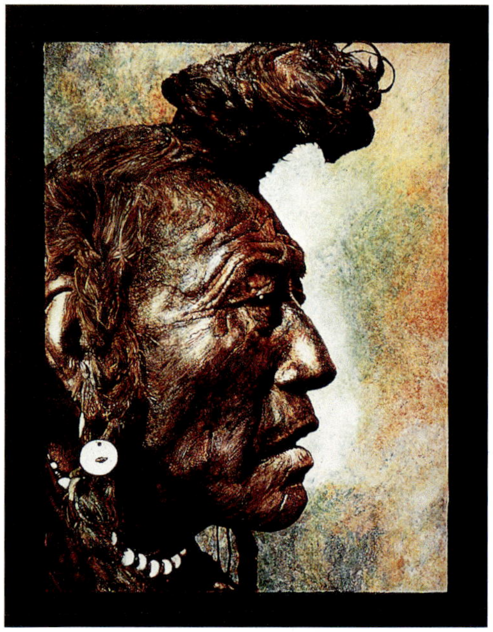

LEFT

96. *Pomo,* 1970
Oil on canvas, 79 x 55½ in. (200.5 x 141 cm)
University of California,
Berkeley Art Museum

ABOVE

97. *Blackfoot,* 1970
Oil on canvas, 80 x 61 in. (203.1 x 154.9 cm)
Joslyn Art Museum, Omaha

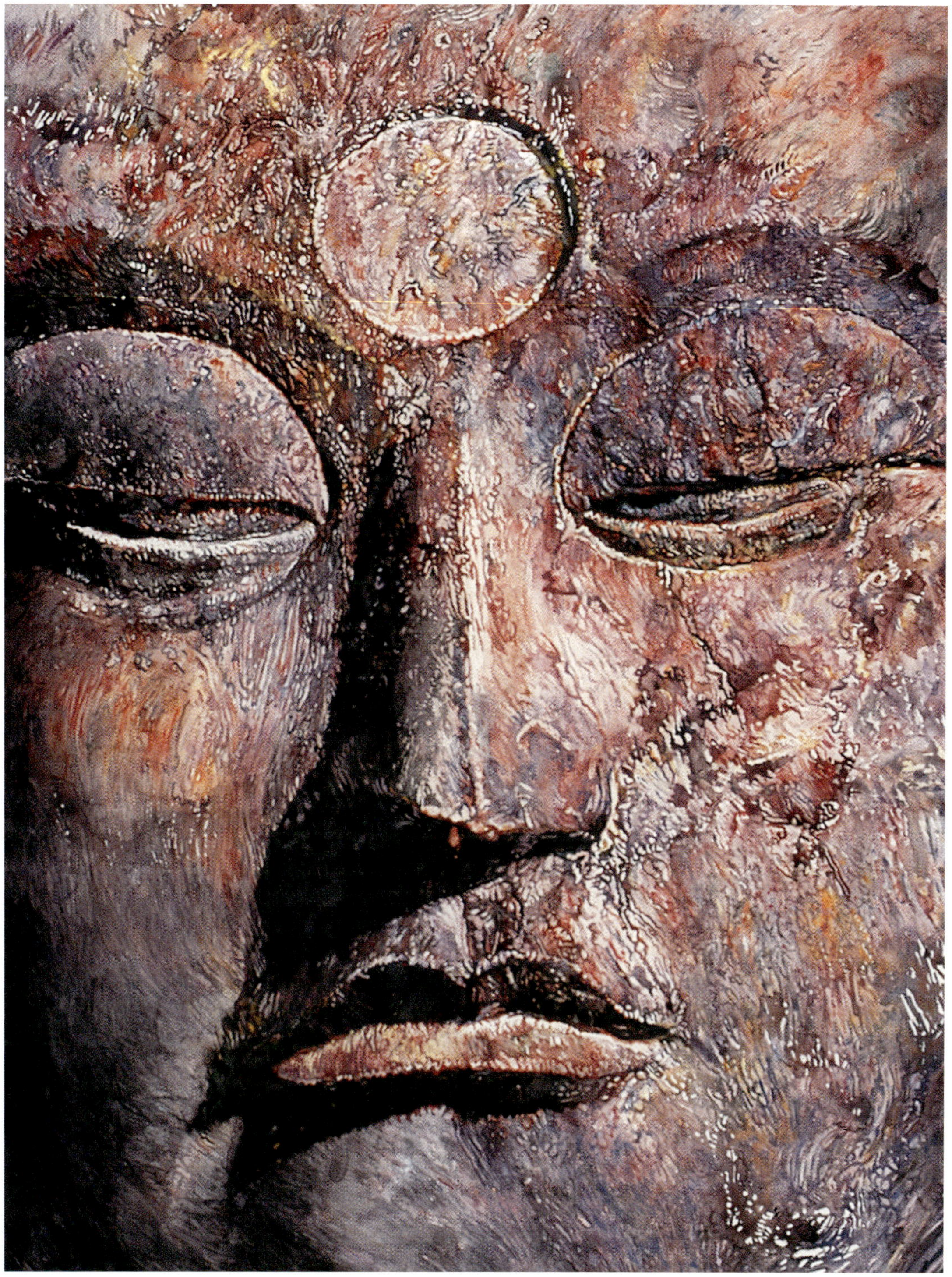

98. *Le Crepuscule,* 1995
Watercolor on paper, 61 x 44½ in.
(154.9 x 113 cm)
W. Brugh Joy, M.D.,
Paulden, Arizona

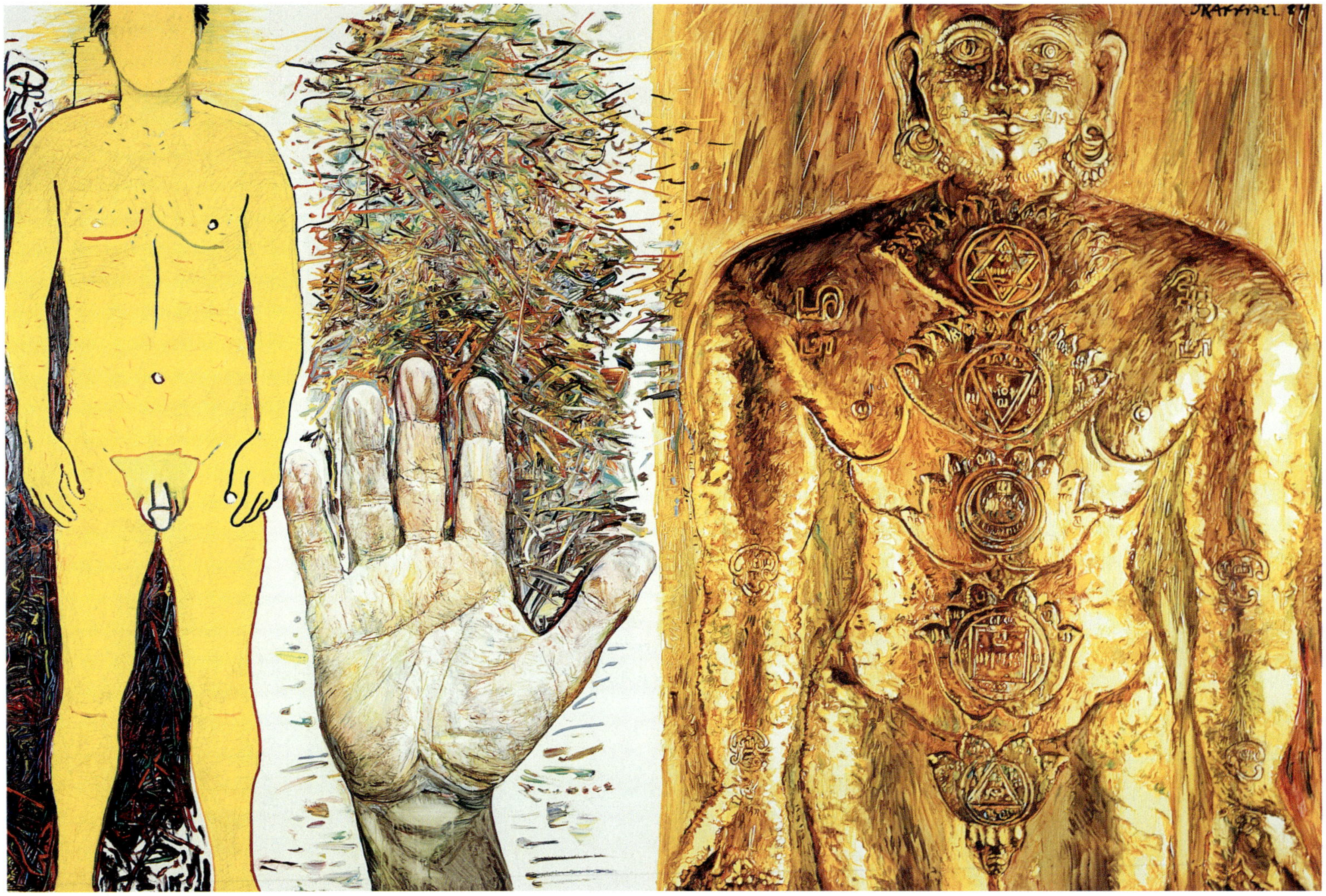

ABOVE

99. *Gateway,* 1984
Oil on canvas, 78 x 114 in. (198.1 x 289.6 cm)
Joseph and Lannis Raffael,
Cap d'Antibes, France

OPPOSITE

100. *The Bridge,* 1986
Oil on canvas, 72 x 48 in. (182.9 x 121.9 cm)
Lannis Raffael, Cap d'Antibes, France

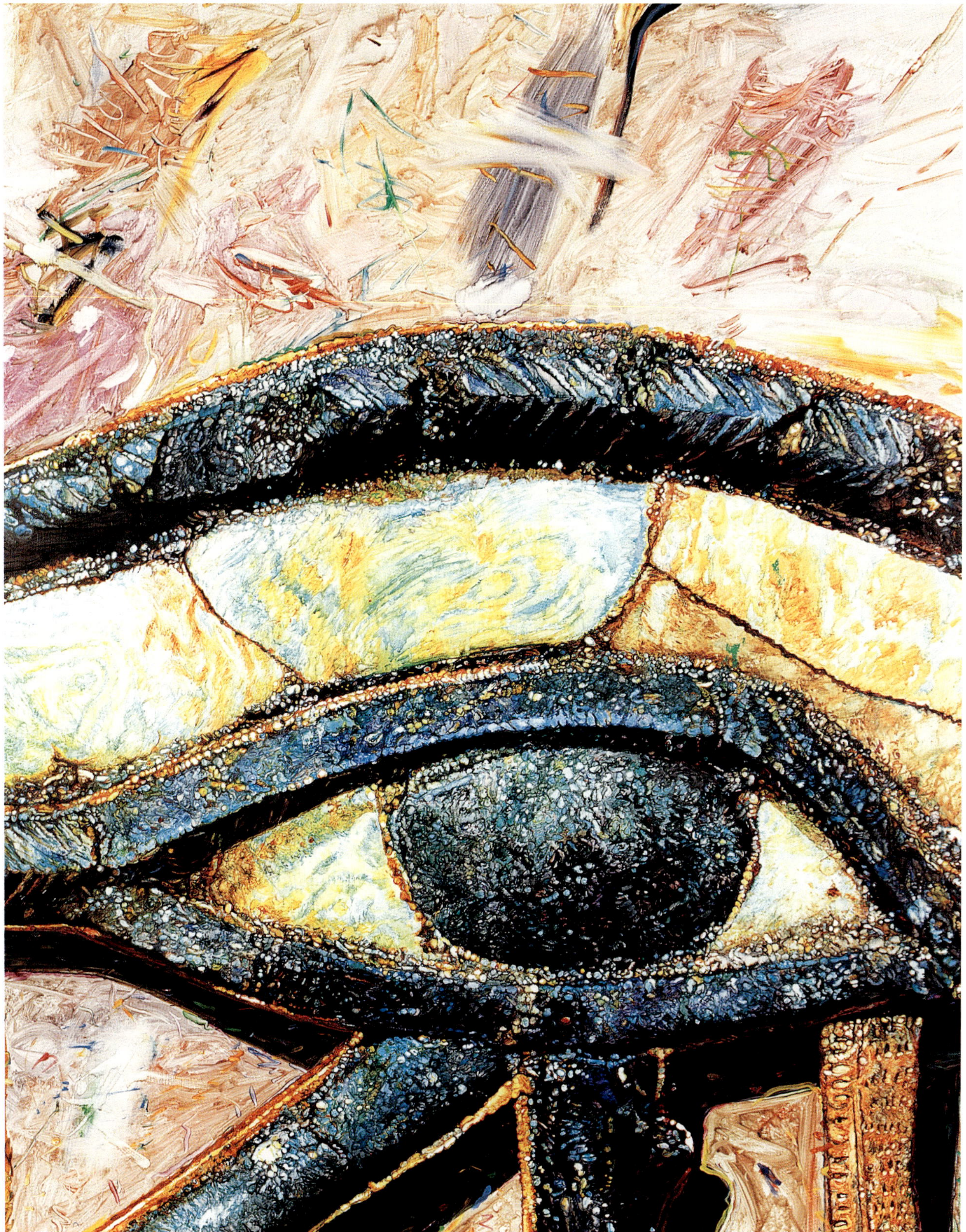

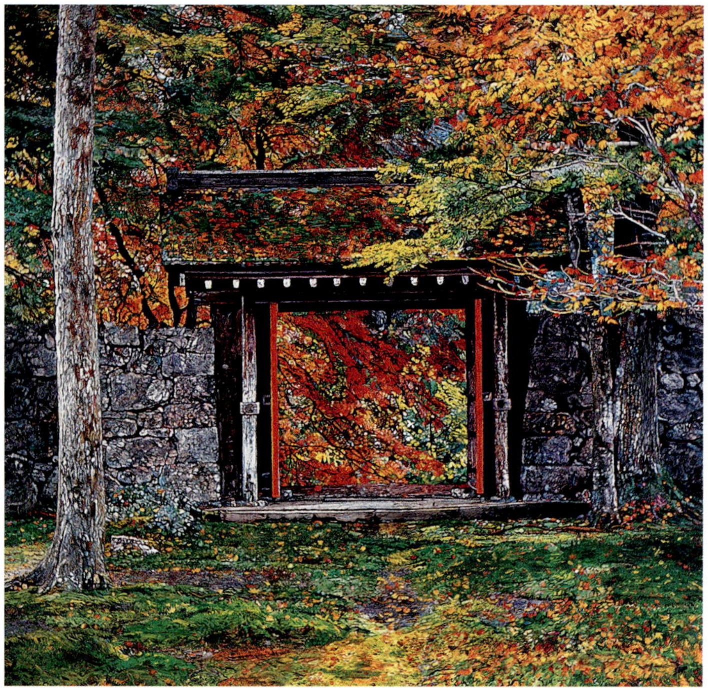

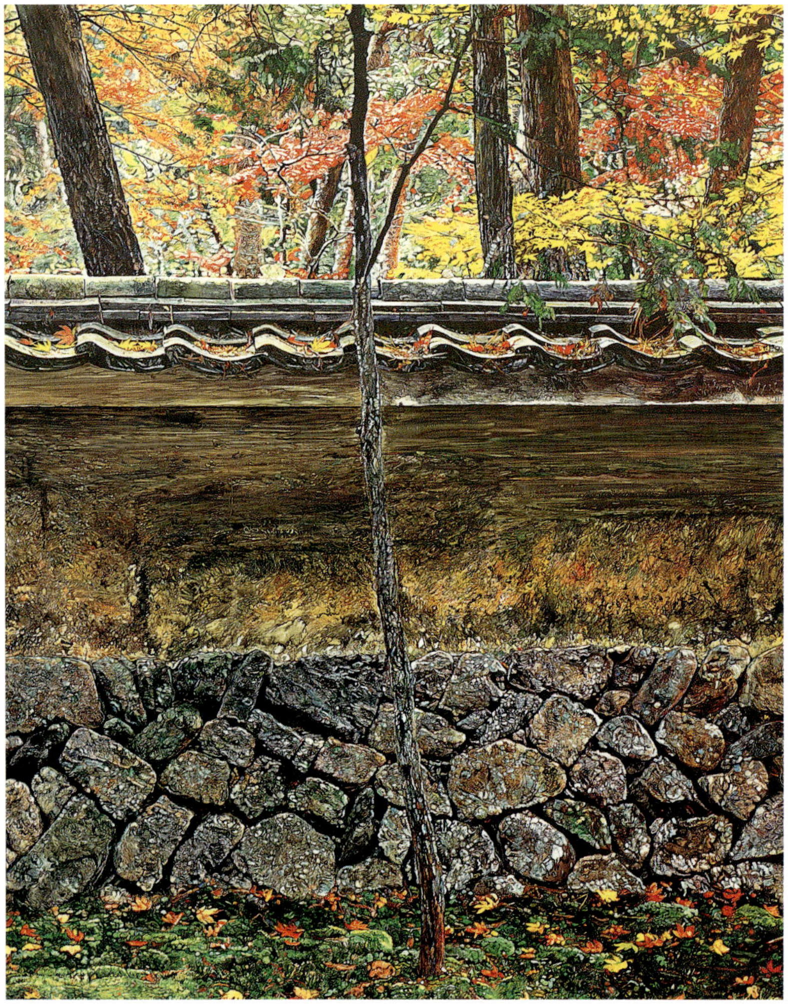

LEFT

101. *Haven,* 1986
Oil on canvas, 77 x 57 in.
(195.5 x 144.7 cm)
Corporate collection, Minneapolis

ABOVE

102. *Threshold,* 1987
Oil on canvas, 59 x 59 in.
(149.8 x 149.8 cm)
Private collection, Osprey, Florida

OPPOSITE

103. *Marriage,* 1986
Oil on canvas, 69 x 96 in.
(175.2 x 243.8 cm)
Francesca Keck, Santa Fe, New Mexico

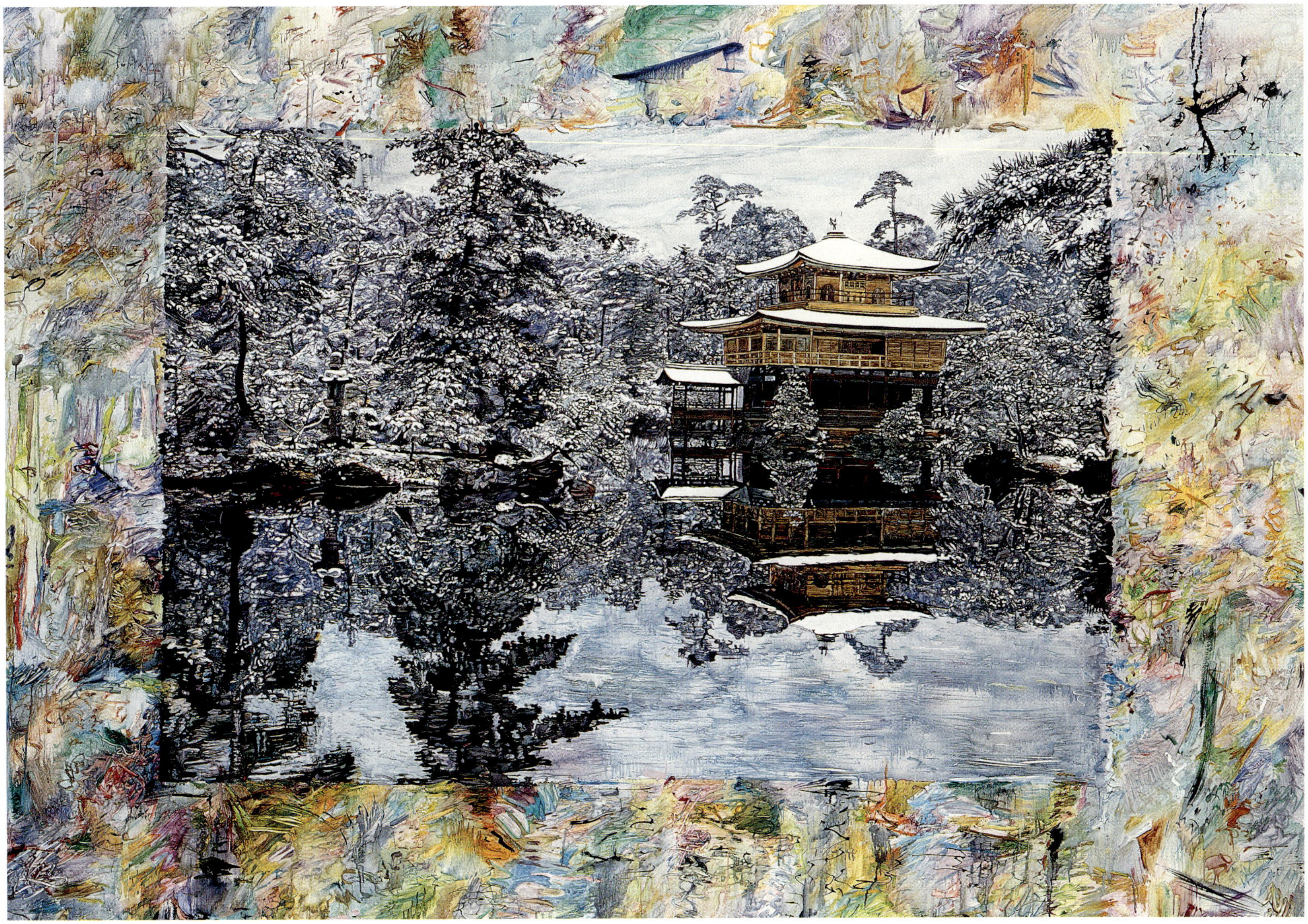

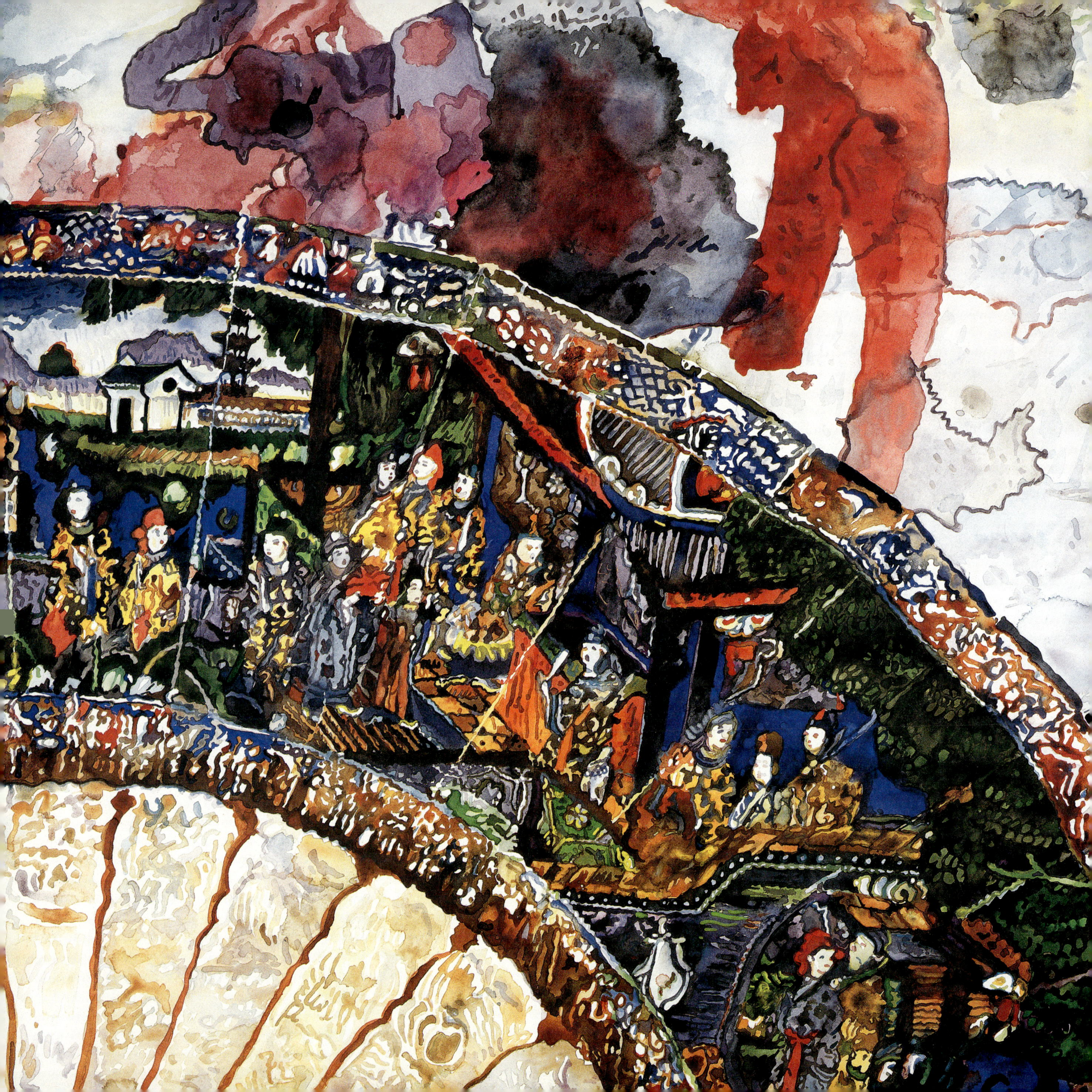

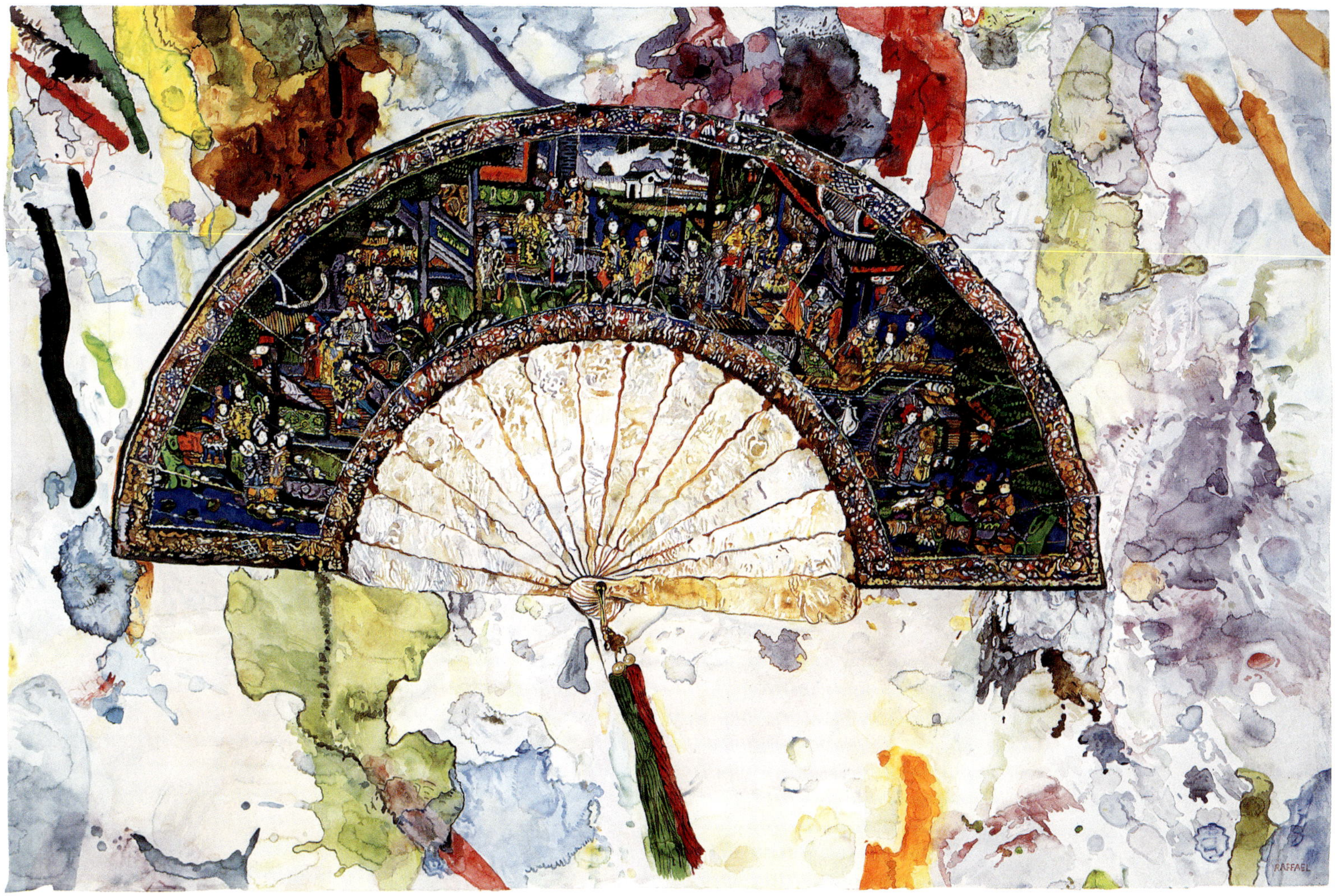

OPPOSITE

104. Detail of *Spring Bridge*

ABOVE

105. *Spring Bridge,* 1992
Watercolor on paper, 44½ x 65½ in.
(113 x 166.3 cm)
Joseph and Lannis Raffael,
Cap d'Antibes, France

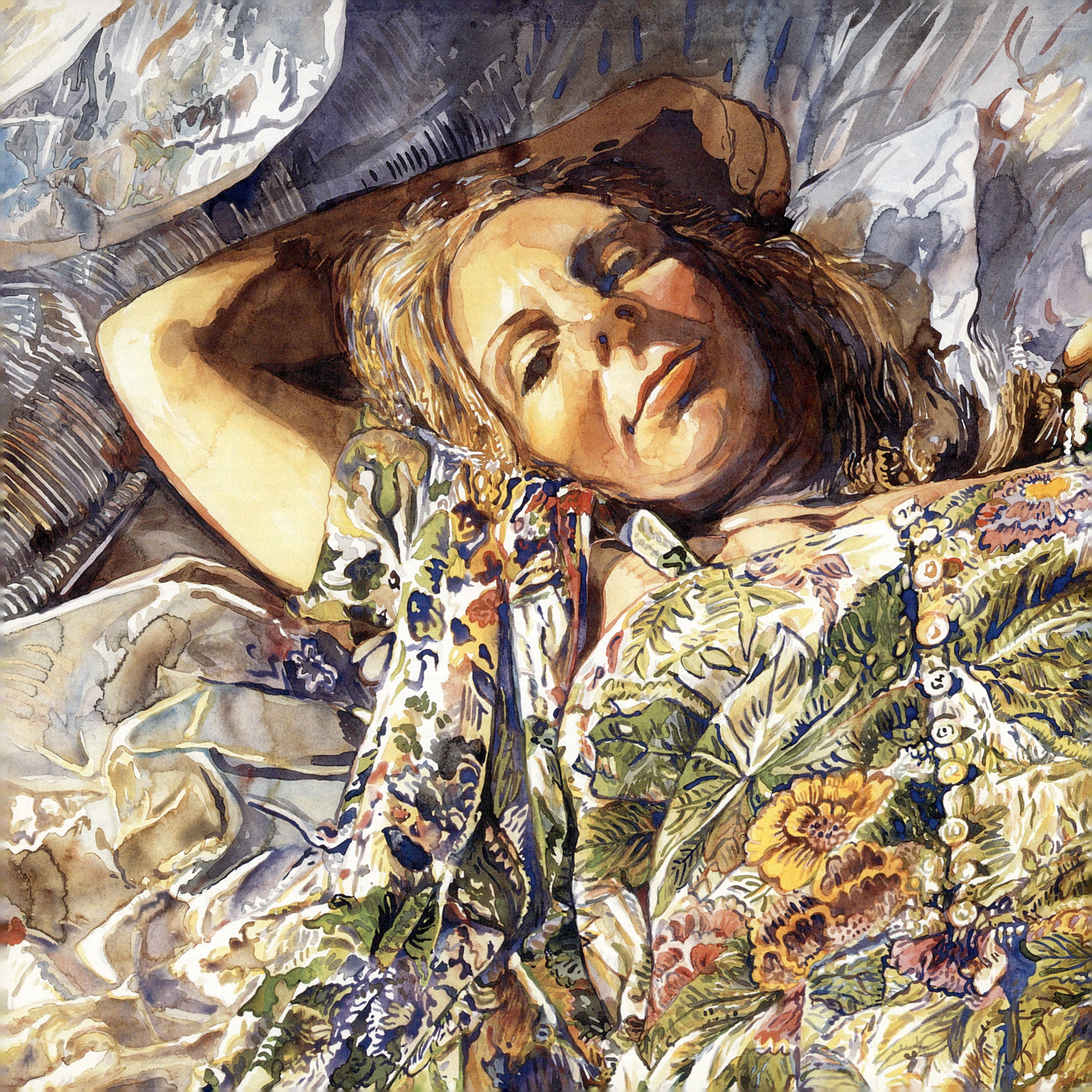

The Lannis Paintings

"The woman in sunshine"

106. Detail of *Lannis in Sieste XIV,* 1988
See plate 110

Through Lannis, Raffael has realized a way to paint the human figure so that, like the mallard or the iris, it is as integral to the painting as to nature. In their sanctuary in the south of France, Lannis is as all-pervasive as water or light. She spends her days in her labyrinthine garden, weeding, transplanting, hefting, and trimming. He spends his days in the studio overlooking the garden, selecting, teasing, building infinitesimal gradations of color into image and metaphor. They come together when the telephone rings or at mealtime, to feed the dogs and the cats, to sift through slides, to retire to the mattress on the studio floor.

"Before we were together, Lannis was my spiritual counselor, helping me go toward clarity in my life. She's really encouraged me to let go of all the facade. Then coming to France has been a terrific exercise in that. Three-year-olds speak better French than I did. You keep things as simple as possible."

In one sense, in France Lannis became the artist's wife, ordering her days to sustain his. But there is nothing in the least docile about Lannis. She cuts to the quick, she prunes away pretense. Lannis is at once the sensibility of their garden retreat and its creator. Raffael paints her as a garden, not so much indistinguishable from nature as at home in it.

He first painted her in 1985, while he was still entangled in the aftermath of the divorce that ended his California years. They had traveled together on a pilgrimage to uncover his Italian roots, and there he saw Sandro Botticelli's *Primavera*. On his return, he painted *Ancient Longing* (plate 107), with Lannis as a particularly apprehensive and implacable version of springtime resurrection, artificially embowered in the flowers that would become integral to her image when he began to paint her in earnest.

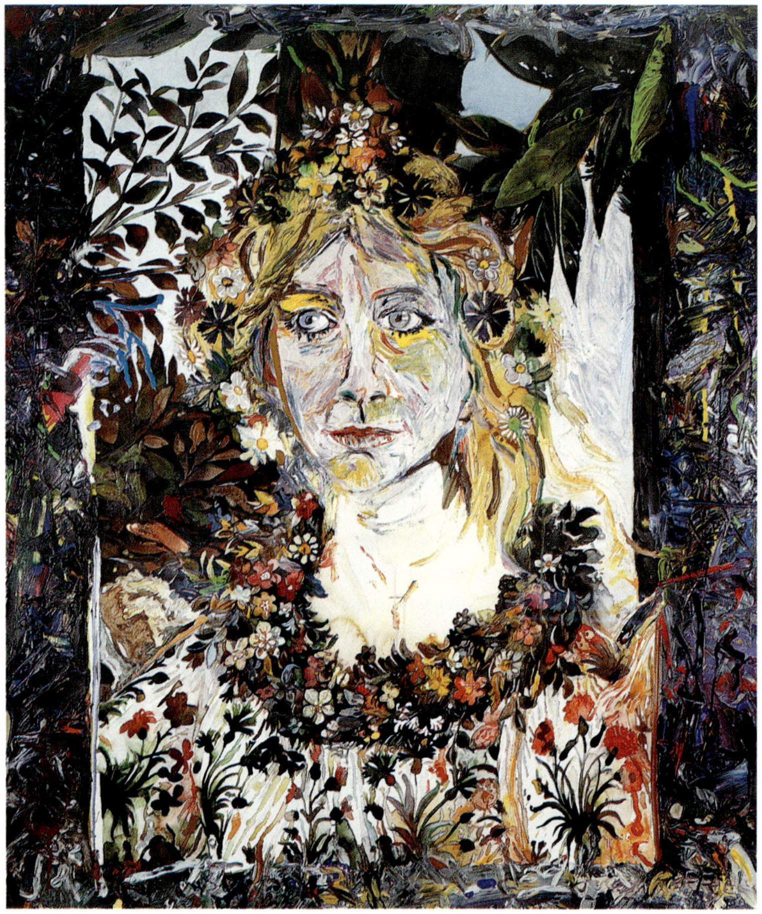

107. *Ancient Longing,* 1985
Watercolor and acrylic on paper, 52½ x 44 in. (133.3 x 111.7 cm)
Private collection, New York

Raffael sometimes gave the cycle of Lannis paintings started in 1988—two years after they had begun their garden idyll—the same name as his new water pictures: Soyez mystérieuses. This was his admonishment to "the feminine in me" to celebrate mystery. Lannis was emblematic of the feminine in him as well as the potency in herself and their surroundings. "Living in this sanctuary, this inner garden, and living with a soulmate, someone who doesn't distract me from my art but helps me return over and over and over again to my artist, I'm able to go into the mysterium of life. And nature to me is part of that mysterium. It's part of this activity of life."

His Lannis in Sieste series catches the woman, asleep in a flowered dress. She is as much a part of her surroundings, and as suggestive of rebirth and reawakening, as the passage of light on water in the Soyez mystérieuses cycle (plates 14 and 38). In this case, the moment Raffael fixes in the cycle of nature that has been his abiding concern is the moment of hot sun and flowers in bloom—even though these are flowers printed on a dress. Under the flowers the shape of the body suggests hillocks and valleys. The paintings are vertical, as in *Metamorphose* (plate 33) or a Chinese landscape. One reads them like a Chinese scroll, traveling over the surface in a manner very like that in which the sun traverses the garden in which they live their lives together. She is not so much object of desire as moment of transformation. Her body is tilted upward and foreshortened, the cloth billowing in folds around it, as in Francisco de Zurbarán's *Saint Serapion.* The practical reason for this is that Raffael stood at Lannis's feet when he photographed her sleeping. With Raffael, however, it is always a mistake to believe in practical reasons. Saint Serapion was one of the Mercedarian friars, who took a vow of blood to ransom Christians in danger of losing their faith.

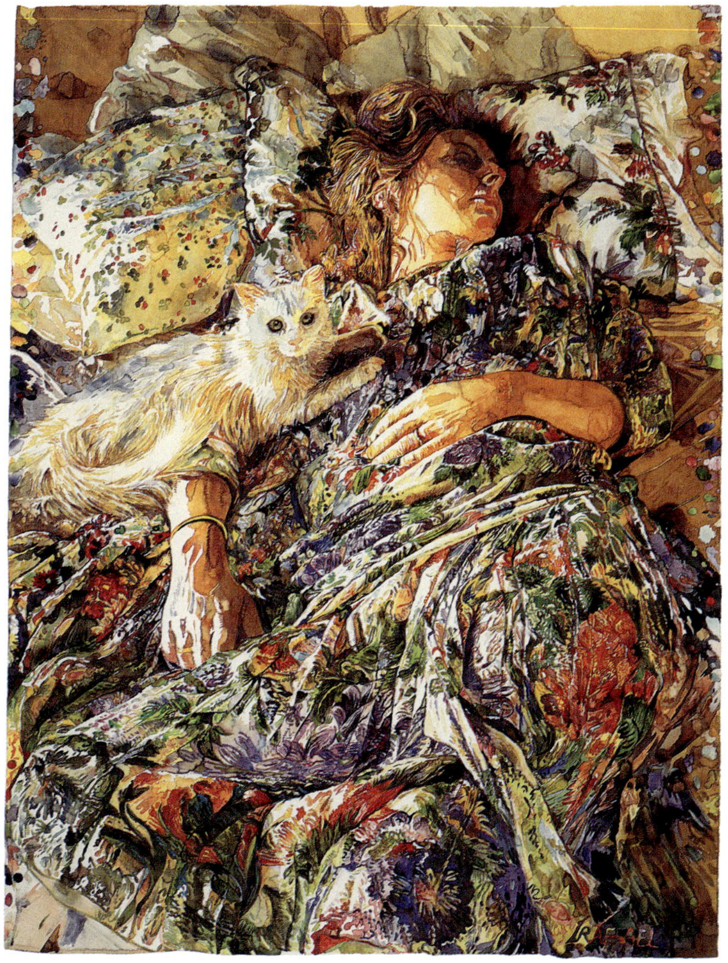

108. *Le Printemps I,* 1988
Watercolor on paper, 61 x 44¾ in.
(154.9 x 113.6 cm)
Public collection, Flint, Michigan

Raffael's faith is in painting that, as a sacred duty, intimates the infinite variety of nature. The Lannis paintings are one more affirmation of his creed:

. . . out of what one sees and hears and out
Of what one feels, who could have thought to make
So many selves, so many sensuous worlds,
As if the air, the mid-day air, was swarming
With the metaphysical changes that occur,
Merely in living as and where we live.[1]

NOTE

1. Wallace Stevens, "Esthétique du Mal," in *Wallace Stevens: The Collected Poems* (New York: Vintage Books, 1990), p. 326.

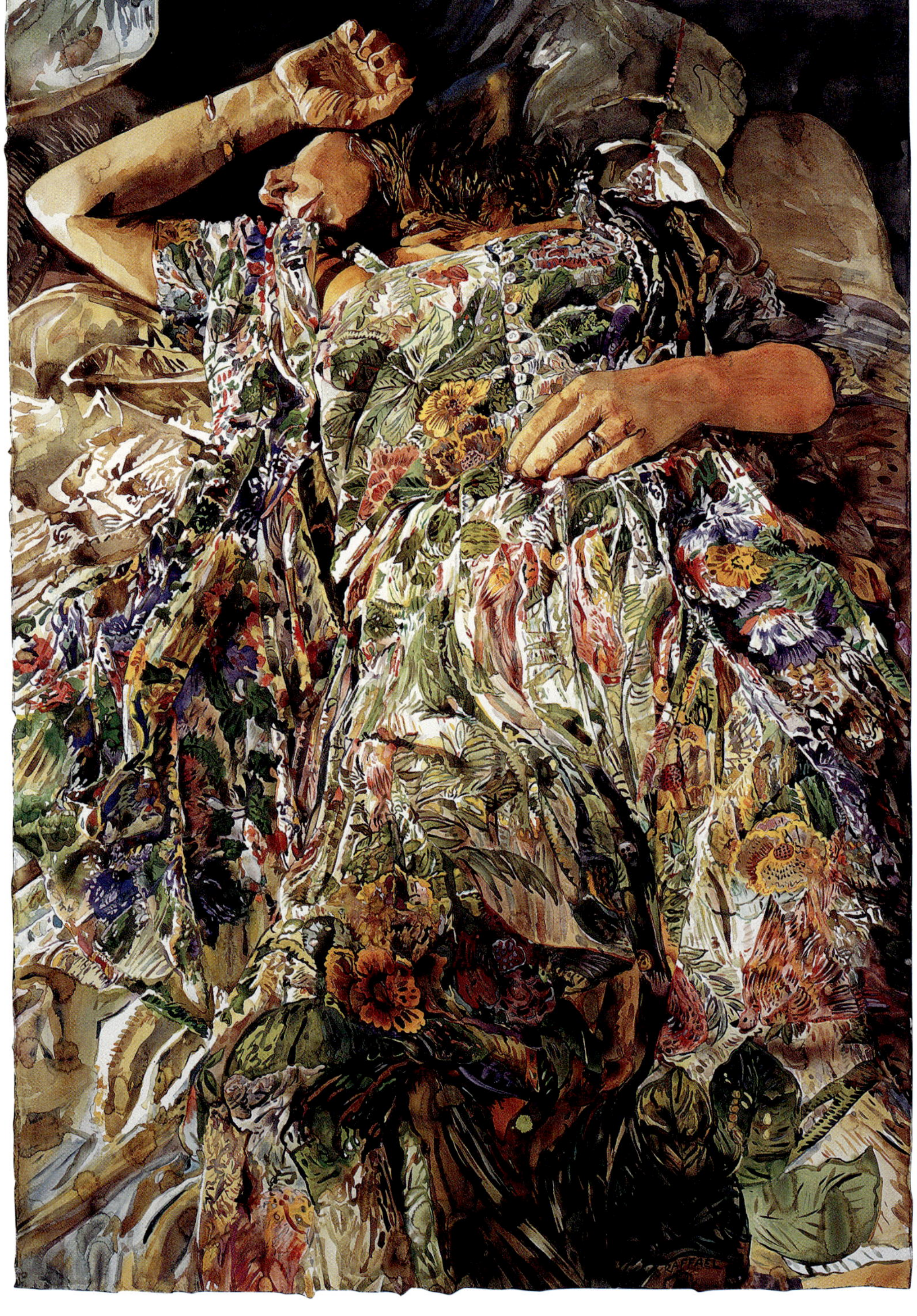

OPPOSITE

109. *Lannis in Sieste III,* 1988
Watercolor on paper, 65 x 44½ in.
(165 x 113 cm)
Corporate collection, Los Angeles

BELOW

110. *Lannis in Sieste XIV,* 1988
Watercolor on paper, 68¾ x 44½ in.
(174.6 x 113 cm)
Joseph and Lannis Raffael,
Cap d'Antibes, France

RIGHT

111. *Lannis in Sieste IX,* 1988
Watercolor on paper, 67 x 44½ in.
(170.1 x 113 cm)
Arlene and Charles Semel, Chicago

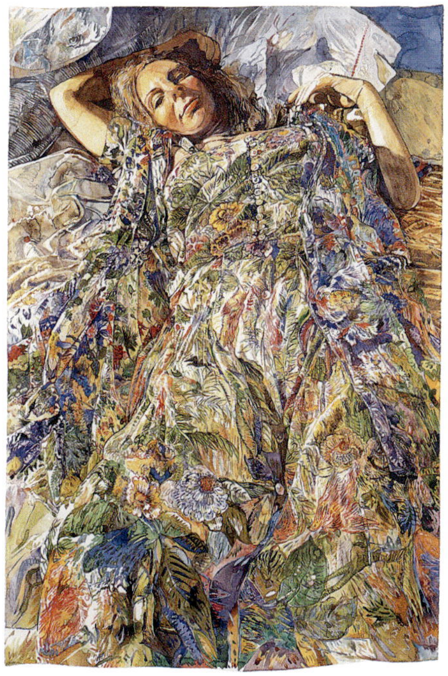

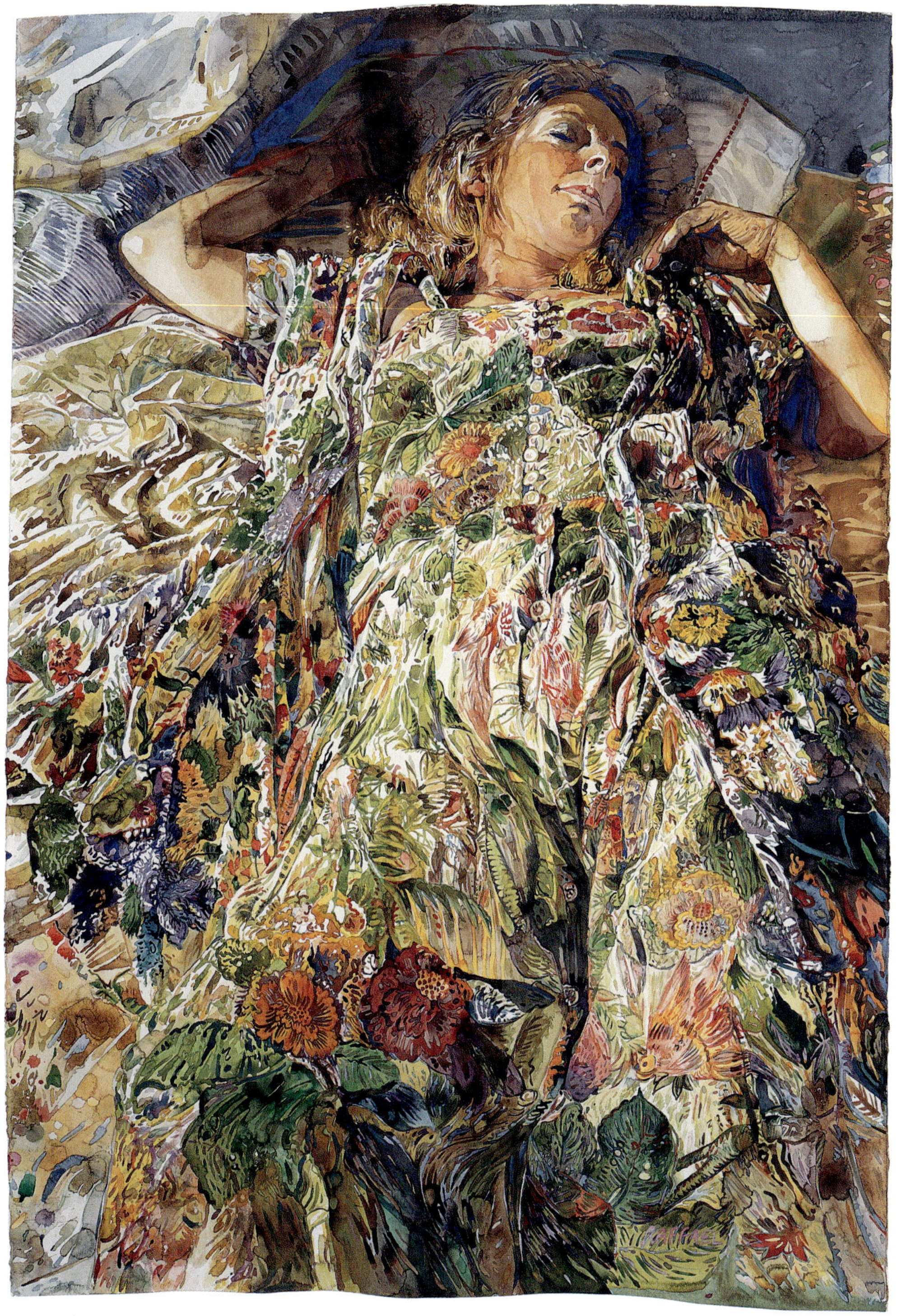

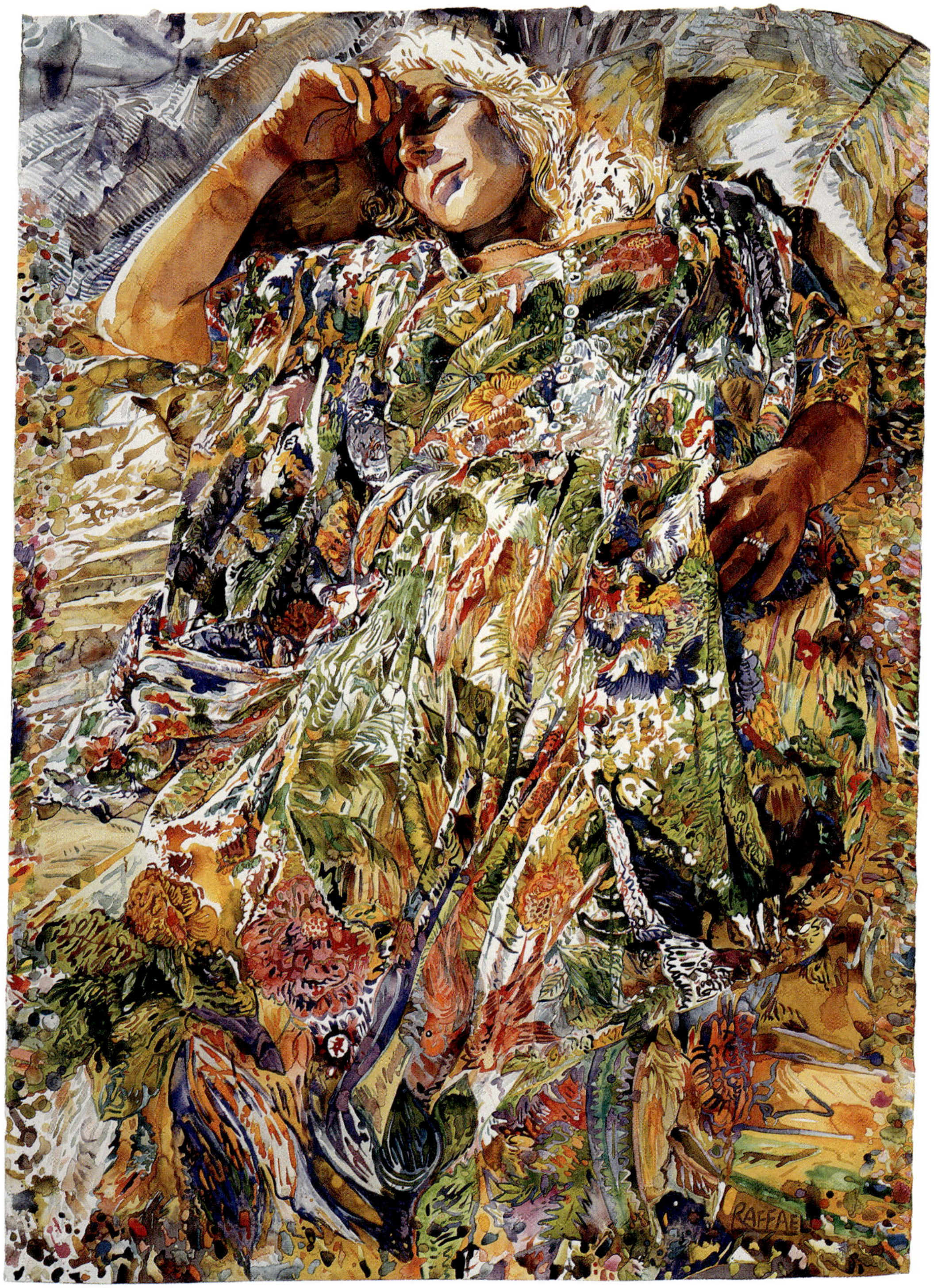

112. *Lannis in Sieste X,* 1988
Watercolor on paper, 62½ x 44½ in.
(158.7 x 113 cm)
Allen and Vicki Samson

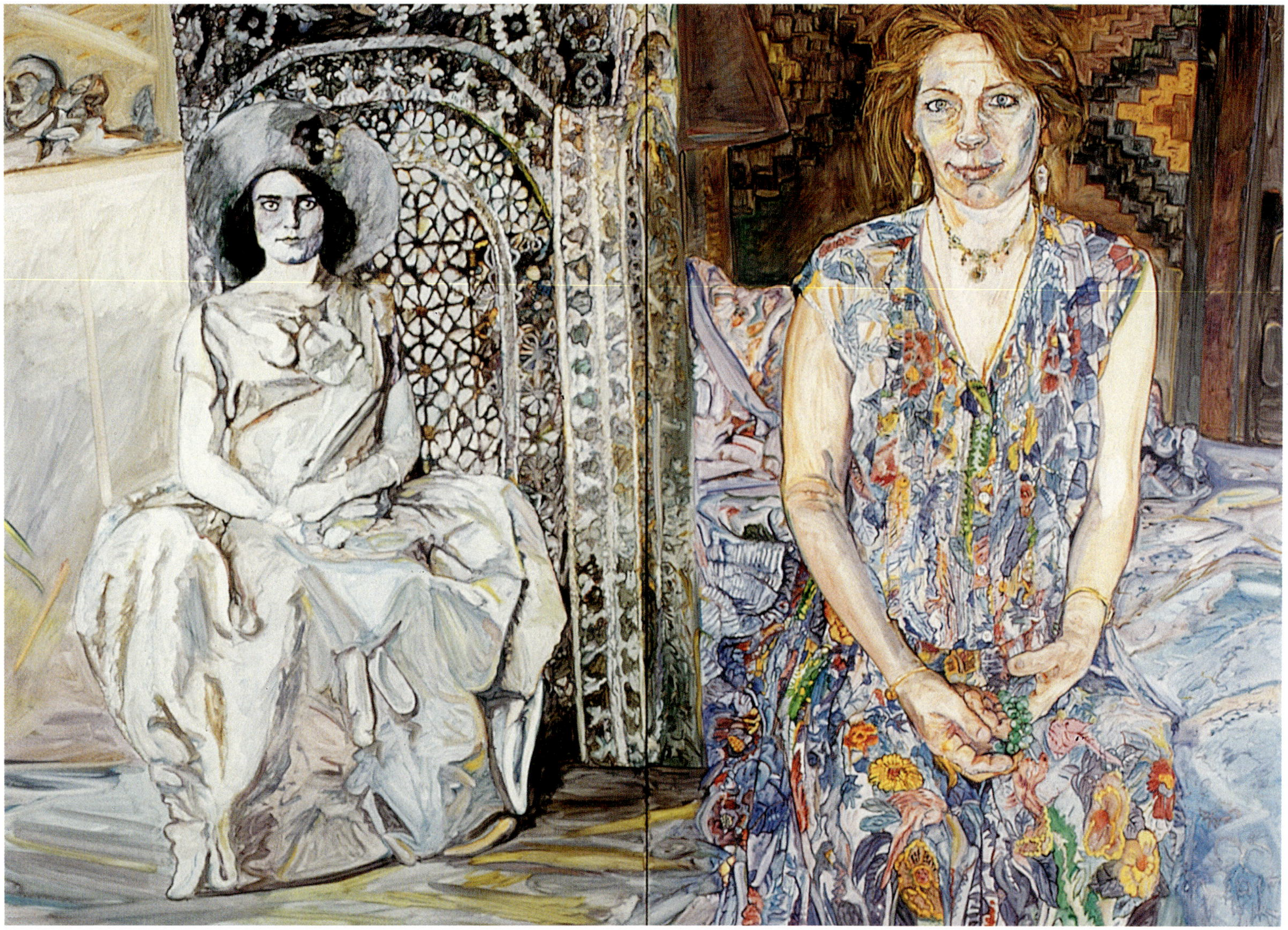

113. *Spring Equinox, Matisse's Model and Lannis,* 1991
Oil on canvas, 77 x 102½ in.
(195.5 x 260.2 cm)
Joseph and Lannis Raffael,
Cap d'Antibes, France

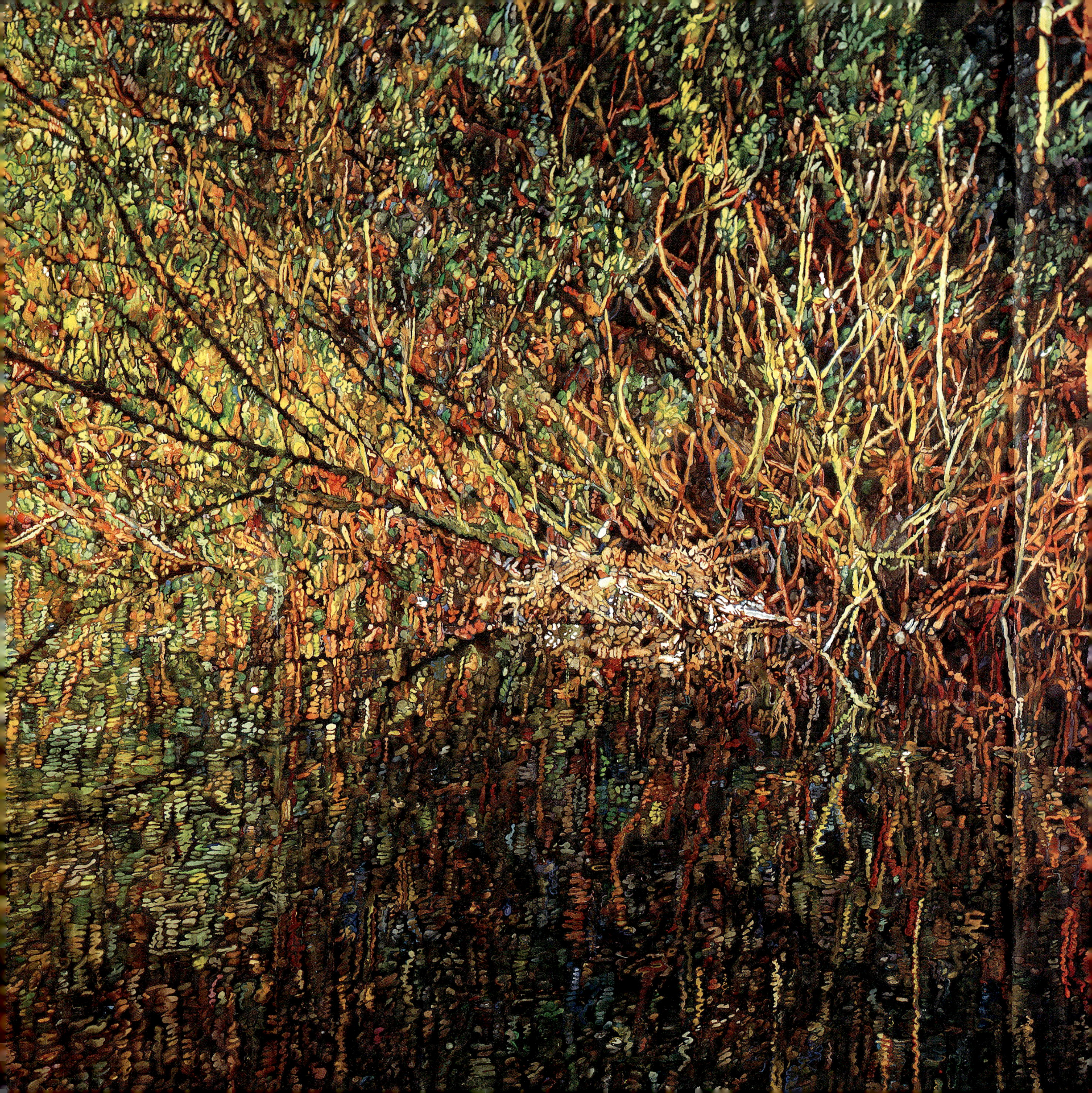

Diary of a Painting

Joseph Raffael

I REGULARLY KEEP A JOURNAL *when I'm painting; what follow are excerpts from the period when I was making* May 4th *[plate 120].*

6 May 1996, Holland

After having finished, for the most part, *Heron's Vision* [plate 66], we are now in Holland visiting the Makkinks. Spring is here.

I returned to the pond where I had seen and photographed the heron last summer. This time there was no heron there. However, as I stood at the water's edge, I saw out in the center of the pond a little island of sorts, and on it an enormous nest built at the shore's edge. On it was perched a black bird. I took pictures.

14 May, Antibes

The slides of Holland trip back today.

There are several which stir me. One or two of the nest amaze me. But they're *so* complicated. Am I up to it? Do I have the energy? Lannis thinks I do and is encouraging. We both feel the import of this image. It is definitely an opportunity to move into a new sphere.

I'll have one of the slides enlarged into a large photo so I have a better chance not to go raving mad with the myriad details.

10 June

I'm so happy to have had the new nest image up on my wall all these weeks. I appreciate Lannis encouraging me to do it. It seems dark to me but I know it can become luminous as a painting. I'm reminded over and over again as I balk at the darkness of it

114. Detail of *May 4th,* 1996
See plate 120

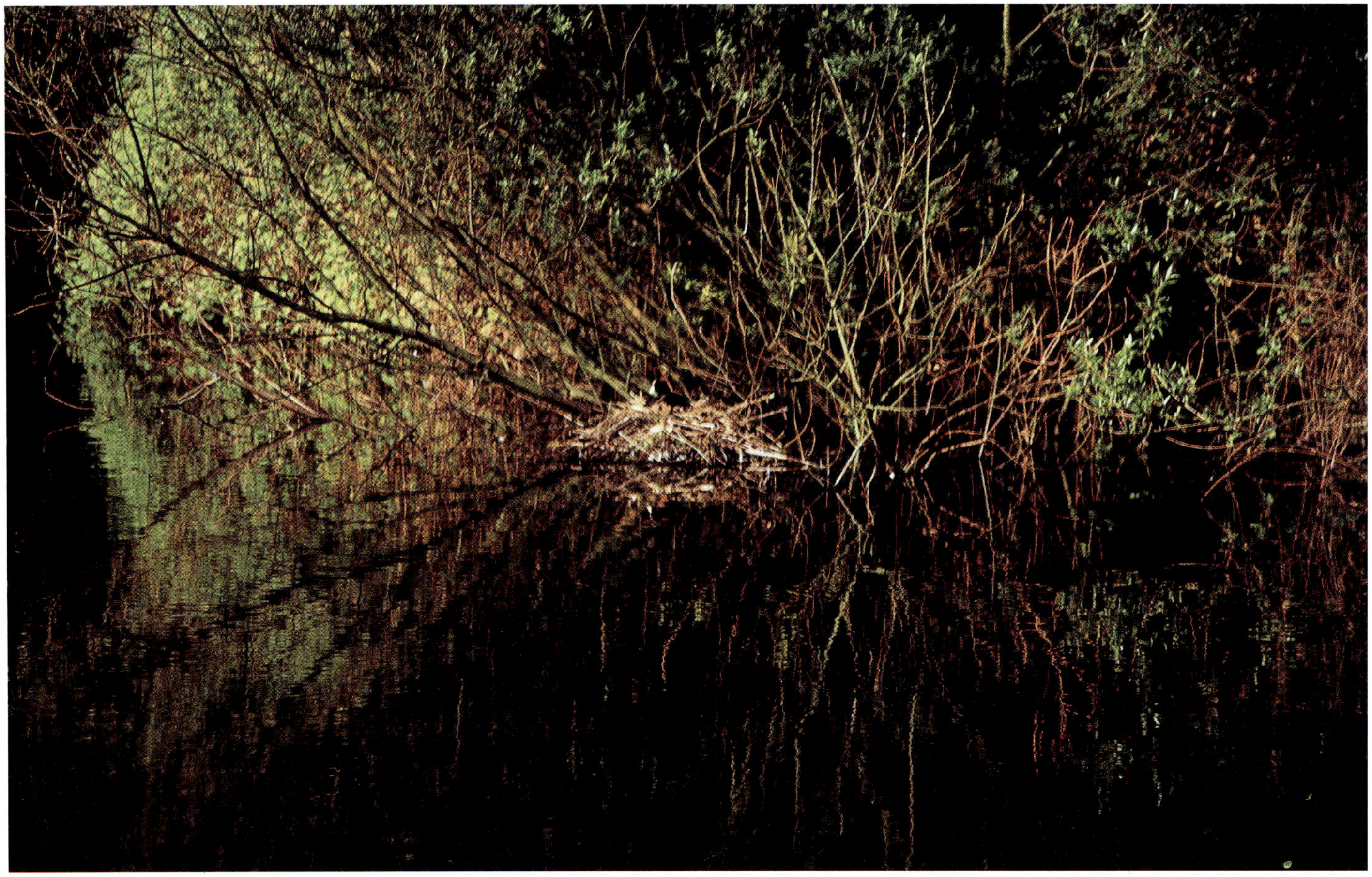

115. Raffael's original photo for *May 4th*

that I've been wanting to do a night painting since seeing Albert Ryder's night seascapes when I was a young student. Also when I look out upon the garden at night I am in wonderment at the beauty and magic of it. The nest photo is not night but twilight. It is these oranges and greens which bother me, although at the time I saw it, I loved it. This quality which irks me a bit actually gives me the opportunity to become very "active," more than usual even, in the painting of it. To make it more "mine." It could end up being a never-having-seen-anything-like-it-before painting.

There will be much iridescence in it, much phosphorescence of a brown, green, and orange nature. Perhaps this is what is scariest for me—these colors. My *critic* inside my head goes crazy. But I remind myself of the excitement and almost sacred sense I had upon seeing this scene, including these beautiful colors. Deep in me I know this will be an extraordinary painting. It could have mystery, passion, complexity, richness, soul. This image is an unrepeatable moment, just as in nature nothing ever repeats itself exactly the same. In what at first glance seems a chaotic complexity, there is a sublime order. I hope the painting shows that and more. Also some evidence of the mystery of being a human being while witnessing nature, perhaps shedding light on our deeper and deepest selves.

Certainly, it's the most complicated work I'll have done.

Now, to start drawing it in.

11 June

This drawing for the painting is the longest I've *ever* done. Already, it's taken almost two days. A third will be necessary. Perhaps even a fourth. It brings up, I don't know why, so much anxiety in me. It's like going into an abyss. Zillions of branches and then their reflection.

12 June

This'll be the 4th day of mapping in the nest and reflection painting. It's been staggering. It will take a *very* long time to paint. It brings up a lot. Well, I have to trust, don't I? There's no choice. I'm going to learn much from this experience and perhaps be new afterward.

I'm not only overwhelmed by the drawing in, the mammoth job of it, but knowing that each time I draw in a line that it is only the barest of outlines, and when I'm actually painting within these penciled structures, the work, the vision will become even more labyrinthine. This is only the simple beginning.

Later

I became so distraught. I went into a dark hole, becoming terribly irritable and negative. I was quite awful to Lannis, who always supports me in my work, encouraging me when doubt afflicts me. With this image in particular she has reminded me over and over how I loved the image since I first had seen it.

Later

I've spent a couple of hours opening to the image and reflecting on how to begin painting it. The aspects of the image for which I had such angst, I see now as question marks and subtle and deep unknowings, which as I approach them with paint, water, and brush will reveal to me how to move through this unexplored geography.

Later
As I begin this nest and pond painting, anguished and uncertain, I hear a bird's song very close to the studio. It's reassuring, connecting me to nature as I do this formidable image of nature in all its mystery. The bird's sound is simple and direct, filled with grace. Hearing it, I fear less. Once again I remember but this time with new meaning, Picasso's words—"Why not try to understand the sound of the bird's song."

13 June
I got into the painting yesterday afternoon. It turned out to be, once *in* it, a very interesting and *very* colorful experience. I realize when the *abyss* appears that it is absolutely necessary to enter it. It's the place where secrets lie. It is the *source.*

23 June
Yesterday I felt such relief when I heard in my head a voice whose message was to paint that which I could readily find and then to paint in the less discernible areas later, when my energy would be more appropriate.

Yesterday morning in the wood walking along an ancient-feeling path, shaded and winding, the dry leaves at my feet were all of a sudden swept up by the wind. They rose and flew through the air, only in that one spot right in front of my eyes. They, the leaves, were like all the small shapes in my painting, moving, moving.

They spoke to me, helping to reveal the process of this painting, to remember that the act of painting is also an act of nature, part of it. That it is also a cycle manifesting.

29 June
I've been working on the first panel of the nest, painting for fourteen days now. Yesterday, I put it up on the wall between its two empty partners in the triptych. I got some perspective. The middle section is about half-finished. I realized I wanted to work on the left panel. I thought a green area. Just greens. But when I got to working on it about 8 p.m., after a long day of painting the middle section, I was attracted to the branches (browns and oranges). It felt less complex. Fresh air.

4 July, 10 p.m.
I just put up the one-third-done left panel next to the half-done middle panel. What a relief to see it together. One can see and sense the span and fan of it. Lannis suggested I begin the third panel tomorrow. She's right. It'll get me out of the detail aspect. As I look at the photograph now I see there'll be a bit less complicatedness, a bit more openness. This will feel good.

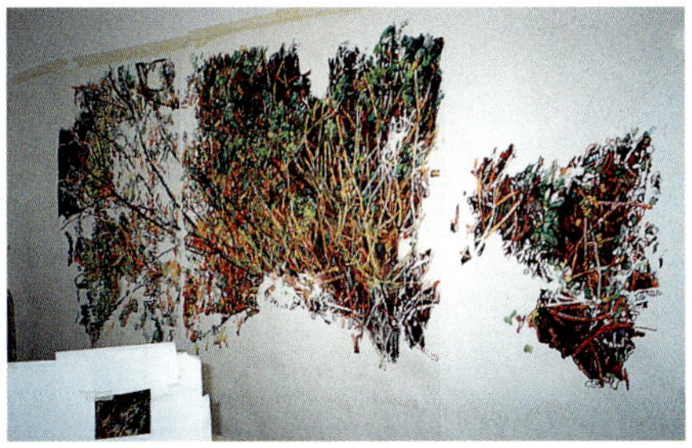

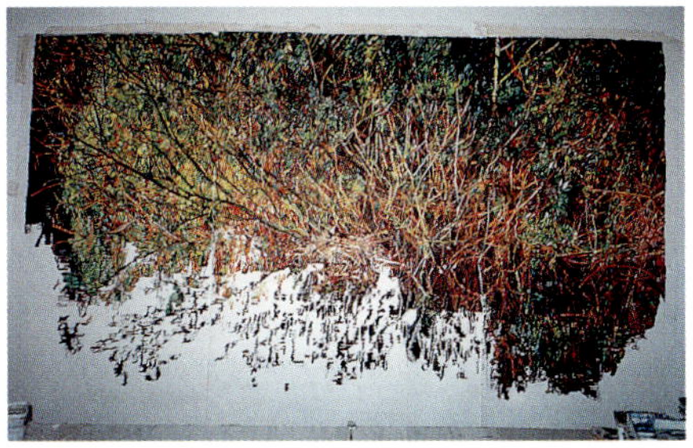

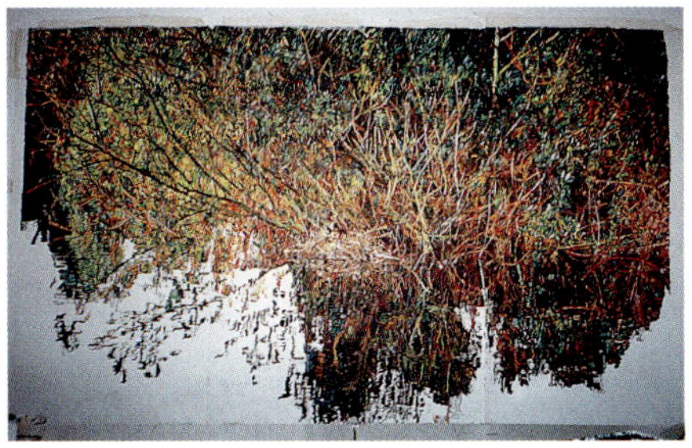

116–18. *May 4th* (plate 120) in progress in Raffael's Cap d'Antibes studio, 1996

5 July

I want to put more purples and blues here and there in the painting. Having it all up on the wall in front of me, I can sense something almost *religious* about it. *Getting back* to some deeper place. *Returning* to something *really* big. Yesterday, not by chance, I heard on the radio a program about Fra Angelico. On it they spoke of his doing the same theme over and over, hundreds of times, but each time they were new. Like the coots making their nests over and over. Or me painting over and over the themes that move me. Yet always differently new and newly different.

7 July

All three panels up (incomplete). Getting a sense of the whole. Will work today and tomorrow, and then hopefully a week off in Holland. A rest is sorely needed. I feel utter exhaustion. Perhaps, a nature recharge. We'll see.

15 July, Holland

After having painted the nest for all these weeks, working from and with the *still* photograph, I am struck, now being at the original site, by the moving-ness of it. Everything is in motion. The fresh air, the breeze blowing over the water, the sounds of the birds, and the whirring and swaying of the trees' branches.

I realize that this aliveness is closer to what my painting is than the photo. The painting has its life and vitality. It moves. Much of this is due to the nature of watercolor. Watercolor has a mind of its own. A "mind" much more creative, inventive, and unpredictable than mine. Its liquidity and original mineral nature give it its own particular character. I like to paint it in a *very* wet and puddly way. When it's wet it looks one way, when it's dry it looks very different. It dries the way it will. I can only bear witness to it. It's a force of nature. One never knows in nature and life what the next moment will bring. Watercolor's the same way.

16 July, Antibes

Just back; into studio already. Ready to paint—to continue nest, after having seen site in Holland. First reaction to the unfinished work hanging on wall is that it is a *painting* and not a site in nature or a photograph of nature. This feels good. This makes a difference.

7 August

7 weeks almost to the day that I began *Spring Nest* [*May 4th*]. It's been quite an experience. It's about two-thirds done.

I've begun to do it upside down, getting a different view, a new angle to approach from.

16 August
I am working now, and will until the painting's finished, on the water and its reflections. It is such an exciting and sensual and freeing experience. I'm in it, in its peacefulness, its luster, its absolute infinity—it takes my breath away.

If there's ever been a painting of mine which can heal, it is this one!

23 August
The nest has become quite visible. The energies definitely pulsate outward from the center. The painting is interesting to look at from different distances, and then it changes dramatically as you look up close or move away from it.

25 August
The painting is winding down or rather up. It is a grand finale, a climax. I'm being swept along with it. Like those leaves in the wood I saw earlier in the summer. It is thrilling.

27 August
Looking through new slides. Chose new very active and stirring scene of lily pond and coot and *wind* at twilight to have a photo made up. I feel like an ancient sailor having just finished an amazing, testing, and vitalizing explorative voyage, getting off one ship and immediately getting on another. This feels good. Actually exhilarating. It's like going with the wind while it's there.

30 August
The painting is basically finished—now for some fine tuning. Then we will be able to see it up on the wall. All three sections together. I can hardly wait. It's been ten weeks plus! It's the largest watercolor I've ever done! Whew!

3 September
Well, it's done. It looks good. And yet it's such a letdown to actually *stop.* To interrupt in a final way this soul-stirring activity. A kind of giant letdown. But I do see it already as a major kind of achievement. I know I couldn't have painted this work until this point in my life.

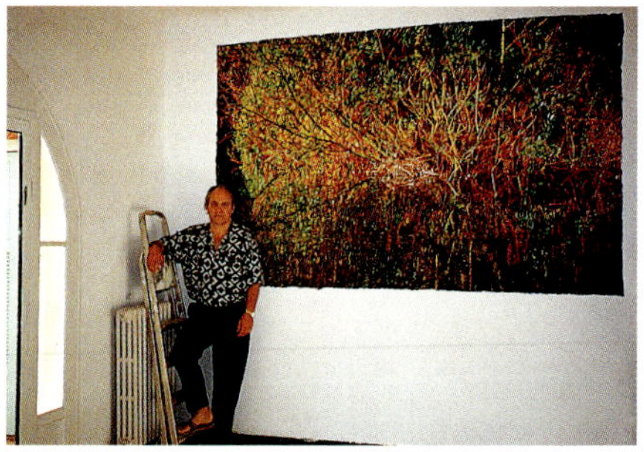

ABOVE
119. Raffael with the finished *May 4th*
OPPOSITE
120. *May 4th,* 1996
Watercolor on paper, triptych: 68½ x 104 in. (173.9 x 264.1 cm)
Private collection, Lincoln, Massachusetts

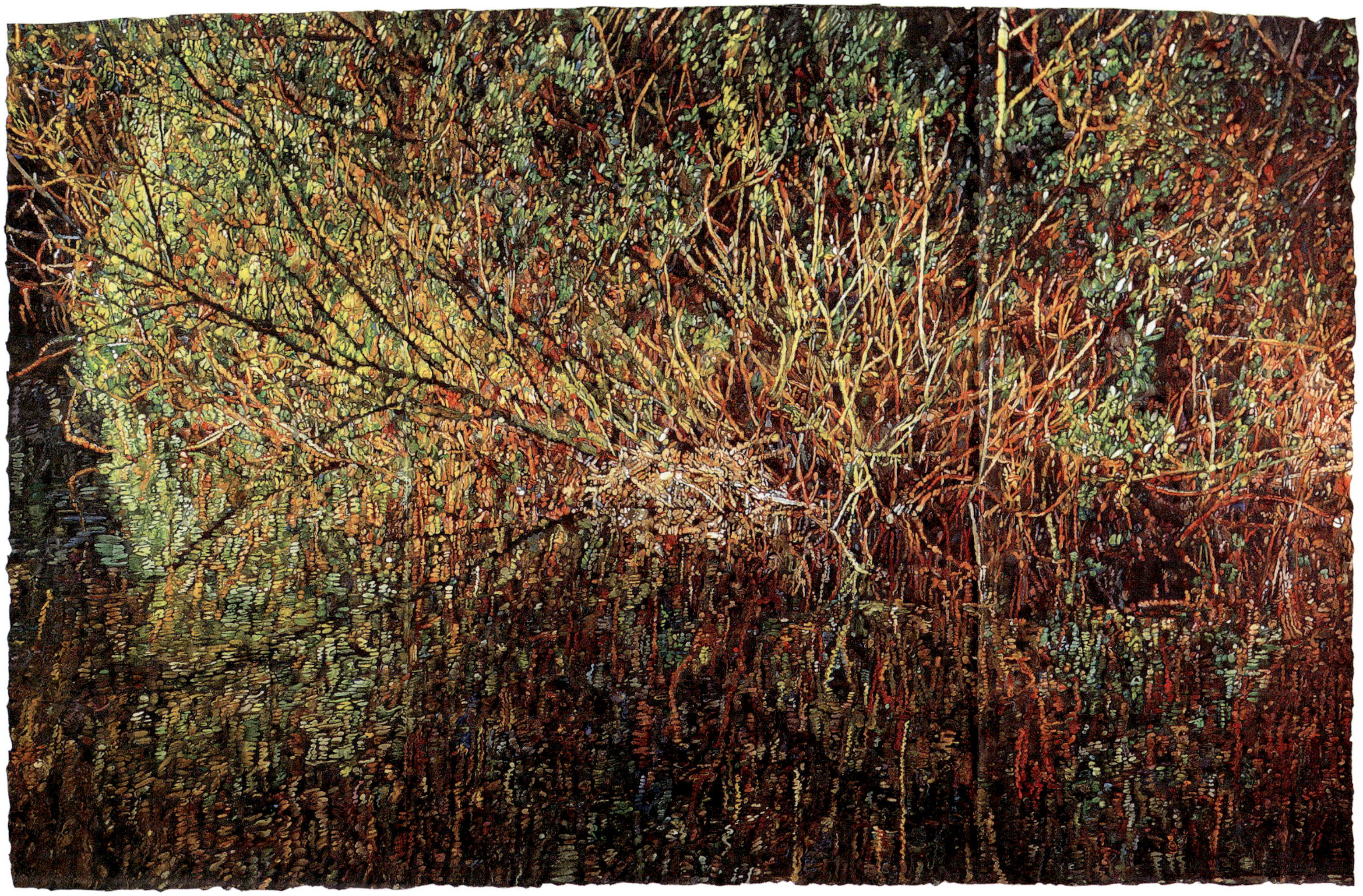

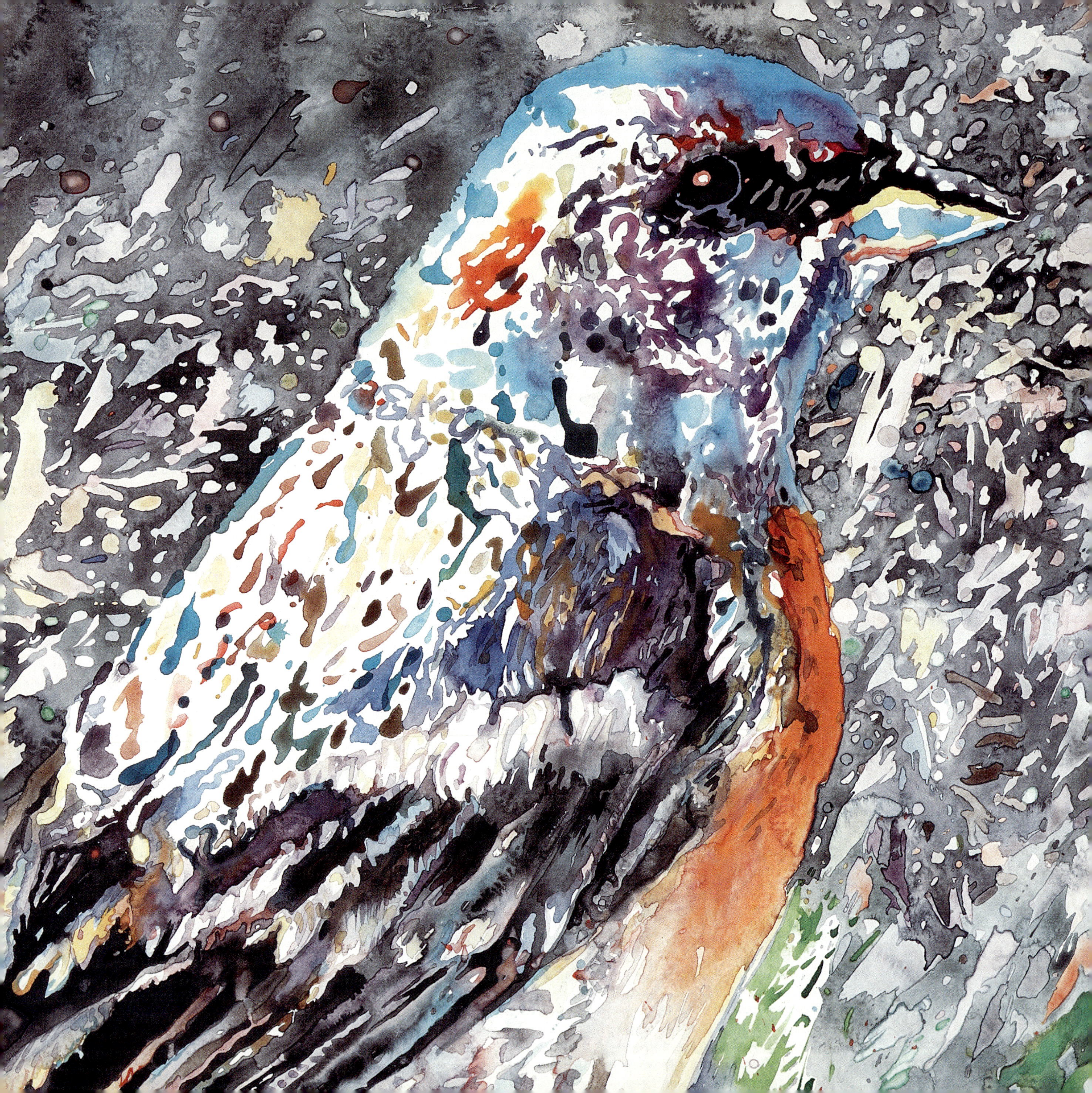

Raffael's Metaphysics of Nature

Donald Kuspit

The paramount relation between poetry and painting today, between modern man and modern art, is simply this: that in an age in which disbelief is so profoundly prevalent or, if not disbelief, indifference to questions of belief, poetry and painting, and the arts in general, are, in their measure, a compensation for what has been lost.

Wallace Stevens, 1951

Where do Joseph Raffael's paintings stand in the history of art? I think the only way to understand their significance is to understand what modern art has done to the object and how Raffael's paintings try to undo it while remaining modern art. Their standing has to do with their beauty, and what beauty means. Raffael's flowers grow in a very different way than those by Odilon Redon and Vincent van Gogh, just as his figures are far from theirs. It is in that difference and distance that we must find Raffael's meaning and his lasting importance. He turns the tide that began to go out with modernism, which left behind a desert of suffering, back to the shore of flourishing life.

After a century of negation, it is time for affirmation—time for Raffael's paintings, time to return to paradise with him. Sigmund Freud once wrote: "Affirmation—as a substitute for uniting—belongs to Eros; negation—the successor to expulsion—belongs to the instinct of destruction."[1] There has been enough destruction in modern art, which since Paul Cézanne and Paul Gauguin has struggled with expulsion from paradise and dead-ended in the inorganic, the ultimate statement of destruction.[2] It is time for Eros, for the force that unites even the most incommensurate beings and forms, affirming the life they inwardly share, celebrating the organic for its own sake. But the task—the task

121. Detail of *Spirit Bird,* 1985
See plate 148

that Raffael's painting accomplishes—is to suggest the simultaneity of the instinct for destruction and Eros, the oscillation between them, and the way each seems to grow out of the other, with the final triumph of Eros over the instinct of destruction in suspense.[3] It is this moment that Raffael brilliantly captures, this "general wish to negate" that belongs to modern art and that, although offering a "measure of freedom from the consequences of repression," can become psychotically destructive.[4]

To my mind, Marcel Duchamp epitomized this nihilism. He was a deliberate "negator," contradicting whatever was affirmed, as he acknowledged. He was anti-life as well as anti-art. Strip the veneer of irony—a very thin veneer, hardly a serious facade—from Duchamp's negation, and one realizes that it—and all the aesthetics that celebrate negation (especially T. W. Adorno's)—is emotionally nothing but the death instinct of modern society. Irony is a refinement of it: the instinct of destruction in intellectually pretentious—quasi-intellectual—disguise.

Raffael's nature poetry is an important alternative to Duchamp's Readymade, the epitome of his negative spirit. The Readymade was found, not made, and then intellectualized, which was not exactly a creative transformation. Its intellectualization is not particularly convincing: the industrial object stays visibly the same, suggesting that, in dressing it in intellectual clothing, Duchamp perpetrated the same cynical fraud as the tailors who gave the emperor his invisible new clothing.

Now having become a sacred cultural icon, the Readymade has lost its power to provoke—its profanity. Institutionalized by the same society it mocked, the Readymade has become what it always clearly was: matter-of-fact—positivist rather than imaginative. This suggests that the Readymade is less negative than Duchamp thought it was. Indeed, it ratifies society's ideology of denaturalization—the Readymade is just another denatured industrial product. It conveys, to the unconscious, the living death that modern life has become. It seems significant that Raffael's nature poetry, with its ecological affirmation of life, has appeared just when Duchamp's negation has negated itself.[5]

When one looks at a Raffael flower one sees it whole: sees that it is a fulfilled, integral, self-consistent being, shuddering with life. It often exists in a field that, however luminous, is intensely black—a lavish blackness that makes the flower's freshness all the more pungent and vivid. Its inner abundance, declared by the overflow of its petals, defeats the dark void. Emphatic against the emptiness, it becomes transcendent—"metaphysically remote," to use Rainer Maria Rilke's words[6]—even as it remains crisply empirical, terrestrial, particular. Raffael's flowers are pure being emerging from and

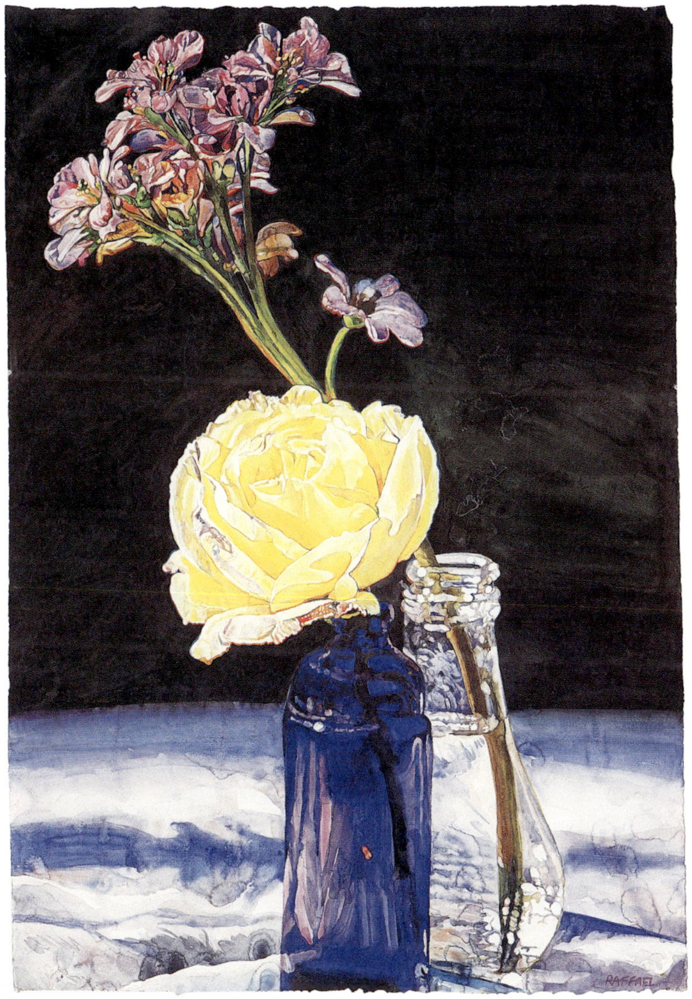

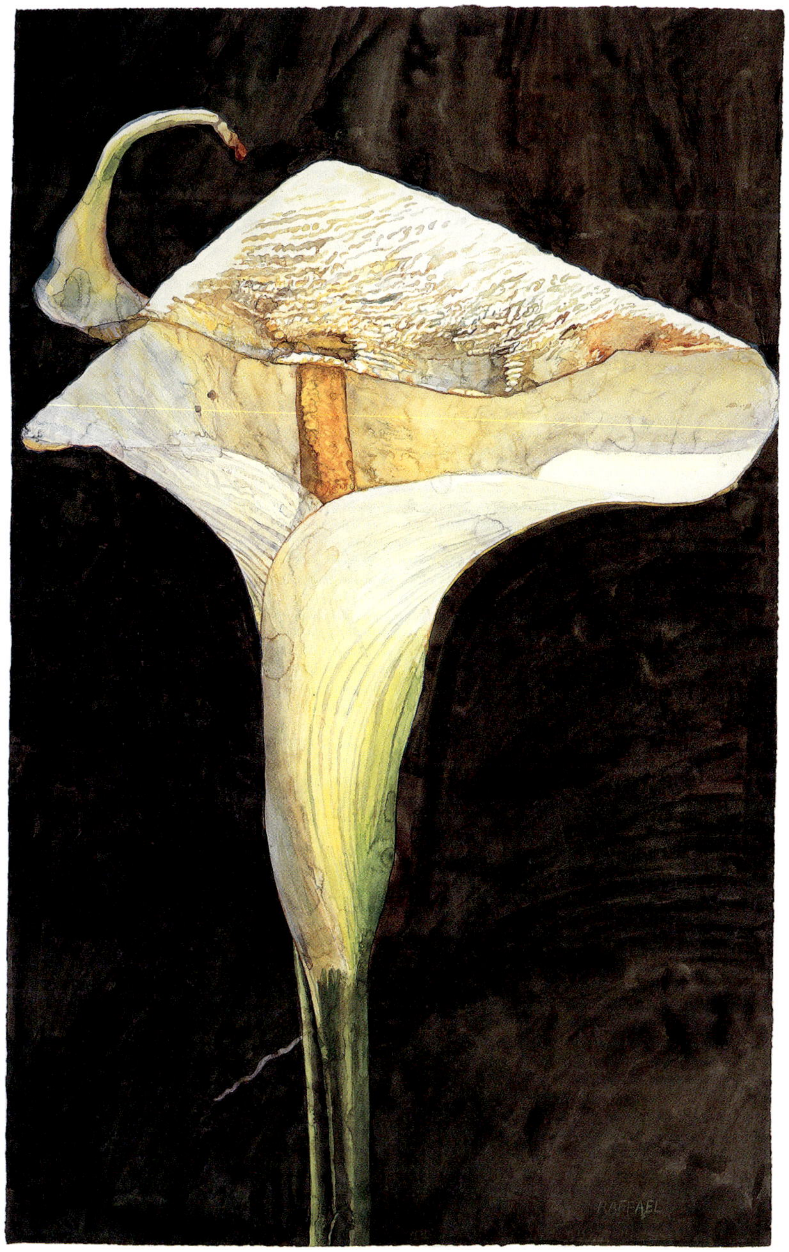

ABOVE

122. *Two Vases, Two Flowers: A Portrait,* 1990
Watercolor on paper, 67 x 45 in.
(170.1 x 114.2 cm)
Private collection, Glencoe, Illinois

RIGHT

123. *The Days Become Longer,* 1990
Watercolor on paper, 72 x 44¼ in.
(182.8 x 112.3 cm)
Courtesy of Nancy Hoffman Gallery,
New York

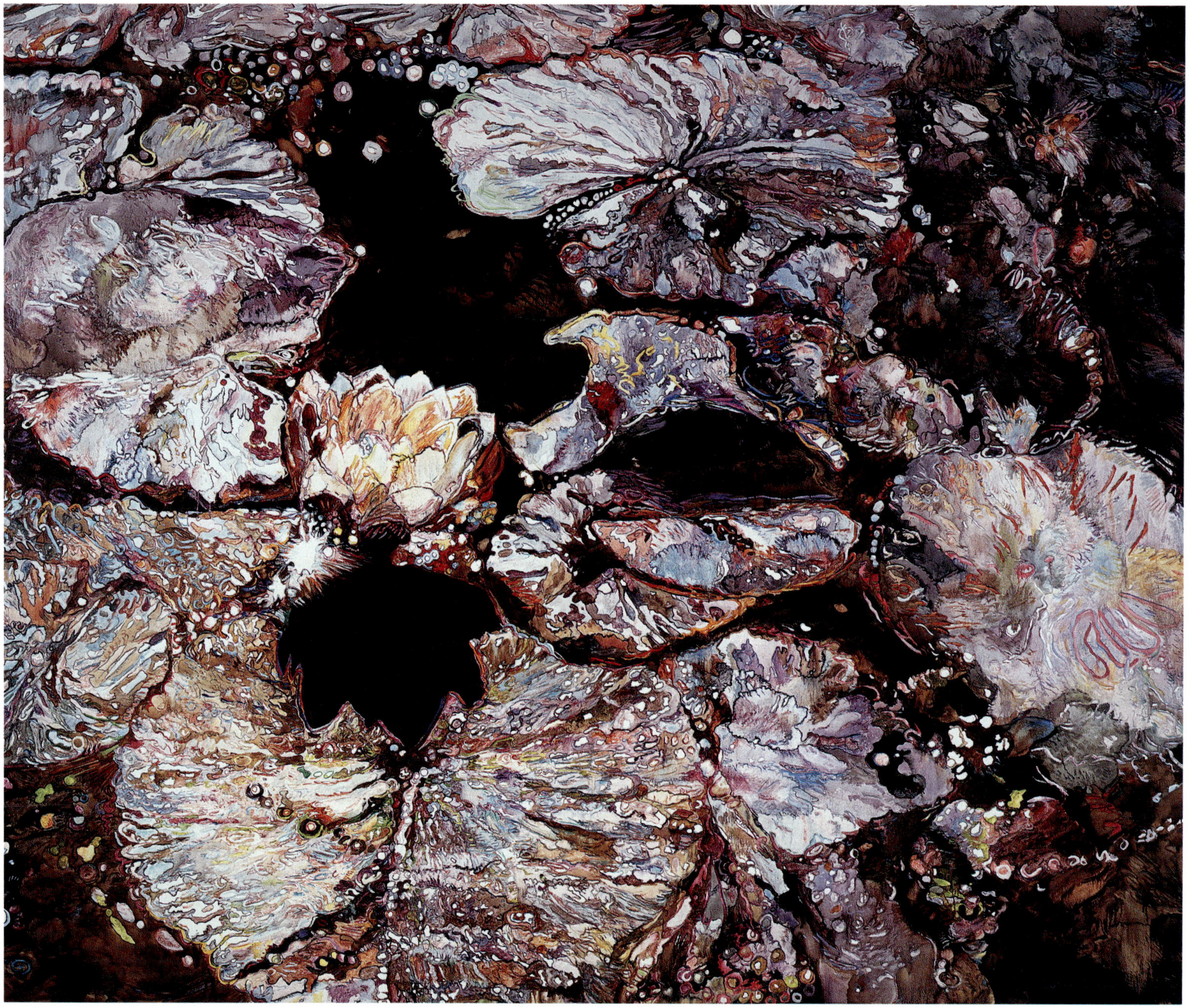

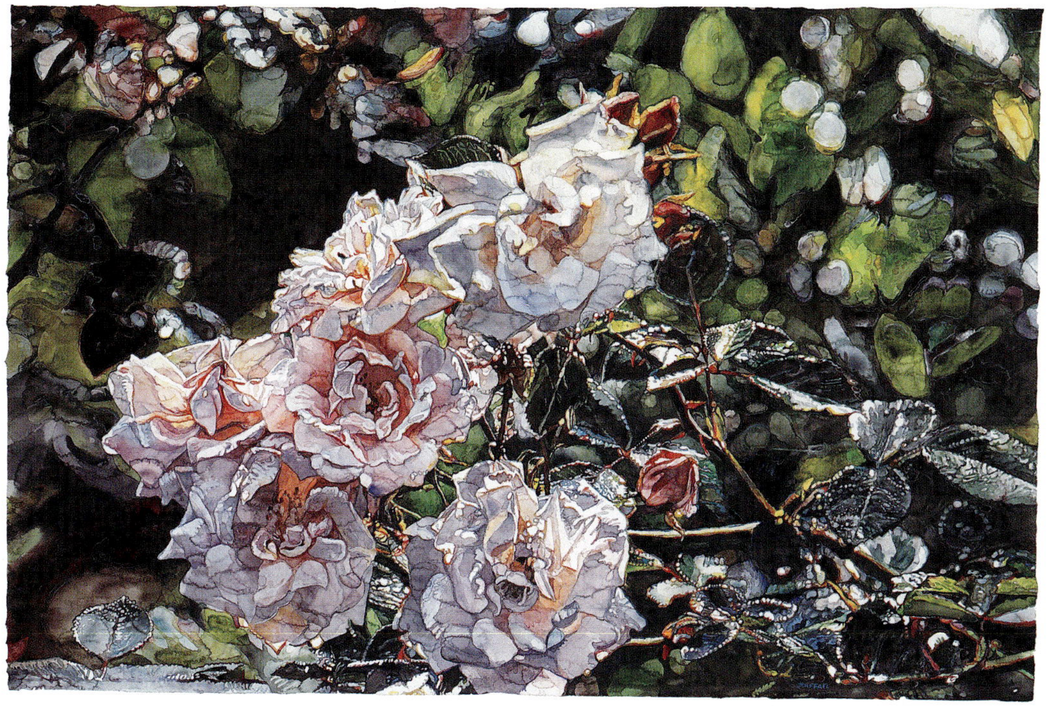

OPPOSITE
124. *Renascence,* 1980
Oil on canvas, 90 x 106 in.
(228.5 x 269.2 cm)
ARCO Chemical Company
Corporate Art Collection,
Newtown Square, Pennsylvania

ABOVE
125. *Renascence,* 1996
Watercolor on paper, 44¾ x 66 in.
(113.6 x 167.6 cm)
The Capital Group Companies, Inc.,
Los Angeles

conquering nonbeing. In his images of flowers, we see art at its best: a fresh discovery of the tangible and the intangible, the immediate and the inevitable, the contingent and the necessary, in all their untranslatable otherness and simultaneity.

Examples abound, from the lilies of the *Renascence* of 1980 (plate 124) through the roses of the *Renascence* of 1996 (plate 125). The title is instructive: rebirth, a triumph over death. Lilies occur endlessly, as though their life could never be exhausted. There are many other flowers as well, from *Orchid* (plate 126) and *Hydrangea* (plate 127) of 1976 through the flowers of the Soyez mystérieuses series of 1989 (looking at them, one cannot help thinking of Stéphane Mallarmé's remark that "every holy thing wishing to remain holy surrounds itself with mystery"[7]) to the begonia, peony, and iris images of the 1990s. "Learn to fathom what a flower infers," Rilke commands,[8] and Raffael has done so. Each of his flowers seems to "endlessly open" into "pure space," with "its decease perpetually behind it and God in front"—to quote Rilke's Eighth Duino Elegy. Seemingly "free from death" because it is so intensely and innocently alive, "it moves into eternity." It is, as Mallarmé exclaimed, "something other than known calyxes," something that is "an idea itself and fragrant, the one absent from all bouquets."[9] But the paradox of Raffael's flowers is that, for all their metaphysical eloquence, they are exuberantly physical.

Listening Lily (plate 77), for example, is a compound of delicate petals and refulgent light. Centered in a liquid darkness, its distinctive calyx holds its own even as it seems about to dissolve into watery details. Similarly, in *Water Becomes the Lily* (plate 128), the flower's substance merges with the seemingly insubstantial water. Nonetheless, its shape remains clear and distinct; it seems sublime and detached from the material in which it manifests itself, a transcendent being even though it remains bound to the water.

Every material detail is meticulously rendered by Raffael. The lily is brought to the picture plane for close observation and studied as though it were a laboratory specimen. No nuance of the water's fluidity escapes Raffael's remarkably searching eye. His pictures are masterpieces of radical empiricism: he is able to capture, with exquisite precision, material process and reality. But more crucially, he renders the interpenetration of the water's flow and the flower's shape; this is the most uncanny, ingenious aspect of Raffael's pictures, their really demanding "subject matter," the true source of their mastery. Even more than Claude Monet, Raffael grasps the transcendence implicit in the floating sensation, the complex metaphysics latent in the physics of a lily floating on water. The flower floating on water seems to become materially one with it but at the same time seems suspended above the water, as though in an unreal space—a cosmic beyond. Raffael's lily becomes an angelic presence in pure space, moving independently of the current of the water while at the same time moved, and shaped, by an invisible power. The lily's fluid shape seems to make the water's fluidity manifest, but it also uses the water as a springboard to transcendence.

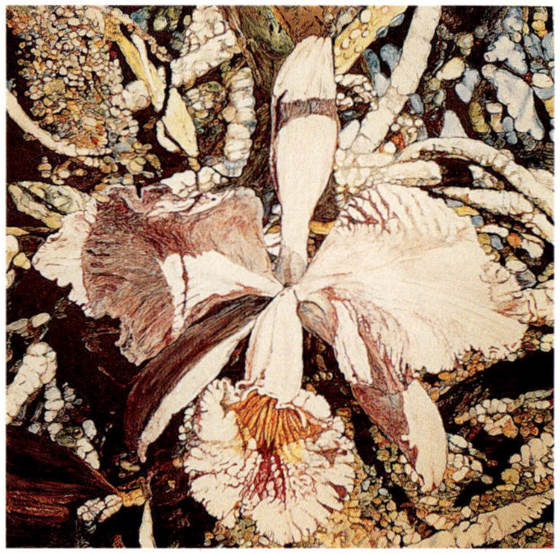

126. *Orchid,* 1976
Oil on canvas, 66 x 66 in.
(167.6 x 167.6 cm)
Private collection

But there is more to the fullness of being—the opulent, radiant efflorescence—of Raffael's flowers than meets the naked eye. It is their self-containment and dignity, their good health and integrity that gives them a metaphysical aura. If we compare them to the flowers by Redon and van Gogh, as I have suggested we do, it becomes clear that those are alien and antilife compared to Raffael's flowers. Redon's flowers are infected by death, explicitly in the dark *Marsh Flower: A Sad, Human Face* (1885), implicitly in the iridescent *Ophelia* (1905). The flowers glow with the iridescence of decay, the darkness of despair—the eerie glow given off by an unhealthy body and mind: in putting "the logic of the visible at the service of the invisible,"[10] Redon put life at the service of death. It is death that is invisible and that always seems illogical when it becomes visible, upsetting the logic of the everyday visible with unexpected ugliness.

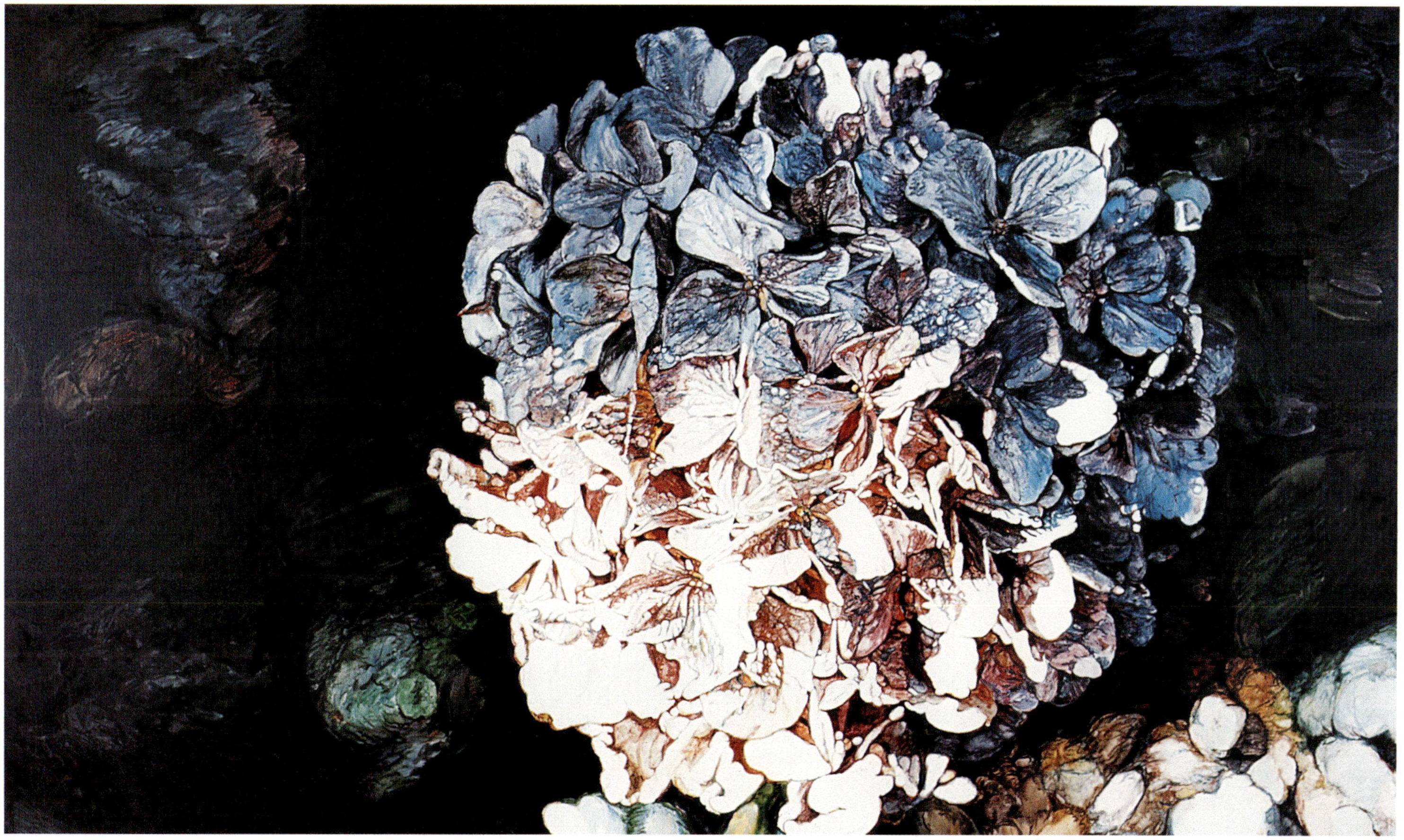

127. *Hydrangea,* 1976
Oil on canvas, 66 x 108 in.
(167.6 x 274.2 cm)
Crocker Art Museum, Sacramento, California; Gift of the Crocker Art Gallery Association with matching funds provided by the National Endowment for the Arts

Van Gogh's *Irises* of May 1890 are full, in his own words, of "violently opposed complementaries," an unresolvable "antagonism" that almost pulls the flowers apart.[11] They seem to be on the verge of dying, and not by a natural process; some are blackened shells of blue, as though rotted from within. Even van Gogh's *Sunflowers* of August 1888 seem inwardly dead—prematurely dried out. Van Gogh noted that "they fade quickly,"[12] which is perhaps why he chose them; they represent his feeling of being psychically dead, however physically alive.

The morbid, suicidal flowers of Redon and van Gogh, symbolizing anxiety about death—Piet Mondrian's weary, turn-of-the-century chrysanthemums complete the picture of premature decadence—are a far cry from the vigorous, lively, end-of-the-century flowers of Raffael. Whereas the former symbolize suffering and psychic disintegration, the latter communicate happiness and reintegration. They celebrate the

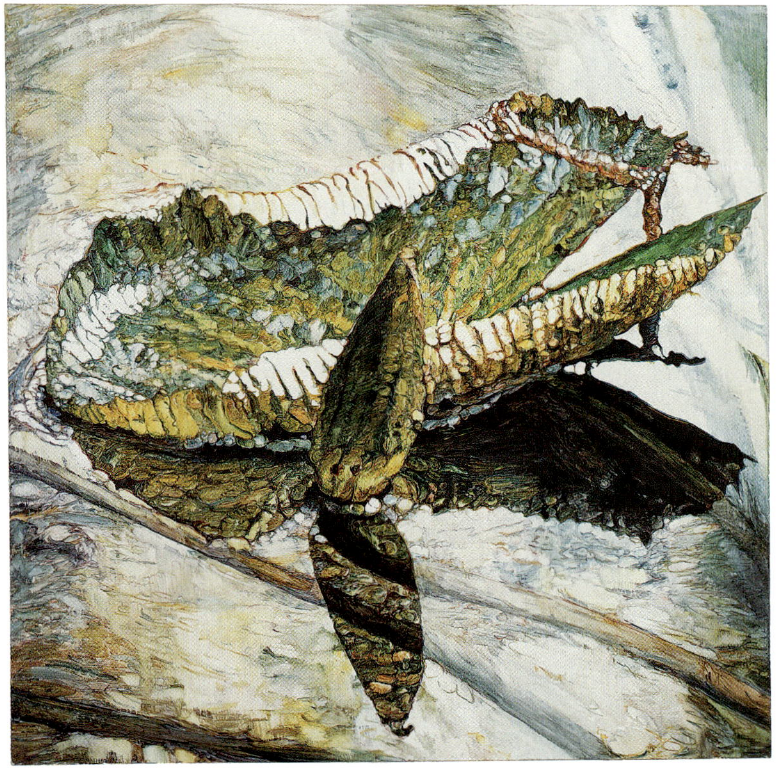

128. *Water Becomes the Lily,* 1976
Oil on canvas, 66 x 66 in.
(167.6 x 167.6 cm)
Private collection

fragility but also the staying power of life. This is the difference between the morbid beginning of modern art and the joie de vivre that must subsume and succeed it. Ironically, this is the difference between a utopian vision of death and a realistic vision of life. One expects decadence at the end of the century—the nineteenth-century decadence ushered in modernism, as has been argued—but Raffael's end-of-the-twentieth-century art instead celebrates the perpetual renewal of life.

Implicit in Raffael's approach is the Symbolist conception of "correspondence," perhaps most eloquently articulated by Charles Baudelaire in his poem "Correspondances," whose first stanza reads (in English prose translation by Francis Scarfe), "Nature is a temple, in which living pillars sometimes utter a babel of words; man traverses it through forests of symbols, that watch him with knowing eyes."[13] Raffael seems to return to the Swedenborgian origin of the notion, though reconceiving it in modern terms. Enid Starkie writes:

> Swedenborgians are convinced that material objects exist in this world only because they have their origin in the world of the spirit, and the hidden relation between things here below and in the invisible world they call "correspondences." We cannot see the objects in the world of the spirit except indirectly through their worldly "correspondences," through their symbols. . . . The true thinker will be the man who can decipher the hidden writings of nature, and interpret the mysterious book of the universe. Swedenborg said in *Divine Love* that hitherto the world had not known what "correspondences" were because it was ignorant of the meaning of the spiritual.[14]

The whole point of Raffael's art is to make the spiritual character of nature "perceptible to the senses," which can be accomplished only by the divine—the artist's religious kind of love.

129. *Eternal Return,* 1997
Watercolor on paper, 44½ x 64¾ in.
(113 cm x 164.4 cm)
Courtesy of Nancy Hoffman Gallery, New York

If, as I think, what Emanuel Swedenborg calls "spirit" is the unconscious, then Raffael suggests the correspondence between nature's material appearance and its meaning in the unconscious. Raffael clearly has an intense investment, conscious and unconscious, in nature. This is why his images of it "vibrate" with "energy," as he him-

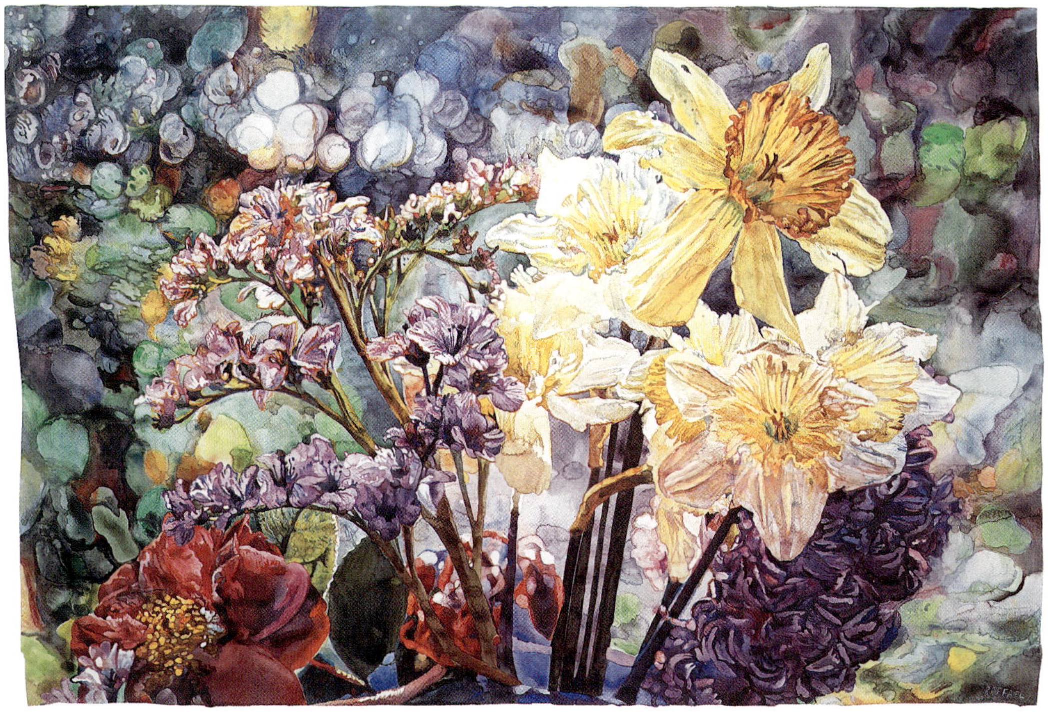

self says. As he has stated, his "inner world" and the "outer world" of nature "join and merge." For him the point of art is to articulate the "edge" where they do so, the "moment" when natural phenomena reveal themselves to be spiritual symbols.[15]

Michael Balint argues that in modern art "the object has been losing more and more its importance as an object; it has become a mere stimulus, unimportant in itself, and important only in so far as it has stimulated moods, feelings, emotions, thoughts, images, phantasies, ideas in the artist."[16] "There is," he states, "a great danger inherent in this narcissistic preoccupation, and this is the danger of regression," that is, the loss of a "mature" and "loving" relationship with the object—a relationship in which it is seen and valued for itself, its separateness and autonomy and particularity respected.[17] Instead, the relationship becomes more and more "immature."[18] Balint believes this is what occurred in modern art:

> The treatment of the object, or the artist's attitude to it, i.e., his phantasies, feelings, emotions, ideas, images, etc., when stimulated by his chosen object, are conspicuously on what psychoanalysis would describe as the anal-sadistic level. The objects are dismembered, split, cruelly twisted, deformed, messed about; the dirty, ugly qualities of the objects are "realistically" and even "surrealistically" revealed . . . less and less regard is paid to the object's feelings, interests, and sensitivities; kind consideration for, and "idealization" of, the object become less and less important.[19]

I believe we see the beginning of this regressive process of dismemberment and deformation in the traumatized flowers by Redon and van Gogh. Both artists were conspicuously narcissistic and all but isolated, suggesting the difficulty they had in relating to others at all, let alone establishing a loving relationship. That they were also subliminally destructive is evident from Redon's preoccupation with death and the violence of van Gogh's painterly gestures. Both were death-in-life artists; they render the death of the object and with it their own "sickness unto death," to use Søren Kierkegaard's term for depression. For Redon death lay on the surface of life, casting a conspicuous pall on it, whereas for van Gogh the death instinct erupted from the depths of nature, as though it was an uncontrollable process inherent to it. Van Gogh's explosive paintings verge on chaos, while Redon's brooding paintings are entropically cloying. Neither artist trusted the flowering of life and nature he saw around him: Redon had to place death at the center of *Ophelia;* van Gogh had to show death sapping the life of his flowers.

Balint argued that "in the development to come we may expect a return of interest in the objects as objects"—an end to "narcissistic withdrawal" from them. Instead of "degrading the dignity of the object into that of a mere stimulus and laying the main emphasis on the sincere and faithful representation of the artist's subjective internal mental processes," there will be "a concern for creating whole and hearty objects." "This will mean a change of attitude" in the artist. He will struggle to integrate "the discoveries of 'modern art' with the demand of 'mature love' for the object." The postmodern artist "will have to learn to feel again regard and consideration for the objects, but this time not because the objects can be used for the purposes of projecting," but because they will be "loved for what they are."[20]

I believe that Raffael's flower represents this new, postmodern, mature art of love, this new and necessary—for survival—attitude of maturity and love. With it comes a new sense of the dignity and unity, the wholeness and integrity, of the object. But also of the subject. Both can flower again; neither will die. No longer possessed by the death instinct, both overflow with life. Raffael's flower is a double symbol: a symbol of the renewal and flowering and wholeness the self experiences when it loves, and a symbol of the renewal and flowering and wholeness of the object of love.

130. *Transition in Spring,* 1996
Watercolor on paper, diptych:
58½ x 85½ in. (148.5 x 217.1 cm)
Courtesy of Nancy Hoffman Gallery, New York

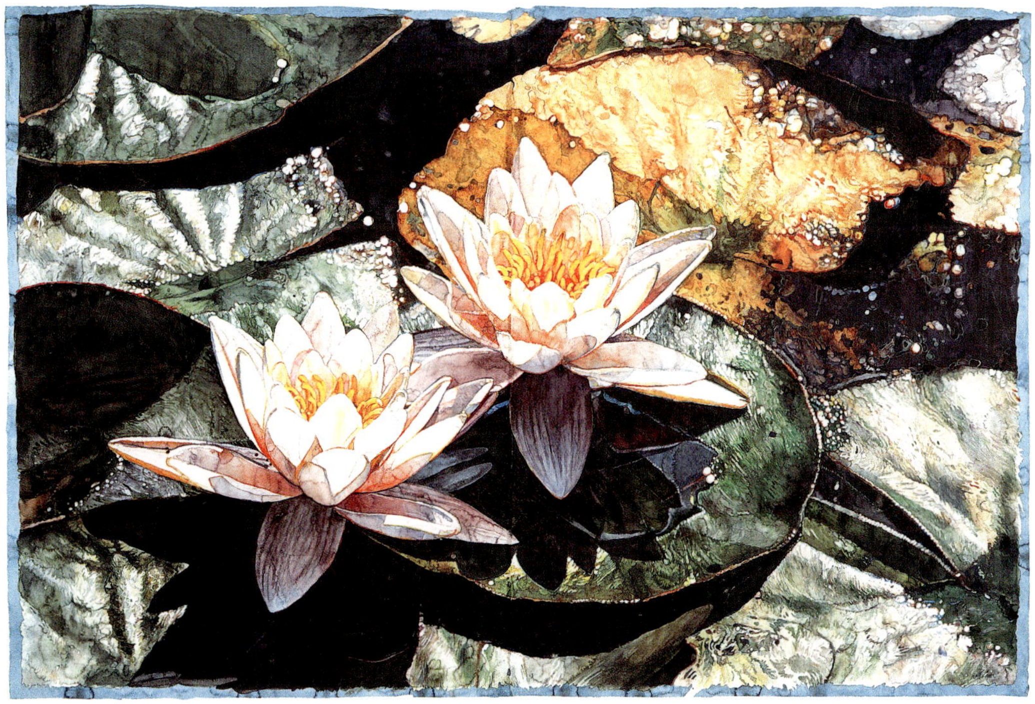

The paradox of this new mature attitude of love is that it restores the object's original power to restore us. When we feel dead and project our death onto the object, we negate it, so that it seems dead; but when we love the object—in effect, re-creating it after we have destroyed it—it re-creates us, making us feel alive, not only in an everyday sense but as though we were reborn. In the creative act of loving the object for itself, it becomes a new "first object," the beloved object of our "earliest experience"—more particularly, the mother when she "functioned as a region or source of transformation," what Christopher Bollas calls a "transformational object."[21] Thus the object repays our love by making us feel as alive and full of potential as when we were infants, taking the modern artist's idea of being like a child a crucial postmodern step further. Of course, it was the Eros in us that came to the rescue of the object and ourselves; but what is unexpected is that it returned us to our origins, as though in re-originating the object we re-originated ourselves.

Raffael's flower conveys the erotic originality of such new life. It carries the mother's power to make experience seem original and radical; Raffael's flower is Mother Nature happening for the first time. It is, in effect, her "good breast."[22] There is a tangled paradox here, an intellectual irony that is an emotional triumph. The paradox of love restores the object, and with it the subject, to wholeness and thus is "progressive." At the same time, it is more "regressive" than narcissistic regression, for the wholeness it discovers belongs to the impersonal good breast, the benign "abstract" breast of Mother Nature. Raffael's flower is Mother Nature's breast, restored and overflowing with fresh life. Indeed, for Raffael the water and milk of life fuse: the lilies live off the water they float on. From the water droplets on *Lily Painting: Hilo (Island Lilies)* (plate 131) to the water ripples of *Spring: Amazement* (plate 132), there is a sense of overflowing abundance—inexhaustible richness and radiance of elemental, maternal, natural being.

In general, the vivid, endlessly proliferating organic details in Raffael's images form a shimmering aura of nourishing compassion. Moreover, Raffael's breast-flower is beautiful because it has been renewed; it is no longer destroyed—wilting, inwardly rotten. As W.R.D. Fairbairn says, beauty "conveys the impression of something *intact, whole, complete* or *perfect*."[23] Nonetheless, there is always a reminder in it of "uncontrollable destruction." Destruction lurks in the flower's transience, which may be why Redon and van Gogh used it to express their feelings of mortality. But Raffael emphasizes the flower's freshness and vitality, which is why his flowers seem so perfect.

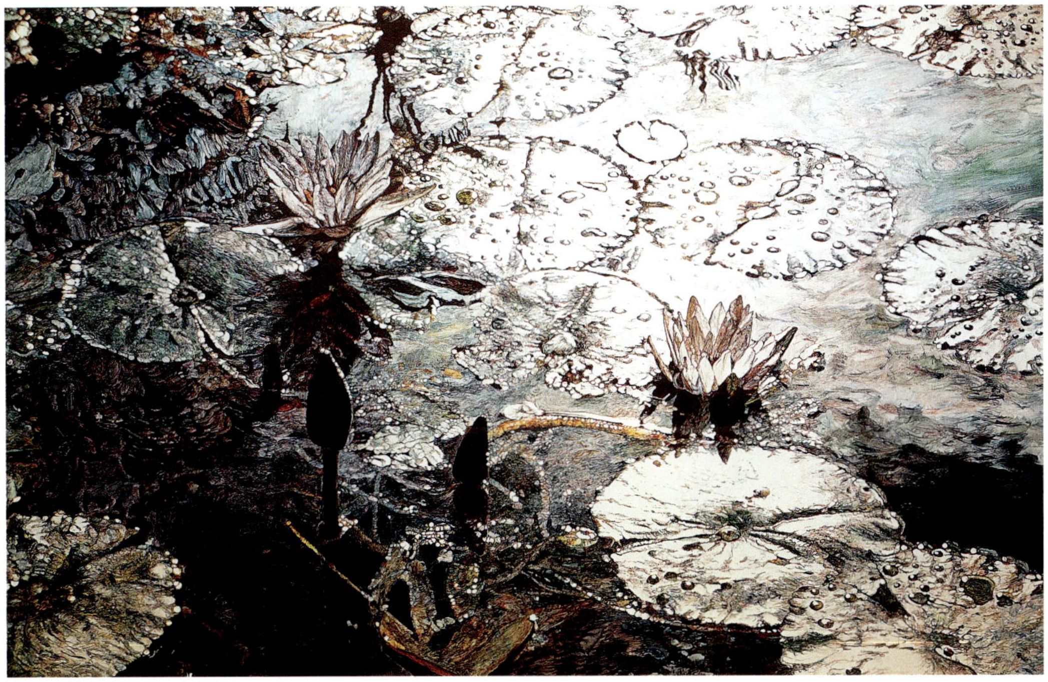

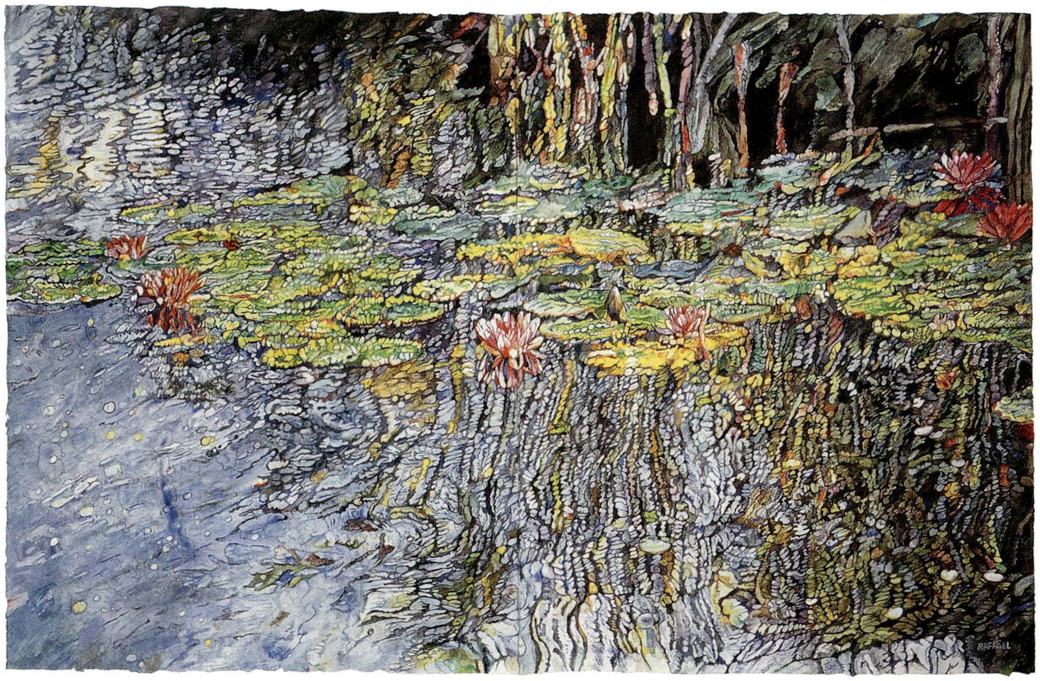

ABOVE

131. *Lily Painting: Hilo (Island Lilies),* 1975
Oil on canvas, 84 x 132 in.
(213.3 x 335.2 cm)
Mr. and Mrs. Graham Gund

RIGHT

132. *Spring: Amazement,* 1994
Watercolor on paper, diptych: 57½ x 89 in.
(146 x 226 cm)
Oprah Winfrey, Chicago

Raffael's flower is the good breast not only because it is bursting with physical life but also because it teaches us a basic lesson in emotional survival, further confirming its motherly character. Raffael takes the raw, concrete experience of the flower and abstractly develops it to make the complicated emotions it arouses comprehensible and controllable. We all approach Mother Nature with the uncertainty of a child, eager for succor and understanding but not certain we will receive it. Raffael's flowers are profoundly reassuring and restorative, for they appeal to our need to believe in the benign character of the cosmos. In general, Raffael's remarkably beautiful art is a mode of memory, a heroic symbolization of the experience of being as such. It is stored for later re-cognition and contemplation, so that the cosmos will never again seem alien and traumatic. Raffael's freshly beautiful nature becomes a source of comfort and consolation, for it evokes all that is good in life. In transforming the flower until it becomes radiantly beautiful, Raffael's consuming gaze shows us how to transform ourselves for the better.

The Animals of Paradise

> *The archetype of spirit in the shape of [an] animal appears in a situation where insight, understanding, good advice, determination, planning, etc., are needed but cannot be mustered on one's own resources.*
>
> Carl Jung, 1959[24]

Raffael's representation of the object, I have suggested, is fundamentally different from its representation in other modern art. His animal imagery, like his flower imagery, is major proof of this. Indeed, Raffael first came into his own as a painter of nature in his animal pictures. As Thomas H. Garver wrote, *Release* (plate 133) is "one of his first images dealing with natural phenomena, plants, animals and landscape, and it is also autobiographical."[25] It was made soon after Raffael moved from New York to California. The painting shows "a young duck beginning its flight to freedom," symbolizing the "new beginning he was experiencing." The human hand that releases the duck is visible to the left, and the duck almost completely fills the enormous space of the huge canvas. Like Leonardo da Vinci in Vasari's account, Raffael gave a captive bird its freedom, symbolizing his own wish for freedom. Outer freedom symbolizes inner freedom, creative freedom.[26] But the moment is ambiguous; the duck is, in fact, not yet free but still struggling to become free. It does not believe that it is being released, even as it is being released.

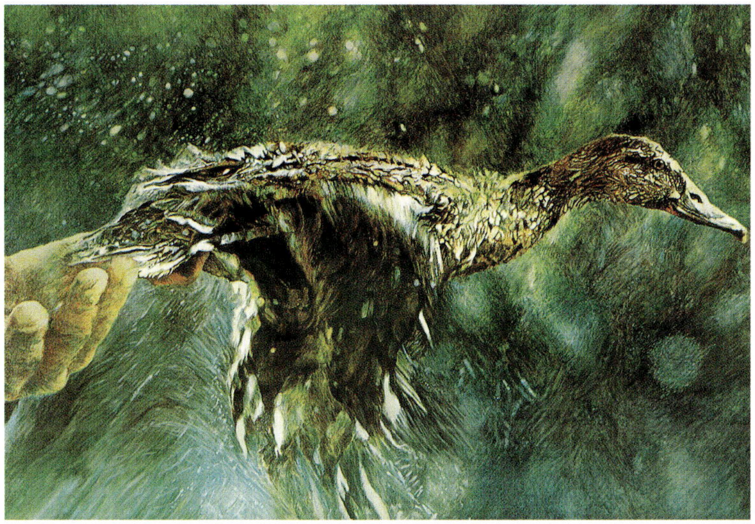

133. *Release,* 1970
Oil on canvas, 75 x 108 in.
(190.4 x 274.2 cm)
Joslyn Art Museum, Omaha;
Gift of FirsTier Financial, Inc.

Even with its wings beating intensely, the animal is remarkably confident and self-possessed, especially considering its vulnerability. Although its fate is in human hands, it seems totally at one with itself. The duck has great presence—much more so than the human presence, which is blurred and vestigial, as though seen through the duck's eye. Its life has been touched by man, but it remains untamed, full of instinctive life, ready to take flight and forget man as soon as it is free. As in the majority of Raffael's paintings, the scale is cosmic yet the scene is intimate; we see the duck close-up, down to the least physical detail. Indeed, Raffael's animals and flowers are usually larger than life, bringing with them a sense of the infinite.

Punctiliously rendered, the duck is nonetheless mysterious. Light glistens on its feathers, making them seem immaterial; thus, touched by the painter's hand, the duck becomes intangible. However natural, in Raffael's hands the duck becomes preternatural. Fact has become fantastic. The effect is startling, as though we are witnessing a miracle. Raffael's picture is an allegory of painting; we see the painter's hand in the act of creating new life, implicitly the painter's own. Restoring the sense of the miraculousness of life, Raffael restores our belief in the miraculousness of art—art as a miraculous creation of miraculous life. Raffael's *Release* is an act of faith, as all his nature paintings are.

Release encapsulates the paradox of Raffael's animal paintings, indeed, of his nature imagery as a whole: invariably they show a finite, elemental creature at home in—instinctively at one with—an infinite, elemental space. Or else they show the great beyond, the implicitly cosmic environment, as in the extraordinary Water Painting series of 1972–74, with its seemingly limitless, changing, luminous water, a macrocosmos shown in microcosmic detail. Each is a morphology of movement, epitomizing the incessant, incalculable movement of the whole scene. Raffael dissected the restless water, as though to discover the secret of its energy and freshness, but it remains unfathomable.

Raffael's duck forms a natural bridge, as it were, between its own limited environment and the larger environment. The two imperceptibly become one: the duck is one with the sky it flies in and the water it floats on. Oceanic experience is suggested, in all its grandeur and mystery. The natural becomes mystical, and the mystical, natural. If, as Sheldon Bach has written, "creativity is the language of serious paradox accepted, understood, and grappled with,"[27] then Raffael is creatively grappling with the paradox that in experiencing nature with mystical seriousness we unconsciously accept and understand our animal nature. What was once split off is reintegrated through the mystical experience of identifying with an animal, which in turn makes us feel mystically at home in nature.

Essentially portraits, Raffael's *Salmon* and *Oyster* (plates 134 and 135) and *Lizard* and *Lion* (plates 56 and 57) seem confrontational. We are only a few inches from these alien creatures, and the question seems to be who will blink or bite first. This disturbing intimacy, and the extraordinary revelation of detail it affords, with the accompanying sense of immediacy, is made possible by the artist's use of photography. But photographs are only a point of departure: his paintings are much more than exact observational records—mimetic triumphs. Raffael is not naively descriptive; indeed, description is not his goal, even superficially. He provides more details than are technically necessary to get the perceptual point—to see the gestalt of the natural object and to recognize it in all its naturalness. Raffael is so extravagant in his use of contingent details that they seem more necessary than the natural object and even independent of it. Indeed, he gives us many more details than the ordinary photograph; a comparison between the matter-of-fact slide (plate 136) and the lush painting *A Frog in Its Pond* (plate 137) makes this clear.

In fact, in *Oyster* and *Salmon* (the touchstones of his later painterly technique) detail almost overwhelms the natural object represented, making it seem strangely unnatural. We must do a double take, as it were, to grasp the objectivity beneath the spontaneous dance of detail. The abundance of detail becomes a veil on the familiar object, making it mysterious and deceptive even as it remains readable. Paradoxically, in being overdetailed—overobjectified, as it were—it becomes evocative and unexpectedly subjective. And unexpectedly abstract: no longer completely compliant to nature, the details can be experienced as the spontaneous gestures and personal ideas they emotionally are. It is this doubleness that makes Raffael's paintings visionary

BELOW
134. *Salmon,* 1969
Oil on canvas, 60 x 60 in. (152.3 x 152.3 cm)
Private collection

OPPOSITE
135. *Oyster,* 1968
Oil on canvas, 70 x 64 in. (177.8 x 162.5 cm)
James and Corinne Schutz, New York

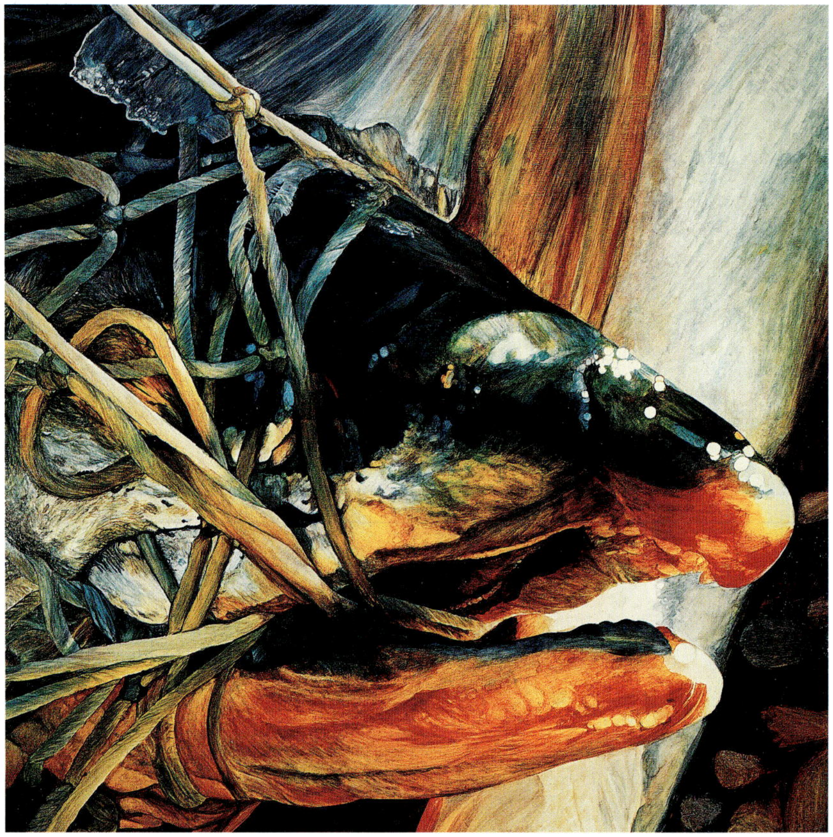

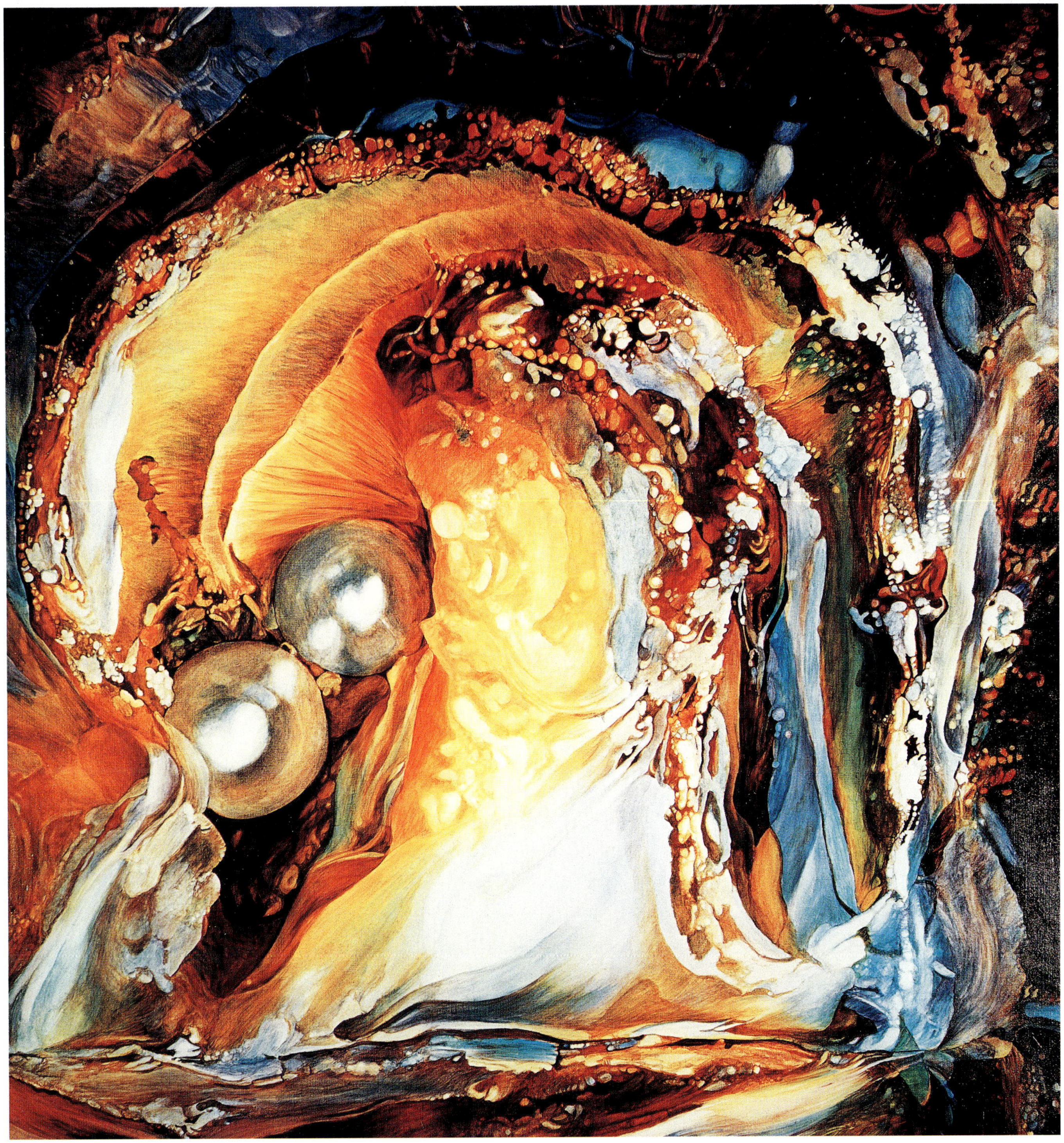

spaces in which objects are at once found and created, separate and intimate, parts of shared reality and radically subjective.

To say the same thing in a cultural way, Raffael's surplus of independent detail turns a natural phenomenon into an aesthetic experience. The excess of subliminally abstract detail makes it clear that Raffael is not a conventional realist representing objects in a practical manner that conforms to ordinary perceptual expectations—which is why he is not a neotraditional painter, however traditional his paintings seem to be at first glance—but a very modern painter.

But abstraction is insufficient for Raffael because it conveys a certain disillusionment with nature, which no longer seems as mysterious and enchanted as it once did. Our relationship with it has become too self-conscious and strained to be organic, spontaneous, caring, worshipful; we no longer instinctively believe in the sublimity of nature the way Claude Lorraine did, nor are we able to establish Wordsworthian intimacy with it the way John Constable did. The Impressionists seem the exception to the modern rule, but their empiricism is distancing—not as warm as it seems—and in fact sets the stage for the later intellectualization of nature. This emerged in Cézanne's late work and was quickly ratified—and reified—by Cubism. It bespeaks a certain distrust of nature or perhaps modern skepticism extended to nature; it is no longer possible to respond to nature instinctively. The modern artist shattered the "Vegetable Glass of Nature," as William Blake called it,[28] leaving in its place shards of pseudo-natural gesture that no longer had organic credibility plus the artist's own construction of art—what Charles Baudelaire called the "artificial paradise" of art. In the twentieth century it came to seem less and less a paradise and more and more artificial. Nature is vanquished by art, but it is not clear that it does art any good, especially in the long run. Art has become a conceptual desert rather than a perceptual oasis. Both have been ruined.

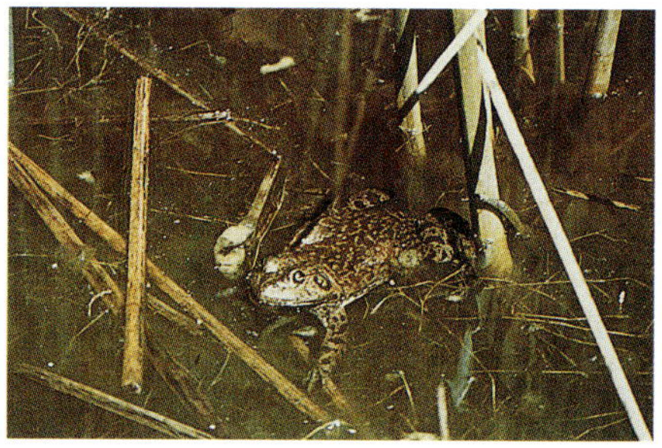

ABOVE
136. Original slide for *A Frog in Its Pond*

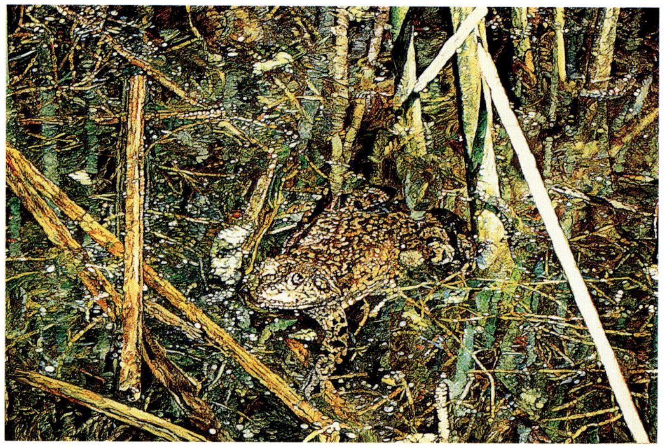

BELOW
137. *A Frog in Its Pond,* 1976
Oil on canvas, 78 x 114 in. (198.1 x 289.5 cm)
Private collection, Hobe Sound, Florida

Raffael knows it is impossible to return to where Claude and Constable were; nature has changed. It can no longer mirror our ideals and emotional needs, at least not as convincingly. And so has art: it is no longer self-expression—an expression of human nature—but pure art selflessly constructed. Raffael accepts the fact that he is, however subliminally, a modern abstract painter; he sees the abstractness in the real. But he raises the question whether abstract art has to look abstract, at least by conventional standards. He transforms abstraction, so that it seems natural, bespeaking the richness and vitality of nature. There is a kind of interplay between free expression and factual observation, an entanglement of the invented and the given. Raffael is a participant observer in nature but also an independent creator. He balances the claims of both nature and art—the found and the created. He is devoted to both, so that neither exists at the expense of the other.

Raffael is a great technician, but his technique serves creative observation. This is apparent in the use he makes of the photograph. It mediates perception through a machine, implying that it is socially constructed. Perception is no longer instinctive, no longer located in the body, but mechanical, a technical rather than organic matter. Perception is no longer a natural response to the given, and the given is always in doubt. The fact that it can be photographed from many different viewpoints, none of which is more valid or essential than any other, casts doubt on perception. Raffael gives the photograph a painterly body, idiosyncratically repainting it so that it reveals details of nature that no photograph can ever show. His surplus of independent detail expresses the inherent vitality of nature.

Raffael shows nature from the organic inside, from the side of instinct. We are no longer at an intellectual distance from nature, but so engaged with it that we feel immersed in its instinctive flow. The static photograph has been turned into a vital process that is comprehensible only instinctively. We can grasp the process only by attuning to it with our own vitality; staying at an intellectual distance blinds us to its intensity. For Raffael, abstraction has become the instrument of his instinctive experience of it. The point of view has radically changed.

Raffael's parting of the ways with the Abstract Expressionists—he was "nurtured" as one, Garver says[29]—has to do with the meaning he gives abstract gesture; it expresses the erotic ripeness of the animal or flower, conveying an affirmative attitude to it. In Raffael's paintings abstract gesture is no longer the manifestation of the death instinct that it usually is in Abstract Expressionism. It is this that makes Abstract Expressionist gesture more compulsive than spontaneous, more impersonal than personal, more accidental than lovingly crafted—the exact emotional opposite of Raffael's expressive gesture. Raffael's gestural excess has an entirely different ambition than that of Abstract Expressionist gestural excess: not to attack and shred the naturally given object but to vividly convey its integrity.

Because Raffael is not in conflict with or conflicted about animals, he can acknowledge their difference, which allows him to have a more differentiated, and certainly less generalized, sense of them. Not feeling alienated from them, he can present them in an unalienated way. At the same time, Raffael's excessive gestural details transcend the creature they describe, and in so doing embody its transcendence of its environment, however much it is nourished by it and remains a part of it. The abstract autonomy of the details bespeaks the animal's peculiar autonomy, as well as its embeddedness in its environment. The frog could not endure without its pond—Raffael rarely shows any animal without its environment—but it is also a unique being in its own right. The complexity of its being is signaled by the complexity of its appearance. Indeed, once we look beyond its gestalt to the level of microscopic detail, the animal becomes unintelligible. Yet every detail is meaningful in terms of the animal's own being. Raffael paints the organic details as though they encoded the creature's inner life.

For Raffael, the appearance of the animal's skin is a direct if cryptic manifestation of its inner world and, above all, of its interface with its environment. It is as though the animal internalized its environment, transforming it in the process, and then reexternalized it. The animal's skin—its external appearance—stands to this relationship and thus to the inner reality of the animal, as the manifest content of a dream stands to its latent content. Raffael is determined to enter the animal's inner world, to get under its skin; he comes as empathically close as he can. His use of the close-up symbolizes this empathy, as does the excruciating attention he devotes to the details of the animal's appearance. He identifies with the animal; its being in effect becomes his own. It is as though he sees the animal's environment through its eyes, experiencing the environment as instinctively as it does. Raffael struggles to internalize the animal's awareness, its complex unity of being, its inner harmony, and its instinctive harmony with its environment; his art is the means to this difficult if not impossible goal.

Are the animal portraits Raffael's spiritual self-portraits? The portraitist of an animal discovers himself in and through his subject as much as the portraitist of a person, inevitably imposing himself on his subject. He discovers repressed aspects of his own subjectivity in the subject or else projects them onto it, so that they come back to him as though in a distorting mirror. Oskar Kokoschka found himself in a mandrill, and Pablo Picasso found himself in a chimpanzee. I am suggesting that painting is a kind of shamanistic ritual for Raffael, in which he becomes an animal in spirit. In doing so, he reconciles with his animal nature, becoming whole—no longer split into instinctive and intellectual, irrational and rational sides. His sensibility becomes whole. He also acquires the animal's power to bridge realms. Like the amphibious lizard, he is at home on land and in the water. Like the oyster, he transforms irritating, potentially destructive impurities into priceless pearls; impinging, overstimulating, almost emotionally overwhelming perceptions become beautiful works of art.

Raffael's animal paintings are, to my mind, subliminally didactic personal allegories, conveying animal wisdom. Each animal represents a strategy of survival, an adaptive lesson in instinctive life—indeed, a demonstration of the strength of the will to life. Each animal embodies a virtue: the lion has the courage necessary to survive in the jungle; the lizard's flexibility allows it to inhabit different environments; the salmon aggressively fights for its life and freedom; and the oyster performs the existential miracle of making something positive out of something negative, thus offering what amounts to a model for art-making. Each animal is triumphant over its circumstances, even as it is dependent on them. Refusing to be defeated by its world, it becomes peculiarly unworldly in the process. It is as though Raffael has learned everything of lasting value about life and art—including the art of life—from them and, more broadly, from nature, with which he always stays in touch. Nature—whether it takes animal, vegetable, or mineral form—is Raffael's self-object, as it had been for many premodernist landscape painters.

To feel like an animal, in order to recover the animal in oneself, with its instinct to survive and its enjoyment of life: this is the "mission" of Raffael's animal paintings—and they are painted with a kind of missionary zeal, even a fanatic intensity. The same empathic ambition is operational in Raffael's flower paintings, but the animal paintings are its first important statement. It is easier to feel affinity with animals, because we ourselves are animals, than with flowers. We can appropriate flowers as symbols, but it is more difficult to become attuned to them as beings with a life and will of their own; their vegetable will to life is biologically and thus emotionally stranger to us than the animal's will to life.

Like Franz Marc, Raffael prefers animals to human beings. "Very early," Marc wrote, "I found people to be 'ugly': animals seemed more beautiful, more pure."[30] Marc's goal, like Raffael's, was "to imagine how nature is reflected in the eyes of an animal. . . . It is a poverty-stricken convention to place animals into landscapes as seen by men; instead, we should contemplate the soul of the animal to divine its ways of sight."[31] This is why Marc said he rejected "unnatural" modern styles—he mentioned Cubism in particular—for they showed how modern man saw, not how eternal animals do. Significantly, Marc began to show the animal world in a modern Cubist way when it was threatened by destruction. Marc, like Raffael, believed that animals "project *their* inner world"[32]—the emphasis implying that we should not project our inner world onto them. Marc's ultimate ambition, like Raffael's, was "to render the predicate of living things," in order to recover the "inwardly genuine plasticity" (as Max Weber called it) that has been lost to modernity, which makes this vital fluidity seem more "mystical" and remote than ever.[33]

But whereas many of Marc's animals seem to exist in a state of anxious tension, while others seem blindly exuberant, Raffael's animals are calm and collected and self-contained. This is because they are the animals of paradise rather than modern animals. Marc's animals react, with either manic optimism or morbid pessimism, to the disenchantment of nature that occurred in modernity. Raffael's animals exist in a prelapsarian state of being, which is why they seem like marvels. They are sacred animals, rather than animals profaned by the world. Above all, they have the fundamental trait of all prelapsarian beings: they are sacred because their *Innenwelt* and *Umwelt* are in balance.[34] This is why their appearance matches their surroundings and why it can be read as a sign of their consciousness. Their outer appearance, inner reality, and surrounding environment are essentially the same, which is why they are beautiful.

This explains their lack of aggression: there is no violence in the garden of paradise. The lion and the lizard live in harmony with one another, as do the oyster and the salmon. The owl is no longer a predator, for it has become a symbol of eternity (see plate 154). Raffael's cats—Claire, Fumé, and Tigre—do not scratch. The fish in his garden cannot be caught, and his cats will never pounce on any bird, as the cat in Francisco Goya's picture of a young prince is about to do. Playful domestic animals, emotionally attuned to their master, they clearly lack the vehemence of the beasts carved on the *trumeau* of the cathedral in Souillac, France—intense animals "twisted, entangled, and unbalanced by their own rapacious energy," as Meyer Schapiro put it.[35] The cathedral's beasts are clearly fallen, even demonic animals—animals at odds with each other and themselves and with the world after the expulsion of man from paradise into the hell of the world. Whereas Souillac's animals are perversely realistic and all too human, Raffael's animals represent a greater rebellion—the insistence on living in a state of paradisiacal harmony in defiance of and apart from the world of human conflict, both internal and external. Raffael's animals represent his revolt against the modern world, with its violence and unnatural way of life. Their beauty is the ultimate rebellion against modern man-made ugliness.

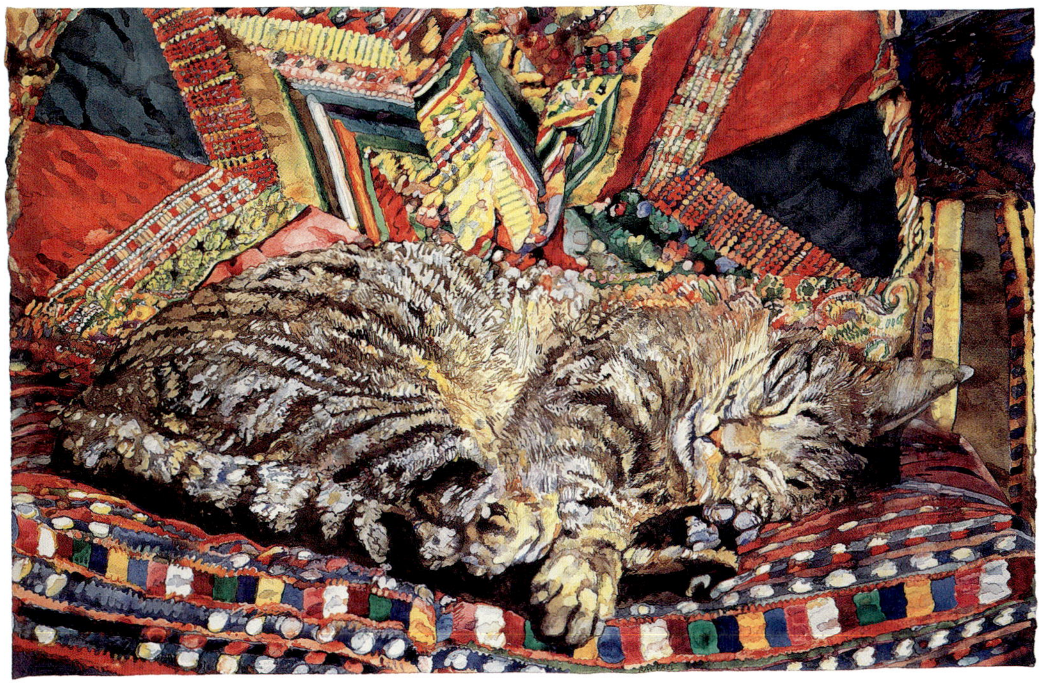

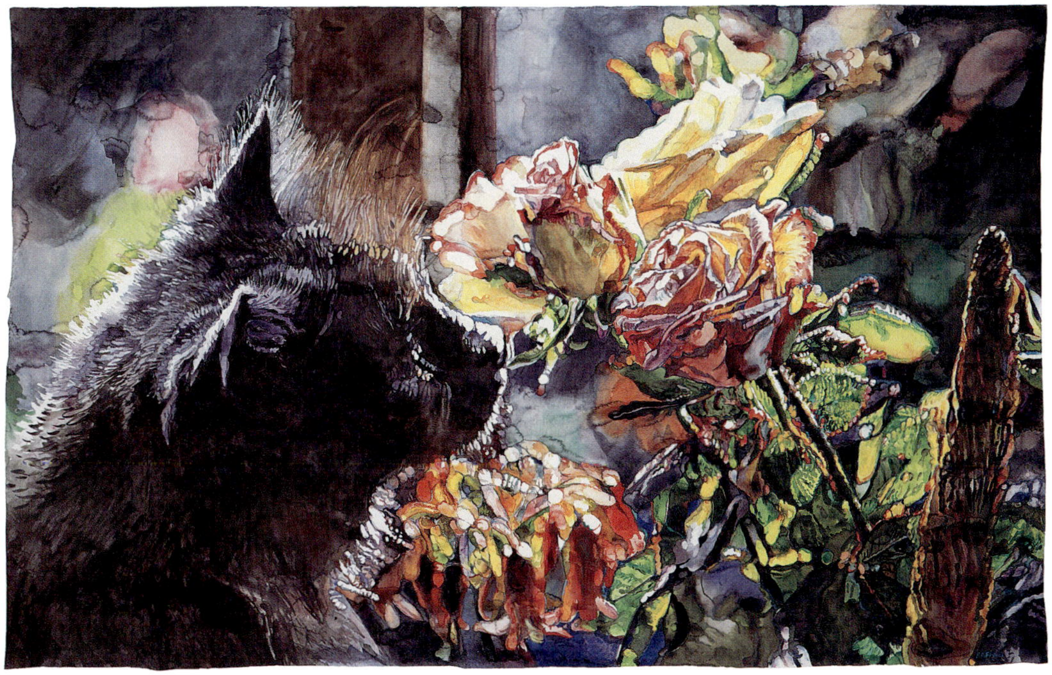

ABOVE

138. *Tigre in Sieste,* 1991
Watercolor on paper, 34¾ x 53½ in.
(88.2 x 135.8 cm)
Corinne and James Schutz, New York

RIGHT

139. *Fumé Watching the Flowers,* 1992
Watercolor on paper, 43 x 66 in.
(109.2 x 167.6 cm)
Private collection

Self-protectively, Raffael has sought out natural paradise: Marin County in California, where his first nature paintings were made, was an early version of it, and Cap d'Antibes in France, where he has been making his nature paintings since 1986, is a new, final version. He wants to keep the destructive modern world—any hint of destructiveness—out of his new French paradise, which is what most of his later paintings represent. Raffael will paint natural paradise wherever he can find it, as *Luxembourg Gardens: Faith* (plate 140) and *Luxembourg Gardens: Truth* (plate 141) indicate. His gardens are all the more poignant because of what we do not see in them—the urban wasteland. In general, his timeless gardens imply a profound rejection of modern society. He insists on keeping paradise pure. Destruction and constraint existed in his California Eden, as *Salmon* and *Release* indicate; paradise was more a possibility than an actuality there. But now he wants the actuality. Raffael is determined to live in a state of prelapsarian grace.

Is Raffael inhabiting a twilight zone? Is paradise a twilight state of mind? Hermann Broch, describing our "animal heritage" in his "phenomenology of the twilight state of mind," remarked that while "the animal copes with its vital tasks in a seemingly rational way, [and] in pursuing its purposes it chooses the most adequate means available," which makes it seem rational, it is in fact "purely instinctive. The animal acts in a rudimentary twilight condition."[36] That is, "animals live true to type." They are not individuals (although that is the way Raffael depicts them). They have little choice but to "accept their environmental conditions"—the environment that Raffael represents in such loving, careful, absorbing detail. The animal is absorbed by the environment; it is nothing without it. It has no consciousness of itself—if it has any consciousness at all—apart from consciousness of its environment. In contrast, "Man is endowed with consciousness of both his self and the world . . . which permits him to penetrate the animal twilight imposed upon him" and transcend his environment. He acquires a history: only man has "historical development and cultural evolution," both of which

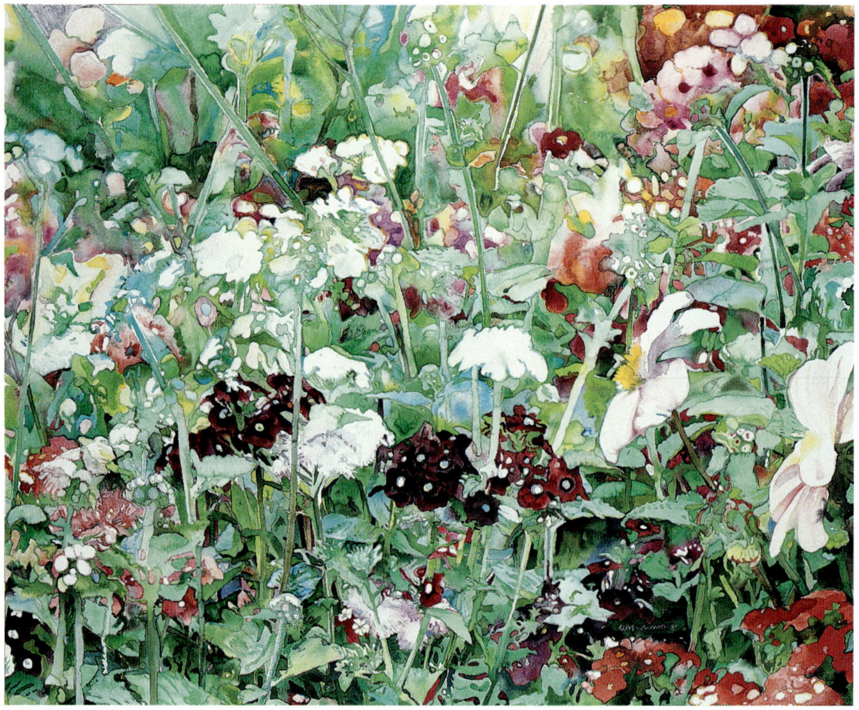

140. *Luxembourg Gardens: Faith,* 1981
Watercolor on paper, 42 x 52 in.
(106.6 x 132.1 cm)
Private collection, Pittsburgh

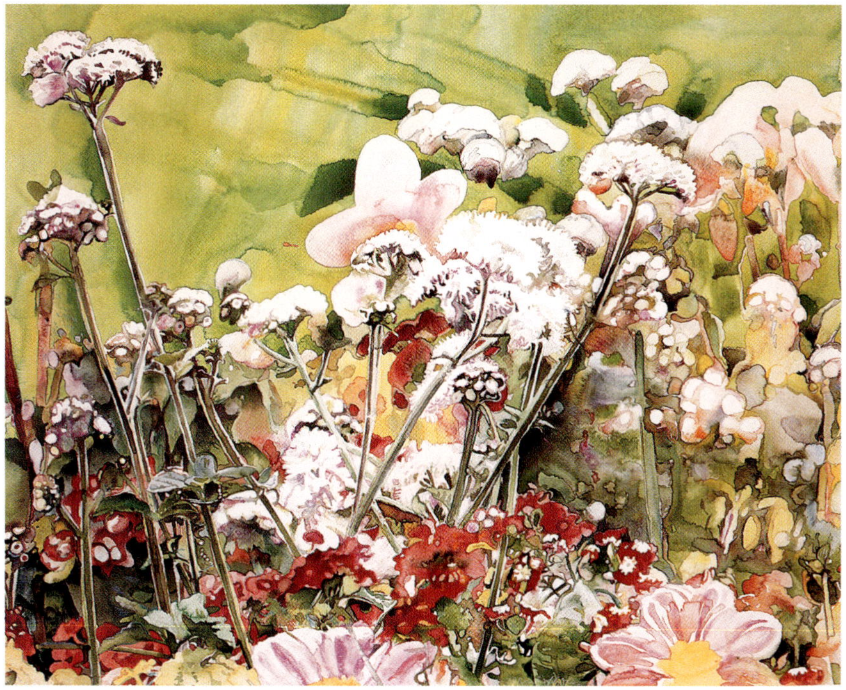

141. *Luxembourg Gardens: Truth,* 1982
Watercolor and pastel on paper,
44 x 53½ in. (111.7 x 135.8 cm)
Patricia S. Callan

are "completely strange to animals." He creates his own environment, rather than depending on the environment that nature supplies. To be in paradise is to be without history and in no need of history—to no longer develop and evolve, indeed, to have no need to develop and evolve. One is complete and perfect: the end of history is to return to the beginning of man, to return to paradise. But from Broch's point of view this is to return to the twilight state of mind, to give up consciousness, to lose one's humanity in nature—to become like an instinctive animal, or even worse, like a flower, with its vegetable instincts.

Why, then, do Raffael's animals—and flowers—seem to possess self-consciousness? If, as Broch says, the "twilight state makes men into mass," why do they not seem part of a mass? Even when Raffael's fish swim together they do not seem to belong to a mass. Each goes its own way, as is evident in *A Secret Path* (plate 142) and *Summers Pond* (plate 143). Similarly, Raffael's numerous Cranes from 1987 (for example, plate 62) act like self-conscious individuals. *Two Birds* (plate 144) makes the point succinctly: the two may look the same, but they are quite different and even have a different relationship to the environment. "Man," Broch writes, "when in twilight state of mind cannot discriminate natural from cultural conditions," but the radiant natural conditions that Raffael depicts look better than ordinary cultural conditions. Indeed, the garden environment is the best of all possible cultural conditions. Raffael's garden is a carefully tended cultural creation, as its calibrated beauty suggests. It is a psychosocial construction, a deliberate harmony between nature and art. Paradise, by definition, is a place from which suffering and death have been banished and where happiness prevails. Raffael creates an illusion that seems real; he suggests that it is possible to be a conscious, cultured individual and still live in paradise, that is, live instinctively—an apparent contradiction in terms.

The question is why Raffael troubles to create this illusion. Does he endow animals with human consciousness in the same way that, according to Meyer Schapiro, abstract works of art can be given more humanity than human beings ordinarily have—

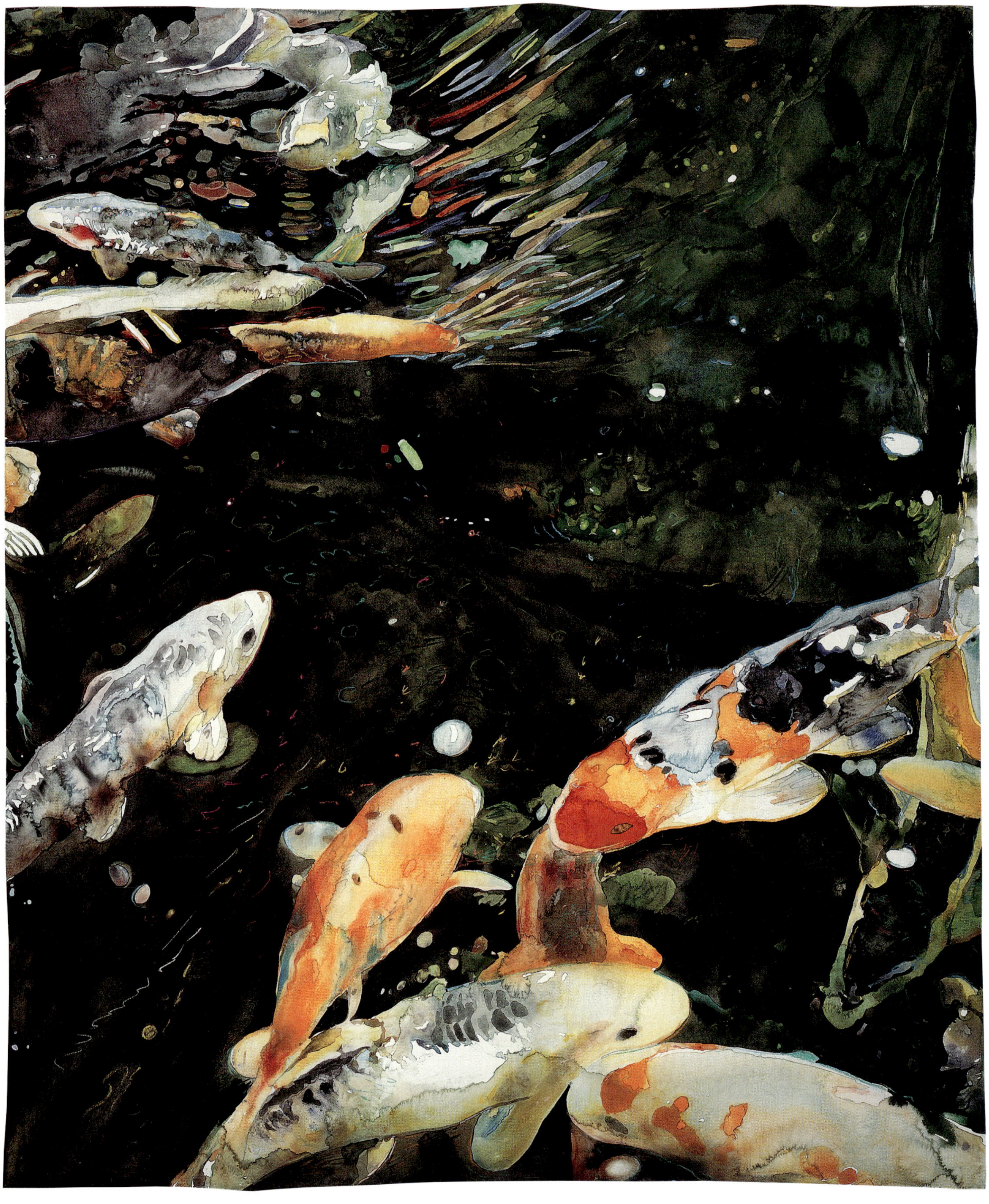

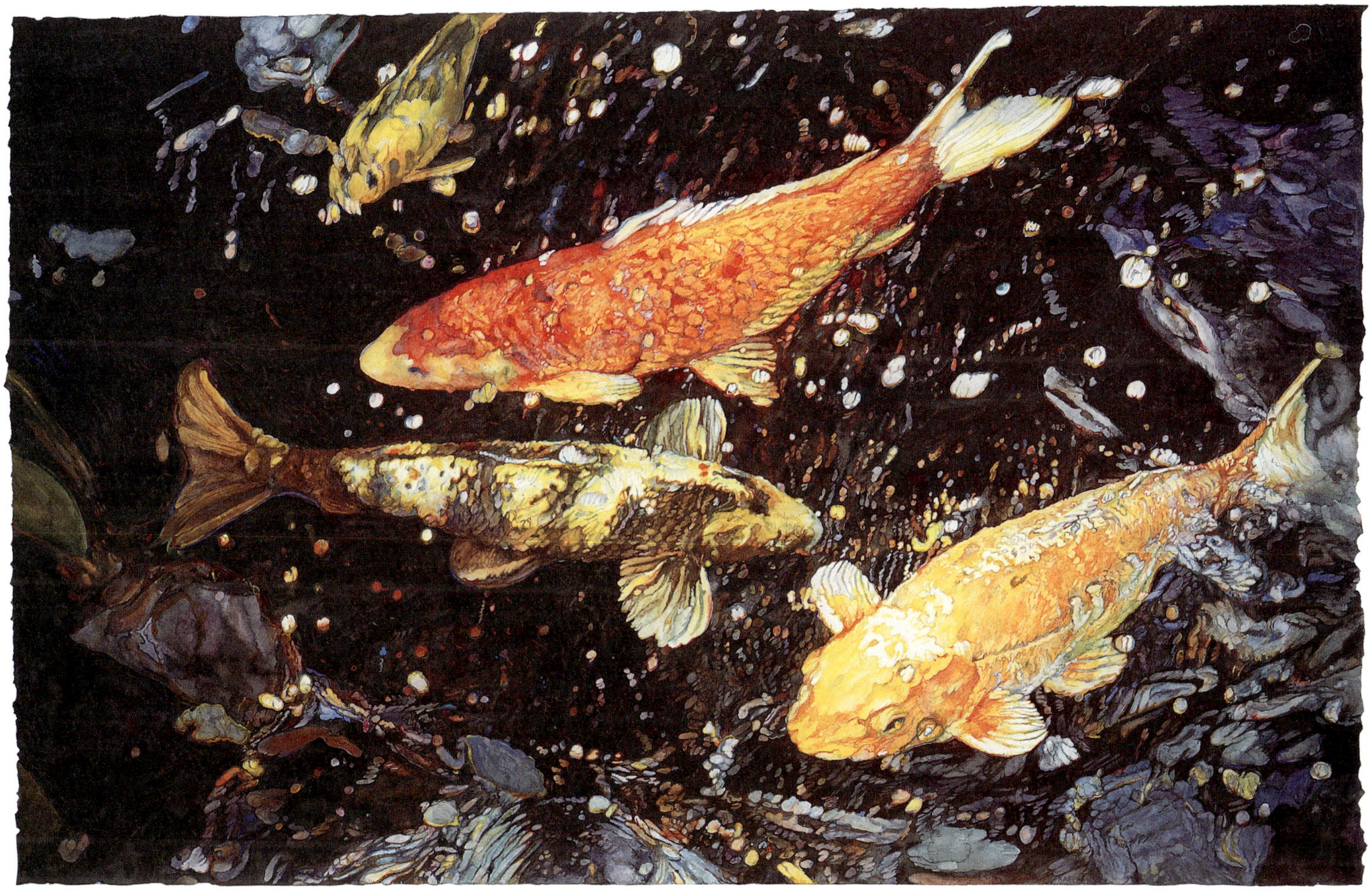

OPPOSITE

142. *A Secret Path,* 1981
Watercolor with pastel on paper,
53½ x 43¾ in. (135.8 x 111.1 cm)
Private collection

ABOVE

143. *Summers Pond,* 1994
Watercolor on paper, 44½ x 68¼ in.
(113 x 173.3 cm)
Commerce Bancshares, Inc.,
Kansas City, Missouri

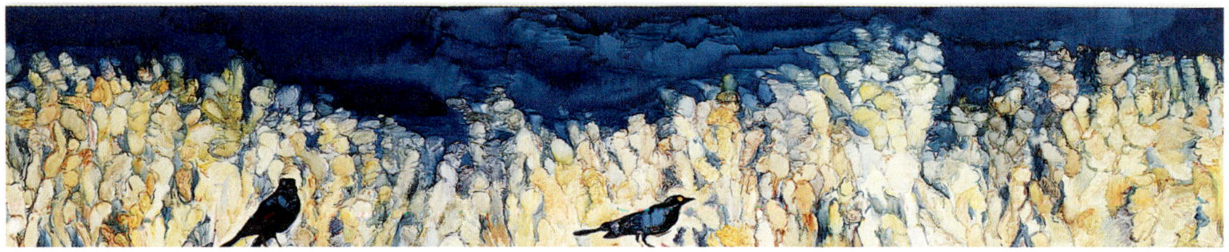

144. *Two Birds,* 1979
Oil on canvas, 20 x 100 in. (50.7 x 253.9 cm)
Wil and Sally Hergenrader

"full humanity"?[37] I think so. It is ultimately out of Raffael's need to keep alive an ideal that has never been realized. Virtue is displaced onto the animal because it rarely exists in history; civilization and humanity—man's compassion and consideration for man—are rare. One needs a garden these days—in every day and age—because one always needs compensation for the horrors of history (one's own history as well as that of society). Like Voltaire, Raffael vigorously tends his garden; it is a place where he can be healed—liberated from social history and free to work through his personal history. The garden is the best of all possible worlds, and Raffael intends to keep it that way.

Can he be criticized the way George Orwell criticized Henry Miller for using sexuality as a panacea for history?[38] Is Raffael's garden a new form of avant-garde polymorphous perversity, as its sensuality suggests?[39] I don't think so. Raffael makes no utopian claims for it. It is just his own private sanctuary—his own personal Cytherea—reclaimed from what Cytherea had become in modernity: "the barrenest of lands, a rocky desert," in effect a new Golgotha on which to be crucified, as Baudelaire suggested in "Un Voyage à Cythère." Again, we see Raffael's postmodernism. The suffering inherent to existence remains visible in Raffael, if one can follow the clues. It is an oblique hallucinatory presence in paradise, often diffused through the scene and emanating from nature itself, giving it a kind of dark edge. Thus Raffael's garden is an eloquently deceptive place.

In his own way, Raffael recognizes what Nicolas Poussin did: there is the threat of death in Arcadia. But in Raffael's case it is the threat of psychic death—not a twilight state of mind but an insidious passivity and sense of meaninglessness and valuelessness, a kind of subliminal depression, perhaps endemic to being human. This threat appears in *Sunset* (plate 145), however beautiful, and it sometimes darkens the water of the pond, as in some of the water lily and duck images. It is an atmosphere that casts a pall on the environment, even as it is inseparable from it. And yet the threat of psychic death (a state of feelinglessness epitomizing the experience of the helplessness and hopelessness that accompany consciousness of suffering) can be overcome by medita-

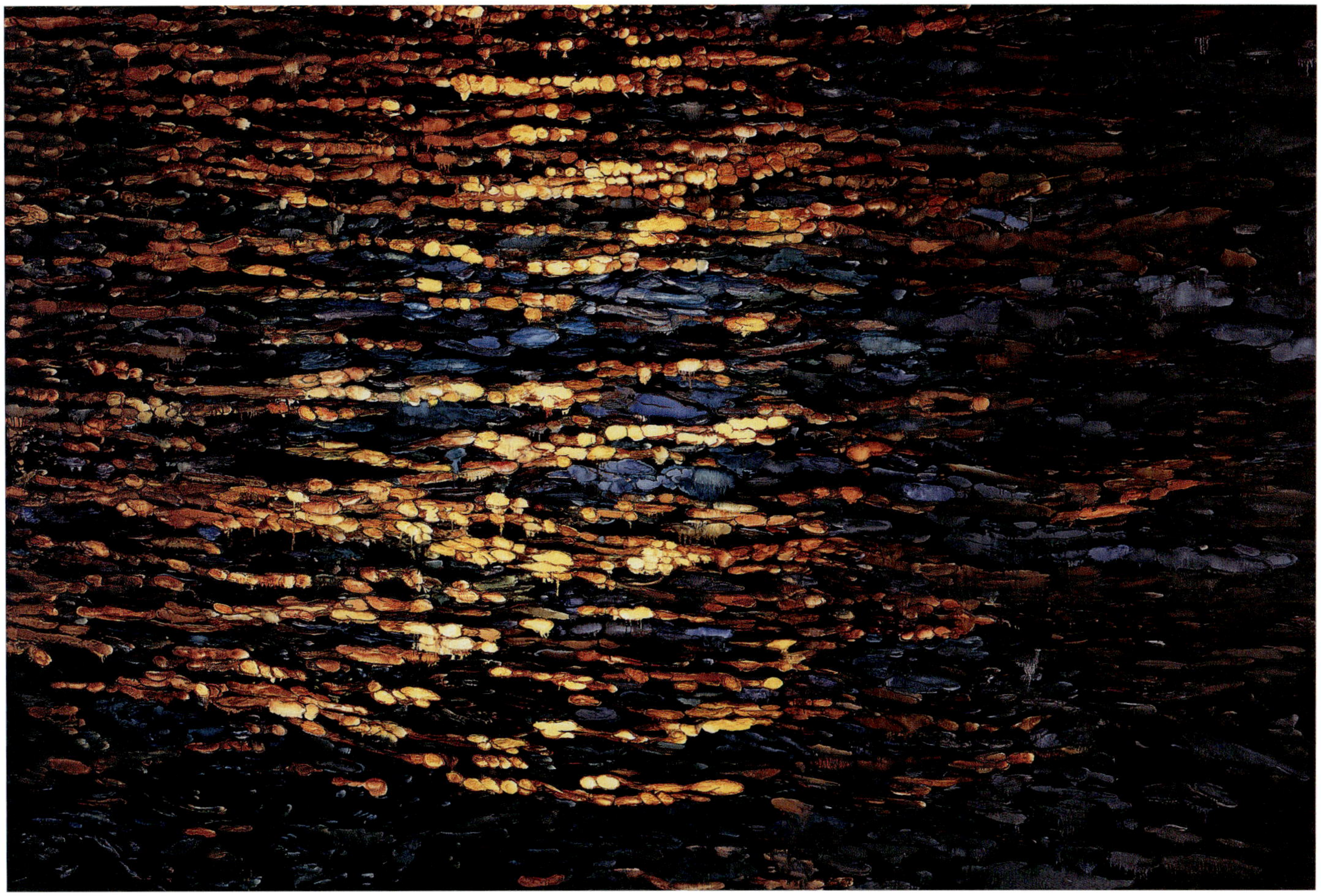

145. *Sunset,* 1977
Oil on canvas, 78 x 114 in.
(198.1 x 289.5 cm)
ARCO Corporate Art Collection,
Los Angeles

tion. There may be no remedy for suffering, but stoic meditation is rebirth after psychic death, or rather the experience of living through psychic death.

Raffael seems to be one of the twice-born people William James describes in *The Varieties of Religious Experience* (1902), and what seems like a transient, even momentary experience of nature in his pictures, and even an idolization of nature, is in emotional fact the record of a conversion experience—a spiritual passage—but one that involves a Buddhist rather than Christian sensibility.[40] Raffael's garden is a place of meditation, in which one learns to accept, with compassion, the inevitable. Hard meditative work is carried out in his garden, as his Buddhist imagery indicates. And the animals and flowers teach one how to meditate, with Zen equanimity but also recognition of the truth of being.

The Metaphysical Garden as Buddhist Monastery

> *"As on a heap of rubbish upon the highway the lily will grow full of sweet perfume and delight, thus among those who are mere rubbish the disciple of the truly enlightened Buddha shines forth by his knowledge above the blinded worldling."*
>
> The Dharmapada, chapter 4

For me, the major clue to the meaning of Raffael's garden is not the animals and flowers that are in it but the fact that it is a place of meditation, more particularly, Buddhist meditation—a monastic place of enlightenment. It has the two qualities of spiritual beauty that result from meditation: not only is there is no "painful clash," emotional or physical, in Raffael's garden, but there is perfect harmony, a synthesis of natural details that makes for a sense of peace, with no sacrifice of the aesthetic intensity afforded by the details.[41] In Raffael's Buddhist garden "the superficialities of sense-experience" become "a message from the Unseen."[42] Paradoxically, the visible animals and flowers, rendered in loving, exquisite detail, represent an invisible, seemingly unrepresentable yet healing truth.[43]

"Peace carries with it a surpassing of personality"; it involves "deep metaphysical insight," which brings with it "the removal of the stress of acquisitive feeling arising from the soul's preoccupation with itself."[44] Without such stress—without the acquisitive urge—the soul becomes tranquil and whole. This is exactly what Buddhism aims at: "a peace which the world can neither give nor take away"[45] because it comes from metaphysical insight into existence, radically changing one's attitude to it. Buddhism has "two major values": "the idea of personal discipline to gain freedom from craving in the ultimate tranquillity of Nirvana" and "the idea of unselfish devotion to the good of others for the sake of their deliverance from ill."[46]

For Raffael, painting is a form of personal discipline. It is a display of metaphysical insight. And it is compassionate: it is a free gift of enlightenment, the fruit of his meditation on nature, lovingly presented to the world. Each painting induces meditation: not passive contemplation, but active meditation. The viewer works through its details to understand the truth they represent. In the process he gains insight into the metaphysics of his desire. Meditating on a Raffael painting, one is liberated from desire: from, as the Buddha said, not only "sensual desire" for nature but also "the desire for existence."[47] One learns to let life be—to acknowledge its *ch'i,* or vital force, which "surrounds [existence] as water surrounds a fish"[48]—which concentrates the mind marvelously. Meditation is a way of concentrating one's mind so that one can let life be. Only by doing so can one gain insight into its being: "see" the metaphysical in its physicality.

Who is the Buddha for Raffael? I think the Buddha personifies the good, helpful father the way animals do—"father" in Jung's sense of the being who offers "insight, understanding, good advice, determination, planning" that one cannot muster "on one's own resources"[49] and thus functions as a god (or ego ideal, always out of reach yet profoundly influential on one's existence). As Freud wrote, the totem animal is "the first form of father-surrogate, the god . . . a later one, in which the father has regained his human shape."[50] The Buddha is the totem animal that has taken human shape but remains sacred because of his wisdom—the wisdom (like that of the animal) of another order of being and thus a wisdom that man cannot muster but can receive only in an intuitive flash. Thus the Buddha parallels the divine flowers that personify the good mother. Male Buddha and female flower become one, and each transforms the other; the Buddha seems as physical as the flowers, the flowers as metaphysical as the Buddha. "Making art is . . . very religious," Raffael has said, in that it is an attempt to "have insights into the universal,"[51] which is to apprehend the particular without aggrandizing it.

A stone statue of the Buddha's head, its hardness softened by light, appears in a 1985 work (plate 94), as does a more nuanced close-up of another stone statue of the Buddha's face in *Le Crepuscule* (plate 98). In *Gateway* (plate 99), the golden Buddha—the Buddha clothed in his aura, an expression of his enlightenment—appears, his "body . . . marked with many sacred and esoteric symbols, radiating the golden light of Wisdom and Enlightenment," as Joyce Petschek said.[52] But, as she observed, Raffael painted only "part of the Buddha's body, that of the lower four chakras, the energy centers pertaining to the physical, emotional, and intellectual vibrations. He paints neither the clairvoyant Third Eye nor the mystical Crown chakra."[53] And yet the Buddha looks at nature with the Third Eye—the eye traditionally in the middle of the Buddha's forehead, representing his metaphysical insight about nature, which Raffael would also like to have. It is within him, signifying his Buddha nature, his achievement of enlightenment. Moreover, *Red Lily in a Buddhist Monastery* (plate 146) and *Two White Lilies in a Buddhist Monastery on an Island in the South China Sea* (plate 147) are, in effect, mystical crowns. Meditation reveals their aura; indeed, the lilies are on the verge of becoming almost all aura. (Traditionally, the Buddha is often represented with a flower, especially a lily, which partially explains Raffael's particular fascination with lilies.) In a sense, Raffael's paintings can be understood as an attempt to make manifest the luminous aura that is latent in natural phenomena. Religiously painted by Raffael, a flower becomes a transcendental icon, the radiant object of transcendental meditation.

In general, for Raffael representation is an act of sanctification and meditation. In a sense, these are the sum and substance of numinous wonder at its most innocent or childlike. For children, ordinary things have an iconic presence. They stand out with sacramental significance. For example, *Blackfoot* (plate 97) and *Ganesh* (plate 95; the Indian god of the threshold) are iconic presences—to my mind they are explicitly "godfathers"—but so is *Mallard* (plate 68), *Orange Fish* (plate 80), *Spirit Bird* (plate 148), the moth of *Re-Entry* (plate 152), and *Le Papillon vert* (plate 149). Every last flower is an iconic presence, an empirical phenomenon spiritualized by meditation; or rather, Raffael's meditative Third Eye brings out the flower's inherent spiritual qualities.

Meditation turns an empirical phenomenon into a numinous presence; it transforms the sensuous into the sacred, or acknowledges that there is no difference between them. This is primary enlightenment—metaphysical insight at its deepest; it is very much in the spirit of the Buddhist sutra that denies the difference between noneternity and eternity, the finite and the infinite.[54] "Everything is relative," states the sutra, which means that empirical "plurality" and ultimate "reality" are not separate. In Raffael's case, this means that there is no difference between painting the plurality of beings and sensations and meditating upon them. If, as the sutra suggests, Buddhism dissolves philosophical antinomies, then Raffael's paintings dissolve perceptual antinomies.

From my point of view, the most Buddhist of Raffael's paintings are his four Japanese paintings: *Haven* (plate 101), *Threshold* (plate 102), *Marriage* (plate 103), and *Passage* (plate 150). The struggle for enlightenment—the attempt to turn an observed phenomenon into a sacred icon—seems evident in them (in the animal and flower paintings, enlightenment has been achieved, as their overtly iconic character suggests). The frame within the frame of *Marriage* and *Threshold* and the divided character of *Passage* and *Haven* suggest a divided consciousness: what is seen is partly of this world and partly "otherworldly." Raffael's subjects exist on a spiritual threshold; they are observed for their details as well as meditated on and appreciated as a spiritual whole. Sight is on the verge of becoming metaphysical insight, but it is still profoundly physical.

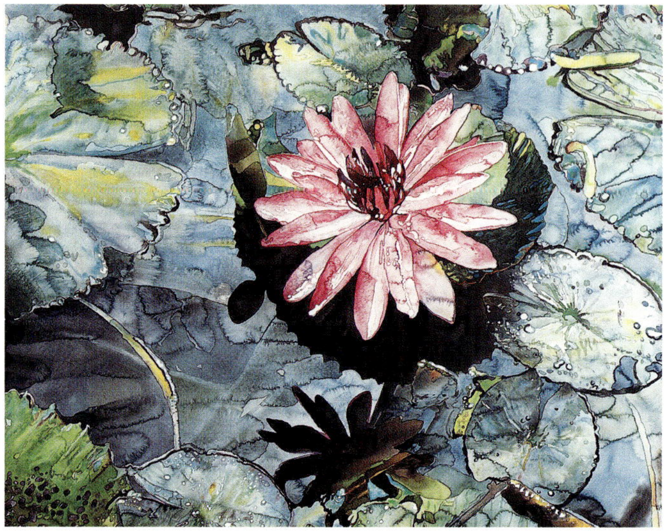

ABOVE
146. *Red Lily in a Buddhist Monastery,* 1979
Watercolor with rainwater on paper,
42 x 52 in. (106.6 x 132 cm)
The Capital Group Companies, Inc.,
Los Angeles

OPPOSITE
147. *Two White Lilies in a Buddhist Monastery on an Island in the South China Sea,* 1979
Watercolor with rainwater on paper,
53 x 44 in. (134.6 x 111.7 cm)
Phyllis and Barton J. Cohen,
Kansas City, Missouri

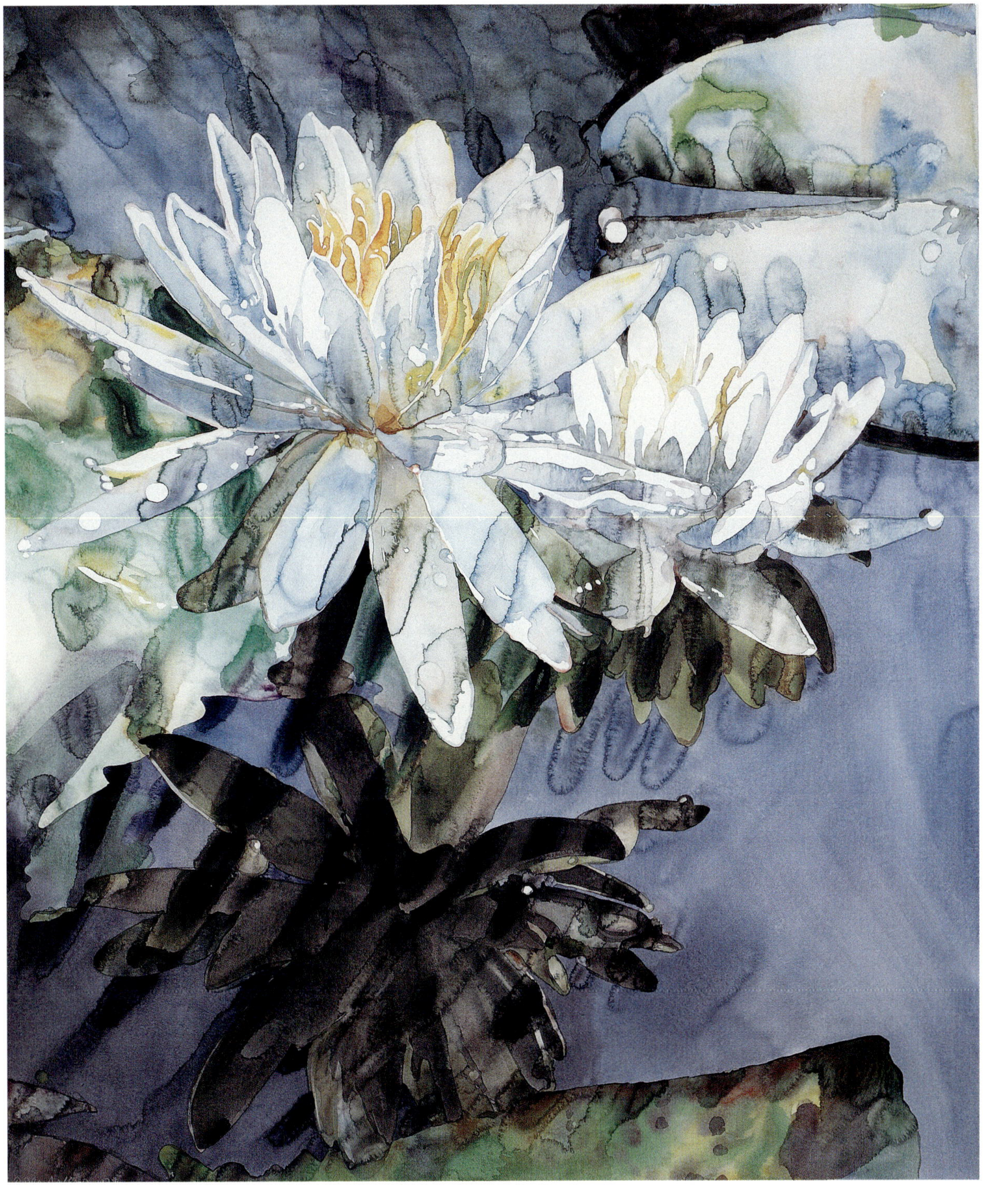

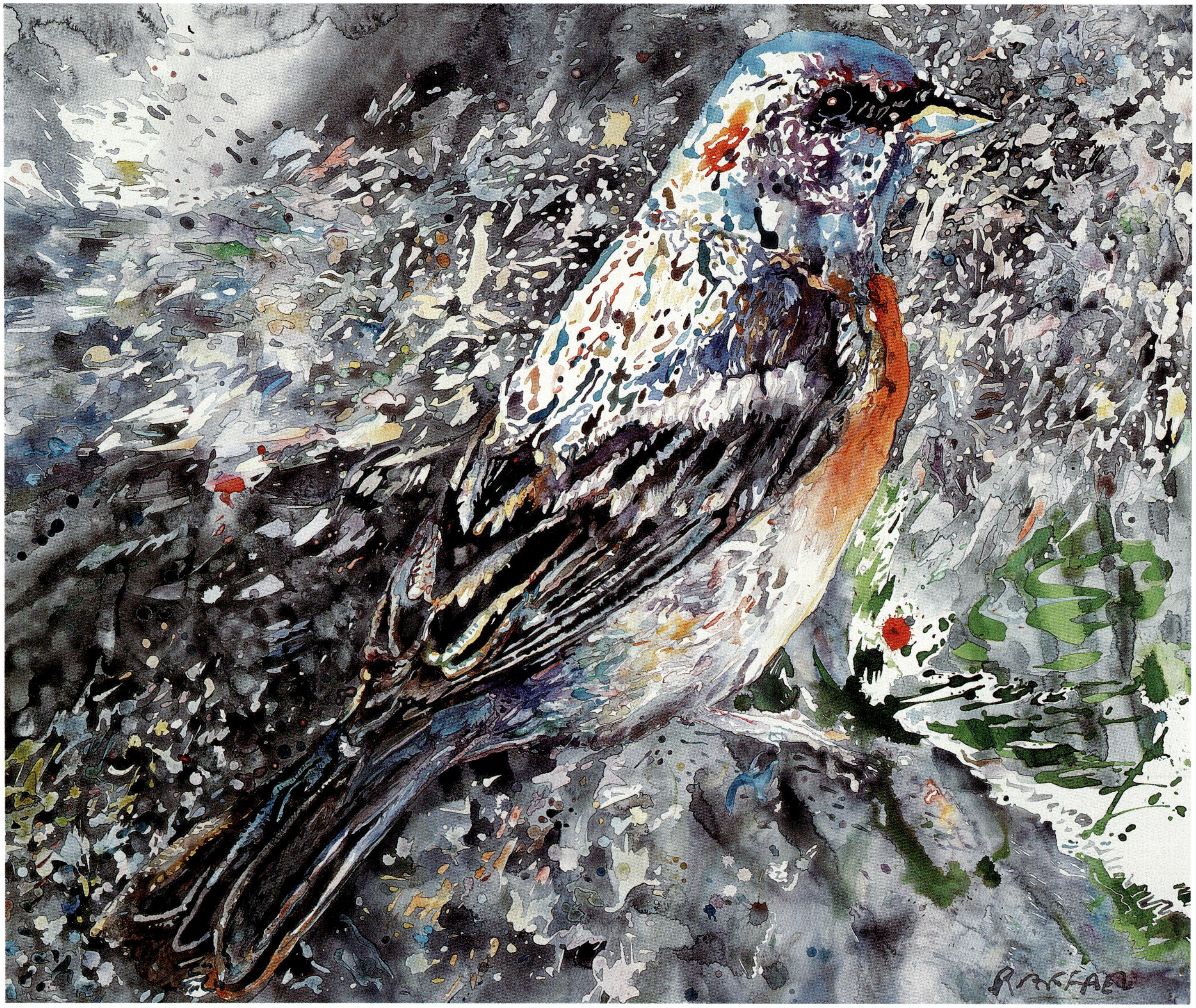

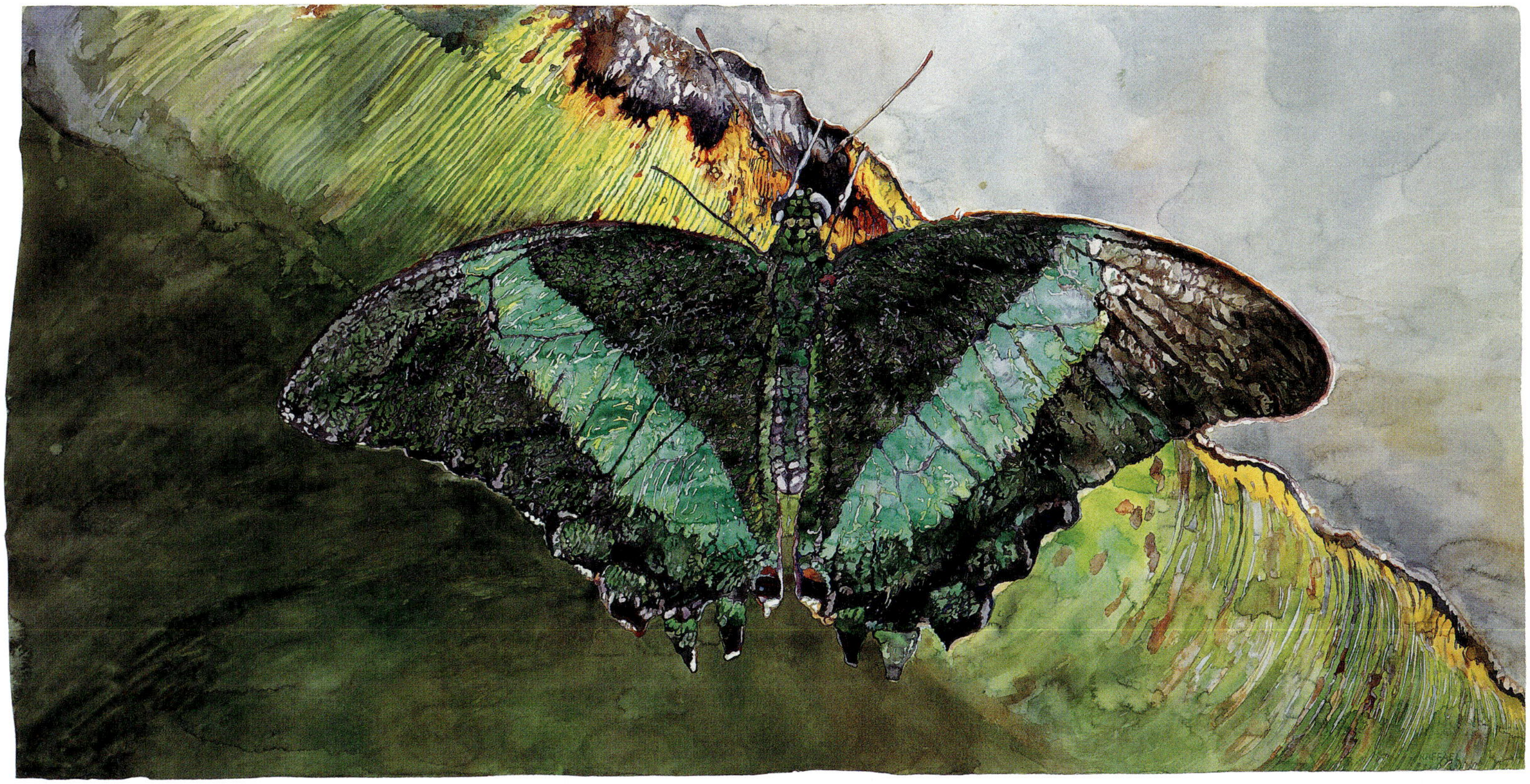

OPPOSITE
148. *Spirit Bird,* 1985
Watercolor on paper, 42 x 50 in.
(106.7 x 127 cm)
Dr. Charles W. Nichols, Philadelphia

ABOVE
149. *Le Papillon vert,* 1992
Watercolor on paper, 44½ x 65½ in.
(113 x 166.3 cm)
Courtesy of Nancy Hoffman Gallery, New York

These paintings have a very complicated personal import. Following the death of his son Matthew in 1980, Raffael became more profoundly spiritual. He had what could be understood, in William James's sense, as a conversion experience—a shift from a mundane to a religious outlook, from perception in a state of psychic death to the vital perception of pure interiority. The Japanese paintings document this shift. *Haven* and *Threshold* represent Raffael's discovery of the garden as a space of monastic consciousness, a spiritual *hortus conclusus.* But it is the wall that is focused on, not the interior space of the garden, suggesting that Raffael is still aware of the outside—still attached to it. The wall is almost dissolved by nature in *Threshold,* but it still remains a disruptive presence. There is an unexpected irony in these works, for Japan is the country where the integration of nature and society has traditionally been a high art.

The figure in *Passage* is a godfather, but a strange, even weird one, from an alien culture. *Marriage* seems to me the most crucial of the works, because of its blackness. Garver says "black is almost never used" by Raffael,[55] but here it dominates the picture,

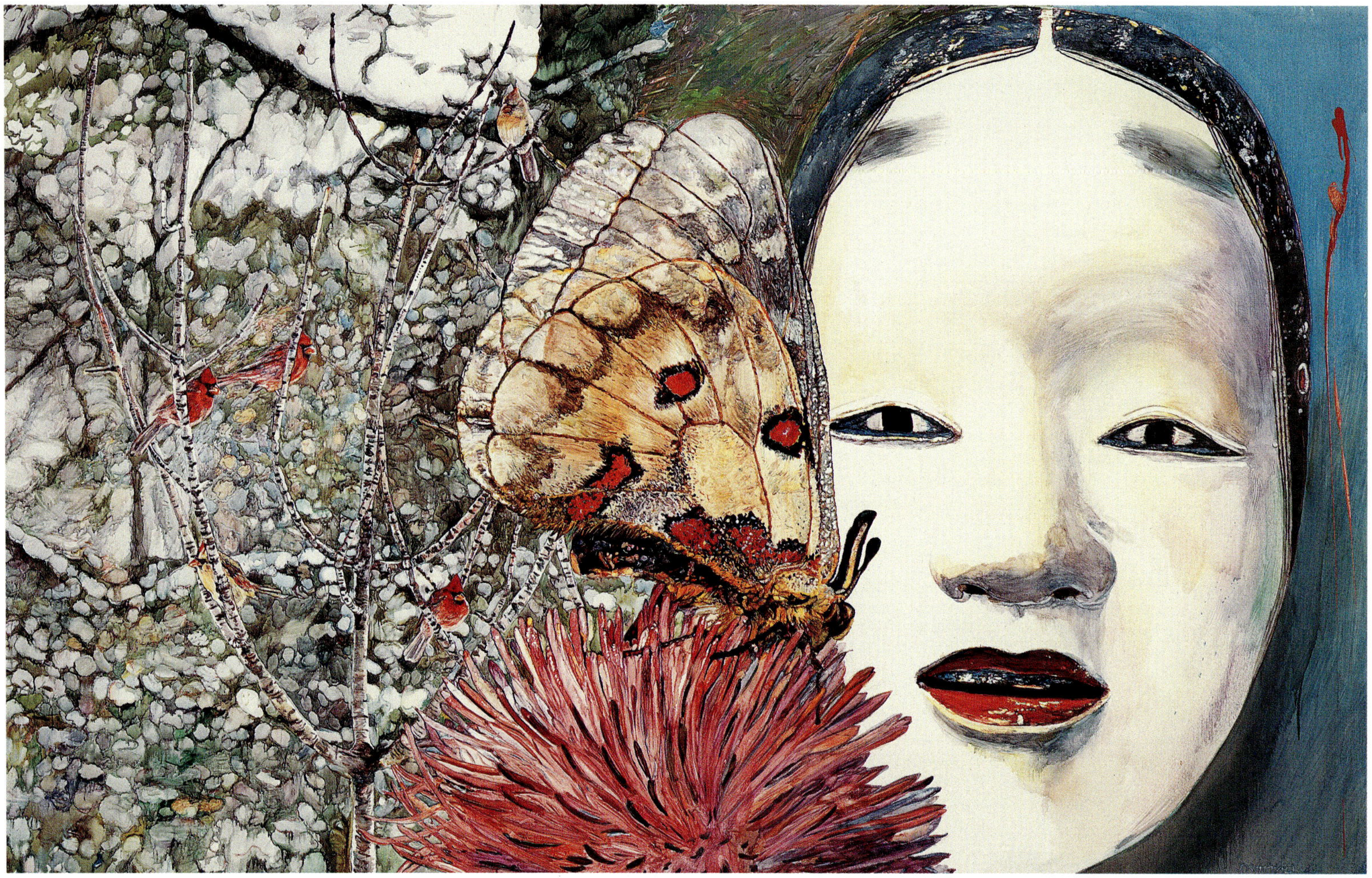

giving substance to the trees and their reflection in the sky blue water, as well as to the lower part of the temple. The issue of the painting is whether the surrounding nature colors of the interior frame and the Danube school–like flickers of snowy light on the trees (there is an unexpected resemblance to Lucas Cranach's images of trees) can counterbalance and finally subsume the temple. No doubt the interior frame, like the garden wall in *Haven* and *Threshold,* can be the "edge where two forms meet in union," as Raffael says, but in the Japanese paintings forms are clearly opposed. The "border" marks the place where the forms conflict. Can contraries—including the contraries of structure and process—be married, if only in occult symmetry? Can nature absorb the alluring yet alien and mysterious temple? The answer is elusive.

150. *Passage,* 1985
Oil on canvas, 63 x 99 in.
(160 x 251.4 cm)
Private collection

BELOW, TOP
151. *Return Again,* 1985
Oil on canvas, 66 x 84 in.
(167.6 x 213.3 cm)
Mr. and Mrs. S. Lawrence Schlager,
Chestnut Hill, Massachusetts

BELOW, BOTTOM
152. *Re-Entry (Moth),* 1985
Watercolor on paper, 31½ x 69½ in.
(80 x 176.5 cm)
Honey and Norman Kurtz,
Scarsdale, New York

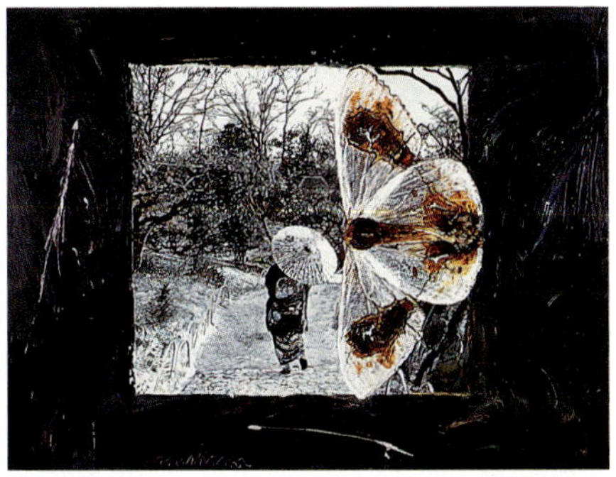

Return Again (plate 151) has the same blackness, even more dense and omnipresent. It now forms the frame and dominates the image within it—the black-and-white picture of Japan in memory's eye, which is not yet the Third Eye. Physical detail is blurred and "off" in memory, in contrast to the clear detail of the vulnerable moth, who vividly exists in the present. The moth looks as if it is bleeding from wounds to its wings; the same moth, looking embalmed, fills the canvas of *Re-Entry*. Psychic death has the upper hand; rebirth is not in the offing. The moth will fly into the light and die; it does not dance in light the way Raffael's many butterflies do.

These are especially intense paintings: light and dark are at odds, with the outcome of their gnostic struggle unclear. I think this is also the case in *Out of the Thicket* (plate 54) and *The Clearing* (plate 55), both 1985, and in other works from this period, including *Listening to Evening* (plate 153), *Spirit (Owl)* (plate 67), and *Eternity* (plate 154). This was the period of Raffael's divorce from his first wife, Judy Davis, and his marriage to his second wife, Lannis. Lannis became the symbol of his rebirth and enlightenment—the triumph of the light over the dark in him, the miraculous transformation of the shadow of the valley of psychic death into a sign of radiant happiness, as in *Two Vases, Two Bouquets, Spring* (plate 155). In effect an allegory of their marriage, it shows that the promise implicit in *Marriage* (plate 103)—painted in 1986, the year Raffael married Lannis and moved to France—has been fulfilled. The darkness in

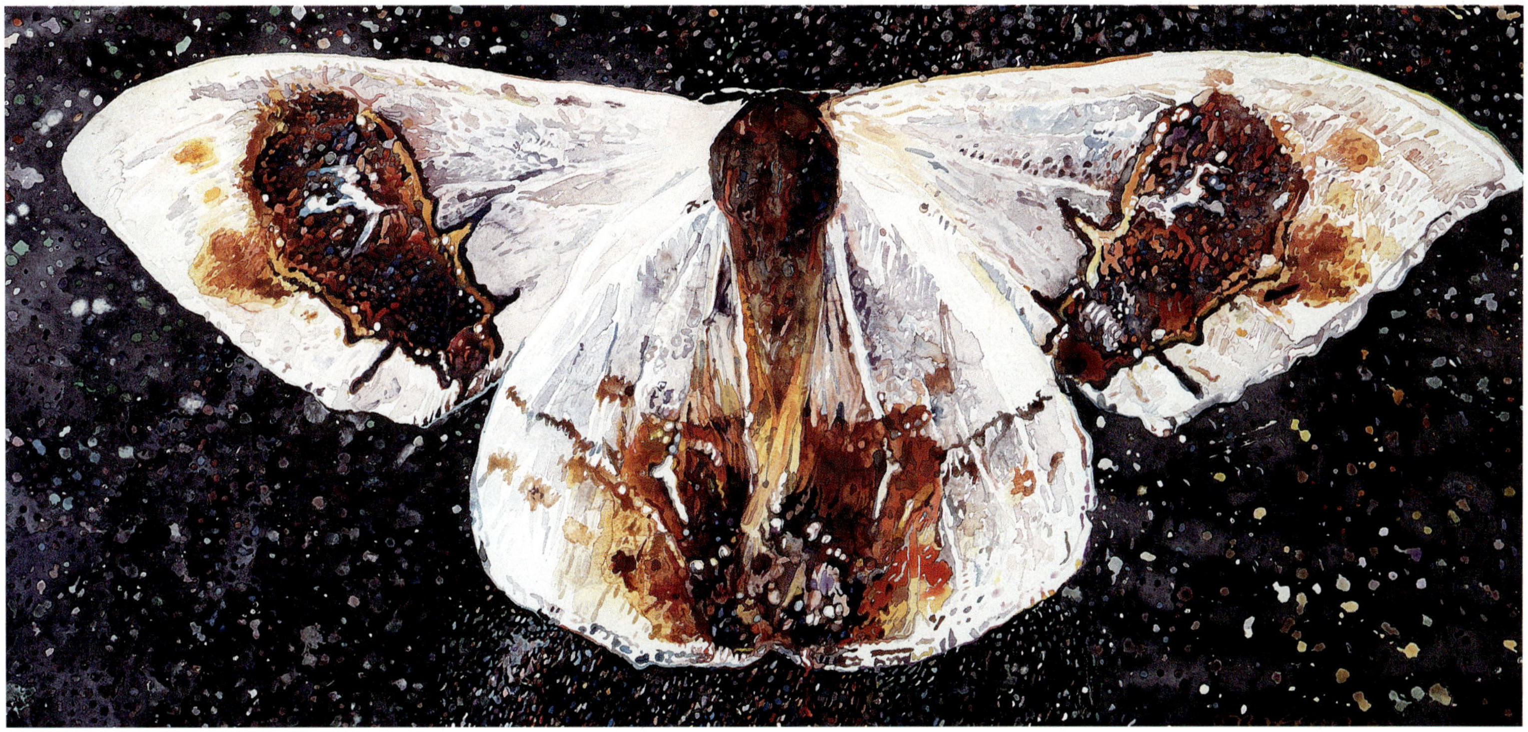

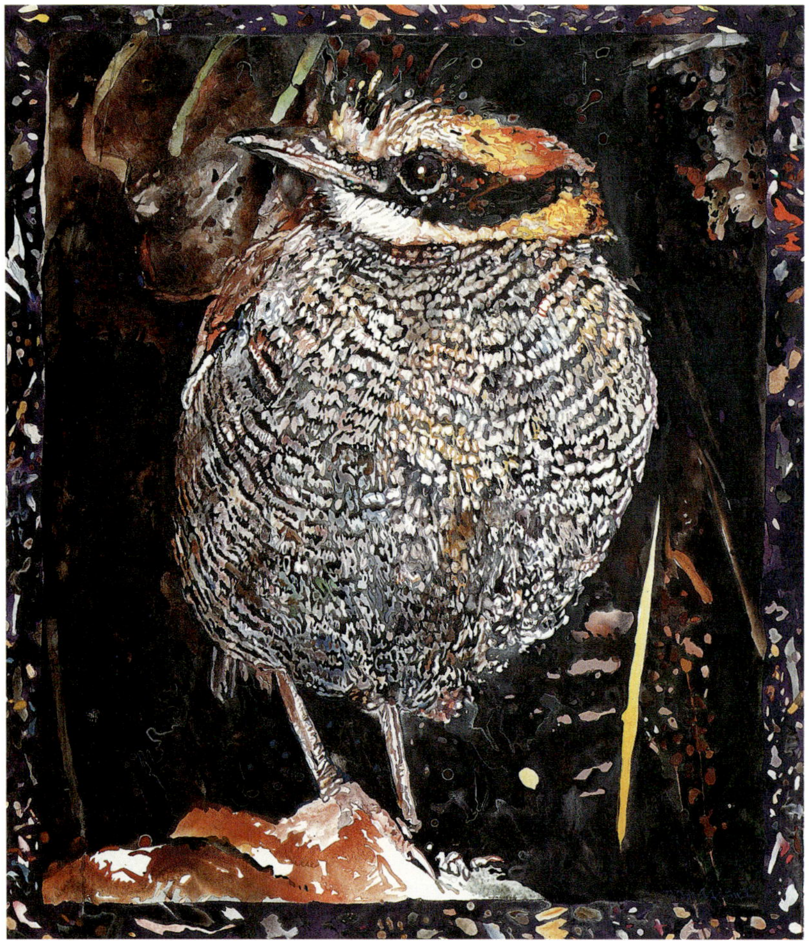

the center of *Marriage* represents Raffael, the colorful brightness that forms the margin symbolizes Lannis. The painting is a question mark: can the margin penetrate the center, lifting its spirit?

The answer is already anticipated in *Ancient Longing* (plate 107), which shows Lannis as Botticelli's Primavera, her colorful brightness at the center of the picture, the blackness relegated to the margin, just as in *Two Vases, Two Bouquets, Spring* it becomes the background. Psychic death, indicative of a profound experience of destructiveness and the sense of nothingness that follows it, does not have to be central to life, however much it must be acknowledged and respected. For only by passing through it can one

153. *Listening to Evening,* 1984
Watercolor on paper, 50⅝ x 42⅝ in.
(128.5 x 108.2 cm)
James and Sharon Hildebrand,
Dublin, Ohio

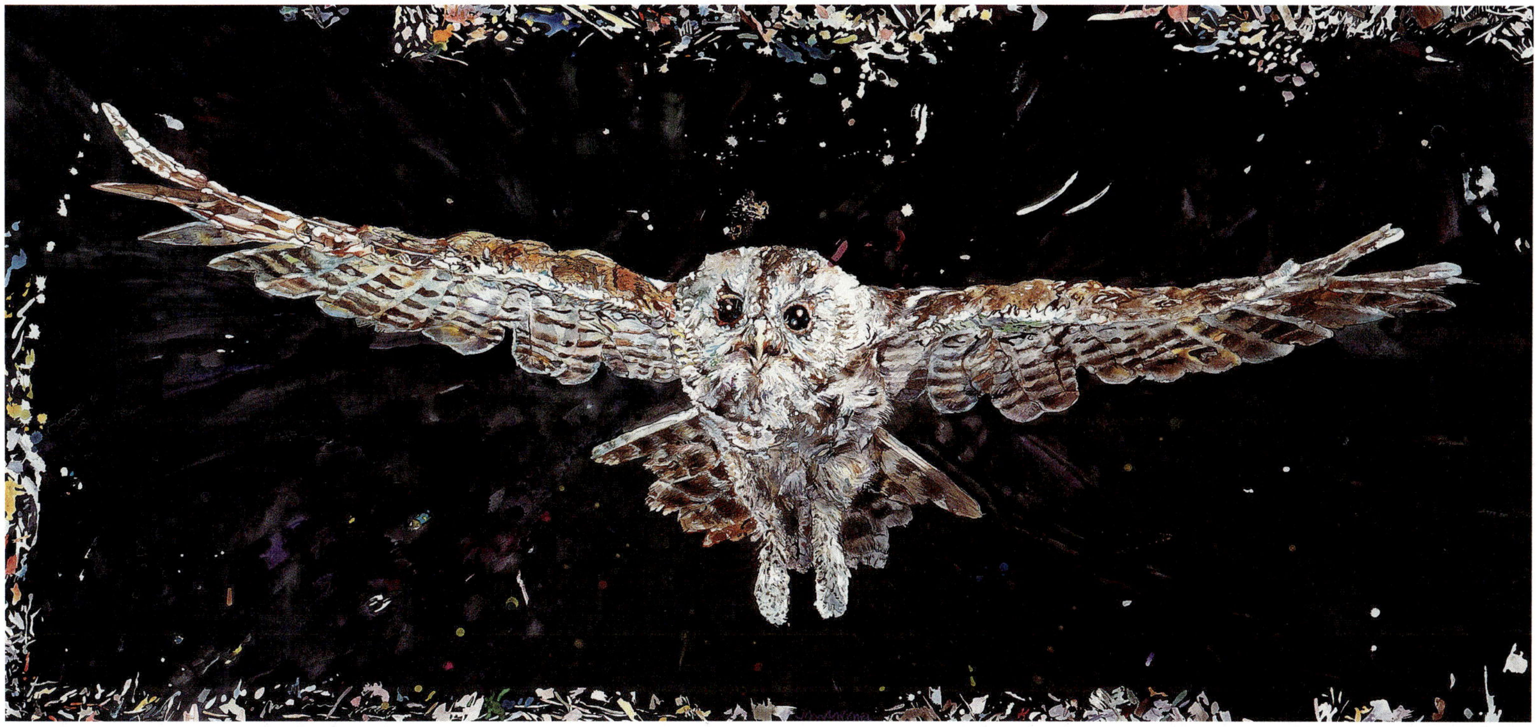

154. *Eternity,* 1985
Watercolor on paper, 42½ x 89½ in.
(107.9 x 227.3 cm)
Hunter Museum of American Art,
Chattanooga, Tennessee;
Museum purchase with funds
provided by the Benwood Foundation
and the 1985 Collectors' Group

reach paradise. The moment of passage (see plate 150) is crucial for Raffael, for it is the climax of the conversion experience, the change in basic state of being. Again and again he suggests this passage or secret path (see plate 142) from psychic death to spiritual life and physical renewal, as in his 1992–93 paintings of flowers after the rain (a begonia, an iris, a peony, and a canna leaf).

Raffael's paintings of Lannis are a tribute not only to woman's power of resurrection and renewal, which becomes man's own, but also to art's power to regulate our perception of the world, making it seem better and safer than it is. Raffael portrays Lannis as a garden unto herself as well as an integral part of his private garden.[56] In a psychopathic age such as ours—an age of emotional regression, as Broch says, for all its scientific and technological progress—true love and a garden of one's own are all the more necessary. Most of all, Lannis is inseparable from the garden. This is evident in his 1988 series Lannis in Sieste, perhaps his most astonishing pictures, in that the human figure and nature are seamlessly integrated for the first time in Raffael's art.

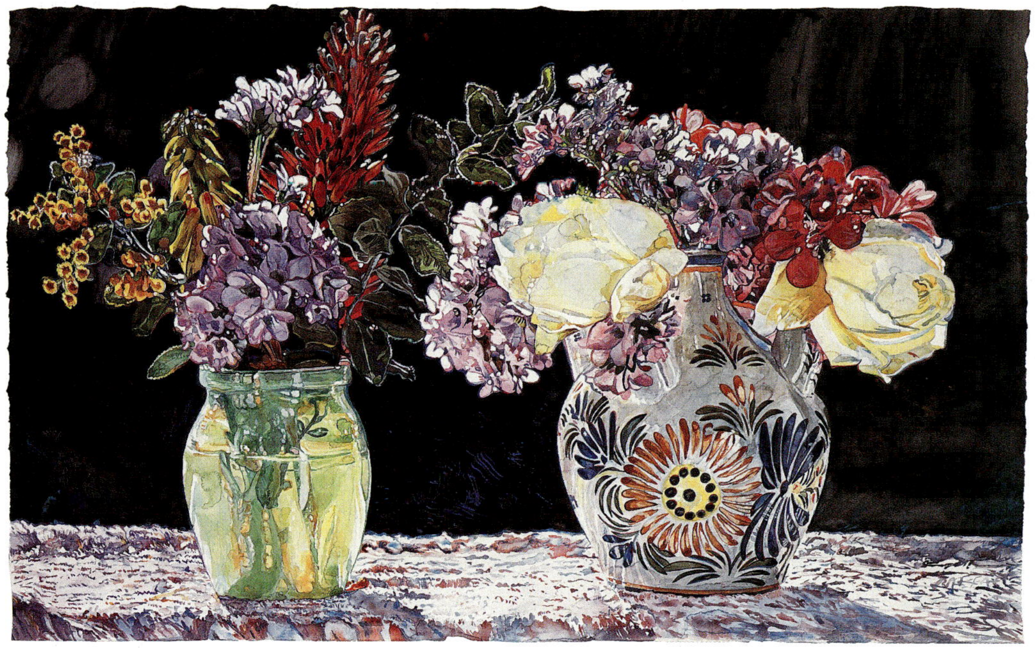

155. *Two Vases, Two Bouquets, Spring,* 1990
Watercolor on paper, 42½ x 67⅛ in.
(107.9 x 170.4 cm)
Mr. and Mrs. Brad Grey, Los Angeles

The decorative richness of these works—which recalls, as though in a distant, refined echo, the decorative wallpaper of Raffael's childhood home, whose "interweaving patterns," as he said, were "his first experience with 'art'"[57]—is the vehicle for this unity. Lannis becomes the personification of nature—a natural phenomenon as well as a human phenomenon. More particularly, she embodies nature in spring, when it renews, and nature in summer, when it is at its ripest. She is nature when it comes to life again after winter death—nature as it appears in the middle of *Marriage*—and nature when it is most flourishing and alive. Her double meaning is particularly clear in *Lannis' Garden with Butterfly* (plate 157). She is implicitly the butterfly, a traditional symbol of renewal, but also the blooming flowers and green leaves. For Raffael, everything connected with Lannis implies the unity of inner and outer worlds and conveys the everlasting life of nature. In fact, Raffael never shows nature in decay, its flowers wilting, its leaves worm-eaten, as Caravaggio, with his attraction to the death instinct, did. Even the flowers of Raffael's *Autumn Bouquet* (plate 41) are intact and alive, as though there is no tomorrow of death. Like the heron in *Heron's Vision* (plate 66), Raffael is constantly astonished by Lannis, more than he is by spring itself—I am

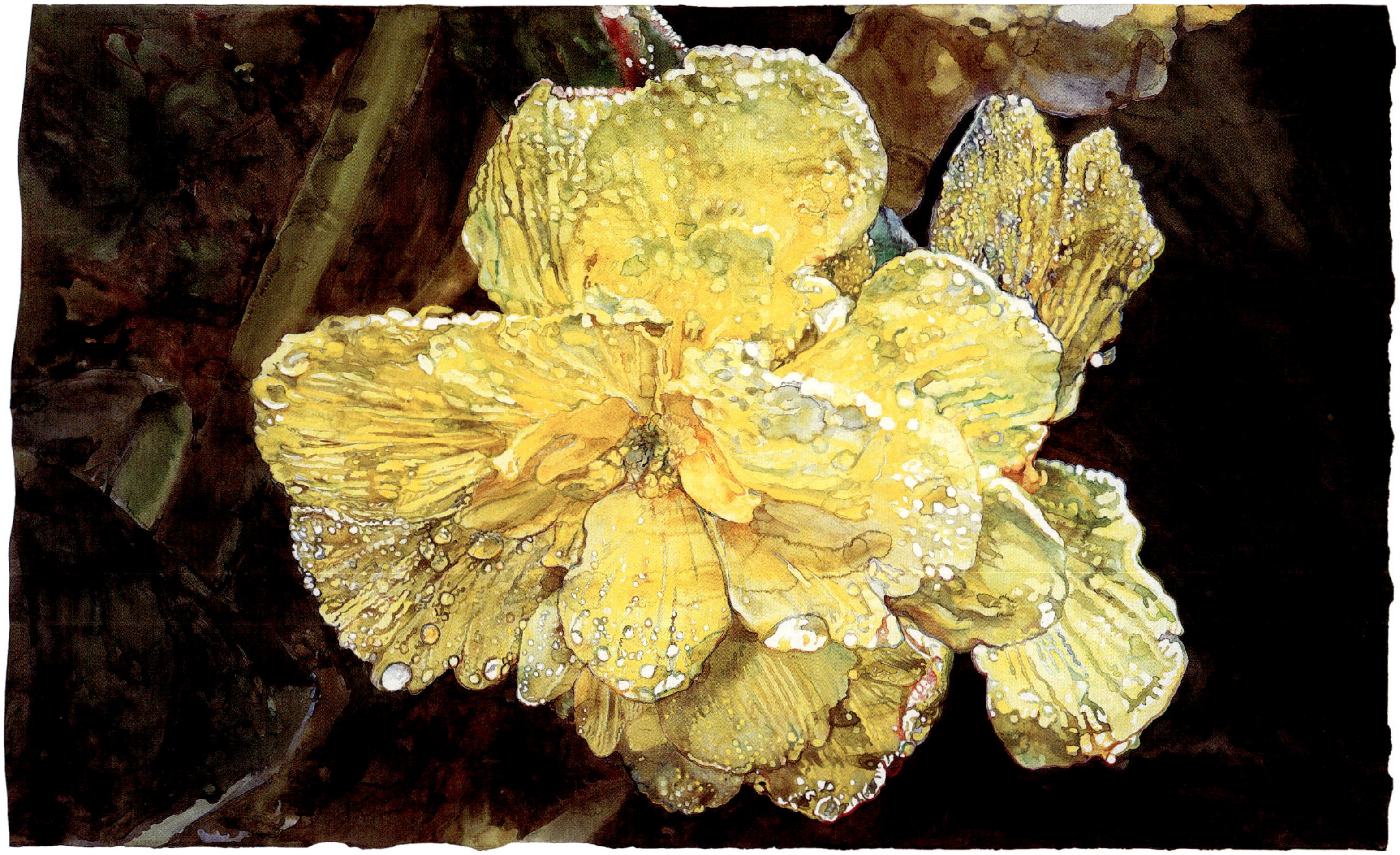

156. *Begonia after the Rain,* 1992
Watercolor on paper, 44½ x 72 in.
(113 x 182.8 cm)
The Capital Group Companies, Inc.,
Los Angeles

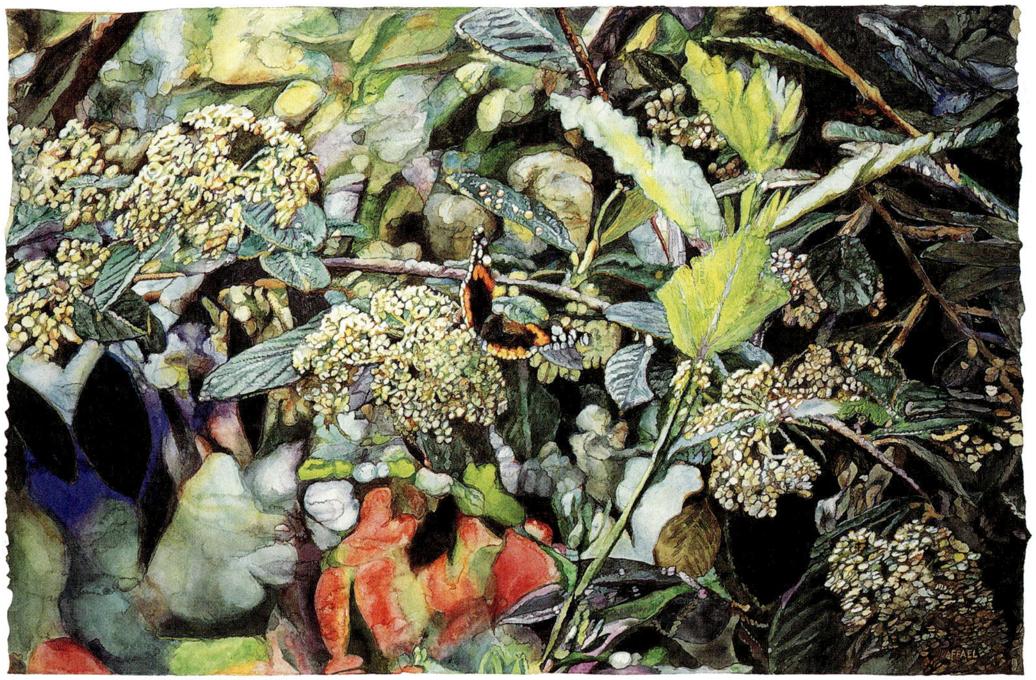

thinking of *Spring: Amazement* (plate 132)—an astonishment that suggests the depth and intensity of his devotion to her. Like the cat in *Fumé Watching the Flowers* (plate 139), Raffael watches her asleep, as in the Lannis in Sieste series. For him, she is being at its most vital and sublime made unapologetically manifest.

157. *Lannis' Garden with Butterfly,* 1994
Watercolor on paper, 44¼ x 67½ in.
(112.3 x 171.4 cm)
Joseph and Lannis Raffael,
Cap d'Antibes, France

NOTES

Epigraph: Wallace Stevens, *The Necessary Angel: Essays on Reality and the Imagination* (New York: Knopf, 1951), pp. 170–71. Thomas H. Garver notes that "perhaps the most important non-art experience of [Raffael's] Yale years was the discovery of poetry, an art of metaphor in another medium, and he felt particularly close to the poems of Wallace Stevens." In a letter to Garver, Raffael quoted from Stevens's "Man with the Blue Guitar" (section 32), declaring that his words "have filled me with their meaning. . . . They've been really helpful to me and my work." The stanza begins: "Throw away the lights, the definitions, / And say of what you see in the dark." It climaxes in the assertion: "Nothing must stand / Between you and the shapes you take / When the crust of shape has been destroyed." (Garver, "The California Years," in *Joseph Raffael: The California Years, 1969–1978* [San Francisco: San Francisco Museum of Modern Art, 1978], p. 12.)

These words, descriptive of the creative process, are Raffael's credo. In creativity the object takes on the shape of the self, and vice versa, in a kind of symbiotic intimacy. Painting and poetry are one and the same for Raffael and Stevens, whatever the difference in medium. As Stevens said, they "move in the same direction." (Holly Stevens, ed., *The Letters of Wallace Stevens* [New York: Knopf, 1966], p. 593.) In other words, Raffael is what Charles Baudelaire called a "painter-poet," "one of the rare elect"—an "imaginative" rather than "positivist" artist. (Charles Baudelaire, "The Salon of 1859," *The Mirror of Art,* ed. Jonathan Mayne [Garden City, N.Y.: Doubleday Anchor Books, 1956], pp. 246, 242.) Raffael's garden imagery is incomprehensible without comprehension of its painterly poetics.

1. Sigmund Freud, "Negation" (1925), in *The Standard Edition of the Complete Psychological Works* (London: Hogarth Press and the Institute of Psycho-Analysis, 1961), vol. 19, p. 239.
2. T. W. Adorno (*Aesthetic Theory* [London: Routledge and Kegan Paul, 1984], p. 311) writes: "Nature poetry is passé not only because it is losing its subject matter, but also because its truth content is vanishing. This helps explain the inorganic character of the poetry. . . . Art's ability to incorporate undespoiled nature—perhaps it never existed—has been lost." Raffael's nature poetry refutes Adorno, suggesting that images of "despoiled nature"—the "dead anorganic matter" of the industrial and postindustrial world (p. 312)—are not inevitable. The whole tenor of Raffael's garden imagery is to conquer the myth of vanishing nature—the modern pessimism that amounts to a decree that nature must vanish. He does not naively regress to the older myth of spiritual nature but shows that nature can still be a "living experience," to use his own words, however much it must be contained in a garden. Such experience is the truth content of Raffael's nature poetry. The image of undespoiled nature—really nature under the best of conditions, that is, cultivated rather than exploited, protected rather than abused—is necessary to counterattack the self-fulfilling prophecy implicit in the notion of vanishing nature. For Raffael the modern issue is not only the despoilment of nature but also loss of the capacity to experience it as alive. That is a failure of modern man, not of ghettoized nature.
3. Otto Fenichel (*The Psychoanalytic Theory of Neurosis* [New York: Norton, 1945], p. 60) writes that for Freud the "proneness to destructiveness on the archaic levels" is due to the fact that "death instinct and eros are still 'defused' . . . they fuse gradually during maturation, eros neutralized death instinct." Raffael represents maturation—ripeness—in creative process, and even though Eros seems to triumph in his work, destructiveness remains far from neutral, however subliminal.
4. "General wish to negate": Irving Howe observes that "the modern must be defined . . . as an 'inclusive negative,' " "an adversary stance" involving "the need to negate" everything, including itself. (Daniel Bell, "Beyond Modernism, Beyond Self," in *The Winding Passage* [New York: Basic Books, Harper Colophon Books, 1980], p. 276.) "Measure of freedom": Freud, "Negation," p. 239.
5. Pierre Cabanne, *Dialogues with Marcel Duchamp* (New York: Viking Press, 1997), p. 32.
6. Rilke, in Donald Prater, *A Ringing Glass: The Life of Rainer Maria Rilke* (Oxford: Clarendon Press, 1986), p. 408.
7. Mallarmé, in Anthony Hartley, ed., *Mallarmé* (Baltimore: Penguin, 1965), p. xi.
8. Rilke, in Prater, *Ringing Glass,* p. 408.
9. Mallarmé, in Hartley, *Mallarmé,* p. xxviii.
10. Odilon Redon, *A Soi-même: Journal (1867–1915)* (Paris: Henri Floury, 1922), p. 30.
11. Van Gogh, in Frank Elgar, *Van Gogh* (New York: Frederick A. Praeger, 1958), p. 181.

12. Ibid., p. 120.
13. *Baudelaire* (Baltimore: Penguin, 1961), p. 36.
14. Enid Starkie, *Baudelaire* (New York: New Directions, 1958), pp. 227–28.
15. Raffael, in Joyce Petschek, "The Knowable Becomes the Unknowable," in *Joseph Raffael* (New York: Nancy Hoffman Gallery, 1990), p. 5.
16. Michael Balint, "Notes on the Dissolution of Object-Representation in Modern Art," *Journal of Aesthetics and Art Criticism* 10 (June 1952): 324. Meyer Schapiro ("Nature of Abstract Art," *Modern Art: 19th and 20th Centuries* [New York: George Braziller, 1988], p. 191) says essentially the same thing: "Common to most of [the] movements after Impressionism was the absolutizing of the artist's state of mind or sensibility as prior to and above objects. If the Impressionists reduced things to the artist's sensations, their successors reduced them further to projections or constructions of his feelings and moods."
17. Balint, "Dissolution of Object-Representation," p. 326.
18. Ibid., p. 327.
19. Ibid.
20. Ibid.
21. Christopher Bollas, *The Shadow of the Object* (New York: Columbia University Press, 1987), p. 28.
22. Melanie Klein (*Love, Guilt and Reparation and Other Works, 1921–1945* [London: Virago, 1988], p. 263) observes that "from the beginning the ego introjects objects 'good' and 'bad,' for both of which the mother's breast is the prototype." "What one might call the 'good' breasts become the prototype of what is felt throughout life to be good and beneficent, while the 'bad' breasts stand for everything evil and persecuting." (Ibid., p. 291.)
23. W.R.D. Fairbairn, "The Ultimate Basis of Aesthetic Experience," in *From Instinct to Self: Selected Papers of W.R.D. Fairbairn* (Northvale, N.J.: Jason Aronson, 1994), vol. 2, p. 408.
24. C. G. Jung, *The Archetypes and the Collective Unconscious* (London: Routledge and Kegan Paul, 1959), p. 216.
25. Garver, "California Years," p. 19. My reading of Raffael's art assumes that he meant what he said when he declared, "The life and the work are not separate." (Joseph Raffael, "Interview," in *Joseph Raffael: A Dream Remembered* [New York: Nancy Hoffman Gallery, 1986], p. 7.)
26. The release of the bird is a "token of freedom," to use Meyer Schapiro's phrase, as is the apparent randomness of Raffael's brush strokes. (Schapiro, "Order and Randomness in Abstract Art," in *Modern Art,* p. 253.) The modern artist is desperate for such tokens of "inner freedom," as Schapiro argued: "The pathos of the reduction or fragility of the self within a culture that becomes increasingly organized through industry, economy and the state intensifies the desire of the artist to create forms [and images] that will manifest his liberty in [a] striking way." (Schapiro, "Recent Abstract Painting," in *Modern Art,* p. 222.) As Schapiro said, "Painting [became] an ideal domain of freedom" because it seemed to escape the "stultifying," "demoralizing" character of modern society. ("Nature of Abstract Art," p. 192.)

    But for Raffael, not painting alone but painting in conjunction with a return to nature can restore the feeling of free life after the avant-garde negation that unwittingly reflects the reduced, of self in modern society. In a sense, while acknowledging and assimilating modern nting, Raffael returns to its Impressionist origins—its "unconventionalized, unregulated of nature as "a constantly changing phenomenal outdoor world of which the shapes ended on the momentary position" of the spectator, thus implying his subjective involvement in hem. As Schapiro says, such a vision was an "implicit [moral] criticism" of modern society, all the more so because it conceived of art as "a field of individual enjoyment." (Ibid.)

27. Sheldon Bach, *The Language of Perversion and the Language of Love* (Northvale, N.J.: Jason Aronson, 1994), p. 71.
28. Blake, in Hugh Honour and John Fleming, *The Visual Arts: A History* (Englewood Cliffs, N.J.: Prentice-Hall, 1982), p. 491.
29. Garver, "California Years," p. 13.
30. Marc, in Herschel B. Chipp, *Theories of Modern Art* (Berkeley: University of California Press, 1968), p. 182.
31. Ibid., p. 178.
32. Ibid., p. 179.
33. Ibid. H. H. Gerth and C. Wright Mills, eds., *From Max Weber* (New York: Oxford University Press, Galaxy Books, 1958), p. 148. Weber was, in effect, describing the sense of deadness that is the psychic by-product of modernity.
34. *Innenwelt* and *Umwelt* are Jakob von Uexküll's concepts. See Thomas A. Sebeok, "Prefigurements of Art," in *The Play of Musement* (Bloomington: Indiana University Press, 1981), p. 232. There is an art to achieving this balance, as Sebeok suggests, art being "a kind of cybernetic device for keeping the organism's *milieu intérieur,* or . . . *Innenwelt,* in balance with its surroundings (*milieu extérieur,* or *Umwelt*)."
35. Meyer Schapiro, "The Sculptures of Souillac," in *Romanesque Art* (New York: George Braziller, 1977), p. 116.
36. Hermann Broch, "A Study on Mass Hysteria," *Erkennen und Handeln: Essays* (Zürich: Rhein-Verlag, 1955), vol. 2, pp. 258–59.
37. As Schapiro says, it is "a feeling-charged whole," "affirming the individual in opposition to the contrary qualities of ordinary experience." (Schapiro, "Recent Abstract Painting," pp. 215, 218.)
38. George Orwell, "Inside the Whale," in *Collected Essays* (London: Mercury Books, 1961), pp. 118–59. Orwell describes Miller as "fiddling while Rome is burning" (p. 151), "a sort of Whitman among the corpses" (p. 159).
39. I am thinking of Daniel Bell's discussion of "the polymorph[ous] perverse," "the unfettering of all instinct," which he regards as "the herald of the postmodern mood." (Bell, "Beyond Modernism, Beyond Self," p. 292.)
40. William James distinguished between "the healthy-minded, who need to be born only once, and . . . the sick souls, who must be twice-born in order to be happy." (James, *The Varieties of Religious Experience* [1902; New York: Random House, Modern Library, n.d.], p. 163.) For the latter, "Pain and wrong and death must be fairly met and overcome in higher excitement, or else their sting remains essentially unbroken." (Ibid., p. 355.) I think Raffael's nature poetry achieves this "higher

excitement." James's definition of religion also goes a long way toward helping us [redacted] Raffael's nature poetry: "The feelings, acts, and experiences of individual men in their [redacted] far as they apprehend themselves to stand in relation to whatever they may consider the [redacted] (Ibid., pp. 31–32.) To which Raffael might add: an animal or a plant can be divine, if it is [redacted] higher excitement.

41. Alfred North Whitehead, *Adventures of Ideas* (New York: Mentor Books, 1955), pp. 251–52.
42. Ibid., pp. 270–71.
43. Raffael has said: "I want to paint what I feel and cannot see. I want to make the invisible visible. I don't know what the invisible is, but I know it's not appearances." (Raffael, in Joyce Petschek, "Cutting Through the Clouds: A View of Joseph Raffael's Recent Paintings," *Arts Magazine* 59 [November 1984]: 80.) Rudolf Otto's famous analysis of the numinous is directly to the point of Raffael's nature poetry. The numinous involves an experience of the *mysterium tremendum,* that is, the sense of being "in the presence of that which is a mystery inexpressible beyond and above all creatures," even as it uses them to make itself felt. (Rudolf Otto, *The Idea of the Holy* [New York: Oxford University Press, Galaxy Books, 1958], p. 13.)
44. Whitehead, *Adventures of Ideas,* p. 283.
45. Clarence H. Hamilton, ed., "Introduction," *Buddhism, a Religion of Infinite Compassion: Selections from Buddhist Literature* (New York: Liberal Arts Press, 1952), p. xxviii.
46. Ibid., p. xxiii.
47. Buddha, in "Pali Literature: The Life of Buddha," ibid., p. 22.
48. Garver, "California Years," p. 9. It is in Raffael's "water-related imagery," as it has been called by Ellen Simak, that *ch'i* is most evident. Raffael notes the "flow and merging of colors, forms, gestures and movements" in *Fish Dream* (plate 79). The flow is emblematic of vital force. Many of Raffael's works are in watercolor, which, as he says, "expresses flow, life as transparency, the ineffable, the transient . . . air, motion, life moving. Watercolor is itself a force of nature." (Raffael, in Ellen Simak, *Reflections: The Water-Related Imagery of Joseph Raffael* [Chattanooga, Tenn.: Hunter Museum of Art, 1992], p. 5.)

    Raffael's idea of the vital force or flow can no doubt be understood in terms of Mihaly Csikszentmihalyi's concept of flow. It arises from the feeling of "being carried away by a current, everything moving smoothly without effort . . . our whole being [focused] in a harmonious rush of energy . . . lift[ing] us out of the anxieties and boredom that characterize so much of everyday life." (Mihaly Csikszentmihalyi, *The Evolving Self: A Psychology for the Third Millennium* [New York: HarperCollins, 1993], p. xiii.)
49. Jung, *Archetypes,* p. 216.
50. Sigmund Freud, "Totem and Taboo" (1913), in *The Standard Edition of the Psychological Works* (London: Hogarth Press and the Institute of Psycho-Analysis, 1955), vol. 23, p. 148.
51. Raffael, in Garver, "California Years," p. 21.
52. Petschek, "Cutting Through the Clouds," pp. 82–83.
53. Ibid., p. 82.
54. Hamilton, "Examination of Nirvana," p. 155.

fragile sense Raffael's water paintings, from *Black*
pure pai (plate 143). It is especially evident in the
vision, as for Henri Matisse, "black is a color," which
depan, as it was for Wassily Kandinsky, "something
thing motionless like a corpse" ("the silence of black
oncerning the Spiritual in Art [New York: Dover,
for Ad Reinhardt, pure "negation," the ultimate
gation" at the root of Reinhardt's concept of art as art. (Ad
cept," *Art as Art: The Selected Writings of Ad Reinhardt* [New
affael, black is not only inseparable from nature, but, like
is 1984 painting *Dying* (private collection) suggests, it can
ed, black seems to offer a space of transition between death and

tings, see Irene McManus, "Joseph Raffael's Lannis Series, Part
1988): 26–28.
ornia Years," p. 11.

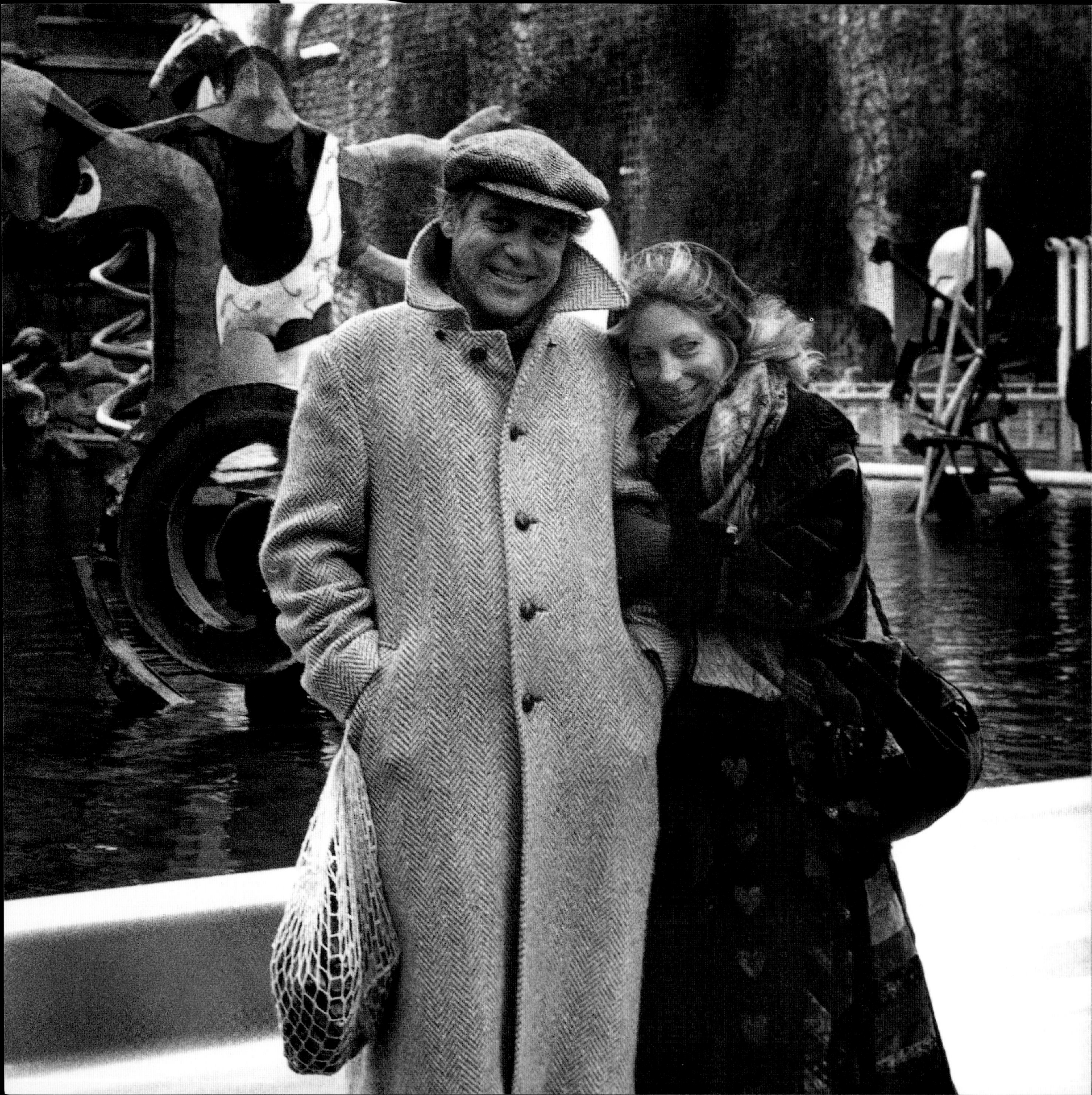

An Autobiographical Chronology

Joseph Raffael

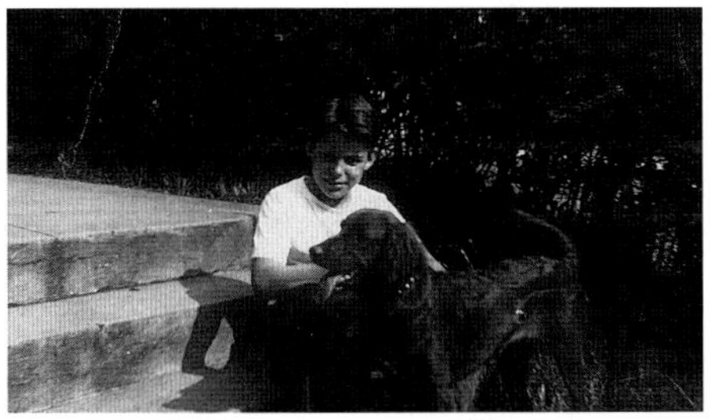

OPPOSITE

158. Joseph and Lannis Raffael in front of the Nikki de Saint Phalle–Jean Tinguely fountain, Paris, 1992

ABOVE

159. Joey Raffaele with his dog Roma, Brooklyn, early 1940s

February 22, 1933

I am born in Brooklyn, New York, to a family in which my mother, Cora Kaelin Raffaele; two older sisters, Jean and Audrey; and an aunt, Mae Kaelin, are the constants; my father, Joseph Marino Raffaele, is rarely present. During a solitary childhood, when I am often ill, I develop my own inner world; nature is my most faithful companion.

1940

I nearly die from spinal meningitis. My father insists that I attend Public School 198 rather than the local Catholic school, which makes me an outsider in the neighborhood but broadens my view of society. Drawing is my favorite subject; I also spend hours drawing at home. I enjoy ice skating, roller skating, and walking—activities that allow me to be by myself in nature. My mother, sisters, and I spend summers on the tip of Long Island, in Cutchogue, Mattituck, and Peconic. I spend most twilights on the beach, watching the sun set, in awe and silence. In fact, I watch nature throughout my childhood—everything from the trees' evening shadows moving along my bedroom walls in Brooklyn to the reflections of summer light on Long Island Sound. Movies become important early in my life, and I see up to five films a week; movie theaters are my first museums.

1947

November—My mother dies after a long illness. The theme of death and near death recurs throughout my life and deeply affects my art.

1947–51

I attend Midwood High School in Brooklyn. The most important and memorable part of high school is Art Club, where (often alone, which is preparation for the solitary studio activity of my later years) I make posters after class for school activities and get my first taste of hand lettering with a brush. At Midwood, I am introduced to poetry, classical music, and jazz by fellow student Stanley Nelson. I begin spending weekend evenings in my room painting scenes of nature. Saturday mornings, I take life classes at the Brooklyn Museum; those afternoons I spend drawing sculpture on my own, throughout the museum.

1951–54

I attend the School of Art at the Cooper Union for the Advancement of Art and Science, in Manhattan. The first year I study drawing with Sidney Delevante, who encourages his students to be artists while also developing their poetic nature. My second year John Ferren, an Abstract Expressionist, teaches painting, concentrating on color. My third year Leo Manso inspires me with the excitement of being an artist. Abstract Expressionism is a strong influence at school; it helps me to "let go," to see the whole picture, to trust the paint and the brush, and to ritualize the act of painting. Evenings and weekends I work as a clerk in the Central Circulation Department at the main New York Public Library.

160. Raffael at the Yale University–Norfolk School of Music and Art, 1954

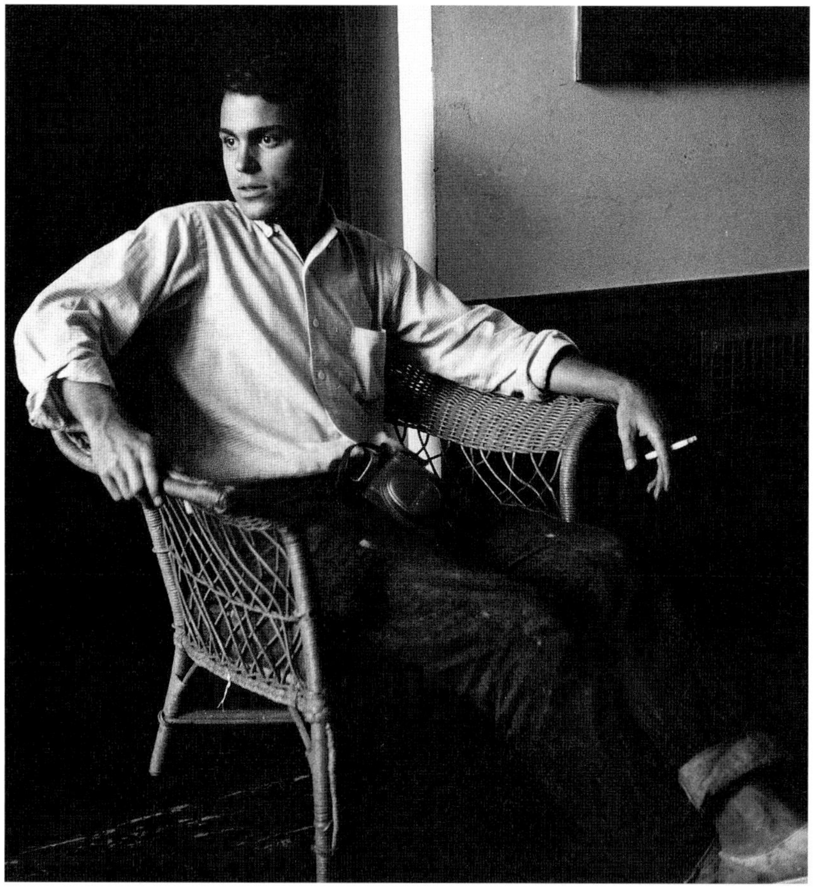

1954

Summer—I attend, on a fellowship, the Yale University–Norfolk School of Music and Art, in the Connecticut countryside; for the first time I have access to individual studio space. I begin to take photographs, which I later paint from. My first photo is of a nun in a landscape (three years later I paint a series of nuns in various landscapes). At the end of the summer Bernard Chaet, artist-instructor, encourages me to go to graduate school at Yale, and with his aid, I receive a scholarship.

1954–56
I move to New Haven, Connecticut, to attend the Yale University School of Art—the first time I've lived on my own. I take Josef Albers's color and drawing courses and study drawing and painting with Chaet; James Brooks, an Abstract Expressionist, is a visiting artist my final year. Albers is a major influence on me. He does not use terms like *hue, form,* or *tone,* but instead speaks of a "feeling" or a "weather" or a "time of day" or a "geographical feel" when discussing student work. Most important for me is his insistence that we not paint in any established way (such as Abstract Expressionism or his own style). His appearances in the students' studios are impromptu and always brief, his remarks pertinent and direct. He speaks to me only twice in two years, saying just a few sentences and once only "Aachhh!! Boy!! SHIT!!!" As a result, I learn not to expect or depend on approval from others, even those I most admire, which is probably the most decisive lesson in my art education.

In the evenings, the Yale Art Library is a haven and treasure house for me. I discover a decrepit volume of Sandro Botticelli's line drawings for Dante's *Inferno;* their extreme complexity and abstract quality appeal to me, as do the grace of the line and the subject matter. At the library, I also discover Edvard Munch, whose color and emotional intensity touch me. Rainer Maria Rilke's *Letters to a Young Poet* offer me solace during a rather solitary and soul-searching time. Gertrude Stein's originality encourages me, as does the fact that she lived in a foreign country.

In art history I study Oriental art, and the landscapes feed my soul; I also take a course in which I see French nineteenth-century art. My graduate thesis is a handmade book with my own calligraphy of Dylan Thomas's collection of stories *Quite Early One Morning*, with collages of leaves from New Haven trees and colored papers from Albers's color course as illustration. (Albers does like and appreciate this.)

After graduating with a BFA, I leave to begin my life as an artist, rather than staying on for a master's degree, as most of the others did in my class. I work as freelance designer at Jack Prince Textile Studio in Manhattan, where the artists Carolyn Brady, Audrey Flack, and Paul Thek are also designers. I learn to do "repeats"— i.e., to copy exactly a freely drawn and painted design within a certain measurement. This is a great drawing lesson that proves useful in making art later on. I also learn how to reproduce colors accurately. I paint on my own on weekends and nights: a series, in oil, of nuns in landscapes and homages to Alain-Fournier after having read his book *Le Grand Meaulnes* (1913) and to James Agee after reading *A Death in the Family* (1957).

1958

I receive a Fulbright Fellowship to paint in Florence. I travel in Europe with friend and photographer Peter Hujar. We share a house with studios on a hillside overlooking Florence, with a view of the Duomo on one side and the Tuscan landscape on the other. I'm very impressed by the Tuscan landscape and by man's effect on it, its order and beauty. My Fulbright project is to study triptychs and altarpieces in Florentine churches, where I discover Piero della Francesca and Giotto. Ironically, while in Florence I also discover the American transcendentalist writers Henry David Thoreau and Ralph Waldo Emerson at the American Library.

Abstraction begins to lose some of its attraction for me. I paint large circular oils of abstracted flowers from the garden and also complexly colored watercolors of flower forms. I make a hand-calligraphed book with flower watercolors of Ernst Juenger's novel *On the Marble Cliffs* (1947). I design and have printed a limited-edition book of Stanley Nelson's long poem "The Passion of Tammuz," financed by ten-dollar contributions, with my line drawings as illustrations; a special edition of ten has a hand-colored frontispiece.

While I'm in Europe, my first exhibition, of the nun-in-landscape oils, is held at Kanegis Gallery, Boston.

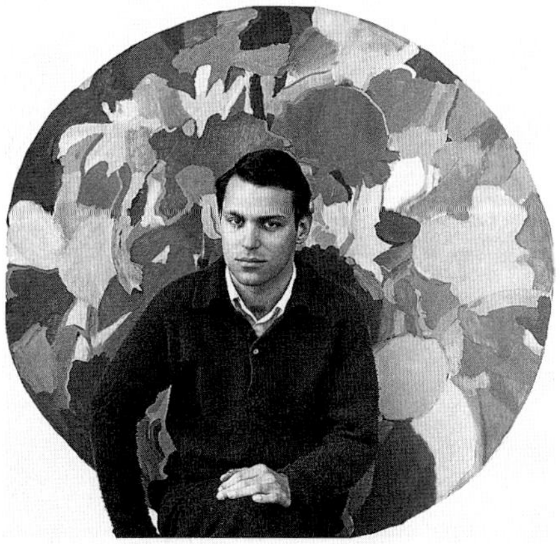

161. Raffael in Florence, 1958

1959

An exhibition of my work done while on the Fulbright is shown at Galleria Numero, Florence.

1960

December—I return to New York City, where I live and paint on West Twelfth Street, sharing an apartment and studio with the Italian opera director-designer Beni Montresor. I work part-time as a freelance textile artist at the Prince studio.

1961

I receive a $2,000 award from the Louis Comfort Tiffany Foundation for my handmade edition of *On the Marble Cliffs.*

1961–62

I spend both summers in Italy. Montresor introduces me to the composer Gian Carlo Menotti, who is director of the Spoleto Festival of Two Worlds. In 1962 Menotti invites me to paint a backdrop for a Jules Feiffer play. In Umbria I paint a series of watercolors of twilight landscapes viewed from a tower.

BELOW
162. *Baby, Man, Man Holding Doe,* 1966
Oil on canvas, 81 x 51 in.
(205.7 x 129.5 cm)
Joseph and Lannis Raffael,
Cap d'Antibes, France

RIGHT, TOP
163. Raffael in New York, late 1963

RIGHT, BOTTOM
164. Raffael, West Twelfth Street apartment-studio, New York, 1966

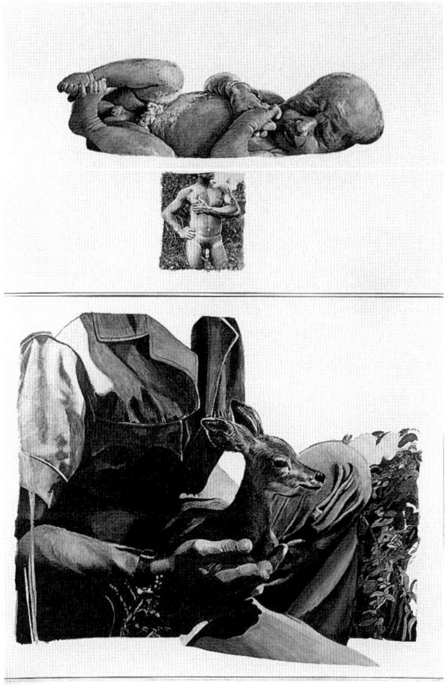

1963
My first New York exhibition, of the Umbrian watercolors, is held at D'Arcy Galleries. Prior to the opening, hepatitis almost kills me; I spend nine weeks in the hospital. Abstract Expressionism's complexity and directness had always appealed to me but now, after this near-death experience, my work becomes more realistic: "real-life" images, fragmented on white-ground canvases, are influenced by my renewed appreciation of life and of being alive within it.

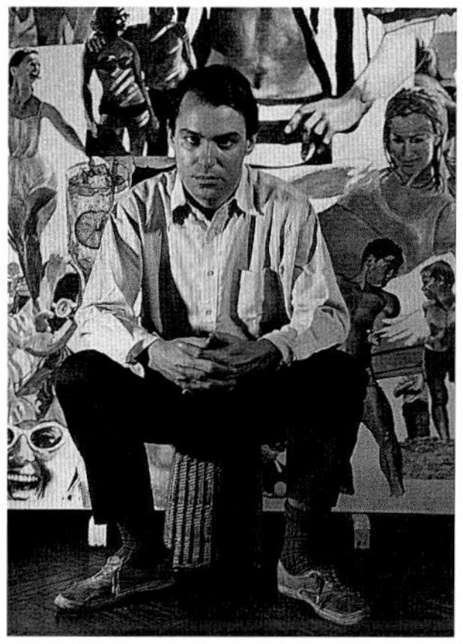

1964
My father dies. I paint *Padre Morto* (my collection).

1965
Stable Gallery, New York, holds a one-person show of my white-ground paintings.

1966
I teach painting for the fall quarter at the University of California at Davis, where I meet the artists William Allan and William T. Wiley and their families, who become good friends. For the first time, I see that an artist can also have a family. I have a studio in an apartment on a hill in San Francisco, overlooking the Bay and Chinatown. I see William Allan's 16 mm film focused on one section of a creek with its water continuously flowing, constantly changing, which reminds me of gazing at the water when I was a child. It evokes something in me that six years later will become the Water Painting series.

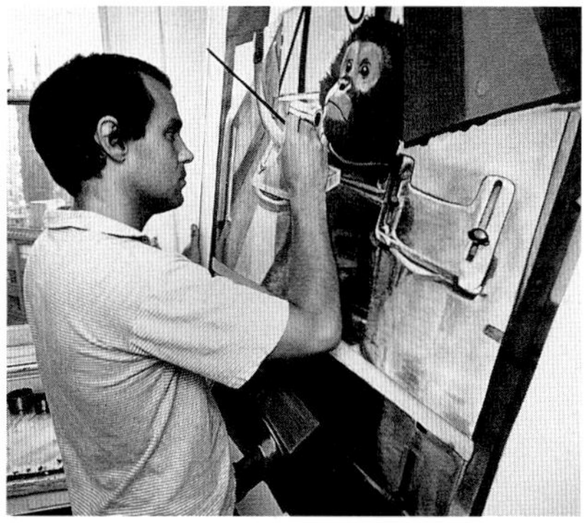

1967
After returning to New York, I practice transcendental meditation and am introduced to the thinking of Krishnamurti and Gurdjieff. I change my name from Joe Raffaele to Joseph Raffael. I begin large-scale, single-image oil paintings, including an Egyptian stone head of a cheetah with a blue tear and a portrait of Tut—both inspired by the ancient view of art-making as spiritual activity.

1968

July—I meet (via Ray Johnson's Correspondence School of Art and also William T. Wiley) Judy Davis, an artist and instructor at Bennington College, Vermont. She introduces me to the writings of Carl Jung. September—we marry; I adopt her two young sons, Robert and Matthew. We live and paint in Robert Frost's house on Bennington College campus. I begin large portraits of Native Americans, inspired by the sense I feel of ancient spirit permeating the local trees and landscape, as well as by a new sense of myself. December—the single-image paintings are shown at Stable Gallery, New York.

1969

We move to the San Francisco Bay area; I teach the summer session at the University of California, Berkeley, then begin teaching at California State College at Sacramento (until 1973). We move to San Geronimo Valley in Marin County, where we have a house and studio on a hill among the redwoods. October—our daughter Rachel is born.

1969–70

Up until this time I have been painting rather opaquely. However, at a certain point I notice that I prefer the way the watercolor dries on the surface of the white porcelain plate that I am using as a palette; it is more transparent and translucent, more fluid and runny than on the paper's surface. So I search out paper that gives a similar effect. Later, I also begin pre-painting my canvases with more than ten coats of white gesso, sanding between each coat. This surface, combined with diluting the oils with turpentine (as one dilutes watercolor with water), gives my oil paintings a look of being lit from behind. I like this. It is also perfect for the Water Paintings, which follow a few years later.

1970

In California I feel a sense of expanded space. I paint *Release* (plate 133), feeling as though I am released as well.

1971

I have a solo exhibition at Reese Palley Gallery, San Francisco. I begin the large animal-head portraits, including *Lizard* (plate 56) and *Lion* (plate 57).

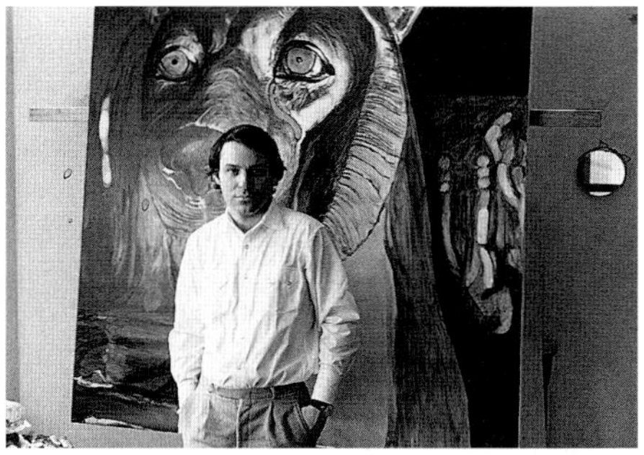

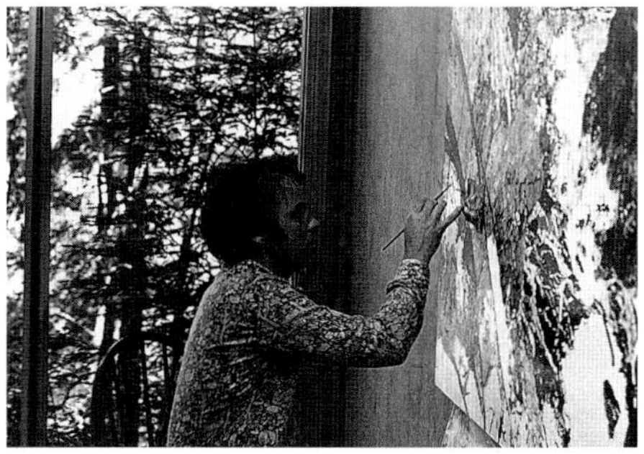

ABOVE, TOP

165. Raffael, West Twelfth Street apartment-studio, New York, 1968, with one of his first "whole-image" paintings

ABOVE, BOTTOM

166. Raffael painting *Leaf* in his first San Geronimo studio, California, 1969

1972
January—I have a solo exhibition of the animal-head portraits at Reese Palley Gallery, New York. March—our son Reuben is born. August—I meet Nancy Hoffman in San Geronimo and join her new gallery in New York. September—William Allan takes photographs of waterways for me to paint; I begin the Water Paintings series. December 8–January 1973—*Landscape* (plate 34) is included in Nancy Hoffman Gallery's inaugural exhibition.

1973
Summer—the first five of my oil Water Paintings are shown at the University Art Museum, Berkeley; Chicago Museum of Contemporary Art; and Nancy Hoffman Gallery. October—we travel to Scotland; while driving in the Highlands I come upon the scenes that inspire *Black Craig* (Art Institute of Chicago) and several other dark Water Paintings. After returning to California, I stop teaching to paint full-time.

1974
I receive first prize, Tokyo International Biennale, Japan.

1975
January—my first visit to Hawaii is sponsored by the U.S. Department of the Interior as part of a Bicentennial program inviting artists to honor the United States. A touring exhibition of paintings by the participating artists follows, called *America 1976;* I exhibit *Island Magic* (plate 22). My return flight from Hawaii is delayed for several hours, so I leave the airport; in Hilo during the wait, I discover and photograph a lily pond. I had taken more than a thousand slides during my Hawaii trip, but when I return to my studio, I realize that the lily ponds are what I want to paint.

April—Clinton Adams, director of Tamarind Institute, University of New Mexico, Albuquerque, invites me to be a guest printmaker there for a few weeks. I'm introduced to lithographic printmaking and create my first print: *Island Magic.* In the following years, I collaborate with various printers, including Will Foo, Charles Gill, Susan Goldsmith, David Salgado, Maurice Sanchez, and John Stemmer, among others.

1977
John Fitz Gibbon, an art historian and writer, invites me to visit Dr. and Mrs. McHenry's koi pond in Sacramento. I take many photos and begin to paint fish, including *Fish Dream* (plate 79), *Luminous Pond* (plate 83), and *Wind on Water Spring* (plate 84).

October—I meet W. Brugh Joy, M.D., a healer and spiritual teacher; I participate in his two-week workshop-conference on transformation in the Mojave Desert. It gives me the insight necessary to help move through the life-changing events that follow.

1978

January—*Joseph Raffael: The California Years, 1969–1978,* organized by Thomas H. Garver for the San Francisco Museum of Modern Art, opens; it will tour to the Des Moines (Iowa) Art Center; Joslyn Art Museum, Omaha; Newport Harbor Art Museum, Newport Beach, California; and Denver Art Museum. I also have two solo exhibitions at galleries: one opens in January at the Barbara Fendrick Gallery in Washington, D.C.; the other runs February 1–March 14 at the John Berggruen Gallery in San Francisco. Summer—I travel to Hong Kong and environs. Inspired by a visit to a Buddhist monastery in the hills of a nearby island, I later paint *Lily with Dragonfly* (plate 76) and other works based on the site.

1980

April—my wife and I separate. May—Matthew dies after an automobile accident. After his death, I undergo a transitional time of spiritual and creative reflection, wanting to connect more deeply to my artist self. I begin deepening my exploration of Eastern medicine and thought, needing to rediscover a "beginner's mind." Closing my studio to everyone, I curtain off the windows, the glass doors, and even the painting area within the studio. I need to paint in absolute privacy to find my original artist again. I paint *Naked* (my collection), *Dying* (private collection), and *Ascension* (my collection). I meet the spiritual teacher Paula Scott.

1981

I paint the oil portrait *Matthew* (my collection) with his face smiling. A friend, upon Matthew's death, gave the family a flowering cherry tree; its first spring blossoming touches me, and I paint *Matthew's Branch* (plate 32). I meet Lannis Wood, transpersonal counselor and tarot teacher, who employs the tarot and its symbols in her work. For the next two years I work with her, exploring life's metamorphoses; during this period a wonderful friendship develops.

April 15–May 16—solo exhibition at John Berggruen Gallery, San Francisco.

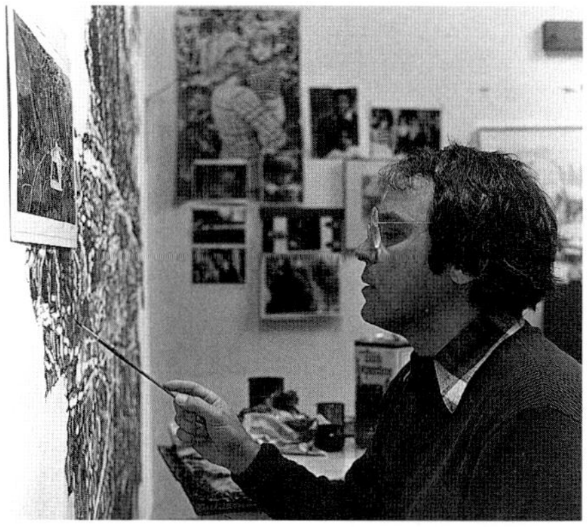

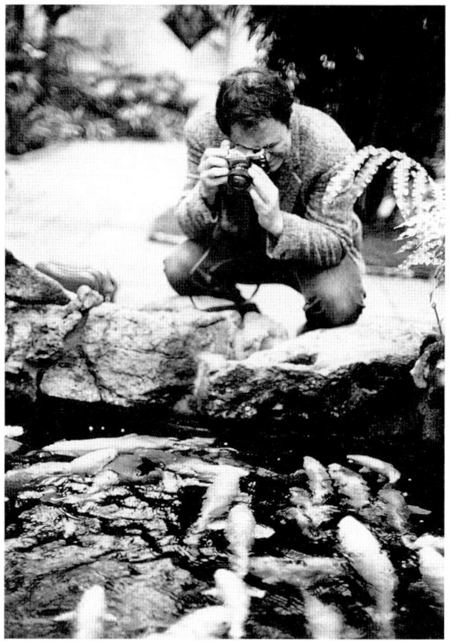

ABOVE, TOP

167. Raffael painting *Ch'i* (plate 26) in his San Geronimo studio, California, 1977

ABOVE, BOTTOM

168. Raffael photographing koi, early 1980s

1982

I visit Paris and southern France, considering buying a house in the South. Ann McLaughlin and Garner Tullis invite me to make my first monotypes, at the San Francisco Experimental Workshop.

April 21–May 22—solo exhibition at John Berggruen Gallery, San Francisco.

1983

During a summer trip to Holland, Italy, and mostly France with Robert, Rachel, and Reuben, I see an Edouard Manet retrospective at the Grand Palais in Paris. I'm particularly struck by two tiny but powerful canvases, one of asparagus on a dish and the other of oysters. After returning to the United States, I paint large oil portraits of myself and the children.

April 2–May 7—solo exhibition at the Richard Gray Gallery, Chicago.

1984

May—Lannis and I begin living together; our family increases with the addition of her three children, Sean, Rachelle, and Casey. November—a show of the figure paintings is held at Nancy Hoffman Gallery. During that exhibition, Lannis and I leave for Italy, to explore my Sicilian roots on my father's side and to revisit sites of my early years as an artist in Florence. After this trip we realize we want to live in Europe.

1985

Back in California, I paint *Ancient Longing* (plate 107), replacing the original face of Botticelli's *Primavera* with that of Lannis. I also paint the oils *Out of the Thicket* (plate 54) and *The Clearing* (plate 55), which relate to Lannis and my psychological states after the tribulations of my divorce and our efforts to leave behind the complications of my San Geronimo life. We set about making a new life, moving out of the "thicket" and into the "clearing." We rent a house on the edge of the Pacific, in Seadrift, Marin County, where we stay until our departure for Europe, scheduled for three months later. We inaugurate a new, much simpler, and more reclusive life, dedicated to the art and to our life together.

1986

January 5—we marry. I paint *Marriage* (plate 103). April—my exhibition at Nancy Hoffman Gallery opens Friday evening; Sunday morning we leave to live in France. We find a small house on the Mediterranean, where we live a private, solitary life. I use two bedrooms facing the sea as studios—one for oils, the other for watercolors. The making of the art becomes our major focus, while we are also learning to live in a new culture. My first painting in France is *The Bridge* (plate 100), then I make many small oils of birds, flowers from the garden, us, and other images from our new daily life.

I have two other solo exhibitions this year: February 28–March 29, Richard Gray Gallery, Chicago; July 23–September 6, John Berggruen Gallery, San Francisco.

1987

I paint three large vertical oils of Lannis—*Lannis and Claire in the Garden, Lannis in the Studio,* and *Lannis with Sunhat Standing in Garden: Summer* (all in our collection). November 14–December 16—my exhibition *In France, the Lannis Series: Part 1* is at Nancy Hoffman Gallery.

1988

We begin regular visits to our friends the Makkink family in Holland. I start the Lannis in Sieste series.

1989

February 18–March 22—the Lannis in Sieste paintings are exhibited at Nancy Hoffman Gallery. After seeing the Paul Gauguin exhibition at the Grand Palais in Paris, I begin the Soyez mystérieuses series. We strongly sense the mystery of life and of our lives in particular. I return to water imagery and also begin to paint large-scale watercolors of the life we share, such as bouquets from Lannis's garden, as well as large-scale details of the interior of the house. On a visit to the Makkinks I see the North Sea at twilight, which inspires *Soyez mystérieuses VIII* (plate 14).

1990

We buy the house we've been renting. The house, studio, and garden become our haven and inspiration. November 1–April 13, 1991—Soyez mystérieuses series is exhibited at Nancy Hoffman Gallery.

1991

I continue to explore the garden, interiors, animals, and Lannis as painting themes; the paintings become clearly a documentation of our daily life. Summer—after having painted mostly in watercolors, I begin several large paintings in oil, including the five-panel screen *Le 2 Novembre II* (plate 44).

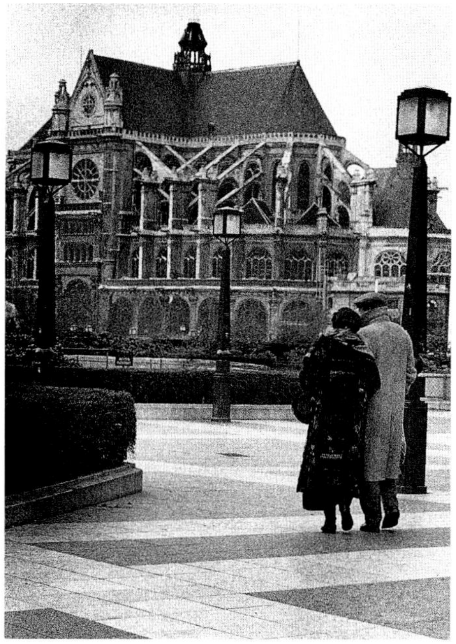

169. Joseph and Lannis in Paris, 1992

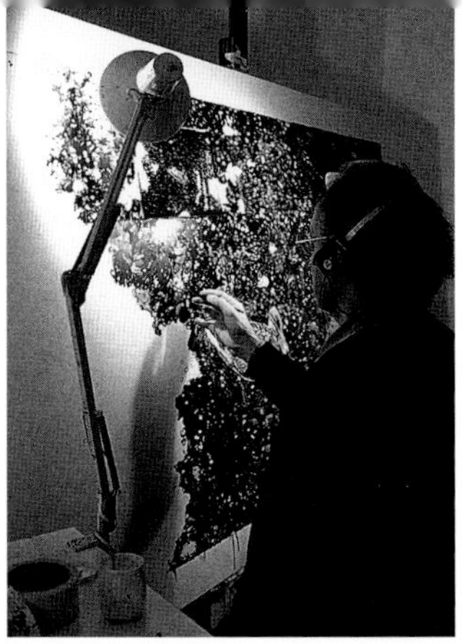

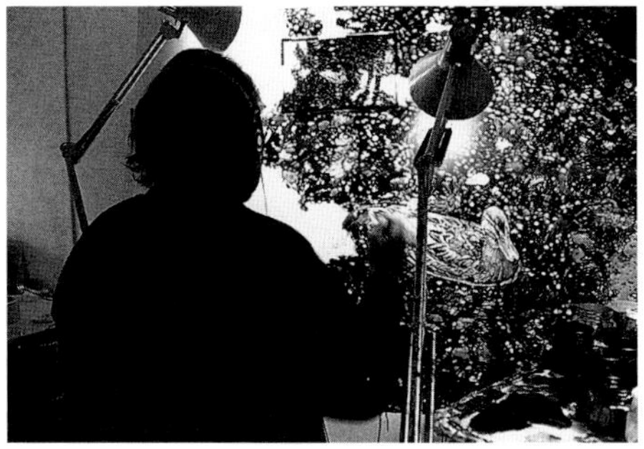

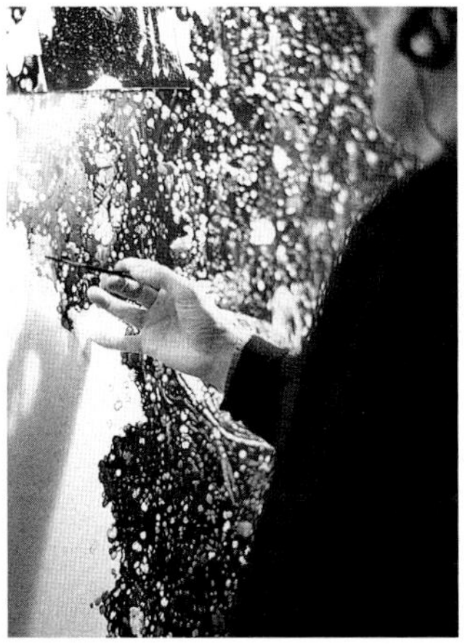

ABOVE

170–72. Raffael painting *Galactic Waters II* (plate 65), 1995

RIGHT

173. *Galactic Waters* (first in the series), completed, in Cap d'Antibes studio, December 1995

1992

April 4–29—these oil paintings are exhibited at Nancy Hoffman Gallery.

1993

August—Lannis has emergency surgery and nearly dies. After her return from the hospital, our life and my paintings progress to a deeper level. An urgency develops to express my love for Lannis and life and art through my paintings. Our visits to the Makkinks in Holland become more frequent; they introduce us to two large lily ponds in the Hague, which inspire *Lily Pond, Lannis, Restoration* (plate 89) and *Lily Pond, Lannis, Light and Shadow Diptych* (plate 71).

1994

March 5–April 13—the Lannis paintings and others in appreciation of Lannis and our life together are shown at Nancy Hoffman Gallery. April—we tear down the wall

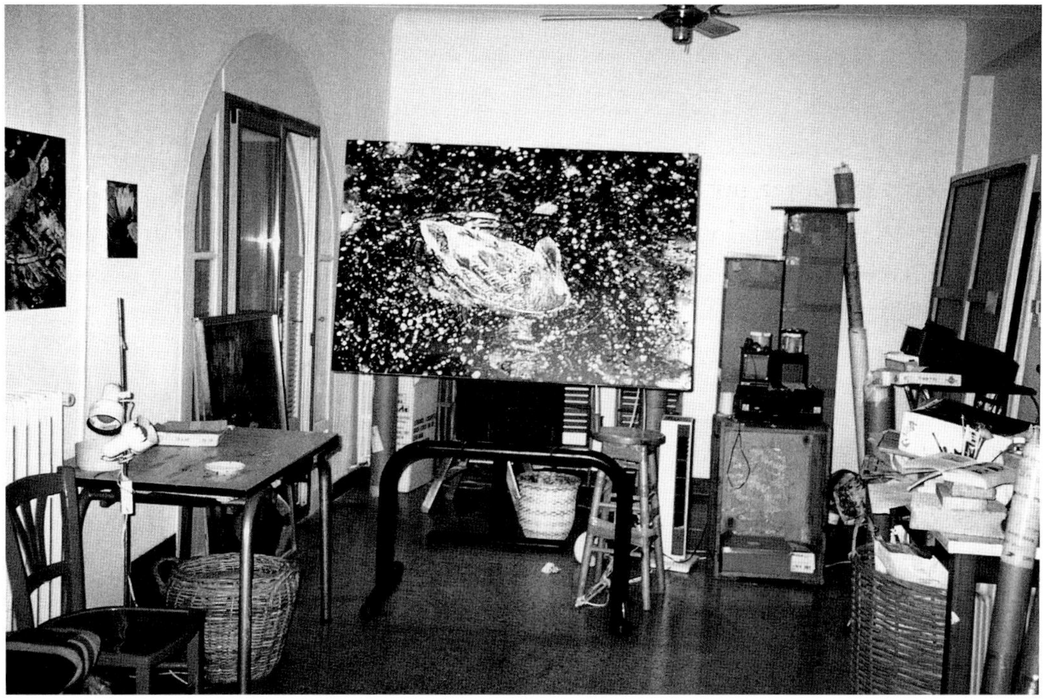

between the two small studios, making one large, light-filled room where I begin working with acrylics on canvas—a longtime wish fulfilled.

1995

January 20–February 28—my first acrylics are shown at Nancy Hoffman Gallery, including *Renewal* (plates 9 and 10) and the Galactic Waters paintings (plates 12 and 65). July—in Holland I photograph a heron by a pond.

1996

April–May—I paint *Heron's Vision* (plate 66). May—we visit the Makkinks in Holland. I see a coot perched on a nest in the pond where the heron had been; this inspires the watercolor triptych *May 4th* (plate 120), which takes three months to complete. December—Lannis goes to Bali to visit our first grandchild; she takes many photographs for my eventual paintings. I stay home to paint; the next year, I paint *La Magie de Bali* (plate 92).

1997

January—our friends the Loizos family invite us to the desert in Borrego Springs, California. There we see an oasis, complete with palm trees and waterfall; I take photos of the oasis, which I later paint. Katina Wood and Chris Desmond take us to the Huntington Gardens in San Marino, California, where in the Japanese Gardens I photograph a flowering tree; in May–July, I base a painting on it, called *12 March* (plate 2). August—I begin the long-planned Lannis' Garden series. October 9–November 5—my exhibition at Nancy Hoffman Gallery includes *Heron's Vision, May 4th, Metamorphose* (plate 33), *12 March,* and the first Lannis' Garden paintings.

Selected Bibliography

Solo-Exhibition Catalogs

An Exhibition of Nine Paintings by Joseph Raffael. St. Petersburg, Fla.: Museum of Fine Arts, 1978.

Garver, Thomas H., and Robert Hughes. *Joseph Raffael: The California Years, 1969–1978.* San Francisco: San Francisco Museum of Modern Art, 1978.

Joseph Raffael. New York: Reese Palley Gallery, 1972.

Joseph Raffael. Los Angeles: Arco Center for Visual Art, 1977.

Joseph Raffael: A Dream Remembered. New York: Nancy Hoffman Gallery, 1986.

Joseph Raffael in Four Southern Museums. Columbus, Ga.: Columbus Museum of Arts and Sciences; Birmingham, Ala.: Birmingham Museum of Art; Charlotte, N.C.: Mint Museum of Art; Jackson: Mississippi Museum of Art, 1980.

Joseph Raffael: Paintings, Watercolors, Prints. Storrs: University of Connecticut, 1981.

Joseph Raffael, Recent Works: 1982. Jacksonville, Fla.: Jacksonville Art Museum, 1982.

Joseph Raffael: Water Paintings. Berkeley, Calif.: University Art Museum, 1973.

Petschek, Joyce. *Joseph Raffael.* New York: Nancy Hoffman Gallery, 1990.

Simak, Ellen. *Reflections: The Water-Related Imagery of Joseph Raffael.* Chattanooga, Tenn.: Hunter Museum of Art, 1992.

General Books and Catalogs

Arthur, John. *Realists at Work.* New York: Watson-Guptill Publications, 1983.

———. *Interviews with Artists.* Boston: New York Graphic Society, n.d.

Battcock, Gregory. *Super Realism: A Critical Anthology.* New York: E. P. Dutton and Co., 1975.

Contemporary American Realists. Philadelphia: Pennsylvania Academy of the Fine Arts; Raleigh: North Carolina Museum of Art, 1977.

Directly Seen: New Realism in California. Newport Beach, Calif.: Newport Harbor Art Museum, 1970.

Eight Contemporary American Realists. Philadelphia: Pennsylvania Academy of the Fine Arts, 1971.

Health and Happiness in Twentieth-Century Avant-Garde Art. Binghamton, N.Y.: Binghamton University Art Museum; New York: New York Academy of Sciences, 1996.

Human Concern/Personal Torment: The Grotesque in American Art. New York: Whitney Museum of American Art, 1969.

Le Clair, Charles. *The Art of Watercolor.* Englewood Cliffs, N.J.: Prentice-Hall, 1986.

———. *Color in Contemporary Painting.* New York: Watson-Guptill Publications, 1991.

The New American Still Life. Greensburg, Penn.: Westmoreland County Museum of Art, 1979.

New Dimensions in Drawing, 1950–1980. Ridgefield, Conn.: Aldrich Museum of Contemporary Art, 1981.

New Images in Painting. Tokyo: International Biennale, 1974.

New/Photo Realism. Hartford, Conn.: Wadsworth Atheneum, 1974.

New Realism Revisited. Potsdam, N.Y.: Brainerd Art Gallery, State University College of Arts and Science, 1974.

1973 Biennial Exhibition: Contemporary American Art. New York: Whitney Museum of American Art, 1973.

The Obsessive Image, 1960–1968. London: Institute of Contemporary Arts, 1968.

The Other Tradition. Philadelphia: Institute of Contemporary Art, University of Pennsylvania, 1966.

Painting and Sculpture in California: The Modern Era. San Francisco: San Francisco Museum of Modern Art, 1976.

Perceptions of the Spirit in Twentieth-Century American Art. Indianapolis: Indianapolis Museum of Art, 1977.

Perspectives on Contemporary American Realism. Philadelphia: Pennsylvania Academy of the Fine Arts, 1982.

Phases of New Realism. Coral Gables, Fla.: Lowe Art Museum, University of Miami, 1972.

The Photographic Image. New York: Solomon R. Guggenheim Museum, 1966.

Private Images: Photographs by Painters. Los Angeles: Los Angeles County Museum of Art, 1977.

Seventieth American Exhibition. Chicago: Art Institute of Chicago, 1972.

Seventy-first American Exhibition. Chicago: Art Institute of Chicago, 1974.

Seventy-second American Exhibition. Chicago: Art Institute of Chicago, 1976.

Thirtieth Biennial Exhibition of Contemporary American Painting. Washington, D.C.: Corcoran Gallery of Art, 1967.

Three Realists: Close, Estes, Raffael. Worcester, Mass.: Worcester Art Museum, 1974.

Twentieth-Century American Painting. Moscow: American Embassy, n.d.

Violence in Recent American Art. Chicago: Museum of Contemporary Art, 1968.

Watercolors and Related Media by Contemporary Californians. Pasadena: Baxter Art Gallery, California Institute of Technology, 1977.

The West as Art: Changing Perceptions of Western Art in California Collections. Palm Springs, Calif.: Palm Springs Desert Museum, 1982.

West Coast Realism. Laguna Beach, Calif.: Laguna Beach Museum of Art, 1983.

Articles

A.A. "Joseph Raffael." *Village Voice,* October 7, 1976.

Adlow, Dorothy. "Raffaele at Kanegis." *Christian Science Monitor,* November 7, 1958.

Albright, Thomas. "A Triple-Threat Artist." *San Francisco Chronicle,* September 15, 1970, p. 38.

———. "Bumper Crop." *Art Gallery* 14 (December 1970): 9.

———. "Jazzing Up the Corporate Image." *San Francisco Chronicle,* March 11, 1972, p. 33.

———. "At the Galleries." *San Francisco Chronicle,* April 3, 1976, p. 34.

———. "San Francisco: Thinking Small: Chamber Works and Futuristic Visions." *Artnews* 75 (summer 1976): 146.

———. "A Flood of Color from Joseph Raffael." *San Francisco Chronicle,* February 4, 1978.

Alloway, Lawrence. "Art as Likeness: With a Note on Post Pop Art." *Arts Magazine* 41 (May 1967): 34–39.

———. "Art." *Nation* 209 (December 29, 1969): 741–42.

L.A. [Laurie Anderson]. "Reviews and Previews." *Artnews* 71 (March 1972): 21, 53.

Artner, Alan G. "An Imagist's Showing While the Battles Go On." *Chicago Tribune,* March 24, 1974.

Ashton, Dore. "An Evolution Illuminated." *Studio International* 171 (March 1966): 114.

Baker, Kenneth. "New American Watercolor." *Portfolio,* September–October 1982, pp. 64–70.

J.B. [Jacqueline Barnitz]. "In the Galleries." *Arts Magazine* 40 (December 1965): 60.

Benedikt, Michael. "New York Letter." *Art International* 9 (November 20, 1965): 44–45, 50.

Bourdon, David. "New Landscapes on the Horizon." *Village Voice,* December 2, 1974.

Brown, James H., and Astrid Kodric-Brown. "Why the Fittest Are Prettiest." *Sciences* (New York), September–October 1985, pp. 26–33.

Burnstein, Joanne. "Joseph Raffael at John Berggruen." *Images and Issues* 2 (fall 1982): n.p.

Butler, Joseph T. "The American Way with Art." *Connoisseur* 175 (June 1970): 162–63.

———. "America." *Connoisseur* 186 (June 1974): 142–43.

Butterfield, Jan. " 'I Have Always Copied': An Interview with Joseph Raffael." *Arts Magazine* 51 (October 1976): 122–26.

Canaday, John. "Art." *New York Times,* December 23, 1972.

Chandler, John Noel. "Notes toward a New Aesthetic." *Artscanada* 172–73 (October–November 1972): 16–25.

Cotter, Holland. Review. *New York Times,* March 25, 1996, p. 101.

Deschin, Jacob. "Photography." *New York Times,* January 4, 1970.

Figoten, Sheldon. "Subject and Technique in Symbiosis." *Artweek,* June 21, 1980.

Frankenstein, Alfred. "Raffael's Watercolors." *San Francisco Chronicle,* July 26, 1973.

———."A Magnified Spectrum of the Beauty of Life Force." *San Francisco Chronicle,* January 29, 1978.

French, Palmer D. "San Francisco." *Artforum* 7 (November 1968): 65.

Fuller, Mary. "The Water Becomes the Lily: An Interview with Joseph Raffael." *Currânt* (San Francisco) 2 (August–October 1976): 16–22.

Garver, Frank. "A Decade in California." *Southwest Art* 9 (May 1980): 88–95.

———. "Mind and Beast: Observations on Art and Animals." *Southwest Art* (July 1992): 82–83.

Gilbert-Rolfe, Jeremy. "Reviews." *Artforum* 12 (January 1974): 71–72.

Glueck, Grace. "Oh, to Be Born under Pisces, with Sagittarius Rising." *New York Times,* December 29, 1968, pp. 25, 27.

———. Review. *New York Times,* November 21, 1980.

Goldstein, Allan L., and Nicholas R. Hall. "Thinking Well." *Sciences* (New York), March–April 1986, pp. 34–40.

Goodman, Cynthia. "Eight Contemporary American Realists." *Arts Magazine* 52 (September 1977): n.p.

Greenwood, Michael. "Current Representational Art: Five Other Visions: Duane Hanson and Joseph Raffael." *Artscanada* 33 (December 1976–January 1977): 23–29.

Gruen, John. "What Painters See in Photographs." *New York World Journal Tribune,* October 23, 1966, pp. 35–36.

———. "The Extended Vision." *New York Magazine* 3 (January 12, 1970): n.p.

Henry, Gerrit. "Reviews." *Artnews* 75 (December 1976): 122.

———. Review. *Art in America* 80 (May 1991): 174–75.

Hughes, Robert. "The Last Salon." *Time,* February 12, 1973, p. 46.

———. "A Slice of the River." *Time,* October 15, 1973, pp. 112–13.

———. "Face of the Land." *Time,* July 5, 1976, pp. 78–80.

D.J. [Donald Judd]. "In the Galleries." *Arts Magazine* 37 (April 1963): 61.

Kingsley, April. "New York Letter." *Art International* 17 (March 1973): 49–50.

Kuspit, Donald B. "Review of Exhibitions." *Art in America* 65 (March–April 1977): 115–16.

———. "Joseph Raffael." *Arts Magazine* 54 (September 1979): n.p.

———. "Joseph Raffael." *Artforum* 54 (March 1996): 101.

L.L. [Lillian Lonngren]. "Reviews and Previews." *Artnews* 62 (November 1963): 48.

Lubell, Ellen. "Galleries." *Arts Magazine* 47 (February 1973): 81–82.

———. "New York Galleries." *Arts Magazine* 48 (December 1973): 63.

———. "Art Reviews." *Arts Magazine* 49 (January 1975): 9.

———. "Joseph Raffael." *Arts Magazine* 51 (December 1976): 34.

Mackie, Alwynne. "Joseph Raffael's Realism." *Art International* (November–December 1978): 20–23, 62, 65.

Mazunder, Asit. "Ripple Effect." *Sciences* (New York), November–December 1990, pp. 38–42.

McManus, Irene. "Joseph Raffael's Lannis Series, Part One." *Arts Magazine* 63 (March 1988): 26–28.

Mellow, James R. "New York Letter." *Art International* 10 (December 20, 1966): 62–63.

Nemser, Cindy. "The Closeup Vision—Representational Art—Part II." *Arts Magazine* 46 (May 1972): 44–48.

"New Talent USA: Joe Raffaele." *Art in America* 54 (July–August 1966): 34.

Oresman, Janice. "Joseph Raffael." *Arts Magazine* 57 (June 1983): 19.

"Painting: Unphotography." *Time,* April 11, 1969, pp. 80–81.

Perreault, John. "Art: Get the Picture?" *Village Voice,* December 18, 1969, pp. 18, 46.

———. "Get Back." *Village Voice,* February 1970, pp. 14–18.

———. "Art." *Village Voice,* February 17, 1972.

———. "Art." *Village Voice,* December 21, 1972.

———. "Postcards and a Plastic Rose." *Village Voice,* October 25, 1973, p. 41.

———. "Tokyo: Paris of Tomorrow?" *Village Voice,* September 19, 1974, pp. 46–48.

Petschek, Joyce. "Cutting Through the Clouds: A View of Joseph Raffael's Recent Paintings." *Arts Magazine* 59 (November 1984): 80–83.

Pincus-Witten, Robert. "Joe Raffaele, Stable Gallery." *Artforum* 4 (December 1965): 51.

———. "New York: The Photographic Image, Guggenheim Museum." *Artforum* 4 (March 1966): 47.

———. "Allusive Structure: A Conversation with Joe Raffaele." *Artforum* 5 (December 1966): 20–21.

Raffaele, Joe. "Letters" (letter to the editor). *East Village Other* (New York), April 15, 1967, p. 2.

Raffaele, Joe, and Elizabeth Baker. "The Way-Out West: Interviews with Four San Francisco Artists." *Artnews* 66 (summer 1967): 38–41, 72–76.

Raffaele, Joe, and Peter Saul. "Los Angeles: Subversive Art." *Arts Magazine* 41 (May 1967): 50–52.

Ratcliff, Carter. "New York." *Art International* 14 (March 20, 1970): 67–68.

———. "New York Letter." *Art International* 16 (April 20, 1972): 34–35.

Raynor, Vivien. "Works Inspired by Religion Show Sophistication." *New York Times,* June 15, 1980, p. 16.

———. "Art: A Tranquil Show of American Landscapes." *New York Times,* May 15, 1981.

Richardson, Brenda. "Bay Area Survey." *Arts Magazine* 45 (November 1970): 54.

Rose, Barbara. "New York Letter." *Art International* 7 (December 5, 1963): 65.

Rosenthal, Adrienne. "Joseph Raffael—Studies in Metamorphosis." *Artweek* 8 (March 26, 1977): 3.

Rubinfein, Leo. "Reviews: New York." *Artforum* 15 (December 1976): 66.

Russell, John. "Reviews." *New York Times,* November 16, 1974.

———. "Art: Beyond Good and Bad Taste." *New York Times,* October 8, 1976.

Saeks, Diane. "Joseph Raffael." *San Francisco Chronicle,* September 1981.

Sajbel, Maureen. "Aspect of Realism." *Observer,* November 10, 1976.

L.H.S. [Lynn H. Schafran]. "Reviews and Previews." *Artnews* 67 (February 1969): 20, 22.

Selz, Peter. "Six Artists in Search of a Definition of San Francisco." *Artnews* 72 (summer 1973): 34–37.

Siegel, Jeanne. "Reviews and Previews." *Artnews* 72 (December 1973): 97.

Stapp, Duane. "Joseph Raffael." *Arts Magazine* 55 (January 1981): 5.

Stevens, Carol. "Message into Medium: Photography as an Artist's Tool." *Print* 24 (May–June 1970): 57.

Stevens, Elizabeth. "The Camera's Eye on Canvas." *Wall Street Journal,* January 6, 1970, p. 16.

Swain, Richard. "In the Galleries." *Arts Magazine* 40 (March 1966): 52.

G.R.S. [G. R. Swenson]. "Reviews and Previews." *Artnews* 64 (September 1965): 18.

Swenson, G. R. "Paint, Flesh, Vesuvius." *Arts Magazine* 41 (November 1966): 33–35.

Tarshis, Jerome. "San Francisco." *Artforum* 9 (December 1970): 83–84.

———. "Nature Upclose." *Horizon,* September 1978, pp. 59–63.

Tatransky, Valentin. "Joseph Raffael." *Arts Magazine* 53 (June 1979): n.p.

———. "Joseph Raffael." *Arts Magazine* 55 (January 1981): n.p.

Taylor, Robert. "Raffaele Paintings." *Boston Sunday Herald,* November 16, 1958.

F.T. [Frederic Tuten]. "In the Galleries: Joseph Raffael." *Arts Magazine* 43 (February 1969): 62.

Ulrich, Lina. "Raffael's Art Really Philosophy of Heart." *Sunday Journal and Star* (Lincoln, Nebraska), March 15, 1981.

Vallongo, Sally. "Watercolors by Joseph Raffael Are Feasts for the Eyes." *Blade* (Toledo, Ohio), August 1995, pp. 21–24.

Wahl, Kenneth. "Landscape Renaissance." *Soho Weekly News* (New York), November 4, 1976, p. 20.

Wasserman, Emily. "Joseph Raffael/Carlos Villa/Hank Gobin: To Make the Painting Look at You . . . ," *Artforum* 9 (January 1971): 54–57.

Wasserman, Jeanne L. "An American Documentary." *Harvard Magazine* 79 (January–February 1977): 45–47.

Wilson, William. " 'Realities' Mirrors a Tragic Flaw." *Los Angeles Times,* September 30, 1973.

Wilson, William S. "The Paintings of Joe Raffaele: In the Franciscan Mood." *Art and Artists* 1 (September 1966): 22–27.

———. "The Paintings of Joseph Raffael." *Studio International* 187 (May 1974): 242–44.

Wolmer, Denise. "In the Galleries." *Arts Magazine* 46 (April 1972): 66.

Wortz, Melinda. "Joseph Raffael at Arco Center." *Los Angeles Times,* March 16, 1977.

Zickerman, Lynne. "In Art with Joseph Raffael." *Daily Californian* (University of California, Berkeley), October 20, 1972, pp. 12–13.

Zucker, Barbara. "New York Reviews." *Artnews* 74 (February 1975): 97.

Index

Page numbers in *italic* refer to illustrations.

Abstract Expressionism, 12, 141, 172, 173, 175
abstraction, 13, 14, 15, 21, 138, 140–41, 147, 174
Adams, Clinton, 177
Adorno, T. W., 124, 165*n*
After the Rain: An Iris with Border, 56
After the Rain: A Peony and Its Leaves, 56; detail, *38*
Agee, James, 173
Alain-Fournier, 173
Albers, Josef, 13, 75, 173
Allan, William, 13, 39, 175
Along the Secret Path, 43
America 1976, 177
Ancient Longing, 107, *108,* 160, 179
Angelico, Fra, 119
Antelope in High Grass, 65
Ascension, 178
Autumn Bouquet, 47, 162

Baby, Man, Man Holding Doe, 175
Bach, Sheldon, 137
Balint, Michael, 132, 133, 166*n*
Bartók, Béla, 40
Baudelaire, Charles, 130, 140, 150, 165*n*
Bauhaus, 13
Begonia after the Rain, 163
Begonia Diptych, 52
John Berggruen Gallery (San Francisco), 178, 179, 180
Bierstadt, Albert, 12
Bird in the Marsh, 66
Black Craig, 169*n*, 177
Black Craig Bubbles, 29
Blackfoot, 98, 154
Black Spring, 42
Blake, William, 140
Blue Pond, Winter Shore, 21, *36;* detail, *20*
Bollas, Christopher, 134
Botticelli, Sandro, 107, 160, 173, 179
Brady, Carolyn, 173
Bridge, The, 101, 180
Broch, Hermann, 146–47, 161
Brooks, James, 173
Buddha, 59, 95, 153–54
Buddha, 96, 97, 153
Buddhism, 9, 12, 95, 151–54

California State College (Sacramento), 176
Canna Leaf after the Rain, 54
Caravaggio, 162
Celebration, 84
Cézanne, Paul, 123, 140
Chaet, Bernard, 13, 172, 173
Ch'i, 34; photograph of Raffael painting, *178*
Chicago Museum of Contemporary Art, 177
Church, Frederic Edwin, 12
Claude Lorraine, 140
Clearing, The, 61, 159, 179
Clemente, Francesco, 18
Close, Chuck, 14
Colour of Transition, The, 92
Constable, John, 140
Cooper Union School of Art (New York), 12, 172
"Correspondances" (Baudelaire), 130
correspondence concept, 130–31
Cranach, Lucas, 158
Cranes, 67, 147
Crepuscule, Le, 99, 153
Csikszentmihalyi, Mihaly, 168*n*
Cubism, 140, 143–44
D'Arcy Galleries (New York), 175
Davis, Judy (first wife), 15, 159, 176, 178
Days Become Longer, The, 125
Degas, Edgar, 8
Delevante, Sidney, 172
Desmond, Chris, 182
2 Novembre II, Le, 50–51, 180
Divine Love (Swedenborg), 131
Duchamp, Marcel, 124
Dürer, Albrecht, 61
Dying, 169*n*, 178

Eleven Fish, 82
Emerson, Ralph Waldo, 9, 174
Estes, Richard, 14
Eternal Return, 131
Eternity, 144, 159, *161*
Expressionism, 18

Fairbairn, W.R.D., 134
Fan Kuan, 18
Barbara Fendrick Gallery (Washington, D.C.), 178
Fenichel, Otto, 165*n*
Ferren, John, 172
Fish Dream, 82, 168*n*, 177
Fish Spirit, 88; detail, *74*
Flack, Audrey, 173
Foo, Will, 177
Fourth of July, 30
Freud, Sigmund, 123, 165*n*
Frog in Its Pond, A, 59, 138, *140,* 142; original slide for, 138, *140*
Fulbright Fellowship, 13, 174
Fumé Watching the Flowers, 145, 164
Fumé with Vase and Camellia, 68

Galactic Waters: in studio (photograph), *181*
Galactic Waters II, 70, 182; in studio (photographs), *181*
Galactic Waters III, 21, *22,* 182; detail, *23*
Galleria Numero (Florence), 174
Ganesh, 95–97
Ganesh, 97, 154
Garden after the Rain, The, 11
Garver, Thomas H., 15, 136, 141, 157, 178
Gateway, 100, 153
Gauguin, Paul, 24, 123, 180
Gibbon, John Fitz, 177
Gill, Charles, 177
Giotto, 174
Gogh, Vincent van, 23, 123, 128, 129, 132, 134
Goldsmith, Susan, 177
Goya, Francisco, 144
Richard Gray Gallery (Chicago), 179, 180
Gurdjieff, G. I., 9, 175
Guston, Philip, 12

Haven, 102, 154, 157, 158
Heron's Vision, 71, 115, 162, 182
Highland Magic, 14, 14–15
Hinduism, 95
Hoffman, Nancy, 177
Nancy Hoffman Gallery (New York), 15, 177, 179, 180, 181, 182
Hommage au Printemps II, 77
Hopper, Edward, 10
Howe, Irving, 165*n*
Hudson River school, 9
Hughes, Robert, 9
Hujar, Peter, 174
Hydrangea, 127, *129*

Impressionism, 140, 166*n*, 167*n*
In France, the Lannis Series: Part I, 180
Interior Department, U.S., 177
Irises (van Gogh), 129
Island Magic, 30, 177

James, William, 151, 157, 167*n*–68*n*
Johns, Jasper, 13
Johnson, Ray, 176
Joseph Raffael: The California Years, 1969–1978, 15, 178
Joy, W. Brugh, 178
Juenger, Ernst, 174
Jung, Carl, 9, 12, 136, 153, 176

Kandinsky, Wassily, 169*n*
Kanegis Gallery (Boston), 174
Klein, Melanie, 166*n*
Kokoschka, Oskar, 142
Kona, 31
Kooning, Willem de, 12
Krishnamurti, 9, 175

Landscape, 42, 177
Lannis and Claire in the Garden, 180
Lannis' Garden series, 182
Lannis' Garden with Butterfly, 162, *164*
Lannis in Sieste III, 110
Lannis in Sieste IX, 111
Lannis in Sieste X, 112
Lannis in Sieste XIV, 111; details, *9, 106*
Lannis in Sieste series, 108–9, 161–64, 180
Lannis in the Studio, 180
Lannis with Sunhat Standing in Garden: Summer, 180
Leaf, 176
Leonardo da Vinci, 136
Lilies Dreaming, 91
Lily Pads and Leaf, 78
Lily Painting: Hilo (Island Lilies), 134, *135*
Lily Painting: Hilo II, 15
Lily Pond II, 78
Lily Pond, Lannis, Light and Shadow Diptych, 75–76, *76,* 181
Lily Pond, Lannis, Restoration, 90–91, 181
Lily with Dragonfly, 80, 178
Lion, 14, 59, *63,* 138, 143, 144, 176
Listening Lily, 81, 128
Listening to Evening, 159, *160*
Lizard, 14, 59, *62,* 138, 142–43, 144, 176
Loizos family, 182
Luminous Pond, 85, 177
Luxembourg Gardens: Faith, 146
Luxembourg Gardens: Truth, 146, *147*

McHenry, Dr. and Mrs., 177
McLaughlin, Ann, 179
Magie de Bali, La, 76, *93,* 182
Makkink family, 115, 180, 181, 182
Mallard, 59, *72,* 154
Mallarmé, Stéphane, 127
Manet, Edouard, 179
Manso, Leo, 172
Marc, Franz, 143–44
Marriage, 95, *103,* 154, 157–58, 159–60, 162, 179; detail, *94*
Marsh Flower: A Sad, Human Face (Redon), 128
Matisse, Henri, 169*n*
Matthew, 178
Matthew's Branch, 39–40, *40,* 178
May 4th, 18, *121,* 182; detail, *114;* journal excerpts on, 115–20; original photo for, *116;* in studio (photographs), *119, 120*
Menotti, Gian Carlo, 174
Metamorphose, 40, *41,* 109, 182
Miller, Henry, 150, 167*n*
modernism, 123–24, 132–33, 143, 166*n*–67*n;* death as preoccupation in, 128–30, 132, 134, 141; relationship with nature in, 140; relationship with object in, 132, 133, 136
modernity: instinct of destruction in, 123–24, 128–30, 132, 133, 134, 165*n;* Raffael's revolt against, 144–46
Mondrian, Piet, 129
Monet, Claude, 128
Montresor, Beni, 174
Muir, 33
Muir Creek IV, 32
Munch, Edvard, 173
Museum of Modern Art (New York), 12
Muybridge, Eadweard, 8

Naked, 178
Native Americans, 176
Natural Paradise: Painting in America, 1800–1950, The, 12
Nelson, Stanley, 174
New Lily, 79
New Realism, 14, 59
Niagara Falls (Church), 12

nihilism, 123–24
Number 22, 1949 (Rothko), 12

On the Marble Cliffs (Juenger), 174
Ophelia (Redon), 128, 132
Orange Fish, 83, 154
Orchid, 127, *128*
Orchid Bridge, 52
Orwell, George, 150, 167*n*
Otto, Rudolf, 168*n*
Out of the Thicket, 60, 61, 76, 159, 179
Oyster, 138, *139,* 143, 144

Padre Morto, 175
Paper Mill Creek, 28
Papillon Vert, Le, 154, *157*
Passage, 154, 157, *158,* 161
"Passion of Tammuz, The" (Nelson), 174
Petschek, Joyce, 153
Picasso, Pablo, 142
Piero della Francesca, 174
Pollock, Jackson, 12, 14
Pomo, 98
Post-Minimalism, 75
postmodernism, 133–34, 150, 167*n*
Poussin, Nicolas, 61, 150
Primavera (Botticelli), 107, 160, 179
Jack Prince Textile Studio, 173, 174
Printemps I, Le, 109
Provençal Autumn: Vaucluse, 48

Quail, 66
Quietude, 57
Quite Early One Morning (Thomas), 173

Raffael, Joseph: abstraction and, 13, 14, 15, 21, 138, 140–41, 174; acrylics and, 39, 182; animal paintings by, 11, *22, 23, 58,* 59–61, *60–73, 122,* 136–51, *137–40, 145, 150,* 154, *156–61,* 176; artistic traditions and, 8–9, 10, 12, 61; autobiographical chronology of, 171–82; beauty probed by, 10–11, 14, 134, 136; blackness in works of, 124, 157–59, 169*n;* butterfly and moth paintings by, *157–59,* 162, *164;* childhood of, 14, 171–72; color sense of, 11, 61; contraries integrated by, 157–61; early career of, 173–74; education and training of, 12, 13, 75, 171, 172–73; excerpts from journal of, 115–20; fish paintings by, 8, *74,* 75, 76, *77, 82–89, 138,* 144, 147, *148, 149;* in Florence, 174, 179; flower and leaf paintings by, *2–5, 11, 38,* 39–40, *41–57,* 123–36, *125, 127–29, 131,* 143, *146, 147,* 154, 161, *162–64;* flux painted by, 11; garden imagery of, 107, 146–64, 165*n;* hand-calligraphed books by, 173, 174; in history of art, 123–36; Japanese paintings by, 95, *102–5,* 154–58; Lannis paintings by, *9, 106,* 107–8, *108–13,* 159, 161–64, 179, 180, 181; lily paintings by, *15–17,* 18, 75–76, *76, 78–81, 90–93, 126,* 127–28, *130, 133,* 134, *135,* 153–54, *154, 155,* 177, 181; meditation induced by paintings of, 151–54; and metaphysics of nature, 123–69; name spelling changed by, 9, 175, 178; near-death experiences of, 10, 13, 171, 175; oil technique of, 39; photographs of, *170, 171, 172, 174, 175, 176, 178, 180, 181;* poetry and, 164*n*–65*n;* printmaking and, 177, 179; relocated to France, 18, 179–80; sacred symbol paintings by, *94,* 95–97, *96–105,* 153–58, *158;* spiritual concerns of, 9–10, 95–97, 151–57, 175, 178; surplus of independent detail provided by, 138–40, 141, 142; water and shore paintings by, *10,* 11, *12, 14,* 14–15, *20,* 21–24, *22–37,* 39, *70, 72, 73, 114,* 115–20, *121,* 128, 137, *151,* 168*n,* 169*n,* 175, 176, 177, 182; watercolor painting and, 39, 119, 168*n,* 176; working methods of, 7–8, 39, 61, 76, 115–20, 141, 176
Raffael, Lannis Wood (second wife), 7, 18, 23, 76, 95, 115, 117, 118, 159–60, 178, 179, 182; husband's paintings of, *9, 106,* 107–8, *108–13,* 159, 161–64, 179, 180, 181; near-death experience of, 10, 18, 75, 181; photographs of, *170, 180*
Raffael, Matthew (son), 10, 15, 40, 157, 178
Raffael, Rachel (daughter), 176, 179
Raffael, Reuben (son), 177, 179
Raffael, Robert (son), 176, 179
Raffaele, Cora Kaelin (mother), 10, 171
Raffaele, Joseph Marino (father), 10, 171, 175
Rauschenberg, Robert, 13
Readymades (Duchamp), 124
Red Lily in a Buddhist Monastery, 153, *154*
Redon, Odilon, 123, 128, 129, 132, 134
Re-Entry (Moth), 61, 154, *159*
Reese Palley Gallery (San Francisco), 176, 177
Reflection, 37
Reinhardt, Ad, 169*n*
Release, 136–38, *137,* 146, 176
Renascence (1980), *126,* 127
Renascence (1996), *127*
Renewal, 16–17, 18, 182
Restoring, 12
Return Again, 159
Rilke, Rainer Maria, 9, 124, 127, 173
Rose Awakening, 46
Rose Bridge, 2–3
Rose-Flow, 4–5
Rose for Lannis Diptych, 53
Rose Outside Matisse Museum Garden, Nice, July 1981, 44
Rothko, Mark, 12
Ryder, Albert, 116

Saint Serapion (Zurbarán), 109
Salgado, David, 177
Salmon, 138, 143, 144, 146
Sanchez, Maurice, 177
San Francisco Experimental Workshop, 179
San Francisco Museum of Modern Art, 15, 178
Schapiro, Meyer, 144, 147, 166*n,* 167*n*
Schnabel, Julian, 18
Scott, Paula, 178
Scottish Falls, 29
Season of the Frog, 64
Secret Path, A, 147, *148,* 161
Site Charmant, Autumn, 49
Solstice, 88
Souillac, France, cathedral in, 144
Soyez mystérieuses VIII, 24–25, 108, 180

Soyez mystérieuses X, 45, 108
Soyez mystérieuses series, 23–24, 108, 127, 180
Spirit (Owl), 72, 159; detail, *58*
Spirit Bird, 61, 154, *156;* detail, *122*
Spirit Pond, 84
Spoleto Festival of Two Worlds, 174
Spring: Amazement, 134, *135,* 164
Spring Bridge, 105; detail, *104*
Spring Equinox, Matisse's Model and Lannis, 113
Stable Gallery (New York), 13, 175, 176
Starkie, Enid, 130–31
Stein, Gertrude, 173
Stemmer, John, 177
Stevens, Wallace, 9, 12, 18, 109, 123, 164*n*–65*n*
sublime, 12, 18, 128, 140
Summer Fish II, 76, 89
Summers Pond, 147, *149,* 169*n*
Summertime (Number 9A, 1948) (Pollock), 12
Sunflowers (van Gogh), 129
Sunset, 150–51, *151*
Sunset in the Yosemite Valley (Bierstadt), 12
Sunset on South China Sea II, 35
Suzuki, Daisetz T., 12
Swedenborg, Emanuel, 130–31
Symbolism, 130–31

Tamarind Institute, University of New Mexico (Albuquerque), 177
Thek, Paul, 173
Thomas, Dylan, 173
Thoreau, Henry David, 9, 15, 18, 21, 40, 174
Threshold, 102, 154, 157, 158
Tibetan Buddhism, 9
Louis Comfort Tiffany Foundation, 174
Tigre in Sieste, 145
Tigre's Dream, 69
Tokyo International Biennale, 177
transcendentalism, 9, 174
Transition in Spring, 133
Tullis, Garner, 179
12 March, 8, 182; detail, *6*
Twilight, 73
Two Birds, 147, *150*
Two Vases, Two Bouquets, Spring, 159, 160, *162*
Two Vases, Two Flowers: A Portrait, 125
Two White Lilies in a Buddhist Monastery on an Island in the South China Sea, 153, *155*

Uccello, Paolo, 76
University Art Museum (Berkeley), 177
University of California at Berkeley, 176
University of California at Davis, 13, 175

Vasari, Giorgio, 136
Vernal Equinox after the Blooming, 55
Voltaire, 150

Water and Reflections, 36
Water Becomes the Lily, 128, *130*
Water Painting II, 26
Water Painting III, 10
Water Painting V, 26
Water Painting VI, 27
Water Painting series, 137, 175, 176, 177
Water with Fish, 87
Weber, Max, 144, 167*n*
Wiley, William T., 13, 175, 176
Wind on Water Spring, 86, 177
Winter Gift, 47
Wood, Katina, 182
Wood, Lannis. *See* Raffael, Lannis Wood

Yale University—Norfolk School of Music and Art, 13, 172
Yale University School of Art, 173

Zurbarán, Francisco de, 109

Photography Credits

The photographers and the sources of photographic material other than those indicated in the captions are as follows (numbers refer to plates):
Thomas Garver: 167; Peter Hujar: 161, 164, 165; Ian Lucas: 170–72; Lannis Raffael: 116–19; Photograph copyright © 1996 Whitney Museum of American Art: 16; Katina Wood: 158, 169.

Cover: Detail of *Renewal,* 1995. See plates 9 and 10.
Pages 2–3: *Rose Bridge,* 1990. Watercolor on paper, 45 x 87 in. (114.2 x 220.9 cm).
Mrs. William C. Janss, Sun Valley, Idaho.
Pages 4–5: *Rose-Flow,* 1990. Watercolor on paper,
69½ x 44¾ in. (176.5 x 113.6 cm). Private collection,
Tulsa, Oklahoma.

Editor: Nancy Grubb
Designer: Joel Avirom
Production Editor: Abigail Asher
Production Manager: Lou Bilka

Invaluable assistance was provided by Nancy Hoffman and the staff at Nancy Hoffman Gallery, New York: Adrienne Drake, Judith Nichols, Cynthia Sanok, Sique Spence, Jeffrey Sturges, and Christopher W. Watson.

First edition
2 4 6 8 10 9 7 5 3 1

Library of Congress Cataloging-in-Publication Data
Wallach, Amei.
Reflections of nature : paintings by Joseph Raffael / Amei Wallach, Donald Kuspit.
p. cm.
Includes bibliographical references and index.
ISBN 0-7892-0280-8
1. Raffael, Joseph, 1933– —Criticism and interpretation.
2. Nature (Aesthetics) I. Raffael, Joseph, 1933– . II. Kuspit, Donald B. (Donald Burton), 1935– . III. Title.
ND237.R117W36 1997
759. 13—DC21 97-42630